Persuasion
Mastery

Inner Patch Publishing

PERSUASION MASTERY

500 PRACTICAL LESSONS IN THE PSYCHOLOGY OF SALES

STEPHAN THIEME

INNER PATCH PUBLISHING

Why Everyone Should Learn Sales Psychology

Persuasion is tremendously valuable. Most people miss countless opportunities to better their lives, simply because they lack the communication skills that can make them more influential.

Even people who think of themselves as *assertive* have no idea how much better their lives could be. **Assertiveness** is little more than inner permission to advocate for yourself. But persuasion moves everything from products to nations. This is why *everyone* should learn sales.

Persuasion, at its best, is invisible. Not because it is sneaking past you, but because the best persuasion is about bringing a person's interests and motives into the foreground. When that happens, persuasion is like **magnetism**. You see things move, but the force is unseen. And persuasive people *are* magnetic. They make great deals, get signatories to treaties, untangle quarrels, and win friends like magic.

Persuasion, once mastered, is easy, like music coming to the mind of a skilled musician. Unconscious mastery comes from practicing persuasion skills. This is why everyone *should* learn sales.

Persuasion can also be work. To prepare for something very important to you, you will work very hard, wouldn't you? Whether it's preparing to negotiate an international trade agreement, or negotiate a deal for a volume discount for your employer or convince your 18 years old son to study hard for his college admission exams, you will work hard for high stakes. Preparation is crucial. This is why everyone should learn *sales*.

This book reveals and teaches the skills behind the magic. With this book, you will build bite-sized skills into the invisible talent of persuasion. Since everyone should learn sales, we have made our best to make this book the only sales psychology manual you'll ever need.

INTRODUCTION

Congratulations! You are holding a pack of 500 concise lessons, teaching the skills of persuasion. These intermediate to advanced skills are written from the sales professional's perspective, but everyone needs to read this book. Skim through the table of contents and you'll see that this book is like an encyclopedia. There is plenty for everyone. *But which of the strengths of this book will wow you the most?*

Many readers will feel that the real beauty of this book is the way it explains these skills in a small fraction of the time of most books. Here, you will not wade through the wearisome padding and long-winded stories that is so typical. The examples are refreshingly real-world, dispensing with the corn-ball and hackneyed scripting so common in books on persuasion.

Readers who know a good deal about persuasion will be happy to find a book that takes the art to a higher level. They will even appreciate our carefully chosen fundamentals. They are written succinctly. They will inspire the experts to reinvigorate the fundamentals in their sales practices.

Most readers will find their efforts at persuasion transformed by the skill of integration. This book will show many examples of how you can weave the skills together to multiply your persuasion power. You will learn to persuade creatively and flexibly to meet varying demands and surprises. All readers will experience dramatic improvements in their lives as they explore these skills.

This book begins with the intent of helping anyone be persuasive, even though it is written from the professional sales person's perspective. But my panel has really brought home to me the immense value these skills offer outside of the sales arena. One of our members is a psychotherapist who keeps returning with news about how this book is not only helping him sell his services, but even giving him new-found powers of persuasion that help him transform his clients. People who have helped us review and edit this book or perform administrative tasks have been gushing with stories of success in their personal lives.

CONTENT WITH IMPACT

This book covers many skills. Let me share a just few of them with you. One of them is **Hidden Influence Factors.** There, you will earn about the amazing amount of scientific research on persuasion. One of the fascinating skills in this section is the ability to trigger automatic behaviors to further the process of persuasion.

In **Hidden Word Magic**, the skills include many word combinations that you can use to activate agreement, building your ability to persuade. **Memory Magic** shows many skills that influence the way people organize and access their memories. This creates incredible leverage for persuasion. That is just two of its 36 topics.

Of the larger sections is a **highly detailed sales process** that contains over 100 skills. It takes you from the cold call to the sale close. It is filled with very specific actions and wordings that cover the five states of the sales process. You will learn very precisely how to transition your sales process from one stage to the next, including **exactly what words to use**.

In another, you will learn to meet the special demands of **group presentation and sales** situations. This section will teach you to establish rapport with groups. You will learn exactly how to make each sales point stand out in their minds. There are skills that move your audience to action. It even provides special voice techniques for persuasion that anyone can learn. Have you ever made an embarrassing mistake in a presentation? You will learn how to recover and "delete" the mistake from the presentation. This is just a sampling of the 36 different strategies for your group presentations.

Negotiation is a big part of sales and persuasion in general. This book provides 86 diverse strategies that take you from your first moves to completing the contract. You'll perfect well-known techniques such as *bracketing*. You'll defend yourself against everything from skilled cons to common negotiating practices such as *good cop bad cop*. You will even turn these potentially devastating moves to your advantage.

Meet Stephan

Let me introduce you to **Stephan**.

Stephan, this is one of our readers. *"Hi, it's great to meet you. I'm really looking forward to sharing this modern, advanced sales training with you."*

Stephan is a real person, but for this book, he is more than that. He will represent the combined wisdom of our panel of sales professionals, writers, and psychology professionals. Stephan will be the voice of his own experience and skill, as well as that of our panel. You are about to receive a wealth of real-world, insights from science that you can use immediately. This book's Stephan, the accumulated wisdom character, will boost your personal motivation and persuasion skills for sales or any other pursuit that requires high levels of persuasion and influence capabilities.

Learning persuasion and improving your communication skills are a part of a journey. Every journey has to start with one single step... here's your one single step: Read the next chapter!

GRATITUDES

Indeed, I am the author of this book and my name is Stephan Thieme. But I have to emphasize this fact: I did not write this book alone in my attic, surrounded by old photographs, chewing tobacco. I had a whole lot of help from my very talented colleagues and friends.

As mentioned in the introduction, the "Stephan" in this book is the synthesized wisdom (a panel) of several highly professional and persuasive individuals. Here's our panel:

Stephan Thieme, a veteran sales person and corporate sales trainer, spent 35 years as an agent selling "hardcore" life and health insurance premiums to middle class workers, the people who need it the most. Now "retired," fishing occasionally, and mostly training sales people in the most historical and artistically gorgeous towns in Europe. It's a dirty job, but someone has to do it!

Isaac Gozlan, on paper an "NLP trainer," but in reality one of the most sophisticated and charismatic corporate sales officers. Isaac can (and did) come to a sales meeting, not knowing what it was about at all or what the product or service was offered, and still come out with a signed contract! This is not an exaggeration, it's his personal work style.

Rose S. Uliel, a wonderful old-fashioned lady that proves you only need to be sincere to persuade elegantly. Mrs. Uliel is a relative of mine who has a store for stones. Yes, stones! Those nice looking colorful gems they dig up in China or wherever. People pay her hundreds of dollars for one tiny piece of rock, so you have to wonder, how does she do it? She's not slick or a con artist, she's just being herself... Well, we have uncovered some of her secrets, and they are described in this book.

Andrea Voncina, an Italian "ideas dealer," was a client of mine almost a decade ago and since then we have remained close. Andrea is unique in my eyes, not only because of his obscene number of female groupies, but because of what he does. For the past 15 years or so, Andrea is selling IDEAS. It's not a product or a service in any manner. Andrea works with product designers in Sardignia, Italy. (But don't say Italy and Sardignia in the same sentence to a Sardignian, though, they'll snap at you). Andrea's job is to pitch his clients' ideas to prospective investors. Obviously, to be good at such a craft one must be a superior persuader--selling ideas that have no vivid or physical attributes! This is what I tell him: He is selling free air!

Robert A. Yourell, LMFT, a professional psychotherapist and one of my dearest colleagues. Bob brought his extensive psychology background and knowledge and made the rest of us ponder for days. The manuscript you're holding is completely different, in essence, from my original plan, mostly due to Bob's magical touch.

There are many people I owe this book to: Shlomo Vaknin, David Harlev, Yaniv Appelboim, Carmelana Voncina, Moses Gozlan, Yair Ashkenazi, Katherin and Steven Montgomery, Robert White, Simona Hudson and every single person working for and with Inner Patch, Inc.

Thank you, too, for reading our book. We would greatly appreciate every comment, compliment and success stories you may have after using the concepts and tools in this book. *Now that we covered the essentials, let's begin...*

KEYS TO
MOTIVATION AND SALES

CORE IDEAS

HOW TO GET STARTED

Your Goals: Let's make sure you get the most from these articles. Do you have goals and objectives for your sales and career? Think about what inspired you to get this book. Write down things that you want to get from these articles; your goals for reading this book.

Unconscious Mastery: I suggest that one of your goals be unconscious mastery. That doesn't mean selling while sleep walking. It means practicing while awake. As with anything you practice, these sales skills can become part of you; skills that you improvise with. As you practice these skills, you will get more and more out of them. You will become more and more strategic. As you get natural with each skill, your brain will make room for more. Brain research has shown us that the skills you practice become like reflexes. Your brain does this so that you can add layers and layers of skills. This makes you able to pick and choose your sales techniques like a jazz musician does riffs.

Practice Right: To practice right, you have to keep *leverage* in mind. Your learning is leveraged by picking a few skills and making them your focus of practice for a week or a month. That means you need to get your highlighter out and mark this book as you go. Mark the skills that you feel you would most benefit from now. I have made them easy to digest with my own *italics*, **bold print** and numbering. But nothing beats your own highlighting.

There is structure and flow to this book. You could go through one article at a time in order. That would work. But you might actually be better off scanning through the titles and picking the ones that most attract you. There are sections that you will want to go through in order though. My sales processes are very engineered pieces that fit together just so.

I'm honored that you have chosen me to instruct you. I'm going to do my very best to make it enjoyable and profitable!

CORE PHILOSOPHY

Right Out of the Box: This book will boost your income at least 20%. This is no idle promise. I admit that there are so many techniques in this book, that you will be absorbing and perfecting them for years. But you'll get an immediate boost because most of them work right out of the box. You can literally pick a few and start practicing them today, with an immediate improvement in your sales. From there, you'll be fine-tuning them and pulling in even more profit.

It's Real Money: As a professional salesperson, you don't have the luxury of saying, *"Well, it's only a couple hundred bucks."* That's because you make many, many transactions. If you make 500 transactions and fail to get that extra couple hundred bucks, you have reduced your income by $10,000.00 per year. If you're just getting started in sales, and making $50,000.00 per year, $200.00 is really 20% of your income. Always be sure to think in those terms. That's the professional way to think. In the customer's life, that $200.00 is pale in comparison to the value that they are getting from the deal.

Do the Math: Apply this formula to your sales work now. How much do you think you can increase the average deal if you consistently and expertly applied a well-rounded set of advanced sales techniques and persuasion methods throughout the sales process? Don't even count the occasional extra big fish that you hope to haul in. Now *multiply* that dollar increase by the number of transactions that you intend to complete over the next twelve months. There you go. Is it $50.00 times 1,000 transactions? $500.00 times 200?

Think about how that little philosophy nugget can drive you. Imagine that annual amount goal injecting more motivation into your every sale! *Every sale equals that annual bonus.* Even the littlest technique equals that annual income boost. Add to that the big fish that you reel in from time to time. *How much might you make from boosting your creativity, charisma, connections, and cutting-edge techniques?* How much will having a more systematic approach bring you? And then there is the sheer joy of becoming more skilled, and having more ways to enjoy your career.

Compliment Your Talent with Technical Prowess

Maybe this is a little basic to say, but I think I'd better say it just to make sure we're on the same page. This book is all about your success in sales, and it's mostly on the more advanced side, as these things go. This means that I can't waste time saying mushy, contradictory things that you hear from some motivational books and speakers. It also means that I will be pulling from scientific research in practical ways. So I'm asking you to remember that when I throw in some verbiage that sounds technical or impersonal, please don't take offense. You can apply what you learn in the most personal and spiritual way that you care to muster, but you need a technical foundation.

The great jazz musicians you hear play with their heart and soul, but their heads are full of technical knowledge. They have spent countless hours practicing all sorts of scales (predictable progressions of notes). But their music doesn't come across as a technical exercise. They have mastered the technical, and expressed the spirit in music. So is it that you can take sales to a level that astonishes your peers and makes you legendary.

Please indulge me in a quick example. Since people identify with their conscious minds, calling the conscious mind an "it" may sound offensive, but no offense is intended. This is a technical manual, so I don't want to waste your time going too far afield, padding this work to make it very politically correct or warm and fuzzy. You will be just as human and spiritual after reading this work as you were before, and actually capable of being a better advocate for your highest values, because you will know more about how to be a leader and motivator; more about how to influence and inspire.

MANIPULATION AND PROSTITUTION VS. YOUR HIGHEST VALUES

I suppose I should also cover the matter of *manipulation* or *prostitution*. Some of my readers will feel, perhaps, that delving into the technical side of influence smacks of manipulation. Perhaps some won't be content with the idea that we are all influencing and manipulating at least by accident, so we would do well to start doing it "on purpose," instead. Well, then, let me add that, **when it comes to ethics, you should look at whether you are harming other people, not whether you are extremely good at influencing.** When people talk about *"taking advantage"* of others, this is generally where they draw the line. If your product falls apart and you know the company will pull up stakes and start conning in a new location, then your customers are not the only ones to suffer; you will, too. But if you deprive yourself of the power of influence, you will fail to reach your potential in sales or any other sphere of life.

For any readers that are still wary, I have one more thing that may help, and that is that much of what constitutes influence is your very humanity. That's right. Bringing forth aspects of yourself that create meaningful relationships. You will find that the self understanding that you acquire during this book, and the improvements in your attitude and relationships, will exceed the value of even your wildest dreams of financial success.

I'll offer just one example. During this book, you will learn to do something that some readers may take to mean that you are acting as if you have special feelings about prospects. But I will be helping you generate those feelings from genuine aspects of yourself. Better yet, by discovering that even your more unpleasant prospect has the same fundamental humanity as everyone else, you will feel a deepened sense of self that enriches you. Ideas from the *Enlightenment* era that led to the creation of democratic constitutions for many nations come into play here. That was not mere political rhetoric. It was resounding and revolutionary. The idea of inalienable rights, of all people being created equal, and of freedom for the pursuit of happiness all resonate to the core of our being. Nonetheless, expressing such lofty ideals in daily life is easier said than done. This book will not only make it easier, but provide you with direct experiences that expand you in very gratifying ways.

Leading-Edge Sales Psychology

I'm going to give you a very special challenge. It isn't one of those effortful challenges, like increasing your sales volume 1,000% or climbing Mount Everest with a Sherpa on your back. It's more about being willing to swish around some very different perspectives. In order for me to share with you the concepts *(yes, they'll be practical, I promised you that)* of modern sales psychology, I'm going to need you to just psych your self up a little bit. That's because of two things that could easily go wrong for a lot of readers. One, they might reject the idea before they have had time to see how right it is, and two, they might not really let it sink in well enough before they sort of toss it aside and move on. Many of the ideas in this book are real game-changers. Our *neurodiversity* section can open up sales with many more people than you currently know how to sell to. Our *Automatic Behavior* section asks you to see how we have triggers that are pretty much hard-wired. This requires a really different mindset that you were probably brought up with. It's one thing to know that people can be irrational, but it's quite another to really get how complicated we are, and how the greater portion of that complexity is a concert of unconscious impulses that you can play a conductor.

Sections such as *Identity Shifting* ask you to try out some things that might be a bit hard to believe, but these are things that come from very serious behavioral and sociological research, as well as scary-successful historical examples. But I'll help out by providing some background that will show just how credible these odd things are. I'm talking about things like actually helping your prospects and customers shift their identities in small ways that can produce big sales success.

So be ready to explore and experiment. That means having an open mind and a little discipline *(or fanaticism, better yet)*. Really give each idea enough time to see how you can start applying it to your work now, and how much it can feed your success.

Beyond Formulas to Flexible Sales Intelligence

The history of business is full of examples of people who had a great formula UNTIL THINGS CHANGED. There are people who were doing great in the stock market, until things changed. Sometimes, these formulas were quite insightful and novel, but the didn't last forever. Nothing can substitute for flexible business intelligence, and this includes some depth in understanding human motivation. We are going beyond formulas such as *"the five key motivations"* (not that that is a bad formula) to more flexible application. That's because you are in this as a career, not as a technician who is disposable. This is your life.

Take, for example, the idea of **value as a core trigger of automatic buying behavior.** We know there are amazing examples of raising the price on an item, and finding that sales dramatically improve. But if you did this to every product with flagging sales, it wouldn't work every time. It might not work for any of the products. This takes us to the core of *"flexible sales intelligence"*; understanding with the depth that you need to choose the right ideas for the right situations. The primary aim of this book is to give you that depth regarding human motivation, because that is where the lion's share of flexible sales intelligence awaits.

We will include some other areas that come from hard-won lessons in the real world. That's because we, too, are being flexible. We will not limit ourselves to motivation factors when there are other valuable skills and ideas to impart. For example, we'll talk about something called *knowledge management*, which is a little bit like 'just-in-time' inventory management, in which costs are saved by investing in less inventory, less storage overhead, and less inventory management. This was made possible for large-scale operations such as *Amazon.com* through IT applications such as databases and bar codes. For the salesperson, **knowledge is your primary inventory,** and knowledge management is one of your secret weapons, as you shall see.

ABOUT FUNDAMENTALS

Wait a minute! You say. Isn't this book advanced? What are we doing with a *"Fundamentals"* article? Thank you for asking. I'll tell you. If we know anything, it's that revisiting *some* fundamentals is critical for the success of even the most advanced sales machines. *Why?* Because it's your foundation. I don't care if you're a concert pianist or a fake wrestling champion, everyone has to practice the fundamentals. Ah, but which? You could fill several books with sales fundamentals, couldn't you? So true! The "which" is the fundamentals that are most critical and ALSO most likely to get lost in the shuffle.

After all, most people that do sales are not there because they dream of being bean counters. They like the action, the people, stalking the sale, harpooning the account. Salespeople need to revisit certain basics the way pilots need a check list to make sure their plane is 100% ready to fly. I think pilots and salespeople have some things in common. One group needs to run down a list of key things to make sure they don't crash and burn, and then there are pilots.

Since I know perfectly well that I am speaking to seasoned professionals, I won't belabor the details when I cover our *"Foundation ideas"* section. We'll run through them as painless as possible, we'll make sure that they are the basics that are often neglected, and we'll make sure they are the things that businesses rave about when they put them in place.

So, let's start by asking you to do a quick mental audit. Can you, off the top of your head, think of some fundamentals that could boost your sales? **Think process, think steps, and think protocol.** Do you have a new product line, but haven't systematically gone through all the potential methods of marketing it and decided which you should invest some elbow grease in right away? Do you have a big contact list, but haven't created a systematic method for tickling that list? Do you have multiple people or departments involved in the sales process, but haven't made sure that the process is happening in a water-tight fashion that doesn't lose potential customers? We'll offer up a few fundamental items in more detail in that section.

MOTIVATION & INCOME THROUGH ADVANCED SELF MANAGEMENT

Vision Motivation

Have you ever noticed how people talk about what makes them tick? Why do people who work hard *work so hard*? Some focus on very lofty goals, like dominating the world market for paint stripper. Others are moving forward, but with the worm's eye view, as it's called; focusing on the very next step, like who they are calling next. Most seem to be somewhere in between, with medium term objectives mostly in mind. Perhaps they are trying to move into a neighborhood where their children can go to good schools. But all three types need all three goals. And all three types can tell you about those levels of goals.

I don't really care which level you tend to focus on, so long as you aren't ignoring any glitches in your follow through. But I do care whether your next best task supports your objectives, and your objectives will contribute a great deal to your big picture goals, whether they are to produce world peace or get your relatives to stop arguing.

In other words, I care if the reason behind what you are doing really shows in what you are doing. Please take some time to think about your long-term goals. Include your contribution to the world, your community, your family, and yourself, in whatever proportion you desire. And give yourself some credit. If you're switching to some green technology, that's not just about saving money. There are good odds that it's good for the world, too.

Then look at your medium term objectives. Do you have some that support your long-term goals? Are they doing something to at least get you into a more advantageous position to go after them? Well good. That's a start!

And how about what you're doing tomorrow. How much of that will take you striding toward your objectives?

Do This with Your Vision for Motivation

You might want to sketch or write some of this out. Even start a file about this if you haven't already. Stephen Covey is a good reference for really running with this kind of thinking.

But why am I going into this? Because the more aligned your tasks, objectives, and goals are, the better your alignment will be. That's because *your behavior, your conscious mind, and your unconscious resources really need to be pointing in more or less the same direction.* You wouldn't try to drive a car if the wheels weren't aligned enough to get you where you wanted to go, would you? It's terrible for tire wear, and those freeway guard rails are really rough on the paint.

Since this book is for sales professionals, I must ask if those objectives (mid-range goals) of yours include your productivity and income. I did not exceed a $250,000.00 sales income by dialing the phone and being optimistic. I'll tell you in some detail what will work a lot better. But for now, work up some mid-term career goals for me and I'll get back to you on that soon. For extra credit, turn those objectives into weekly production quotas and schedule the items into your week as time blocks. If your current sales position doesn't work that way, I'll trust you to adjust these instructions according you your best instincts for the moment.

But right now, I'd like to ask everyone for a moment of silence, to appreciate all the things that a high-income professional salesperson can do in their off time. However much you may love your career, isn't it those things that drive you the most? The kind of home and community you want to live in? The kind of travel and learning you want to do? The things you want to get or yourself and your family? The kind of car you'd like to drive? And let's not forget your sales career. How would you like it to expand you with skills, knowledge, experiences, and wisdom for more career satisfaction and even better income?

Don't worry if any of your desires sound petty. It's human to have desires. **It's spectacular to be 100% aligned!**

THE BEAUTY OF ALIGNMENT

I just won't be satisfied if you are wildly financially successful, and nothing more. I want you to be happy and fulfilled, too. And I'm sure the people around you will be a lot happier about it, too, as a general rule. Since I try to get right to the point when I write, I'm happy to say that **alignment serves both financial success and joy.** It is amazing to see what happens to people when they are aligned. When their dreams and objectives are lined up, and they are actively pursuing them, they open a fount of energy and enthusiasm that just can't be found in a pill. If that changes, let me know, okay? I'll invest!

If you feel stuck in life, and you have heard more than enough motivational types trying to give you a shot in the arm (or maybe a pill), I can only tell you what I have seen. I have seen many people who were really stuck for a long time finally come across that alignment. And you never know what will trigger it. But when they find it, it's as if the power and lights all came back on! So I encourage you, *no, I implore you* to continue your quest. Upgrade your sources of inspiration. Go for something technical rather than inspirational, maybe. Consult with someone who really gets your issues and get to the bottom of it. Most importantly, keep changing your tactics until you start getting a footing. This is too important. **Life is too amazing just to survive it.**

I'm happy to tell you that this book will provide you with many ideas that can help with that. Yet only a little part of it is about your motivation. That part probably has some things you've never come across before that will really speak to you. But the rest of the book is filled with so many ideas that you can use to improve your effectiveness and income, that I just don't know how anyone could help but feel more motivated and excited. Nothing succeeds like success.

FULL-SPECTRUM GOALS

Most of my readers will have already gotten some kind of training on how to establish personal and professional goals. It was pretty good, I'll bet. But if you have, you will still find some nuggets in my version of goal-setting. And when is the last time that you dusted off your goals and got them up-to-date? This might be the perfect time for you to use this section for exactly that purpose. And if you haven't had a good grounding in goal setting, you'll be able to learn and develop goals at the same time.

I make a very big deal out of something called *alignment* in this book, and in my life. When your subconscious and conscious are aligned, it opens up a lot of energy and creativity. When your long term and short term goals are aligned, it produces very great amounts of accomplishment. When your highest values and dreams are aligned with you smallest tasks, this produces incredible integrity and satisfaction, as well as more certainty that you are really going where you want to go.

Full-spectrum goals are all about producing alignment.

I think *Stephen Covey's 7 Habits* approach is very helpful in this regard. *Tony Robbins* does something similar in the form of an audio program called *Time of Your Life*, if you prefer his style of presenting. These go into plenty of detail.

But a brief overview of this kind of full-spectrum goal setting goes like this. As usual, I'm putting my personal interpretation into this based on my life experience.

Take time to write down some of the following. This is something that you'll want to make a part of your life, so I wouldn't try to be comprehensive. It would be better to leave this task feeling energized and interested in returning to it.

1. **Highest values and dreams** for your personal and professional life. What is your vision? How does it reflect what you want to have, to be, and to do? What kind of life do you want to lead?

2. **Big picture goals** that are the major accomplishments toward those dreams.

3. **Objectives** that will take major steps toward those goals.

4. **Projects** that contribute to your objectives and goals.

5. **Milestones** that will tell you how you are progressing on your projects and objectives.

6. **Tasks** that you can begin doing now to work toward those milestones.

EXPERIENCE COMPELLING GOALS

You want your goals to be compelling, so that they will inspire you to pursue them, inspire you to think resourcefully, and inspire you to move others with your vision.

Here's an example of a NOT compelling goal: To make as much money as possible. At least it isn't very compelling for most people. Not by itself. That's because it implies that your goal is to do a little as necessary. There is no reason to work any harder than necessary to make an arbitrary number of dollars. Also, it makes no connection to any other values or purposes.

Ask why you want a goal like that, and you'll get closer to your driving values. Ask *why* again and you'll get closer still.

"I want the money for an addition to my house." Why?

"I need a study to clear more room in the house." Why?

"For the family. The kids need a play area in the house and we need a place to relax that isn't so cluttered." Why?

"I want my family to be happy." Why?

"What are you, some kind of idiot? Who wouldn't want their family to be happy?"

Well, there you have it, the driving goal is family happiness. And if you could get him to tell you more, he probably has good feelings about his children benefiting physically and intellectually, his wife having less stress, and them all being able to have more togetherness because the space is conducive to it. Those values are connected dreams like college for the kids, long and healthy lives, and a harmonious, close lifestyle.

Full spectrum goals bring out more of you because you have MORE reasons to succeed. You need goals that create a sense of *urgency*, motives for expanding your skills and wisdom, and motives for expanding your connection with people and society.

THE POWER OF BEHAVIOR LEVERAGE

Behavior leverage is what you get when your mind and behavior automatically react *without* will power. It can be good, or it can be bad. Scientists have learned how to create behavior leverage with something called *behavior modification*. This work has enabled people to train animals to do very complicated tricks, and to train themselves to achieve much more. The key to behavior leverage is that you can do much more and enjoy it much more if you don't have a fight on your hands. If you don't need to muster a lot of will power, you will have more energy and creativity with which to succeed.

The first and most important thing for most people to do with behavior leverage, is to discover the ways that they have been "behavior modified" into bad habits. Procrastination is a perfect example. It is a collection of habitual ways of feeling, thinking, and acting that eliminate certain tasks that you really need to or want to be doing.

People who are very busy can still be procrastinating. In fact, people who are very busy and very focused on doing what they are supposed to be doing can be procrastinating. Even people who are making plenty of money can be procrastinating. I know of a fellow who was very busy, very focused on what he needed to do for success, and was succeeding wildly with bookings and profitability, but he went to federal prison for tax evasion. You can guess what he was procrastinating on. *What have you been procrastinating on?*

The reason procrastination is such a good example is that it shows how unconscious behavior leverage is. You can produce it consciously, just like animal trainers do. But it *works* unconsciously, just like trained animals' minds do. That's a very, very important distinction. Understanding this makes all the difference.

EXAMPLE: PROCRASTINATION BUSTING

So consider how procrastination works unconsciously. People who untangle themselves from procrastination tend to discovery that little discomforts and anxieties gradually shaped their behavior until they eliminated or greatly reduced certain thoughts and behaviors. Unfortunately, these things that get eliminated tend to be tedious, unpleasant, or negative in some ways. Those things tend to be the things we have to do instead of want to do. This is why procrastination is such a problem. It has the *power of the unconscious* working *against* you to make it very hard to take care of some of your responsibilities.

This deep subject really requires at least one book all on its own. But I want you to start applying behavior leverage on this level. Note down the things that you tend to have trouble getting done, and come up with ways to reward yourself for taking steps in the right direction.

Here is where the word "leverage" comes in. This is because of how the subconscious works in regard to behavior and habits. You reward even very small steps in the right direction, such as creating the space on a desk for completing these tasks. Also, you reward immediately. Your subconscious mind responds to short-term rewards a lot like an animal does.

The reward does not have to be something fattening. It doesn't even have to be an actual thing at all. It can be you taking a moment to give yourself a big, emotional pat on the back. You can pull your fist out of the air like you're activating an air horn, and shout, *"Yes! You're fantastic!"* I don't care how silly that sounds. Your subconscious likes it. Get your conscious mind out of the way long enough to do something that will build your success. Don't stand on principle, you can be right and dead, as the expression goes. **Reward yourself for every increment in the right direction and your subconscious mind will start building momentum in that direction.** You will need less and less willpower, and you will then be able to apply yourself more to other things, building leverage in those areas.

This kind of technique is not just for spot work. This is something that builds your success momentum in more and more areas until you are almost like a different person in terms of your energy, creativity, resourcefulness, and *results.*

DISCOVER ANY GATEWAY PROBLEMS

We talked about getting out of procrastination by using rewards. Now, let's look at obstacles to success in terms of what I call the gateway problem. When you move in the direction of some kind of success, you could say that your first moves are like going through a gateway. Once you are through, you are on your way. But sometimes, the gateway has a challenge. It might be a little troll or a big dragon. But somehow you need to defeat it in order to pass through.

The gateway problem against having a meaningful and intimate conversation with a family member can be your ability to experience a confident, open, creative state. If you find yourself in a closed, insecure, defensive state, you will probably end up trying to manipulate them, rather than experience a deep conversation. Many of us manipulate others without even realizing it, because we are feeling too reactive to notice.

The gateway problem against focusing on your one top priority of the moment might be a habit of feeling like everything is a top priority and having your brain turn your day into a crush or priorities. The same kind of thing might happen with your need to pull out your biggest objectives or greatest dreams. Some other automatic reaction interferes.

Solve Gateway Problems

People try to solve gateway problems by talking to themselves. This works from time to time, but not often enough. My favorite way to defeat a gateway problem is to find what the automatic mind-body reaction is, and resolve that reaction. I use techniques that accomplish this pretty easily. *Emotional Freedom Technique,* which you can learn about online, is a good example. If the problem is more challenging than a self-applied technique, therapists know various reprocessing techniques such as *EMDR. Shimmering* is an excellent method that uses guided experiences.

Let's say that you have a colleague who has trouble with rejection. Each time she experiences rejection, she gets a little less motivated. This is behavior modification at work. Each rejection is like a little electric shock training her subconscious to go in a different direction. Anything that moves her toward rejection, such as making a sales call, becomes less and less desirable. Some people become completely paralyzed in their career because of this negative kind of behavior leverage.

It can be so automatic, that somehow the person just doesn't get around to really identifying and deciding to get rid of the anxiety. It's as if negative behavior leverage can make people dim-witted when it comes to their gateway problems. Hopefully, someone will come along and really get her excited about resolving the anxiety so they can get on with their career. The anxiety about rejection is like a weak link in a chain that is perfectly strong except for that one little link.

The funny thing is, that it might be a fear of rejection that makes her mind have trouble dealing with priorities. Clarity on priorities could lead to more appointments, which would mean more rejection. It's like a domino effect.

EXAMPLE SOLUTION: DESENSITIZING

Fortunately, she doesn't have to figure this out. Surprisingly, if she can get one or more of these gateway problems to be less sensitive, her behavior and thinking may automatically change. That is a very interesting thing. Because that often happens without actually working directly on thought patterns.

Let's say that she first takes care of her reaction to priorities, and she no longer reacts to sorting them out and looking a deadlines with that quick tickle of anxiety. As a result, she does not experience the tendency to hold back from looking at the big picture. This causes her to recognize that her success can benefit from tackling the way she experiences rejection in sales situations. So she goes for the gold and decides to take on this bugaboo about rejection.

She might use *Emotional Freedom Technique,* or need to escalate and see a therapist about it. Once resolved, she ends up with a completely different feeling about rejection. And I *don't* mean on a logical level. Just about anybody can be logical about a problem and still have it. A famous talk show host used to call his cigarettes *"coffin nails,"* but he still couldn't stop smoking. What I mean is what you get at a gut level; **bone-deep feeling and knowing that comes right out of you spontaneously.** Now that's a real change.

REPROCESSING RESULTS

Now I want to you take a moment to imagine the results of this. First, she has an easy time thinking about priorities items in a calm state of mind. That means that her mind naturally gravitates to them at various times, like when she's taking a shower, and, eureka! She has more brilliant ideas for moving her career forward. In fact, she has all sorts of other breakthrough, problem-solving ideas as well.

Also, her performance with prospects improves because of less anxiety. That helps her establish rapport and think on her feet. **More sales result!** And that's not to mention the beauty of simply enjoying life more.

It's very interesting to see how thoughts can change spontaneously when an automatic feeling reaction gets resolved. Our colleague's new state might produce new thoughts such as, *"They aren't rejecting me. They are rejecting something that I can pro-actively take care of as I get more skilled about this issue. For example, I know that if I show them that I'm concerned about not abusing their time, they will not reject me."* or, *"Now that I don't have bad feelings about rejection, my attitude is going to keep getting more upbeat and attractive. That will naturally cause more people to want to talk with me."* Now that's the kind of bone-deep change that brings out the salesperson in a person.

Wouldn't you love to just naturally feel that way? I mean, your colleague. Wouldn't you love to see your colleague just getting more and more "juice" as their funk lifts? Imagine watching their sales figures climb as their natural energy and motivation start revving up!

This basic change in her relationship to these seemingly little personal reactions could dramatically change her life. That's because these little reactions have a *leverage effect over time,* to produce big limitations. That's why I take them so seriously and make sure to become aware of them and deal with them early and often.

See if *you* have any gateway problems that might benefit from a desensitization technique like *Emotional Freedom Technique.*

KNOWLEDGE MANAGEMENT

Knowledge management is a little bit like 'just-in-time' inventory management, in which costs are saved by investing in less inventory and less inventory storage. This was made possible for large-scale operations such as *Amazon.com* through IT applications such as databases and bar codes. For the salesperson, **knowledge is your primary inventory,** and knowledge management is one of your secret weapons.

As technology becomes an ever-greater part of our lives, and as information becomes ever-more available, many sales positions are becoming flooded with knowledge. On top of that, customers are becoming more knowledgeable and sophisticated. Emotion will always be an important part of sales, but the analytical side of customers is more prevalent than ever.

Luckily, the very technology that threatens to overwhelm us can also save the day when it comes to being prepared for a specialized customer. Consider my work in life insurance. Many customers have extraordinary control over their assets, making changes in investments on the fly, and observing trends and allocations on fancy pie charts and the like. They also go to sites that tell them about life insurance, including Consumer Reports, which takes the analytical consumer to a whole new level of knowledge in comparing products, brands, and services.

Many of you are already experiencing the *death of the salesperson* who knows all about their product line and is ready to answer any question. Now more than ever, an important role of the salesperson is to prepare for the specialized customer. It means inhaling a lot of data. You research your customer, and this may include detailed interviews over time, not a brief appointment and quick sale. You research industry trends and competitors' offerings. You even research your company's offerings and knowledge. Knowledge management software and your own ability to acquire knowledge and sources can serve you in all three of these areas.

You customer will be impressed with your specialized knowledge, unaware that you didn't have it until you crammed in the preceding couple of days. But don't be shy about bringing your data with you. You can't be certain that your customer won't throw you a curve ball. Your Internet-enabled device, loaded with your company's data, could save the day.

The take away message is that a knowledge management philosophy that includes "just in time" knowledge acquisition may allow you to save time and focus your sales efforts where they can have the most impact. In some sectors, the days of being "well-rounded" are over.

State Management

You may manage your time well, but **you must manage your emotions,** if someone cancels and that puts you into a state of frustration or disappointment, this will drain your energy and affect your presence and creativity with prospects. It can wipe out your self discipline. *"Discipline your disappointments."* Turn them around so they empower you, because success comes from managing yourself.

The way you feel largely causes the results you get, because of how it affects not only your behavior, but subtle cues in your body language that affect people. Managing the things that affect how you feel can dramatically improve your results. One of the major things that affect how you feel and what you communicate to the world around you, is what you have on your mind.

The way you feel affects your physiology and vice versa. So change your physiology and you change the way you feel. Physiology is just short hand for referring to everything about your physical state, such as your body language.

When you change your body language, it changes how you feel. I'm not talking about your unconscious, subtle body language, rather, you can directly manage your conscious aspects of body language that you can control. On the other hand, by learning to mange your state, you will also generate subtle body language that helps build rapport and increase your sales, even though no one is consciously aware of the influence.

I'd like you to think about what states you enter into at various points during your day. How do they affect your sales, your energy, and your focus on success? Throughout this book, you will have the opportunity to practice and learn many things that give you greater control over your state, and as a result, your success. *Success results from managing your state so that it is relevant to what you need to do a particular place and time.*

STATES ARE YOUR PLAYTHINGS, NOT THE WEATHER

Many people treat their states like there is nothing they can do about them. Worse, they amplify them into Greek tragedies. It reminds me of the old joke, *"Everybody talks about the weather, but nobody ever does anything about it."*

Successful people will tell you, though, that you can exert a great deal of influence over your states. A good place to start is to look at the words that you use to describe how you react to negative experiences. Some people say things like, *"I was shattered,"* or *"I died on stage,"* or *"I feel like such a failure."*

Stop right there. *What does a failure feel like?* How do you know you feel like that? If you actually stop and ask, you'll notice that you have very specific thoughts and feelings, and they are not the weather. They are a part of you, and you can influence them a great deal.

Just shifting your words can begin to give you a taste of how that works. Instead of *"I feel like a failure,"* how about:

"I'm really reacting pretty intensely to this. My breathing is shallow, my posture is droopy, and my thinking is fuzzy. I really had my self esteem attached to this outcome. I need to get my body and mind back into a good state for what is coming up next. Let's see, how about taking a break and walking while I plan? That sounds good."

This keeps you from reinforcing the pattern of habitually going into a destructive state. That is totally different thinking. Your body will respond to that, and your thoughts will begin to catch that positive drift. You won't have to work at it once it becomes a habit.

WORD-STATE WORKOUT

If you blew it, you can move into a problem-solving focus instead of wasting time on self-recrimination. There's a big difference between self-reproach and taking responsibility. Suicide is not actually the most sincere form of self criticism, it's taking responsibility. Consider this language:

"I was not prepared for the questions, I'll really need to bone up before I try that again. I'm really concerned about what this did to my reputation. I suspect it's going to take me a while to regain enough trust to have another crack at that group."

Wow, is that language ever different. It's constructive, it's about your power, it's about possibilities, it's about accountability, and it's about action and desired outcomes. it connects with your power and desire.

At first, it may seem artificial or forced, but it is a much more realistic pattern of thinking than, *"I feel like a failure."* All that means is that you have a collection of feelings that are so overwhelming in your current skill set that you feel like you can't cope and need to escape the situation, but it is intolerable because it would be devastating to you to give up. So you're stuck.

You don't need to be stuck. You can start getting unstuck by managing your state. Thoughts are a nice way to start, and you'll learn more as you go along with this book. Since you're a salesperson, sell yourself on your own success with this straightforward approach.

TIME MANAGEMENT

You know that time management is important. But do you have an approach that really works for you? Many people find that someone else's book or program works for other people but not for them. Don't assume that it's because you aren't trying hard enough. It might be that you need something that fits you. You might not be able to work in their shoes, either.

Of course, you still have the same bottom-line need to spend most of your time selling. That usually means spending most of your time eyeball to eyeball with customers. The more influence you have, the more money you earn. This means you must use a system in which you manage your activities in a time-sensitive manner.

Successful people always have more to do than they can possibly get to, so most people focus on tasks. The problem with this is that tasks expand into the time you give them. You need to make sure that the things that will truly make a difference to your income and career have their time. That means that you must not be intimidated by the little tasks. This is the kind of thing that you want to desensitize as we discussed earlier.

To create results that go beyond surviving the tasks that come at you, you have to get beyond just being reactive. That means shifting your focus from tasks that come at you to outcomes that you desire. It becomes much easier to discern what you can postpone or overlook when you have an outcome focus.

A BIG TIME MANAGEMENT REFRAME

Becoming a celebrity is a great example. When people become extremely famous, they have to focus on their craft, not answering thousands of emails. They have people for that, and if they are using their people wisely, their people create systems for filtering in only the most important contacts. They have no choice. It is not a struggle for will power or better judgment. It's the only way they can continue on. What if you felt like that about the tasks coming at you. Imagine your discernment as to what would really have the best bottom line results being so acute that you simply had zero tolerance for any task that would waste your time?

You can do that, but you have to have compelling reasons. That means that you use full-spectrum goals, and think in outcomes rather than tasks. The more you think in outcomes, the more sense you can make out of all the tasks that come at you. When I got this into a habit, I was amazed at how many tasks I could postpone or bypass altogether. At first, I was having this twinge of doubt. This nagging feeling that I was being irresponsible. Then I realized. There will always be infinitely more than one can do. You must have boundaries, like a cell has to have a wall. You must accept the responsibility and wield the power. There is no alternative, because failure is not an option, and profit is your mission.

Try this little assignment to begin acquiring a taste for this. Take your list of tasks, and group them into outcomes. Then spend your day thinking exclusively in terms of what outcomes you are working towards. This gets interesting, because you are then in a much better position to ask yourself if those outcomes are in line with your truly meaningful projects, objectives, longer term goals, and your vision and dreams. In other words, are your outcomes really part of your full-spectrum goals? Is one of your goals how many hours you will spend in front of customers? How many would that be, and what income would result? We'll talk more about that later.

This is truly revolutionary. And people need revolutionary time management these days.

TIME AND SELF MANAGEMENT TIPS

Account:Value Ratio: Which is better, lots of accounts that you don't follow up with, or less accounts that are really happy with their service? Ask yourself if you are following up where it matters most.

Do it on Hold: I'm glad you can do more than one thing at a time, but are you doing the best *"more?"* For example, I know you hate paperwork, but imagine how caught up you would be if you insisted on holding for those big fish that don't call back. Put the phone on speaker, but only until they pick up. In the mean time, shuffle paper. Your boss will love this, and your blood pressure will, too. Make sure the operator knows that you have all the time in the world, because you are working on a deadline at the office and won't be leaving your desk.

Protected Time: Do you have *uninterrupted* time set aside for productivity, concentration, and fostering creative ideas. Do you need it? Most people do. Think about what it could do for you at work or at home.

Sneaky Rhythms: It is very important to sniff out time patterns that have unintended consequences. For example, does your company have a predictable rhythm for offering specials? If so, you may have predictable sales slumps because customers are waiting for a special! Some companies need to disrupt their pattern, while others can actually benefit from being predictable.

After all, if you *"entrain"* your customers into a buying pattern, keeping their eyes out for that email that tells them there is a special, then maybe they'll pay less attention to the competition. Habits can be hard to break.

But, if you are somewhat unpredictable, maybe they will watch even more carefully. **And the competition may not be able to counteract you as easily if they can't predict what you'll do.** Create ripples in their time-space conundrum!

More!

Quota Crossings: Don't coast just because you passed a quota, or because the quota is far off. Learn lots of tricks for keeping yourself fresh and motivated.

You are an Athlete: You are a sales athlete. You need all the TLC (**T**ender **L**oving **C**are), fine-tuning, conditioning, and training that an athlete does. That means creating the kind of holistic lifestyle that health fanatics have. If you had a multi-million dollar race horse, would you let it watch TV all evening and stay on the phone all day? Would you let it drink and stay up late? No way! You're worth multi-millions too, and that ain't hay.

Sleep: Sleep is the biggest secret to mental health and motivation. You won't hear a motivational speaker say it's the secret to success, because that would be boring, but it's one of the top secrets to success.

The problem is, it has to be quality sleep. You need to be on a good rhythm, not stay up late watching talk shows, and if you aren't waking up feeling well-rested, then you need to find out why. It could be there are some old issues that aren't letting you get through your REM sleep.

Context: How well does your work environment promote your productivity. No person is an island. **Environment makes a difference.**

Are you getting interrupted too much?

Is there too much chaos for you to keep a clear head?

Do you have a good system for tracking your obligations and opportunities?

How about your ergonomics?

Meaning: Do the people in your life inspire you and chare your values? Do they bring out the best in you? Well, they better, or you need to hang with a better class of people!

MORE YET!

Beware Metaphysics: There are people who want you to give them your money so they can tell you that you can make money come to you with your mind. Every minute you spend learning what they believe is a minute you could spend getting in shape, honing your skills, and loving your family. Tell them that you *already* make money come to you with your mind. *It happens when you plan your work and work your plan.*

I have heard them say that if you protest war, you will actually cause more war because you're putting *energy* into war. That means your thoughts alone can make people kill each other. Now that really kills me. If this magic worked, every teenage boy would have a lingerie model for a girlfriend. If you want to influence events with subtle energy, learn to manage your state so your personality will exert subtle influences.

Needy vs. Charismatic: Have you ever noticed that it can be easier to sell to folks when you are not attached to the sale? Think about how that applies to the 80/20 rule.

When you deal with the roughly 20% of accounts that are worth around 80% of your income, I'll bet you get 100% more nervous. If you do, you could be working poorly on 80% of your bottom line productivity! Try hard, not too hard.

Number or Percentage Quota: Perhaps you can consider a percentage improvement for your next quota. An arbitrary number is more likely to be intimidating or seem meaningless. There's something more inspiring about going for a percentage gain. It works for me 20% better than an arbitrary number. *Just kidding.* But, maybe it's just a psychological trick.

Wait.

Did I say JUST a psychological trick? That's like accusing a baker of cheating by using dough. Of COURSE it's a psychological trick. Sales is all about psychology. Motivation is all about psychology. That means sales motivation is psychology cubed.

Get Out of the Box

Have you been in a little too much of a rut? You may be missing some great opportunities to boost sales, just by looking a few feet over the fence called your "role" in your organization or profession. For example, is there some force field stopping you from communicating with employees who can have an effect on sales? Surprisingly, many salespeople ignore these staffers, because they are so involved with their own motivation, techniques, and processes.

Take a little time off from that right now, and think about what people in your organization could do something (or STOP doing something) that could make a difference to your bottom line right now. How hard would it be to develop a little bit of a relationship with them. You could thank them for things they have done that were helpful.

Maybe remember their birthday and give a little gift. And then ask for a little favor. You'll be learning about the beauty of reciprocity in triggering helpful responses. In one of my positions, I was very nice to the receptionists.

When I came back from a meeting, I usually had a nice snack for them. I was very consistent in responding to their requests for appointment times. The other agent in the office gave them the feeling that he was not exactly excited about appointments. Sometimes he was late.

The receptionists wanted to take pride in their job, so my performance reflected well on them. I made them feel good by being reliable. I became their first pick when a new appointment came in, My colleague got second pick. Now and then, there was only one appointment at the same time, so I was picking up more business. Meanwhile, my colleague kept up his night time drinking schedule and his daytime hangover schedule. I brought home the bigger commission check.

Good thing I was not content to limit my idea of my role to the obvious one: go to your appointments and sell. I added an "intrapreneurial" objective of building staff support where it could make a difference.

There's a classic example from *Disneyland*. Stop me if you've already heard this one. It's about a janitor who would yell at the visitors when they dropped garbage on the ground. I suppose he thought that was part of his job. Or maybe he was just frustrated. Or maybe he was potty trained at gunpoint. Whatever the case, his manager pointed out to him that his paycheck was basically written by the people that were walking through Disneyland, and that the better they felt, the more people would come and help write that check. Is there anything you can do to help your staff feel more excited about giving your customers and potential customers a truly satisfying experience?

The moral of these two stories is, "everybody sells." But there are plenty of different ways to get out of the box. I'll bet in just the next minute or two, you could think up a few out-of-the-box ideas where you could win by stepping over those artificial lines that seem to define your role. *Why not?* Somebody has to do it. And it's profitable. Start now. **Those bonus checks don't write themselves, you know!**

What are You?

If you could create your own job title, what would you like it to be? Try coming up with a title that does NOT have sales, representative, or account in it. This is a mind stretch that will get your subconscious mind more creative. Who knows what little brilliant ideas will come to you in the shower when you least expect them. *And just because of a little silly creativity.*

Of course, I'm not suggesting that you change what you say in public. Not unless you come up with something that's just irresistible. I'm certainly not suggesting that sales is a bad word. I'm just saying that you get a mental stretch from finding other names for what you do. For this exercise, it's okay to be funny and creative.

Sometimes, people do this, and like the results so much that the decide to use the title as an attention-getter.

It's good to sell shoes, but aren't you really a personal mobility broker? Or maybe a foot longevity consultant? Maybe a paparazzi escape facilitator. (If you've ever sold an athletic shoe to a celebrity, there you go.) Selling vacations and timeshares is good, but how about being a dream fulfillment expert, a dream agent, or a *dream proofer*?

Bankers, real estate agents, and executive head hunters are salespeople. They don't call themselves salespeople because their products and industries define them. What should define you? You and I know that sales is not just transactions, unless you spend the day at a cash register. But the word "sales" sounds like a transaction and can limit some people's thinking. So try this little experiment. Do it for the fun, the motivation, and maybe a way to create more attention, more conversations, and more sales!

Just so you know I'm not crazy, there are many people who have done this very thing in order to create a professional identity that attracts attention. The first *"success coach"* could have just gone by the old moniker of counselor. The first *"glamour consultant"* could have stuck by cosmetologist or make up salesperson. And how many people have put celebrity or "of the stars" in their title? They didn't find that in a federal pamphlet about work titles. Maybe tax collectors should call themselves "infrastructure fund-raisers." As in, *I get money for streets, bridges, and everything else you take for granted.*

SHEER PERSUASION

HIDDEN INFLUENCE FACTORS

MASTERY OF INFLUENCE

You will become a master of influence by moving beyond old-school formulas. Find the needs and fill them? Make sure the customer knows about all the advantages and features? Help the customer see that the advantages outweigh the disadvantages? Motivate the customer? That's all fine as far as it goes, but in order to achieve great success, you must learn the deeper secrets of motivation. And you will, as we help you understand the vortex of forces that culminate in that moment when the prospect becomes a real customer; when they cross that threshold to truly and deeply wanting your product. In fact, I want you to learn to connect them with their *existing*, driving passions that are *waiting* fuel the sale. This is the force that overrides the objections and makes the customer justify their purchase. This is the force that makes them desperately desire your product. This is the force that makes the financial commitment just that, a real commitment.

THE TWIN FORCES
THAT DRIVE ALL BEHAVIOR

I will start with the simple premise that **we do everything to avoid pain or pursue pleasure**; that these twin forces drive all our behavior. Seen from that point of view, all sales techniques begin coming into focus; this is foundational.

Try this perspective now. I'll argue for the *pain* of *doing* it. You argue for the pain of NOT doing it. Because in both these examples, the pain of NOT doing it wins, I'm sure you will agree.

If you drive, why did you take the time to put gas in your car? It's smelly, it costs money, and it takes time. If you wear clothes, why do you buy them? Shopping for clothes involves crowds, a lot of time, and tedium. And then there's hemming. And they might go out of style!

Isn't it interesting to think about the pain of NOT doing something, instead of the usual motivations FOR doing it? And we're just barely getting started. People will go farther to avoid pain than to gain pleasure, generally. Most of us would go farther out of our way to keep someone from stealing $1,000 than we would to earn it. It's just human nature. This is a key to persuasion, as you will see soon. This is a key to a powerful force for change.

THE PLEASURE ELEMENT

Let's start with the more obvious of our twin forces. You could say that, as a sales professional, you are selling consequences. Those consequences are positive and negative. When conveying the positive side of your offering, how do you make it attractive. First, take a big step backward from *making* anything into anything, and ask yourself how well you know your prospect. What drives them? What is most likely to be attractive about your product *to them*. Persuasion is the process of getting your customer to clearly associate their most desired feelings and states to you product or service. But first, you must discover those *"most desired feelings."*

We'll be uncovering many ways to discover just that. Our People Reading section will give a great deal of insight there. I want to start with you as a person. In order to really make the positives shine in their mind, it helps for the prospect to know that you really have their best interests at heart. A key way for you to get into this state of mind is to be willing to lose the sale. That may sound crazy, but desperation and pushiness will only alienate most people. But a lost sale, lost properly, may become a good referral. Remember this, your focus on their best interest appeals to the prospects *"what's in it for me"* roots, and generates interest and trust.

So, of all the things that might bring them pleasure, confirmation of their most treasured beliefs about themselves ranks number one. If they see themselves as savvy shoppers, the pleasure of a BMW does not lie in its status, but in its reliability and safety. It lies in the extraordinary training of its mechanics, the availability of service shops, and the remarkably generous guarantee. You must instinctively appeal to the values and identity of the prospect, not merely those of the sales brochure, for therein lies the biggest pleasure principle of all.

The Pain Element

When it comes to pain as a sales force, the heart of the matter is that most prospects start out associating more pain with the purchase than with refraining from the purchase. That means that they will not buy until this balance of pain shifts. As important as the pleasure factor is to the buying decision, the less obvious pain factor is usually that one that actually rules over the sales process.

This gives you the essential mission of bringing the pain of *not* buying into the foreground of their mind. A good way to do this is to discover the problem that must be solved, and the pain of that problem. That pain will be the source of their desire. Once their dissatisfaction is strong enough, it will outweigh any pain still connected with buying. They will feel compelled to produce a change.

To rephrase a statement from the pleasure piece above, persuasion is the process of getting your customer to clearly associate their most painful feelings and states to *not* buying your product or service. The place to start for associating not buying with pain, is to *seek and activate* the pain.

Pain Element Workout

Think about your own purchases, especially any that kind of took you by surprise, perhaps because of a persuasive salesperson; maybe a person who you didn't even realize was a salesperson.

A friend of mine got a dog some time after he was divorced. He did not do this on his own. He was persuaded by someone who knew how to activate his pain. It was his ex-wife. Yes, she definitely knew how to activate his pain. That's why she was his ex. But I digress. She played the kid card, making him think about his son visiting him without a dog.

She activated the loneliness by talking him into "just going to see" a dog that she felt he would want. You know what happened next. He came home with the dog. It caused him to get more exercise, meet more people, and have more company, so this ex-wife was, in effect, a salesperson that did him a big favor by activating some hurt. She didn't really hurt him at all. His son was happier, and he was happier and healthier.

You could make a very long list of places where such hurt hides. Perhaps for your next prospect it will be in the form of a potential missed opportunity. Don't miss out! ...the ability to use it now. Don't wait! ...someone else getting it and showing it off. **Don't be showed up!**

Whether the hurt appears to come from petty or saintly origins, it is a key to sales. And remember, the hurt will usually be one that neither you nor the customer knows in advance is there.

TIPPING THE SALE

Your first and greatest obstacle to the sale is usually the primary objection. At first glance, it appears to be an unbreachable wall or uncrossable current. But it will not be expressed clearly or directly, not usually. If you hear, *"I don't really need this,"* don't assume this is all there is.

Your job will be to find out what you can use to tip the scale of their buying decision so that the primary objection becomes neutralized, but first you must clarify their primary objection. Remember that it is probably not rational. The most powerful objections are the irrational ones, because they drive the prospect unconsciously, and may be rooted in bad experiences. Is this starting to sound like psychotherapy? Maybe in a way it is! But, fortunately, you can ferret out their primary objection in any number of ways.

Using my sales system (in detail later in this book) and the section on objections, you will gain excellent methods for uncovering these pests. For example, test closes, done repeatedly, can take away the layers covering the true issue. As you gain experience, your intuition may lead you to the objection, and you can work on it without necessarily ever putting it into words. My *People Reading* material will help here.

What about the most obvious objection, that they don't have enough money for it? That is rarely the true objection, especially when they came to you with an interest in your product. As a matter of habit, you should translate that objection to mean that they have not gotten to the tipping point that makes the sale; they have not overcome their deeper objection, have not really connected enough pain to not buying, or have not really connected with the pleasure factor. They might even be trying to soften you on price. To reduce the power of that technique, and its cost to you, you will be promoting the value of your product.

GET READY TO RESOLVE OBJECTIONS

Any number of objections may feel legitimate to your prospect. And they are usually quite rational and respectable. They may be important enough to need direct attention. You are likely to encounter at least some of them before you get to the primary objection. The objections may fade when the primary objection is resolved, or need additional attention or tipping point work as I described.

Think about a time when you wanted something, but didn't buy it because you couldn't justify it. This happens when your emotional reasons aren't strong enough to overrule your more rational or logical reasons. In this case, the domain of the primary objection was logic, unless you had a hidden emotional objection that you expressed by turning to logic. *Can you think of an example of that?* I suppose you'll notice immediately that you usually can't afford things that you have little excitement about, but find a way to afford those that you do.

PAIN ELEMENT WORKOUT

When we dig a little deeper, we find primary objections are usually fears or pain of some kind; financial hardship, fear of betrayal and buyer's remorse, self doubt, and concern about how others would judge the purchase.

If you have enough experience with the product, or you size up your prospect in advance, you may be able to preempt the objection, so that it does not become a primary objection. You may be able to outweigh it with a stronger dose of existing or anticipated pain for not buying or pleasure for buying.

It is easy to see a want from the positive side. I want it because of this or that good benefit. But to activate more hurt, your primary vehicle for resolving objections, you must find the hurt that the need implies. If your prospect is a young professional who just took a job in Honolulu, and is looking at one of your surfboards, perhaps the hurt in the want is the loneliness of being in a new town. The surfboard could cure the hurt by getting him involved with people who are learning, and teaching, surfing. You don't have to tell your prospect that they are lonely, but by focusing on the social aspect, you may drive away that concern about cost like a good off-shore breeze.

TIPPING POINT WORKOUT

Many sales are lost because the salesperson does not realize how close they are to crossing the tipping point. You have learned that activating hurt is often the answer. You know that you can find hurt within a desire, as we did with our potential surfer. I explained that you could activate them by focusing on the benefits that would heal that hurt, or, put another way, resolve that need. Another way is to ask questions that arouse that pain, especially when it brings out beliefs and values that are tied to the need.

Consider this language:

"From what you've told me, Bill, it sounds like taking care of your life insurance now will mean an end to the frustration of not having time to research the subject. As you know, I have done the research and my customer's are very happy with my expertise. And if you learn more and decide there is a better policy, you can change without a penalty, anyway."

The hurt is that the prospect already feels the need for life insurance hanging over him, and he has been procrastinating with the excuse that he needs to do research. This is a double whammy of failure that makes him dig in his heels, because he feels like making the decision based on his own research will prove something. At least that's my best guess, based on what he's said, and because it is a common kind of subconscious "logic." It certainly isn't something he has thought through.

Since I had already established my credibility as an expert, I used that to resolve the conscious concern about research. I activated the hurt about the decision hanging over him. I neutralized the need to prove something by telling him he could choose a better policy after he did his research.

Think about your prospects' likely primary and other emotional objections, and what kind of language would mollify them. Write some brief scripted statements from that, and try them out on your prospects when they appear to have one of the emotional objections you have identified. Remember that these objections are usually irrational, like my prospect who felt a need to prove something.

YOUR MOTIVATION FOR ACTIVATION WORKOUT

It's time for a brief break for motivational philosophy; your reasons for being a master of influence. This material about healing hurt is really more important than you might realize at first. By getting people into action, you are acting as a healer of hurt that is already there, you don't actually create the hurt. That's helpful to know in designing your sales approach, but it is also helpful to know in terms of the human condition.

When people get into action, they enjoy being more dynamic. It feels good to be engaged in solving problems and meeting needs, especially your own. Participating in life is the opposite of the doldrums. By putting what is significant on deck, we pick up the winds of success and joy. This expands us as people and connects us with society.

As a good persuader, you are not a nag, but someone who ignites desires that will motivate your customers to improve their lives. Sometimes all they need is more information, but you almost always need to activate the hurt. Pain is part of growth, and the pain of desire has a cure: action.

When you get people motivated to buy, how does it jibe with your highest values. *Does any of this piece's philosophy apply to you?*

THE LOGIC ELEMENT

You may need to apply some logic at any point in your sales process, but there is a special place where it is almost always helpful. That is at the point where you want to give them that last push over the tipping point. This is because you have provided them with the emotional momentum and the pain. They already have some logical reasons for making the purchase. **But by invoking a key logical reason as you close, this provides them with the feeling that their**

conscious mind is in control. People really like this illusion. In fact, evolutionary psychologists think that we evolved to treasure this experience. Since the conscious mind controls the pen with which they sign, you should make sure it feels like it has the final say.

Did you know that the energy to act in a specific way builds up in the brain before you are aware that you are about to act?

Scientists have commented that we have more of a "free won't" ability than we do "free will." That's because most of our self control takes the form of consciously preventing ourselves from doing something that we are geared to do, rather than to consciously create the action to start with.

Providing the conscious mind with that logical justification at just the right moment keeps it from doing "free won't" (which is a way to experience power and justification), and gives it the freedom to "take charge" by allowing desire to carry the moment. If that sounded contradictory, that's because **being human has its contradictions.** This is one of them. Understanding this contradiction as you do now will net you many more sales.

BELIEFS

For this book, **a belief is a solid sense of certainty about something.** Since we're dealing with the motivational power of feelings, needs, and logic, we don't need to get academic. Since the bottom line is sales, we don't need to split hairs.

You have already learned that people base their actions on the twin forces of pleasure and pain. So, where sales is concerned, we want to affect beliefs about pleasure and pain. We want our core skills as masters of influence to affect these beliefs.

Since beliefs are about certainty, we want our prospect to have the certainty that our product with bring pleasure and avoid pain.

BIG SCALE BELIEFS

For the sake of understanding people, and for the sake of our own personal development, we can take a broad view of beliefs. Think about people you know who tend to be very happy and proactive. What makes them different from those who are generally unhappy and lack personal power? Look at the beliefs that drive these states. What do they have certainty about? What are they certain will bring pleasure and avoid pain, and vice versa?

And, since the subconscious looms so large in these equations, what certainty might be encoded in their unconscious minds that drive them. Unhappy people tend to have limiting beliefs that actually take some work for them to put into words, because those beliefs are so buried in their subconscious minds.

Consider the ways that you tend to be happy and driven, or unhappy and prone to failure. I'm sure you can find some of both in your life. *What conscious and unconscious certainties could be driving you into these states?*

YOUR BELIEFS AND YOUR SUCCESS

One of the greatest things you can experience in life, is to find a belief that would make a tremendous difference in your life. One of the things that were holding me back early in life had to do with trust. I'd had some experiences that had encoded mistrust into my unconscious. It causes the bad things people do stand out more in my mind than the good ones. I lived on the same planet as my more successful friends, but it might have well been a different one, since I was looking through cynical eyes. This held me back from seeing my life and career as being part of the good contributions that people are making in life.

Once I made the shift to fully embracing the fundamental goodness of people, and accepting the fundamental badness, I could accept a sense of mission; I could expand my identity and career;

I could meet people with a fuller openness that made me more attractive; I made more sales. I wanted to bring out the best in people, because I felt the certainty that it was there. I wanted to connect with that, because I valued it; it made me feel really good.

The personal growth guru Tony Robbins says that his big shift was in getting a sense of urgency. This came from him becoming certain that he could succeed if he made a high level of commitment. Commitment and certainty are kissing cousins.

Prior to that, he was becoming crabby, depressed, and felt put upon. He had to get more than a sense of urgency, though. He had to connect it with his driving values, and create certainty that urgency would take him where he wanted to go.

BELIEF WORKOUT: YOUR SUCCESS

What pivotal belief might change your life? Write it down, and discover the ways that you can create a profound shift in your life from this book.

What would you do if you had the certainty that, by becoming a master of persuasion, you could become who you most want to be; that you could create what you most want to create; that you could do what you most want to do; that you could have what you most want to have?

What if you knew that you could take your income into the stratosphere?

What kind of quotas and goals would you set for prospecting?

What kind of effort would you make to master the tools in this book?

Your can achieve superior success by having more certainty, by having more reasons, by having more certainty, that you will use your tools and hours to produce your desired income and other achievements.

Your first step in producing that certainty, is to get clear on what you value most. This is essential. Because certainty about achieving something that is not 100% in line with your highest values will not take you 100% to success. You may not be completely sure about that. If not, you will know more as this book progresses.

But however much you know about your highest values so far, take a minute to put them into words, and write them down. Throughout this book, I want you to apply these sales techniques to yourself to enhance your certainty about living these values, your development of a plan to live those values, so that you have the certainty that your plan fully serves those values.

Take a simple example. If you thrive on adventure, and you were considering some vacations, you would really be excited about one that you were certain would be an adventure. If you are totally fascinated by exotic people, you would get worked up about one that would get you involved with another culture. Kicking this up beyond vacations, think about how such values drive your life, and how they can fuel your success.

PEOPLE READING
FOR FUN AND PROFIT

IT'S REALLY IMPORTANT TO READ PEOPLE

Your sales career depends on how good you are at sizing people up. I have had the experience of banking on a judgment about a prospect that turned out to be as wrong as peanut butter on poker chips simply because I had not been observant enough, and missed a crucial clue. This section is intended to give you the acuity you need to predict how a prospect will respond to your sales techniques and your approach to them. More to the point, it exists to help you decide how to approach each prospect.

And, as you can imagine, this skill goes beyond sales. It will spill into your personal life, too. You'll make better choices about friends and lovers, employers and employees, and in all other areas of life. This talent will fuel all the skills that I am offering you in this book. No business wants competitors that are highly curious about people.

As a salesperson, I have learned to be a people-reading fanatic. I am truly obsessed. Perhaps it is my inquisitive people nature, or perhaps the rewards have given me the same dogged, relentless pursuit of people knowledge that you would expect from a well-rewarded hunting dog. I think it's both. The former sounds like a gift, but anyone can cultivate this, because the rewards will turn this into an addiction.

This section will give you not just reasons for reading people, but plenty of ways to do it. I want you to become fascinated by all the details of the people around you. Nothing is off limits to your inquiring mind; not physical appearance, vocal quality, behavior style, style, social class, mental and emotional strengths and weaknesses; nothing. Combined with your knowledge of meta-programs and other factors that tell you how to communicate effectively with various types of people, this knowledge has explosive potential.

Here is where I want you to start: Understand that your sense of a person will emerge from many factors that you take in. Do not expect a cook book approach, like some cheesy dream analysis dictionary. The purpose is to see more deeply into people so that you can tailor your sales approach to them as unique individuals rather than simply placing them into a category that a certain sales approach supposedly goes with.

This way, you will not be confused when their traits seem to contradict and mismatch. It will also keep you from taking your cues from one or two traits that stand out, causing you to pigeon hole your prospect too easily. The brain always wants the efficient path (remember efficiency pressure?) so don't fall victim to this urge. This section counsels patience in sizing people up.

KEYS TO ACUITY: 20/20 PEOPLE READING

Why is it that people reading, one of the most important skills anyone could have, does not grow into a full skill set the way playing games or learning to cook does?

If you have a weak back hand, your tennis game will suffer in a pretty obvious way, and you'll make a big priority out of developing that. The stakes are even higher with people, so why don't insights into people reading weaknesses emerge just as readily? Perhaps because it is more subtle and complicated. Perhaps because the reward is not as obvious and immediate. Perhaps because most people don't realize that there is so much to gain, that the time it takes to develop this skill is well worth it.

And bear in mind that I am not talking about simply having a good general understanding of human behavior and motivation, or typical ways that people respond to sales techniques, or even the ways people are mentally organized by things like meta-programs. I'm talking about becoming a true people reading expert. You can do this. Remember that people rise to the top in their profession because they take their gifts and hammer them into skills. Gifts alone are not enough. And it takes time, development, and practice to hammer out those skills. The people who make this look easy fool us. They make us think that we shouldn't have to practice so much in order to develop an esoteric skill, whether it's people reading, comedy, art or anything else. Re-set your expectations AND your standards to get the greatest benefit from this section.

The Discipline of the People Reading Craft

Start your people reading craft with these disciplines, or should I say, *fun* activities:

1. Spend plenty of time with people who are similar to the people you call "prospects". If you sell to everyone, then you can hop on your horse and gallop off in all directions. Do you live in a big, impersonal city full of scary, crazy people? Fear not. There are plenty of ways to get out there and connect with worthwhile people. If you're at all timid, then go to events and meetings that appeal to your own interests. And remember, people watching does not require you to interact; At least not at this stage.

2. Spend less time talking and thinking about how you are perceived by others, and much more time taking in what they are presenting to you. Of course, I am not talking about what's on the surface. Don't just understand their words, look at every kind of information they present to you, right down to their shoes. Yes, shoes are information when you are reading people. But I'm getting ahead of myself.

3. Get these people to reveal more of themselves to you. Learn to get the conversation going deeper than their interests, activities and opinions. What about their dreams and fears? What about their attitudes about people and relationships? What about their struggles to improve themselves and tolerate the stresses of life?

What are they ashamed of; proud of? Start this opening by doing it a little yourself. Most people will not open to you unless you open up to them first. Does this guideline seem to contradict the previous one? It doesn't have to. It doesn't take long to reveal a detail about yourself. You probably already do this in some ways without giving it much though. Have you ever said, "Oh, yeah, I hate it when that happens." You just revealed that it happens to you, too, whatever that was.

ENHANCING YOUR CRAFT

What to look for: As you enhance your people reading skills, learn from this section what to look for. You don't want a jumble of facts or observations. You want it all to begin fitting together so that a meaningful picture emerges.

Nurture your objectivity: Without objectivity, you will not read people effectively. People reading is such a delicate art, that your emotional reactions can throw you off, at least until you learn to distinguish fully between intuition and personal reactions. Yes, these are two very different things, and this contrast is one of the biggest secrets to reading people.

Biases: With that in mind, begin observing your own biases. Stalk your prejudices. The better you know them, the sooner you can transcend them in order to master the objectivity that is crucial to people reading.

Take action: Let's throw in an advanced step, just to sweeten the pot a bit. Begin taking your impressions of people, and use them to take actions, but carefully track the results to see how well you are doing as a budding people reader. This makes it a little more like a game, and gets you focused on getting feedback, which is the most important way to improve your skills. After all, you want to know more about people than they know about themselves. This means that you can't rely on them to tell you what you need to know. You also want to generate motivation within yourself. The game factor can help fire you up and maintain your interest.

From Practice to Benefits

Practice: Only with ample practice can you build and retain these people reading skills. I know that it is more difficult than ever to be disciplined to a practice of any kind. There are so many distractions from technology, and the technology itself means that much more of our interaction eliminates the kind of face to face contact I've been encouraging. But don't let that phase you. If your contact is not fact to face, this need not stop you from taking in your people reading information and observations. It just means you are using media to learn what you can for this purpose. You can still ask questions and notice things about how your prospect communicates. There is also video and pictures.

Expect acuity: As with any skill, it will grow on you. But people tend to underestimate just how much of an impact skills like this can have, and how much it can improve with practice. This reminds me of the story of a young intern who was becoming a heart doctor. When he first listened to heart sounds, all he heard was *lub-dub, lub-dub*. But his teachers, highly experienced cardiologists, could hear all sorts of diagnostic meaning that he was oblivious to. It took a lot of practice to hear the wealth of information in those heart sounds. But it was worth it. His patients certainly think so! Their lives depend on it.

Threats to Objectivity

Now that I've gotten you off to a good start, let's preserve your objectivity. As you'll recall, I made a really big deal about how important it is, and how vulnerable it is. It truly is a gift to cultivate.

You must start with patience. It isn't just that it takes time to put your impressions of a person together, but that if you jump to conclusions you'll end up jumping to conclusions. We can't have that.

We evolved to make snap decisions, but not about in-depth people reading. Our brains are constantly scanning for physical threats to our well being. Unfortunately, a high-pressure environment, or an internal sense of pressure about sales activates this ancient and primitive aspect of ourselves, and banishes the subtleties of people reading.

This explains many improper shooting events by police officers. Even trained police officers can get their survival potential so intensely activated that they will think someone is pulling a gun when they aren't. They may be more tense than they realize and fire their gun unintentionally. They may even have an ancient pack mentality activated and act more fiercely in a group than they would on their own. Stress psychology has come to a similar conclusion about many heart attacks and other health problems. Because our ancient survival potentials can mistake a deadline or verbal confrontation for a physical threat, those of us who spend too much time activated that way can develop heart disease. Perhaps you've heard of the *type A personality*. The idea of the *Type A personality* got started when two cardiologists discovered the pattern in their heart patients.

PROTECT YOUR OBJECTIVITY

This means that, in order to cultivate your objectivity, you must first protect your objectivity. You do that by creating a more spacious mentality; by developing the patience that people watching requires. But let's say you are in a rapid-fire sales situation in which you only have a small amount of time to size people up. That's all the more reason to create the internal space I'm talking about; to "make haste slowly." The more you take time to size people up in various situations, the more you will be able to do it faster without jumping to conclusions.

You'll also know your limits. You will have a good sense of what chances you should take; when is it worth risking being wrong as opposed to when you should take the conservative tack.

With your growing acuity, you will notice things that slip by people who are less observant. Many of your observations will prove vital to your sales.

THE FOUR PILLARS OF OBJECTIVITY

Now we know that we must keep cool to be objective. That means, that the higher the stakes, the more internal pressure mounts against staying objective. Also, our minds can play tricks on us where we unconsciously don't want to see something. One of the scientists at Chernobyl saw radioactive soot raining down and, because it was "impossible" that it would be a breach of the system, believed at first that it was something else. But he died within hours.

This is how our minds cope with a mismatch of what we want to believe with the evidence. It's called cognitive dissonance. It happens when we refuse to accept evidence. You could even say that it is delusional, since we come up with untenable alternative explanations, and adhere to them.

Once you have defended your objectivity against time and money pressure, you must defend it against this more subtle threat. This leads us to the positive side of the coin, which is enhancing the four pillars of objectivity:

1. Emotional vacations

When you are too emotionally attached to something or someone, your mind will play tricks on you. How many people have you met who stay in terrible relationships for terribly silly reasons? There's nothing wrong with emotional attachment, but you must be able to take an emotional vacation when ever you want to size people up, so that you will think clearly.

2. Independence

No one is an island and we are all interdependent, but you must be able to take a vacation from your needs whenever you want to maintain your objectivity. When it's about your needs, it isn't about objectivity. You have to need objectivity more than you need anything else.

3. Fearlessness

Fear is natural, but you must learn to realize when it is trying to steer your boat. You need to learn to temporarily step outside of the fear, so that you can size up the person.

4. Responsibility taking

If ever there were an automatic behavior, it's defensiveness. Practice taking responsibility rather than jumping into defensiveness. A good way to start is by being curious about criticism. This shows others that you are thoughtful and responsible. This builds trust. They, then, become more open with you.

These four pillars, or mind-sets, will serve you well as you practice your people watching, no matter how advanced it is.

THE ZEN OF OBJECTIVITY

There is a story of a Westerner who came seeking enlightenment from a Zen master. The Zen master offered to pour tea, and the visitor accepted. The Zen master peacefully filled the man's cup, and continued pouring as the tea overflowed onto the table. The visitor said, *"Stop, you can't pour any more tea can go into that cup!"* to which the Zen master replied, *"And so it is with the mind. For when it is full, nothing more can go into it."*

And so it is with objectivity, for a salesperson who subscribes to stereotypes cannot know his prospect. If you'd like to know more, please visit me on my mountain in Tibet. *On second thought, just read on...*

Biases and prejudices are like rust. They accumulate so gradually, that we may not even realize they're there, at least not until we have a personal or professional judgment go awry because of one. Our news outlets, television, and movies appeal to our biases, or help to cultivate them. And our minds play tricks upon us based on how we create statistical errors.

For example, the more extreme situations we hear about seem to be more commonplace than they really are. The more unfamiliar a person is, the more we tend to judge other similar people by our experience with that person. That's why a few bad experiences with salespeople so strongly color the attitude people have toward salespeople in general.

SERIOUS STAKES

During the immediate aftermath of *Hurricane Katrina* that devastated New Orleans in Louisiana, reports of looting cause a small white area's population to think that blacks were going to come and loot their homes next. Nothing like that was going to happen. In fact, many believe that the news media portrayed the people who were looting as black criminals when they were actually mostly people trying to get basic supplies because help had not arrived and they were desperate.

The criminal looter side of the story made the government look a little better, and appealed more to the existing prejudices of the population as well as to avoid offending people with a strong law and order attitude. The sad result of was that approximately eleven innocent black men were shot by these paranoid folks in the white borough.

How many sales are lost because salespeople evaluate their prospect as unqualified simply because a single feature, such as race, gets them thinking that the person can't afford what they're selling, or doesn't have the intelligence to appreciate it?

Put your bias detector on high for a while, watching vigilantly for your own biases. No one is completely free of them. Practice looking past them, to see more deeply into people. I don't mean to automatically assume everyone is nice or rich, I just mean practice your objectivity to see what more there is to learn as you practice your people watching.

Start with the working assumption that pretty much everyone has at least one trait that will miss-cue your biases.

For every person you meet for the next month, look for a trait that gives the wrong impression about them. Start with people you already know well. *Perhaps yourself?*

SUCCEED WITH PROSPECTS THAT MAKE YOU CRAZY

Do you ever have customers that make you feel as if you've taken a trip down the rabbit hole? These are the folks who seem to send a buying signal, and then back off; or they seem closed off and disinterested, only to buy as soon as a salesperson approaches them; or they seem like simple, straightforward people, but turn into a time-consuming hassle of demands and resentment from out of the blue.

Well I'm glad you are able to feel crazy, because that is a signal to you that you have a crazy-making customer. You can think of it as a kind of intuition. The sooner you sense it, the sooner you can do something about it. Don't be so caught up in the sales process that you miss subtle internal signals. In time, you'll find that your intuition is your friend; a friend who brings in sales.

I'm going to share some techniques for responding to crazy-making customers. They will help you discriminate between the ones who are just wasting your time and the ones who aren't. And for the one's who aren't, you need to know how to approach them.

Is the prospect an eccentric person who needs to be understood? ...directed with a firmer approach? ...directed with a more informative approach? Or is it just more of a misunderstanding that needs to get cleared up?

The main concern I have is that you may default to the wrong attitude, because these crazy-making prospects trip one of your biases. It really is easy to jump to the conclusion that the prospect is just wasting your time, playing mind games, or too crazy to be a real customer, when they are actually a sale waiting to happen. This happens with some regularity.

TRY THESE ANTIDOTES TO THE CRAZY-MAKERS

For starters, you need some canned responses that you can try with your crazy-making prospects. The ones below are a good selection. One of them should work with just about every oddball prospect, including the ones that seem odd but really aren't.

By the way, don't forget about the *neurodiversity* section. That goes a long way in helping your understand eccentric prospects and what to do with them.

1. Pointing to the elephant in the living room:

This means commenting or asking about the thing that is bothering you. To do this, you must first let your uncomfortable feelings guide you to what it is that's getting to you.

Or perhaps it's obvious to you already. Next, you think of a way to bring it up that will not alienate the prospect. I'll tell you a story about that soon.

A good time to use this is when you suspect that you need to better understand your prospect, or when you feel that whatever's going one is threatening the sale, and your prospect seems to rigid to respond to normal methods.

2. Gentle redirection:

You can gently direct a prospect away from a pattern of thinking or behavior that is hampering the sales process. You can ask them directly to do something

3. Break the state (usually with redirection):

This is a classic method to loosen people up for a new approach. You occupy their mind with other ideas that are stated in a sensory-rich fashion. Let's say your prospect and his family are thinking of buying a yacht, but all they seem to want to do is walk around the marina with you in tow, wasting valuable time on a Sunday when there are other prospects due. "This marina is a great place to walk. Now, I'd like to take a break, and get you into our nice, cool office, where we can get you all something nice and fresh to drink, and show you some yachts and features that you've probably never seen before in your lives. And the kids will love our play area. Have you met Betty? She's so great with kids, and she's been with us for years. We have a great set up there."

4. Gentle directness:

Sometimes our belief that salespeople must always be nice can get in the way of being direct when we need to. Sometimes, it's best to be direct about your own needs or concerns, or unmet needs of your prospect.

Consider the marina scenario. *What if my redirection and state breaking hadn't worked?*

Ultimately, I'd have to try being direct:

"As much as I am enjoying providing this tour, I have to get us back to the office, because the boss requires me to get back within half an hour so I can service buyers, especially on a busy day like Sunday. I hate to rush you, but then, we've seen everything that you were interested in, except of course for those catalog items I mentioned. Let's head back now."

Some Advanced Antidotes

Careful, these are for when you have the intuition, or the stakes aren't too high. They really take some practice to use constructively.

Creating potential humiliation

If a person is acting or talking inappropriately, but you aren't ready to give them the boot, you might just want to make them a little more self aware. You might respond with some discomfort. But if they don't read you, you can comment on their behavior just loud enough to make them think about how others might view them.

If that doesn't work, maybe you should get on the phone and ask your boss, right in front of them, how to respond to someone who keeps doing whatever they've been doing.

Self disclosure

We are so programmed to preserve our own security and dignity, that revealing feelings like confusion or self doubt tend to be automatic taboos (but then, we know a lot about automatic behavior now, and how important it is to be aware of it).

Sometimes it's best to reveal a feeling like this, and turn it into a sales point. I had a prospect who seemed to want to turn our session into a reality TV show, where she bent my ear about how much she hated her family.

I could have asked her why she wanted life insurance for these rascals, but instead, I made other comments, such as, *"Think how bad they'll feel when they see that you took care of this and it's too late for them to admit that they were wrong."*

"Oh, no," she responded, *"I'll be rubbing this in their face as soon as I get home."*

EXAMPLE: CREATIVELY MIRRORING THE CRAZINESS

If you've never tried this, you'll find it can actually be rather liberating. I mean, don't you deserve to be crazy from time to time? In this antidote, you borrow a page from the rapport-building technique or mirroring to mirror what is making you crazy or uncomfortable.

I have done this with various unusual prospects. I had a prospect who was tense and judgmental. He seemed to like being intense, because he had a really short haircut that made him look like he longed to still be in the military. As soon as he took a seat, he demanded, *"Are you a patriot, son?"*

I had already adopted a tense ramrod posture, and responded, *"I tell everyone in the military, that if they ever have to pull a coup to restore democracy in this country, they should use me a their front man, because I know what people want and I could help to keep the peace."*

The only reason I was able to think of this was because of a joke I happened to have going with a friend the night before. A strange coincidence, but I use what I have, and it is often something that happened recently. Color me opportunistic.

I knew that this was a risky gambit, because he might think what I said was UN-patriotic. I took the chance based on the feeling I had that he identified with the military and probably thought the federal government was letting everyone down, infested with liberals (or conservatives, who knows). But, he started laughing. He laughed to the point that I was a little uncomfortable. Then he slapped the desk, and said, *"Well then, I hope they give you some good Kevlar"* (a brand of bullet-proof clothing). He made a few comments about politics from time to time, and I took the time to point out that I understood what he was saying. We completed the sale.

I think perhaps my "front man" comment worked because I was acknowledging that he was the tough alpha male, and at the same time,

I was asserting that I was in charge of handling public communication, symbolically reaffirming my role as being in charge of the sales process.

Handling a Crazy-Making Prospect: A Success Story

Here is an example of exactly how I handled a crazy-making prospect. And note that this person wasn't crazy at all. Most crazy-making prospects aren't. But they make you feel crazy, invalid, insecure, angry, or some other objectivity-threatening emotion.

Here's a slightly more detailed learning example of handling a crazy-making prospect. As you'll see, there was a very good reason for his behavior. Let's call him Ted. I could never seem to get into a groove with this fellow. Every test close just seemed to take me into another process that seemed disconnected from everything else. It was as if Ted had multiple lives to service.

I finally said, *"I don't know about you, Ted, but I'm starting to actually feel confused. And that's really odd, because I have been doing this for a long time. I have the feeling that maybe I'm totally missing something, and causing us to go in circles or something."*

Notice how I blamed myself for going in circles. You might be pretty sure that it's your prospect's fault, and it probably is, but they have to be the ones to take ownership of it, otherwise, you'll risk making them dig in their heels even more. But you aren't being dishonest, because you can assume that you are playing some role in the dysfunction.

I didn't not expect Ted's answer. But, in retrospect, maybe I should have. He said that was the kind of person who had to look at every angle before making a decision, and that sometimes he drove himself crazy. He chuckled about it, and this told me that my discomfort with being confused did not match his inner experience very well. That was a very important piece of information, because it helped me set the tone for the discussion. Good thing I didn't inadvertently make him feel like the bad guy for confusing me. I have to admit, I had some temptation for a moment to express my displeasure with him for wasting my time and interfering with the discussion, as if he were a saboteur.

Now I was able to feed Ted's hunger for details and scenarios, watching him very carefully for any signs of fatigue. I was impressed with his stamina, because this ended up being a long presentation.

However, I know that people who have to look at every angle become increasingly invested with each new idea.

After all, they are working; they consider this their job. It is their highest responsibility to make sure that they make the "right" decision, and that means putting together a lot of information until they have what psychology calls a "gestalt" or a comprehensive overall view of the situation, where the pieces are all relevant to each other.

But I was not just a passenger on this ride. I related each answer to his needs, so that his gestalt would help him move to buying now, and not falling back into a position of needing to gather more information.

After all my work, I didn't want him to get the last piece of information he needed from someone else and close the sale with them another day.

One thing that kept me going was that these analyst types tend to be very faithful to a decision they have made. Unless there is a significant change in the situation, they have done their homework and will not be fickle. In my business, we want customers with that kind of staying power. And since life insurance lends itself to an analytical approach, I knew how to feed the prospects information hunger.

As you can see, I was using my people reading to make decisions, because there was little risk that my stereotypes about analytical types was going to take me too far astray if I was wrong.

From Observation to Impressions to Sales Presentation

I'm going to have you start putting your observations together into values that your prospect probably holds, and then decide what sales pitch is most likely to appeal to those values. But we've only begun to hint at what you're looking for when you do people reading. That's hard to do, since everything about a person is fair game. Every detail through every sense modality tells you something about the person. The more you consider, the better. The trick, of course, is to look and start noticing things that you would not have otherwise bothered with. For example, do you notice people's finger nails. If so, then what percentage of people chew their nails? Ah HA!

You can take in specific observations like nail biting, but ultimately you must put them together into an impression. And remember that observations, in addition to coming in as sensory information, can come in as *information* information, like when the person tells you their income, or your boss gives you a folder on the client company and its principles, so you can know all sorts of things about everybody.

From Specifics to Impressions

The more you look for specifics, the more you'll see that their meaning is not so specific. For example, let's say your prospect is very short. That doesn't tell you how he was treated, or how he developed his personality. On the other hand, things that are less specific, such as the cultural and religious significance of their clothing or accessories, may tell you very specifically what their religion is or where they are from.

Sometimes, a collection of behaviors, attitudes, and physical signs (like their mode of dress) will tell you enough that you can guesstimate about their personality. Consider, for example, signs of

impairment, signs of alcohol or drug abuse, level of education, attention
to detail, spiritual attitudes, empathy, analytic ability, leadership, and
how outgoing they are. Any of these things could have a bearing on
how to approach them, or whether you should approach them at all.

Now we have moved beyond collecting facts and observations,
and gotten more of a big picture of the person. Consider the prospect
who is very invested in showing the world that she is a classy person.
Make sure she is impressed with what a great impression her purchase
will help her make. Consider a prospect with a minivan that has the
upholstery worn down by the family dog. *Won't he respond well to a
pitch that helps him express his enjoyment of his family? We could do this
all day, once we get started, right?*

Well then, take this on the road and start putting observations
together into impressions about values. Then ask yourself what sales
approach would most appeal to those values.

What Jumps Out at You?

I want to talk to you about really making the transition from
being a good judge of people to becoming a real people reader. That's
why I call this piece *"What Jumps Out at You?"* Because your first
impressions are what currently jump out at you. It's intuitive and
automatic. I want you to think about the last person you sized up;
someone you had never seen before. Imagine that you can observe
your mind in slow motion. This way, your first impression turns into
a series of smaller impressions that merge into an overall impression.
What if you could see that happen so slowly that you could name
which senses went into action first, and how they combined? Play with
that in your memory, and see what aspects of the person your mind
automatically emphasized.

There is a reason cartoonists exaggerate features. Neuroscientists
have come up with the theory that our brains remember people by
exaggerating their unique features. For the people reader, this can be a

problem, because our automatic exaggerator may not be directing our attention to the features that will help us predict their response to our various sales approach options. It is for this reason that I want you to break away from your normal way of getting to your first impression. That's why I want you to start with the slow motion exercise. That way, you can get to know your own automatic exaggerator more intimately, and become better at trying a new approach.

That new approach is this: Next time you're out in the world, people reading, just ask yourself what their most striking features are, and then ask yourself to look for the next level deep. That is, the runners up that you didn't notice on the first go. Perhaps their edgy hairstyle and pert walk got you thinking they were dynamic and rebellious. *But what about the next level, the careful makeup and the awkward social skills. Is somebody compensating?* You'll want to approach her with some grounded gentleness, because she might actually be insecure. Scratch the surface with some reciprocity, and you might find she's a people-pleaser when she feels safe.

AND WHAT ABOUT THE SUBTLETIES?

Once you have practiced going for that deeper layer of impressions, you'll want to practice coming from the opposite direction. *What are the subtlest things about the person?*

The easiest place to start is to go for **small**. Yes, small things like fingernails, accessories, scuffs, tears, stains, mismatches of socks, and color match or mismatch. While you're at it, notice breathing patterns, gestures, and other body language.

Remember context. People may act quite differently in a sales showroom than out in the wild. So is their tension because they are worried about being manipulated, or is it that they are not very aware of their body? If it's the latter, is it because they were potty-trained at gunpoint, or because they are just superficial people that you should approach totally based on how thing will affect their status and appearance? If it trauma, how can you structure their experience so that they will feel in control and not vulnerable?

I understand that taking you out of your familiar way of people reading can be uncomfortable. The first thing you might feel is sensory and choice overload, as in, *"What good are all these details? It's like reading tea leaves? I can predict ten different possibilities from these factors."* Well, that's a fine place to start. Don't give up your first impressions, just begin a parallel project of pulling in more details and making predictions. You'll get better and better, until you start surprising yourself and amazing your friends.

THE PEOPLE READING GAME

A fun way to play with this is to sit at a patio table on a street that has good foot traffic, and make up stories about the people walking by. Base the stories entirely on things you can actually see, from what they're wearing, to their demographics such as age, to their stride, posture, and other body language.

When you make up your story, talk about where they live, where they are going, and what is on their mind. Expand that into their values and motives. Then talk about the ideal sales approach for them with a specific product in mind. Imagine what kind of objections they might throw up to a luxury item, or what they might say to justify the purchase.

Kick it up another notch by asking them a question based on your story.

"Excuse me, do you live on a boat?"

"Pardon me, ma'am, I couldn't help but notice your hat. It's really unique. Are you a writer?"

If they converse with you, you'll have the pleasure of finding out where you were right, and how far off you could be as well. That's fine, it's about sharpening your powers of observation first, and building accuracy second. Have a relaxed attitude about it, because this is a life-long pursuit. Rather than being a one-semester learning project, it is something that becomes a wonderful part of you.

Remember that this game goes from specific details to you imagination. And it goes from inventing more details, to guessing about their values and motives. Take turns with your friend, and you'll have your mind opened to even more details that you missed, and even more possibilities that you wouldn't have thought of. That surprise element makes the game even more fun.

This is a great way to emerge from detail-overwhelm, and have some fun. Also, you are weaving your conscious, detail-oriented mind with your intuitive, creative side. That's a formula for mastery.

AN EXAMPLE: UNCOVERING A BIAS

I recall, early in my career, when my automatic people reading was taking me in the wrong direction. I worked in a company in which one of the principles was a very successful man who was involved in health care as an entrepreneur. He drove an expensive care, wore expensive clothes, and all I ever heard him talk about was administrative matters. The only people I ever saw him with were big money people.

But one day we had a team-building person come in to teach us some communication techniques. Part of it involved talking about an experience that defined us and how it played out in our lives. This fellow who I had only seen as a 100% materialist talked about learning how his ancestors had been lost to Nazi Germany in concentration camps.

He talked about his involvement in a charity for children affected by war, and how much of his life he had devoted to it. He became tearful, surprising himself, as he spoke about it all, including how his mother had been affected by the disruptions in her own parenting. He had revealed a lot of vulnerability, talking about his own mother's emotional problems and how they had impacted him as a child.

This was one of the experiences that taught me never to think I knew someone based on the obvious things. An important part of the lesson was that some of the traits I knew him for were what helped him go in that charitable direction. His administrative talents, communication skills, vision, and leadership were all necessary for that role.

This experience speaks well for the art of conversation. It's the flip side of your people watching skills. As we learned in the sales process sections, building trust and being inquisitive will yield valuable information as well.

LOOK FOR EXCEPTIONS THAT DIS-PROVE THE RULE

Our brains must be designed to ignore little exceptions, even big ones sometimes. When people see psychics, they ignore all sorts of errors and are amazed at the correct guesses. Watch for that automatic filter when you are people watching. Look for the little exceptions that you might automatically discard. Look for the details, actions, gestures, and tones that don't fit your overall impression. Make a practice of trying to find out what they mean.

Sometimes you can ask directly about them, but you wouldn't ask, *"Mamma, you're voice almost sounds like you need a good cry. Did someone die, recently?"* But you might say, *"That cameo looks like an heirloom. Is it special to you?"*

When it comes to tattoos, I'm tempted to ask, because I'm inclined to assume that they mean something. Many people, however, are not happy about what their tattoo means, because it was an act of youthful excess. If you know them well enough, you can say, *"Well, for something from youthful excess, it sure beats the heck out of syphilis."*

Behavior Signs and Intuition

Remember to watch for deviant behaviors, not just traits or appearance factors. A friend of mine was considering hiring an outfit to build her website and online store. They wanted a very high amount of money, and I was suspicious. I looked over their materials, and saw that they made a lot of promises that they wanted monthly fees for. When I showed up to the meeting between my friend and the salesperson, he said, *"Oh, I see you brought your guard dog."* Now isn't that an unusual thing to say? I thought it meant that he was the thief and I was there to protect his potential victim. It turned out that I was right. I was learning about Internet marketing when many people were quite naïve about it, and found that his approach was a common rip-off. I saved my friend a very large amount of money.

As you can see, sometimes a small thing that deviates from the overall impression speaks volumes, and can dramatically change your course.

When you have a prospect that is not comfortable in their dressy clothes, and one of them is a woman who is a little wobbly in high heels, perhaps they are telling you that they are not actually there for the big purchase they are talking about. *Could they be there just for information? Could they be con artists? With this couple, you'll want to be very cautious with your qualification process and maybe save a lot of time or grief.*

Traits vs. States: Character Matters

What do you think of someone who has a fit of anger. Does that mean he is an angry person, or was he having a really bad day and someone pushed him too far? Be very careful not to take a single incident and assume that it is a character trait. With a little more information, of course, you'd be in a better position to predict more about him. If you got him to open up and tell you why he was so stressed out, it wouldn't take but a few moments for you to have a very good idea about it. If he was doing a lot of blaming and showing that he was not very worldly, that would tell you not to use an approach that is for more sophisticated people. You might be part was through the qualifying process right there. People like that are usually not in well-paid positions. But don't assume anything. At this point, you do know, though, that he will respond best if you appeal to his desire to be the hero, to feel rich, and let him carry on thinking that other people are entirely responsible for his failings.

Here's a tip that can save you some overwhelm. Remember that the most optional things are the least core to the information they are transmitting. An ear ring is less permanent than a nose ring, a suit is less permanent than a forced confident attitude. The most telling features are the ones that a long-term. On the other hand, those temporary things tell you more when you have context to go with them. *Why is that lady going into the office building in sweats?*

TAKING PEOPLE READING INTO THE SALES PROCESS

We could get a Ph.D. in people reading without becoming better at sales. I say this, because sales demands special people reading skills. If you were picking jurors, you would be concerned about how they would react to the way the defendant and others act. If you were a police officer, you would be very attuned to who is guilty. But sales professionals develop a great deal of flexibility in their personality. They are occupied with what approach will draw in the prospect, not how the prospect will react to a given person. Sales professionals are concerned with **how** to present the offer, and even *what* exactly to offer, rather than *how the person will respond to the product itself.* Usually, when salespeople say, *"this product sells itself,"* they are taking their role in the process for granted, because they have developed unconscious mastery.

In the section on automatic behavior and elsewhere, you have been learning about many ways to be a catalyst for the sale. So this piece should come as no surprise. What it means is, that you want to take your people reading farther into the sales dimension. You have been thinking about what values people may have based on your people reading, and what sales approach might be best for them. Now I'd like you to add another cluster of factors. How well do they respond to leadership and guidance. How easily are their minds occupied by others' speech, especially when it is sensory rich or idea rich. You'll discover that some people become quite engrossed when you use abstract ideas, others, when your story really appeals to the senses. You'll find that some people become very cooperative when you get them relaxed, while others become more anxious with the same moves that would relax most people. Now you are looking for more subtle characteristics.

You'll recall I recommended experimenting by trying out your theories about people to begin getting feedback right away. Now I want you to experiment with what people respond to. Based on your impression, decide what kind of content would most occupy a person's mind for the equivalent of a light trance, and then see if you can get cooperation for some kind of a request, such as a request to give you their contact information so you can discuss your product with them.

You'll recall that, especially in the automatic behavior articles, you have learned a lot about additional elements you can add in to help make sure they follow through when you contact them. Keep practicing, and what now seems complicated will become unconscious mastery.

MORPHOLOGY FOR SALES

As your people reading skills blossom, you'll want to focus on the traits that have the strongest value in helping you choose your sales approach. You could say that you want the traits with the strongest predictive value. What sales approach will have the best odds of getting a favorable response? You already have a variety of sales skills, but you want to hone them to the individual. Ideally, you want to do that preemptively, that is, rather than blunder and make a correction, you prefer to have a seamless approach that does not make the prospect feel that you adjusting too much. I call this "morphing" (shape shifting), hence the title of this section, Morphology for Sales.

I think you'll find that the best traits to start off with in your search for tell-tale traits are these: caring adjustment, and class.

Caring means the ability to experience others' feelings, and value their needs. Adjustment refers to how well a person is adjusted to life. Class is where they sit on the social totem pole. These three very general traits really affect how people judge and respond to other people. That's why I am focusing on them now. These traits transcend those that are easier to stereotype such as race or sexual orientation.

Think about your sales experience in terms of these three traits. What general conclusions can you draw about how these three traits respond to your various sales approach options. Have you noticed that people of a lower social class will tend to be more suspicious of you? Do they respond better when you characterize the competition as costing more because they spend so much on advertising? Are they more likely to believe that they are getting a deal when it's because your company doesn't squander it's money on things that rich people squander money on? Do they resonate to a narrative that shows how they live high on the hog? Does it matter much if that narrative involves bad math?

Ask questions like this for all three traits, based on your experiences. Bring it on home and think of your own experiences as a prospect. Where do you fit on each scale? How empathic, well-off, and well-adjusted are you, and how does that affect your response to various sales approaches?

MORPHEUS WORKOUT: CARING

Morphing means shape changing, but Morpheus is the Greek god of dreams. The Morpheus workout is about learning to connect people with their dreams by accommodating to their traits.

Let's start with caring. If someone has no caring, they will not be moved much by your feelings about anything. You will need to de-emphasize the relationship, and emphasize how you are a tool of their fancies. There is a magician in Los Angeles whose business card says, *"Plaything of the Rich."* Apparently he knows where he stands, and he's making a living at it, too.

But there is a paradox here. People who are low on caring about others, that is, people who don't see the validity of others' feelings except in so far as they are able to use them to their own advantage, are not called caring. However, they may be highly empathic, that is, acutely aware of other people's feelings. The problem is that they only use this information for their own interests.

These people have no problem with being con artists, so long as they can avoid punishment. The best con artists have excellent social skills. The better they are at acting, and the more experience they have, the smoother they are. I'm sure that you've noticed two general types of salespeople: the ones who care about their customers, and the ones who have no moral code outside of necessity. Like a pick pocket, the money in the other guy's wallet is really theirs. They just have to figure out how to get it.

If your prospect is low on caring, you must appeal to their sense of entitlement. For prospects high on caring, you will do better by bringing this out by developing a relationship. Even if your contact with them is fairly brief, you can emphasize relationship-building opportunities through your warm welcome and voice.

These tell a low-caring person that you will appeal to their sense of entitlement, so you don't "save" these niceties for high-caring people, but you do not attempt to gain concessions from a low-caring person based on the relationship, only their self-interest. You do not "save" self-interest only for the low-empathy person, but you do emphasize it above all else.

To learn more about this fascinating spectrum of experience, look up antisocial personality disorder, sociopath, and psychopath. This knowledge could save you a bundle, maybe more.

Another thing that is quirky about caring is quirky people. Some people, who seem rather cold, actually are high on caring, but they do not experience empathy in the emotional way that we do. They may lean towards the autism spectrum personality of Asperger's syndrome that we'll learn more about in the *Neurodiversity* section. Don't be fooled. You can easily think that these people think very little of you, when actually they just don't experience the world the way you do.

MORPHEUS WORKOUT: ADJUSTMENT

Adjustment is a profound idea. How do you sell to a generally happy person as opposed to a generally unhappy one? Let's start by making the distinction between people who have a jovial attitude and people who are generally happy. Very unhappy people may use perfectly normal social skills and laugh about things. But scratch the surface, and their unhappiness leaks out. Their jokes are cynical. Their insecurities show in little self-revelations. Their suspiciousness flashes at a test close.

It's very important to get the feel for the unhappy person's perspective, because these people tend to bond around their pet peeves and perspectives. You don't have to launch into a diatribe. Just drop a comment that shows you get it, I mean really get it. Even if you have a different perspective, you are certainly aware of the issue. Whatever country you're in, you might not think the government is turning into a fascist internment camp, but you are aware of factors that might make someone think that, like all the cameras.

Since people who are generally unhappy are likely to be impatient, your sales approach will most likely need to emphasize relaxing the prospect; getting them into a less time-sensitive state of mind. The rapport-building techniques in this book will go a long way in that department. You might be surprised to know that there are plenty of hypnotic techniques that you can actually use for conscious sales work. The rapport-building work relies on this background.

UNHAPPINESS STYLES

It's important to ascertain whether the generally unhappy prospect is an underachiever with a limited scope of experience, or an accomplished person who has mustered the social skills to have a broad collection of life experiences. You'll find this our fairly easily. For the underachiever, you will want to very carefully limit what you reveal about yourself so that you stay within his boundaries, unless you are fairly certain that establishing yourself as someone to look up to will actually function as part of your sales approach.

This is often true for selling motivational seminars, products that represent a lifestyle that the underachiever aspires to, and businesses for which your success is emblematic of what the business buyer can achieve. However, it is usually important to establish clearly in the prospect's mind that your roots are humble and that it is your product that enabled you to become what you are today.

Here is an interesting pair of questions.

Is it hard to sell to a generally happy person because they are already happy?

Or is it easy, since they have no problem with becoming even happier?

Overall, selling to a generally happy person is no harder or easier than to a generally unhappy one. The challenge depends on the product as much as its pitch.

MORPHEUS WORKOUT: CLASS

An interesting thing about class is that it affects health, but not simply because the person has less resources. Research tells us that the relative class in the society has more to do with health that just how much money they have.

Apparently, there is a social and psychological dynamic that strongly affects well being that comes from where you are in your society, not just whether you can afford good food. This tells us that there is a lot to the psychology of class. It shapes our perspective and values a great deal.

Don't assume that a person who is well-off now has always been so. Their background will have a stronger impact upon their attitudes than their current situation.

People with a lower class background do not have the same point of view as those higher class folks. Wherever you live in the world, you live in a class-based society. Some societies are just more shy about admitting it, because equality is a politically useful illusion. In societies where equality is a vision, there is more honesty, because vision thrives in an honest environment.

The place to start morphing based on class, is to put yourself in their shoes, relating to their experience. You must be able to relate to the pull-yourself-up-by-your-bootstraps mentality of someone who has struggled up from poverty.

Paradoxically, you do not need to pretend that you have had all the experiences of someone born with a silver spoon in their mouth in order to relate to the upper crust, however. Unless it's true, you would be nothing more than a poseur in their eyes.

However, the better breeding you can show, and the more you can know your place as a service professional, the better. The higher the class of the customer, the more you are likely to be a statistic. A quote, falsely attributed to Abraham Lincoln, goes, "God must have loved the common people, he made so many of them." Don't take it personally, just explore how that can color your approach. But if your upper-crust customer really connects with you as an equal, don't be too surprised. Remember, the caring dimension is separate from social class.

Coping and Adapting: Don't be Blinded by the Un-chosen Trait

Many of the traits you observe are not exactly optional. Since people reading is not a cookbook skill, I can't tell you that a person of short stature will have a personality warped by overcompensation, or that they will be bigger-hearted people because they know to not to read a book by its cover. I can't tell you that an ugly person will be jealous of others' beauty, or that they will have a monopoly on compassion because they have experienced discrimination. I can tell you though, that challenging traits give you a place to look for clues as to the person's values and character.

That's because they are likely to telegraph to you how they have handled the challenge. You don't have to tickle their defenses to see how they will react, there is no point to taking such a risk, but you certainly do want to have your radar out.

It is important to practice relating to people with unusual features and disabilities, so that you can be desensitized.

The last thing you want to do is put out an uncomfortable vibe because you are distracted; especially since your prospect is sick of that distraction intruding into their relationships.

If you are smooth, you will be providing a refreshing experience, and farther along in your goal of establishing rapport.

BECOMING TRUSTWORTHY

Introducing Rapport

Rapport happens when people feel good being around you. This kissing cousin to charisma is so valuable that anyone who could bottle it would be wealthy indeed. Rapport is a key to sales success. People act from their hearts more than their heads, especially when it comes to sticking around long enough to hear what a salesperson has to say. It also encourages them to buy from you.

If you could take only one sales skill from this book, you would want the ability to build rapport with your prospects. They will be less edgy about negotiating, and less fussy about features. They will be less defensive about your probes and test closes. They will reveal more to you and be in less of a hurry to leave. They will be more likely to refer others to you. They will even make your job less stressful by being more pleasant to be around. Most important, they will be happier about buying from you.

Your prospects respond to your rapport building skills before they respond to any of your other sales skills. That's because your ability to establish rapport enhances their sense of you as a person. More specifically, it is their ability to connect with you, to trust you, and to relax into relating with you.

Technique-Based is Good

The word rapport was first seen in English in 1894, referring to a relationship that is one of mutual accord and trust. Most people rely on chemistry to luck into rapport, or good manners to give it a boost. But you can do a great deal to create rapport with just about anyone. Fortunately, the art of rapport building has been developed into a near science over the past few decades, and taught with great success to sales professionals.

In these pieces, you will learn exactly what you can do to create rapport with nearly anyone, and reap the benefits in your sales career. At first glance, it may appear like a simple trick of imitation, but the more you explore it, the more you will discover additional depth. Each rapport-building ability you master will become unconscious mastery, making room for another skill, and another, until you have profound rapport-building abilities. If you are already good at establishing rapport with people (and if you are, you are probably well aware of that), then these pieces will give you more accuracy, flexibility, and speed.

THE UNCONSCIOUS AND RAPPORT

Two professors popularized rapport building after discovering and analyzing the unconscious talents of famous psychotherapists. One of the best was *Virginia Satir.* When they told her what they had learned about how she established a good therapeutic relationship, she didn't believe them. She really felt that their attempt to boil what she was doing down to skills left out how much she cared. She thought it cheapened the relationship and underestimated the human element.

The next day, she tried doing her work without the techniques that they had identified, and she was unable to create the kinds of relationships she was used to creating. Apparently the professors were right. She was using observable techniques to create rapport. It was just that she was taking them for granted. She had developed her skills unconsciously, and had no idea how much she depended on them.

Satir used rapport skills unconsciously, and customers respond to rapport skills unconsciously. If they don't want to buy a car from a used car salesman because he's in a loud suit, that's mostly a conscious reaction. They could tell you that they don't trust used car salesmen, and the ones in the loud sports coats are the *worst.* They don't have to be right, of course. It doesn't matter if they're right or wrong. A lost sale is a lost sale. But if they overlook the loud suit because they feel a personal connection with the salesman, they probably got that rapport connection unconsciously. That is, factors outside of their awareness influenced them, causing them to have a sense of affinity with their salesperson.

RAPPORT IS ESSENTIAL

This means that it is pretty much a requirement to learn and improve your rapport building skills for sales. But what about those of us who are already excellent at pacing, because we've been practicing it pretty much all our lives? Even these natural unconscious pacers stand to improve by learning more about it. They can improve their flexibility and efficiency.

People want to do business and spend time with people they feel rapport with. Since so much of the sales process is managed subconsciously, rapport has deep implications. Rapport is the life blood of the sales relationship. Unless in your business everything hinges on price and you never meet your customers, rapport is key. And even if you get a job that doesn't connect you with customers, rapport-building skills will serve you well with your supervisor, colleagues, vendors, and in your personal life.

Imagine what it would be like not to be able to establish rapport with anyone. That would be a lonely, frustrating, and maybe deadly situation. You are far beyond that. But how much farther might you be able to go in life with well-polished, well-informed rapport skills? Many people from all walks of life have reported profound improvements in their work and family lives as a result of making a conscious effort to develop these skills.

RAPPORT AND TIME

The first moments of an encounter are intensely affected by your rapport abilities. That means that even brief sales encounters can depend on your rapport skills. However, as valuable as first impressions are, rapport will also serve you in the long haul, with sales relationships that last over a long period.

Speed is important, because most salespeople, even the ones who want long-term prospects, only have a short time to make that first impression and start building their initial rapport. The more powerful and flexible their rapport-building skills are, the more prospects will respond, and the more diverse ranges of prospects will respond. That's where the flexibility comes in. An unconscious pacer may not have the flexibility that comes from technical pacing fluency.

The less time a person has to size someone up, the more they will rely on the most obvious clues. That includes the gut feeling that they have from their initial, mostly unconscious reaction to you. This is important, because the tipping point that I talk about applies to brief sales encounters as well as longer sales processes. This is so because of how often people feel that they should look around just a little more to see if they can get a better deal, better features, or the latest model. They are on the verge of buying, so a little rapport may make all the difference as to whether they soften up and take care of the purchase. Often, it will be that gut check that determines whether they decide to be done with their search and take their bounty home.

RAPPORT AND RELATIONSHIP

Some of my readers are in jobs that involve fostering long-term relationships with internal or external customers. Other have relationships that last a few hours, as may happen during a time share tour or prolonged automotive sales process. Still others have only very brief contact such as a little consultation to a customer seeking vitamins.

Whether your relationship lasts a minute or years, you can improve sales with rapport skills. You will develop unconscious mastery of these skills, as well as managing them consciously as needed. For your prospects, the effect will operate subconsciously. They may be able to consciously say that they feel good about working with you. They may be able to say that you were very considerate, understanding, or motivational. But their good feelings will almost entirely arise because things you do that they don't notice. Which is to say that they processed your behavior mostly unconsciously.

As for those prospects who are especially observant, few, if any, will notice any but your more obvious efforts to connect with them and be good-mannered. The few who know about rapport building techniques will notice them and appreciate that you know what they know and use. You may find them very likeable for some reason.

WHAT TO DO NOW

Begin applying the following rapport-building skills immediately. You may already be doing them. If so, you're ahead of the game.

People must sense that you care about their interests. They don't expect you to be a saint, but there are many ways that you can show your concern for their welfare. In some businesses, your attention to the details of their account scores points. ...or your ability to show warm feelings to them. ...or sending them something thoughtful in the form of a gift or online resource that is clearly relevant to their needs. ...or your ability to show how you are similar to them. Of course, that means knowing how you are similar. Do you make enough chit chat to know some things about them? If you don't tend to remember things like that, do you write them down and go over them before a call? ...or giving good service before they have made any commitment to you. ...or just listening well and expressing your understanding of their needs.

Whether it is over a minute or over years, you want your prospects to develop an emotional investment in you.

These are the most obvious and basic (and conscious) skills. Most experienced salespeople already use them, but I wanted to set them down here to make sure we're on the same page. Besides, a brief review or self-audit of fundamentals never hurts.

Congruence

When things are congruent, it means they are in some kind of alignment or agreement. This term has some to mean that a person is congruent when their body matches what they say. By body, I mean anything physical: tone of voice, facial expression, posture, gestures, hand temperature, you name it. Everything about you comes together in meaning. This produces a powerful message that you are sincere. Nothing expresses sincerity like congruence, except maybe paying bills on time. Since you are so sincere, you must really be certain about what you are certain about, too! **Certainty is a very attractive trait, unless you have poor judgment.** This book assumes that you have basic good judgment. If you have trouble there, get thee to a therapist.

Now here's something that is really great to be certain about, especially when you are congruent. That is that you are providing something that is worth more that you are asking for it. Rev up that certainty before you make contact. If ever boredom should begin to soften your intensity, take the time to rev up that certainty factor. You'll learn wonderful methods for managing your state during this book.

Pacing for Rapport

Pacing is the most influential skill in rapport building, unless you consider things as basic as good manners, but that's for a Sales 101 book. It relies on expressing yourself in ways similar to your prospect, but don't confuse pacing with simply imitating people. The deeper you get with pacing, the more you experience that it is a true art.

Pacing is done subtly, but you will be surprised at how direct you can be about much of it without causing any distraction. When you do it unconsciously, it works, and when you do it on purpose, it works. Up to a point, it comes naturally to most people. But you can speed up and enhance your connection-making by following my instructions.

A great side benefit of pacing is that it helps you tune into people's unconscious attitudes. Bodies communicate a great deal about attitudes, and they have a funny way of not censoring themselves quite as well as mouths do, despite our best efforts. Pacing will also sharpen your people watching acuity, because of the practice you will get in paying attention to them in new and meaningful ways. Both these benefits will help you understand people and how they experience the world.

Even without the other benefits of pacing, you have a valuable aid for building rapport.

PACING WORKOUT: GETTING STARTED

From now on, notice how people move and express themselves. Without being really obvious, find those qualities in yourself and let them out a little. Keep doing it, don't stop. Notice what happens, and how many seconds or minutes it takes. Do they seem to connect with you easily? Do you feel more at ease with them? If not, it could be that you are trying on a way of being that is too unfamiliar. Or it could be that you are self conscious about it. Either way, it will pass.

Do you feel that this assignment is a bit much? Then focus on body positioning only, for starters. You'll take on more as you get comfortable with pacing this single trait. How do they fold their arms? What is their posture like? Which way do they lean as they sit with you? Now you have the idea!

Here's a good tip. Remember how I said you should be subtle about it. Think of yourself as lightly coloring your *existing, actual* personality and body language with theirs. This is not imitating. Not quite.

Practice pacing people throughout your day. Do it with friends, coworkers, and prospects. Why not? You're starting out subtle. You'll probably be too worried about being obvious to do anything that would offend anyone, anyway.

When you are in situations that are more anonymous and the stakes aren't too high, then be adventurous and try more extreme pacing. Start a conversation as you drink some coffee or wait in a waiting room and pace more obviously. If they get uncomfortable, you can always gently break off the pacing.

By the way, you don't have to connect intensely to pace someone. How intensely do they connect with you? You can pace that, too!

When I travel in Latin America, I feel a little uncomfortable, because I am not used to sitting so close during conversations, but I do as the locals do, and they appear to be perfectly comfortable. I'm starting to get used to it now.

PACING WORKOUT: GETTING PHYSICAL

For this workout, we'll take pacing to another level than you practiced in the previous section. Let's get technical about it. I want you to practice pacing one or more of the following things, and I want you to keep building this ability until you can pace all of them with anyone. Yes, that will take some practice, but it will be one of the most important disciplines you ever practiced.

1. Keep on practicing body position, as in the previous piece.

2. Body language: gestures, posture. *How animated are they? How sweeping are their gestures? What kind of meaning are they conveying?*

3. Breathing: Yes! Breath at the same rate as they do. I know, that will take practice all on its own.

4. Voice timbre: The basic quality of the voice. This is definitely a subtle one. Just take on a little of the quality. Is it soft, edgy, nasal.

5. Voice pitch and lilt: What kind of musicality does their voice produce. Are they a monotone, or do they rise and fall? How quickly? How expressively? Don't get carried away and imitate their accent, though!

6. Volume and dynamics: Are they loud. Do they shift from loud to soft? How so? How many *words* do they *emphasize* per *sentence.* Three? What *kinds* of *words* do they *emphasize?*

7. Tempo and rhythm of speech: How fast do they talk? What kinds of rhythms animate their speech?

PACING WORKOUT: GETTING EXPRESSIVE

These pacing items are more mental, so they might be a little more difficult. But they'll grow on you. As they become easy, they really are enjoyable because of the comfortable connection they build.

1. Facial expressions: Start with their overall expression as their mood changes, rather than trying to imitate every fleeting nuance.

2. Vocabulary, plus: Definitely stay within their educational level. But you can go farther than that. What kind of expressions do they use? Is there a lot of slang? What kind? How about metaphors? Do they compare things to football? Are they very academic and abstract or technical? Do they add sound effects to substitute for fully explaining things that happened? How long are their sentences? Are they simple, or not?

3. What senses to they mostly appeal to? Vision, hearing or feeling? Consider these sense references: I see. I mean, I hear you. I mean, I feel for you. I can picture it. It sounds good. He's getting under my skin. Which sense does the person tend to talk in? Use that sense as you speak, especially for key points.

4. Perspective and mood: Do they look through a glass gleefully or darkly? Do they talk big picture or details? Short term or long term?

5. Chunking and idea flow: How much do they try to get across in a sentence. Do they stroll along one idea at a time. Is it all very clearly following a time line, one event at a time? Do they try to put several ideas into a sentence? Do they jump around among their ideas or change the subject easily?

Keep noticing what happens. I find that I do this so naturally, that I have to be careful with my time. I keep getting into relaxing yet animated conversations that I don't feel motivated to end. My prospects tend to add information in a relaxed way, and it is much easier to know what they need and will respond to. I could go on, but you get the idea.

EXPERIENCE AND VALUES

People prefer people who are like them. Generally, people are more likely to buy from people who are like them. The more ways they are similar, the better. So consider the ways you can emphasize your similarities. As you size up your prospect (the section on People Reading will help you with this immensely), you want to look for traits to match.

For this piece, think about behavior, attitude as what you see on the outside, while values and life experience are what you have on the inside. So far, we've been talking about qualities of behavior without considering where they are coming from. That's a good way to start. But you can expand your pacing abilities by looking at the "inside" factors as well.

Consider these: social class, region or origin, educational level, profession, extroversion or introversion, happiness or seriousness, pace of speech and sense of urgency, religious orientation, etc.

EXPERIENCE AND VALUES: FINE TUNE IT

When pacing the experience and values of a prospect, you have two basic aspects. There are the mannerisms and mood of your responses and probes, and there are direct expressions of opinions and facts. These are very different. It's one thing to show that a religious comment touched you, and another to directly profess faith in their religion. If you do share a faith, you can reveal that, but you must be subtle, because it is not classy to appear to be using your religion as a sales tool.

Even if your prospect seems very different in their values and background, you can find something in yourself to match them. Sometimes it is as simple as side stepping a difference so the commonality is more obvious. I once had a prospect who had a charming personality, but said something that I felt was bigoted. I focused on appreciating her charm and brought out that aspect of my personality. This will be a much more relaxed, sincere approach, than pretending to harbor an ignorant prejudice, unless you're some kind of master of disguise who got tired of working for the CIA. No matter how different your prospect is in these three areas, you can find ways to improve your connection through similarities.

PACING WORKOUT: EXPERIENCE AND VALUES

Think of ways you can pace people based on the following factors. Remember, you do not need to pretend to have values you don't have, only to bring out qualities that you can find in yourself that match where they are coming from in terms of experience and values.

1. Cultural factors: If they are religious, good things are blessings. If they are an atheist, good things are good things. If they are worldly, you can drop a hint here and there as to your scope, if not, you can stick to things they are familiar and comfortable with. If they are from someplace you aren't, you can at least express your interest and appreciation. That's fine, too.

2. Values: This is, maybe the most advanced of all, because values often divide us. Challenge yourself to find their values in yourself, even if they are not your dominant values, and have them color the things you say. At first, just focus on how their values leak into their speech. Take your cues from that. As a result, you may have to fend of an invitation to an LDS meeting, spouse-swapping party, or political fund raiser, but at least that will clue you in to how well you're doing.

3. Keep going. You'll notice more things that you can pace as you get comfortable with what you have so far.

You'll have to exercise a little extra care with cultural and values pacing. This is mainly a concern in your lasting relationships, especially in your personal life. You don't want your friends to think you're a chameleon, or that you have different values than you actually have.

Rapport Story: Identity and Stigma

One of my prospects knew that there was a large gay population in the neighborhood, and he sounded a little judgmental when he asked about it. I wasn't willing to pretend to be anti-gay or any other kind of anti-people, but I wanted to maintain enough rapport that I could say something that might open his mind a little. So I made a joke about one of the men who went running in the area, saying there seems to be a special gay way of running. Then I said, "...but seriously, yes, this is a very gay-friendly area with a lot of businesses that cater to the gay population. They are very political and organized in this city." And I said it in a pleasant tone, rather than judgmental.

Later, I found out that he had just begun to struggle with his own gay identity, and that was the real reason for his tone. He was feeling awkward and confused, or testing the water with me to see if

I was judgmental. This goes to show that pacing values can be trickier than more obvious things. But then, some people are very obvious with their values. I feel bad about the joke that was intended to help him identify with me while I tried to open his mind. But I feel good about the good things I said about the community. And that prevented me from alienating him too much to close the sale.

PACING WORKOUT: ATTITUDE

You don't have to change your mind anything to bring out attitude qualities that match your prospect. If they are liberal or conservative, evangelical or Jewish, you will find that their attitude has little to do with this. Look for their attitude to life, the world, and people, and match that up as a general quality, regardless of your opinions.

If they are a little stand offish, then give them space and allow time for them to warm up to you, as though you were stand offish as well. Find other ways to engage them, without trying to force warmth into the relationship.

Perhaps your idea of warmth is different from theirs. I have had plenty of customers who were very formal, cold, officious, or robotic, but who bought my products. They prefer to relate in other ways, such as by analyzing the features of the product or being very efficient. Many probably have a limited ability to experience or express warmth, and some of them feel more than they express to you.

But what about people who are in a bad mood?

Can you build rapport with a mean, irritated, or impatient, person by acting that way yourself?

Almost. You can express commitments and awareness that align with these attitudes, without being so negative that the person loses faith in you.

Rapport Workout: Loud and Dominant

I had a prospect who was pretty impatient and irritable. He was a decision-maker for an employer that could mean a big sale of an insurance carve out. On the phone, he got it across to me that he was very knowledgeable and experience, and I could tell that he actually was pretty smart.

I accommodated him by telling him that most of my business customers needed a dumbed-down sales presentation that, frankly, gets a little tedious to deliver day in and day out, and that I was looking forward to getting right down to brass tacks. This probably helped me get my foot in the door.

Despite my best efforts to establish a warm atmosphere and provide some information that I felt would improve the image of my company in his mind, he was fairly short with me, and spoke in a somewhat loud, dominant voice. I used a similar voice from the start, and with a little more volume, I said:

"Well, I'm glad you've done your homework, because the last thing I want to do is waste a lot of time on a motivational sales pitch. I'd just a soon get right to the point..."

Then I pick up at a somewhat more advanced point in my sales process.

By complimenting him on doing his homework, I was acknowledging that I didn't need to tell him more about the company or the general product information. And I moved forward to a point that would create an accelerated feeling. By maintaining a similar intensity in my voice, I contributed to our rapport. A person who did not like loud, dominant voices would not think we were developing rapport. But I have been through this enough times to know that it can lead to a strong bond. But remember, I did not clash with him, I directed my intensity at something outside of us, never at him. That's key to this kind of rapport!

RAPPORT WORKOUT: DISGUST

I had a prospect who had an attitude of disgust towards salespeople that came out pretty easily, but unexpectedly. But I didn't let it throw me. He made a caustic remark about my industry, and the kind of scheisters that run it.

I got in touch with my own disgust about unethical insurance outfits, and I let that disgust show on my face and in my voice. Then I said:

"I am so relieved to work for an outfit that actually gets the kind of customer service ratings that we do. I left my last employer because they didn't walk the walk. (That's true.) Here is our list of the reviews we've had from major magazines, even Consumer Reports, oh, and the Better Business Bureau, and these larger websites."

A little mismatch between what you appear to be about to say and what you *actually* say can hold the prospect's interest. My sentence started with, *"I am so relieved..."* even though I was showing disgust, and even though the prospect probably expected me to be defensive. Surely he was used to invoking various awkward responses in people.

Until it was clear why I was saying that I was relieved, the prospect was, briefly, in that sort of suspended animation that people experience when they are mentally dealing with some ambiguity, confusion, or contradiction.

This served as a bit of a pattern interrupt, which allowed me to inject something positive AND credible into the dialogue without creating resistance in the prospect. At the same time, I was pacing the prospect with my actual feelings of disgust, at first, and then moving toward positive feelings to see if the prospect would follow me there. He did, and started getting interested in what I had to offer him.

Experience: Look for anything that you can relate to in their sphere of experience. Anything about them, or any comment they make, or any information that you can get out of them about their experiences and current interests is fair game. Get to know about things that your prospects are typically into. If you don't follow football, but many of your prospects do, then learn about the local team and where they stand so you can make comments that show your understanding. If you want to appeal to the upper crust, then take a course in cultural literacy or peruse the Internet, library, or bookstores for information of cultural interest.

GET SOME INTELLIGENCE AND RUN WITH IT

In many sales relationships you can steal a moment or two to find out about your prospect's personal interests. It can be as simple as asking about a ring or sun tan.

"Oh, you went to Louisiana State? Still following their team?"

"Your vacation must have been somewhere far from here, we haven't had a day of sun around here for two weeks."

You can count most people to respond to a comment or question like that with some information.

This can help you establish a bond of common interests or experiences, because you can respond about anything that you have in common, even if it's just a comment about football.

But you can take it farther than that, in the interest of pacing. You can find the qualities in yourself that match that kind of person, and put them into the foreground of your personality.

If you're from a city of similar size, you can dispense with the ways big city living has rubbed off on you, and be more like you would be if you were visiting that city. If you are talking to a construction worker, make some extra effort to be like you are when you are with friends involved in the construction or other blue-collar trades.

STAYING IN BALANCE

A fellow who was role playing with a therapist in a training, noticed that she was very good at pacing. He also knew that she did it unconsciously. So he tried a little experiment. He kept moving over more and more to the side of his chair until she fell off of hers. I suppose that's one way to teach someone that they are an unconscious pacer.

The more adept unconscious pacers tend to be other-centered. I'm not talking about the normal unconscious pacing that most of us are perfectly good at, when we are comfortable enough to do it. We should be, because it's part of the glue that holds society together. But the extremists are self-sacrificing, going too far and neglecting their own needs in the bargain. This happens in their personal lives as well as their business lives. The more conscious you are of your pacing, the better you can decide how much to pace, and what kind of signals to put out. You will have an easier time negotiating or setting limits with someone if you are not too easily entrained into being like them and taking on their feelings at the expense of your own. People who have trouble *"hanging on to their own reality"* are not merely unconscious pacers, they are compulsive pacers who feel responsible for even the thoughts of others.

You're more likely to find compulsive pacers in nursing or social work than sales, but if this applies to you, now is your chance to liberate yourself with a flexible, technical approach to pacing. I say this because, done right, your pacing can actually help you be more assertive, if it is conscious.

Conversely, you can come out of self-centeredness through conscious pacing. Pacing tends to build empathy, which you'll recall is your ability to pick up on how other people react and feel. That kind of acuity is important to sales. It doesn't turn you into an instant doormat. Understanding others' feelings can do the opposite, tuning up your BS detector.

You don't have to change you personality to take these benefits from pacing. But you will expand your skills and improve your style.

WHAT WENT WRONG? BIAS?

I guess we have all had the experience of feeling really out of rapport with someone, and it was pretty obvious that they were out of rapport with us. You could almost feel it in the air. The atmosphere was cold, awkward, or even hostile. When you master rapport building, you are less likely to experience this, at least not when you want to avoid it. However, sometimes rapport building just seems to shut down. If this happens to you, it may be a good learning experience.

It is possible that the person has a very anti-rapport personality, or that there is some factor that is more powerful than your rapport building skills. But let's focus on what you can directly control: those situations when you magically lose your skills.

Consider some possible reasons for a rapport skill shut down. Put another way, consider some reasons for your unconscious to be reacting negatively to the person. I mean, if you aren't turning your rapport skills off on purpose, then you must be having some kind of subconscious reaction to the person or situation.

Start by mentally scanning your thoughts and body for clues about your reaction. Do you have judgments, discomfort, fear, or other negative responses? Ask yourself what might be triggering your reaction. One woman who had an instant negative reaction to someone, and I mean a really hateful automatic reaction, realized that he was a movie star and she had seen him play a very despicable villain.

With enough knowledge of pacing, you can experiment and adjust your approach. Perhaps you are doing the body language well, but you are not putting out the right value signals. Perhaps you are not comfortable with this person for some reason and you have unconsciously shut down your unconscious pacing. Since unconscious pacing is vulnerable to any judgments that you make about people, you will benefit immensely from my state management skills that bring out your ability to appreciate very diverse people.

We all have biases or prejudices that we are not entirely aware of. These can be ethnic, racial, political, cultural, gender, disability, etc., etc. By discovering and working through such automatic reactions, you will be expanding your flexibility and, thus, your effectiveness as a sales professional, as well as your comfort in the world.

FINE TUNE IT: ASYMMETRY!

Another problem with unconscious pacing happens when the pacing is not working. This is not a failure to use the skills, it is a failure of the skills being used.

But what was failing?

Were you too artificial?

Was there something about you or the situation that was too negative for this person to have gotten comfortable with you, despite your efforts to connect?

Or was it something more advanced and subtle?

The answer may lie in asymmetry. Some people want to have a very asymmetrical relationship. They want to be very much in charge. They can be like those lizards that flare their necks and charge at a mirror image of themselves. Acting like a peer of a person like that can actually cause them to feel enraged. I've experienced this myself. There are several things you can do.

You can pick up on this early in the encounter and act like the servile service person that this domineering person wants to see you as. **What does it cost you? It's your choice.** If you have been showing your *alpha* aspect to him, then perhaps you're best off deflecting it sideways, that is, by expressing it about a separate target.

For example, inferior customers who don't understand what he does, or inferior staff of another business that he was displeased with.

You could even deflect it into something inadequate in the packaging, and rush to hand him one that has no defect (real or imaginary). This deflection gambit is a very good one to have up your sleeve.

But bear in mind that many dominant or attacking types can be lonely, and really want someone to step up and meet them directly. The trick is that, if you have gotten intimidated or aggravated, this may take some practice. But what you want to do is to show your intensity in a was that is directed to a positive outcome.

"This delay is ridiculous, I can't believe we haven't scheduled enough checkout staff for today! Let me take care of this immediately!"

A strong attitude, eye-to-eye, with a dominant person will work much better this way. Even if you have to redirect them, when there is no other choice, you can be strong if you use positive, outcome-oriented words.

"Some of the staff can't handle an animated discussion! Here, let's hash this out over in the side office, I'm sure we can get take care of you."

GROOVE SET

Sometimes, a sales relationship becomes so natural, it's like two old friends. You can't force that, and it doesn't come in pill form. But you can watch for it, and promote it. And when you recognize that it is happening, you need to act accordingly.

Here are the symptoms of the groove set: you and the prospect blend your comments a little bit like a single mind processing the possibilities; your prospect becomes more spontaneous, less cautious in expressing their reactions to the sales process; the whole interaction seems more natural and warm; you and the prospect feel more of a natural urge to make concessions; you both have the feeling that if you were stuck in an elevator, it wouldn't be so bad.

The way to act when this is happening is to not be too entranced by it. If you are, you might actually start to act like this is a well-worn friendship, and try to be too funny, too insulting, or too distracted into time-consuming banter that could cost you this or the next sale. Instead, enjoy it consciously, while maintaining a tight rein on your technical sales process. Remember, you are being intuitive and technical at the same time. At least that is your goal for unconscious sales mastery with conscious method application. Those are the two sides of sales.

TRUST

Let's move into an expanded dimension of rapport. You know that people buy from friends, and that part of rapport is trust. But, besides trust developing from pacing, we need to expand trust by how we relate to our prospects. This is really important, because people will buy from a poor salesperson if they like them enough. They will even tell you how to sell them, by pointing out what really matters and asking how well the product fits their needs.

If I can risk being a little philosophical, I believe that the starting point for building trust is to find your love of humanity within yourself first, unless you're a con artist. That may seem like a tall order, but it really isn't. I'm serious.

It's about finding the part of you that cares about people and putting it into the foreground of your mind while you are with that person. It means learning to set your judgments aside, recognizing that you are not in any position to know what heroic things they may do or already have done, or what sacrifices they may make, or what their potential really is.

Once you do that, you can see them as a potentially unlimited person who deserves to have people bring out the best in them. Don't be fooled by a gruff exterior or slimy personality. Just assume that there is a good person inside who isn't being very obvious at the moment.

EARNING TRUST

It's been said that love is not enough. You need skills to go with it. One of the best skills is to learn not to push. You don't want to trigger a pushing back response in your customer, and you don't want to raise your own stress level. It is also helpful to have some language so that the customer knows they can trust you.

Consider the example of a customer who you call, but who is very gruff. Imagine saying this:

"Oh, perhaps this is not the best time. I don't want to disrespect your time. I just have a method that is increasing productivity in your industry by 20%, but it's clear that you don't care to hear these comments at the moment. When might you want me to provide this?"

This shows that you respect their feelings, are not a high-pressure type, that you are surprisingly classy, and that they could be missing out on something so good, that you are fine with moving on to your next call. This gives you much better odds that they really will have a time in mind, or just relax a tiny bit and say, *"Make it short, I'll listen."* Well, that's a start, no?

FOR TRUST, ALIGN AND REDIRECT

Here is a basic principal to use when you get a response that you might want to argue with: Always get into alignment with them and then redirect them. Align and redirect. Never push, pull, or argue. As soon as you feel off center, this is a red flag signaling that you could be on the verge of alienating your prospect and getting one of those defensive, push back responses.

But what if they say something that is simply incorrect, like, *"These products always break down right after their warranty expires."* You don't want to say, *"Always? Come now."* And you don't want to say, *"That's untrue!"* **Remember, first get aligned, then redirect.**

Try this, *"Many people are very concerned about the reliability of these products.* (You're telling them that they have a legitimate concern, and that you here their concern. This keeps them from tuning you out.) *In fact, another country trying to corner the market on these gave them a bad reputation. We took the bold step of being the first company to offer a three-year warranty for parts and labor, and to have a no-questions-asked return policy. Our customer response is the highest, as you can see on sites like Epinions.com."*

RAISE THE ENERGY, TURN DOWN UNWANTED PAIN

Our nervous systems work like gates. That's why those hot or cold ointments can reduce pain. They actually distract us from sensing the pain. Not like a mental distraction, but a biochemical one that closes the gateway for the pain to reach the brain.

You can use that ointment effect to promote sales. Consider the pains that might make them apathetic, crabby, or fatigued in talking to you about your product.

1. They've been burned.

2. They are pinched for time.

3. They have been hit with high-pressure sales.

4. They are torn about spending money, even though they want it. That was just a few examples.

Let's tone down that pain so they can be fully connected with us for the sale. Apply the ointment to get them out of touch with their pain. Some examples:

1. Raise the energy level with an infectious (but not overdone) attitude.

2. Raise their self esteem with a nice compliment.

3. Fill their senses with a sensory-rich description of a benefit, feature, or outcome of the product. I'll bet you can come up with even more.

Notice how nicely this approach jibes with the idea of starting with the pleasure factory, THEN going for the pain factor, and finally, the logic that helps them through the closing of the sale. (We'll be coming back to that sequence in my sales process.) In this step, we are providing pleasure (and excitement) to get things rolling. Once we have some rapport and get to know them a little better, then we will be in a position to activate the pain factor.

GENERATE HIGH QUALITY AFFECTION VIBES

One of the most important signals that shows that you like someone is eye contact. You don't stare, but you have a good amount of it. You do it with a relaxed quality, in which your positive feelings for your prospect and your product shine through. Practice bringing your relaxed and positive feelings into your face and eyes. See how this looks in the mirror or on video. Learn to turn this on by finding it within yourself. After all, it is always there, waiting for you to enjoy it. This is not a dramatic or extreme thing that you apply to your face like a mask. It is something that you find and allow to be expressed.

Practice this and you will learn to connect with this state of mind at will. This way, if you wake up on the wrong side of the bed, it won't throw off your work. You will be able to connect with people, establish rapport, and concentrate on your work.

You probably have some of this ability already. Haven't you ever been in a bad mood, then interacted with someone from a positive state of mind, and then found yourself right back in your bad mood as soon as you were away from them. And I'm talking about an interaction with someone who wasn't so charismatic that they were responsible for your good mood.

All I'm saying is, most of us have a good start on this ability; the ability to psych yourself into a state of mind. So try this at work. What am I saying? It might be even more important, for your own peace of mind, to try it at home, too!

WISDOM FOR GENERATING A GOOD CONNECTION

Sometimes, coming from a fully accepting or loving place is easier said than done. Please allow me to offer some ways generate that quality. These bits of practical wisdom will help you find acceptance of others within yourself, no matter how judgmental you might tend to be.

1. Be willing to recognizing the fundamental humanity of others, even if you don't understand them. We're all in this together, after all.

2. Find things that you approve of or enjoy about them. See them in terms of how they are special, talented, witty, likeable, or at least trying. Give them an A for effort if nothing else. Catch them being those things, and give compliments about that.

3. Practice having the intention to bring out the best in them. You've seen how kids with a mean teacher under-perform, and how a good teacher can really bring out their cooperation and motivation; even their compassion for others.

4. Know that they want to have a good time, and that you can help them do that.

5. Know that anything you don't like about them, they express for reasons that you can never fully understand. Recognize that they are on their own path, and wish them well in achieving their own kind of contribution and greatness.

6. Know that they want you to have a good time (most do). Notice what they are doing to help you enjoy the experience or to bring out the best in you. Pay attention to those efforts, since attention helps to reinforce that cooperative behavior.

7. If they do things to give you a hard time, then perhaps they would prefer to see you squirm, but this has nothing to do with you, really, since they don't know you very well. So, instead of taking it personally, assume that they came about this grudge honestly, and that they are applying it to the wrong people, and wish them well in overcoming their obstacle to enjoying other people.

Being "Only Human"

People like people who do not take themselves too seriously, except when that person is generally perceived as a superior, special person. If you talked about your product the way Martin Luther King talked about civil rights, your prospect would either walk away or want to take you down a notch. If you make a mistake, then make a joke about it.

Drop a humorous self-deprecating comment, like comics to, just not one that is too colorful or extreme; it should match your prospect as much as possible without appearing to take a pot shot at them. For example, *"Watch your step through here. First day on the job, I did a face plant right in front of a group of five. Now the office will never let me live it down."* (Smiling in a good-natured way that conveys amusement and shrugging it off.)

Ever watch talk shows? The hosts are incredibly charming and make lots of money, yet they make fun of themselves. They really play up their weaknesses. Many comics do that and it wins people over. And think about the really major proponents of peace, like Martin Luther King. Great leadership requires trust, and the right blend of confidence and humility inspires that trust.

Look for opportunities to be "only human" so people know that they can trust you.

LIKING IN STAGES

If you switch on your good vibes of acceptance 100% from the very beginning, this will only appeal to people who think this is normal. That is a fairly small proportion of people. If you start pleasant, and then find excuses to become more approving, this has several advantages.

First, it validates your approval, because the person had to earn it.

Second, it shows that you are aware of their best qualities and are responding to this. This enhances their self esteem in ways that associate their good feelings with you as the source.

Third, it creates a sense of their earning your appreciation and respect. People value what they must earn. This approach does not set the bar very high, but you should not set the bar too high or you will screen out good prospects.

The reason that hazing rituals in the military, gangs, and fraternities are so harsh, so sociologists say, is because they produce very strong bonds. These bonds, from an evolutionary point of view, have been necessary for survival for millions of years. It's no wonder that, no matter what the administrations of colleges do, these rituals continue to take place, in secret if need be. You may not be able to have a ritual that tests your prospects' desire for admission to your sales presentation, but you can at least emulate that by having them earn your respect and admiration as you discover admirable things about them.

For example, "Oh, this loan indicates you are a veteran. What branch? You were in... oh, yes. Thank you for your service. Seriously, I had asthma and couldn't enlist. One of my friends from high school died in that conflict. Well, anyway, I know you want to get moving... Here are those options I mentioned. The most popular one might be just what you're looking for, from what you've were saying."

Positive Arousal Workout: Approval, Warmth, and Chemistry

I'm beginning to feel a little aroused. No, not that way. I mean I'm feeling some excitement. Just the right amount of excitement. That's because I get to go to work today and practice something. I call it "balanced arousal generation." That means I do my best to inspire just the right amount of excitement in my prospects; the amount of excitement that keeps them engaged with me and moving through the sales process; excitement about the pleasure the product will bring them; even the arousal that comes from the pain of not having it.

Arousal is important. Done right, it creates a stronger desire to act; more *attunement* to emotional meaning; more attraction to the salesperson. Yes, with the right kind of excitement, you are helping the prospect bond with you and vice versa. From what the eggheads know about evolution, the right excitement probably triggers some ancient, instinctive bonding that can be good for our survival.

If the excitement is colored by too much fear, the brain's threat detection jumps up, and the ability to pick up on subtle social cues drops. That makes people defensive, and they dig in their heels.

Think of some things that can increase the balanced excitement level in your prospects. Here are some examples:

Your own attractiveness. Sorry of this sounds shallow, but the research and practices speak for themselves. Why do UPS men tend to be hunky and wear shorts? They are delivering to predominantly female clerical settings. Why do pharmaceutical agents tend to be slinky females? They are pitching to predominantly male physicians.

Approval from you or anyone else.

Anticipation of the rewards of the sale.

The symbolic entry into a higher status represented by the possible sale.

Being right about something.

The sales pitch, loaded with some exciting words.

Bonus item: the Emotional Speed Ball. Alternate your direct connection with them, with moments of withdrawal and seriousness where it seems like they might be losing their connection with you. Then come through very clear and connected suddenly. Watch their reaction to see how it works for them.

Warmth, Not Just a Trait

Take warmth to another level. Of course you already have a warm personality. But have you examined the words you have been using in your pitch? Research has shown that even a single warm word can alter a person's perception of another person. This is extra important during your first minutes with your prospect. Use warm words. Find cold words and find warm substitute words.

Consider the translation of, "*We aim to secure your business with a policy that fits you to a T,*" to, "*I'd like to tell you about a policy that I think will provide just the right amount of protection for your family, and it's really affordable.*"

How do they make you feel?

Compare the words and phrases:

1. aim to secure, business, fits, and T.

2. tell you about, provide, right, protection, and family.

You can warm things up by taking your emotions about getting the sale and diverting them into your love for your product. This helps you eliminate that needy feeling that alienates prospects. The more you need the sale, on an emotional level, the more you prevent it. By directing your prospect's energies with factors such as automatic behavior triggers and relationship building, as we describe in this book, you are also taking the unpleasant feeling that the time for the purchase decision is approaching. The desires that you fan and the needs you stir carry the customer along without provoking protective, resistant responses in the customer.

Warmth, Physical Warmth, as Your Secret Weapon

Warmth is a very powerful first impression tool. But this time I'm talking about physical warmth. I always make sure that my handshake is warm. The handshake is a big part of your first impression. I go into the washroom and run hot water over my right hand and then dry it well, so that when I shake the person's hand, my hand is very warm and dry. If I'm in a situation where my hand may be cold from being outside or a cold building, I will put one of those little chemical hot packs in my pocket and warm my hand. It's a small investment for an important sales relationship.

There is some very interesting research on this. In one study, a person would hand the subject a cup of coffee. The coffee would be either hot or cold. Either way, the person acted the same with the subject. After the interaction, the subject filled out a questionnaire about the person.

If the subject had received hot coffee, they rated the person as being a warmer person than if the coffee was cold. But the coffee had nothing consciously connected with what they were rating, which was the person's personality!

Similar research has been done with words. If a warm word was used along with other adjectives to describe someone in advance of seeing them speak, the person received a nicer rating than if a single cold adjective was included among the adjectives.

Scientists suspect that this happens because an important pleasure area in the brain is very close to the area that registers the temperatures that you feel with touch. Perhaps there is an intermingling that affects our judgment. Whatever the reason, you now have a valuable secret weapon for improving your connection with your prospects.

HOW MUCH OF WHAT ATTRACTIVENESS OR AUTHORITY?

Have you ever wondered where to draw the line on amplifying your own attractiveness? If you look like you put too much effort into looking attractive, will people think you are egotistical? In my experience, it depends on your customers.

If they expect you in a suit, you should be in a suit. If they are suspicious of people who have exceptionally perfect grooming, clothes, and accessories, then you want to tone things down and appear less severe to them.

This takes us outside of the realm of pacing. If a construction worker stops by to get an engagement ring, and finds the jeweler at the counter wearing grubby blue jeans and a sweaty t-shirt, that mash up will be to confusing to sell well.

And how fast can you change your clothes for the next customer, who happens to be a cross-dresser?

Did you bring your gold lame teddy?

There is also the matter of your authority. The more professional your position is, as when it involves some consulting, the more upscale your clothing should be. This is not the same as matching the clothing choices of an upscale clientele.

I'm talking about when the clientele, regardless of their clothes, expects you to be upscale. But even when high class is not required, you want to have clothes that provide you with some authority that will help your customers follow your lead in the sales presentation. For this, you should experiment in order to fine tune your image. Be scientific.

YOUTHFULNESS AS AN ATTRACTANT

There is a kind of attractiveness that is not in your clothes, makeup, or accessories. It is your youthfulness. This is one attraction factor that you can have without appearing self conscious. And you can reign it in at will, depending on your prospect. Cultivate youthful qualities through exercise, flexibility, and health. You can be 17 or 70 and have a youthful quality. It's about your flexibility, comfort in your body, and your attitude. You cultivate these traits through your lifestyle.

You already know that people are drawn to, and more cooperative with, people who are more attractive. But this is not just about the clothes you wear or the face you were born with. It's about a relaxed attractiveness that you live. It's about who you are. It's the result of how you live and what you experience. If you do the things that enhance your youthfulness at every level, then you will be more attractive. At the time of your contact with your prospect, you will not have to try to seem attractive, because it will be part of your nature. You are not posing or pretending, it just comes out of you.

People are attracted to youthful qualities because they are more desirable from an evolutionary point of view, and because of the social capital afforded to young, attractive people in the media and elsewhere. But this is not just sexual attraction. It applies to overall attraction.

This means that there is a certain amount of asymmetry that can work in your favor. People who seem older or frumpier than their years are still attracted to attractive people. The trick is to reign in qualities that they are not comfortable with. If you are quick-witted, you don't want to try to dazzle someone who does not relate that way. A somewhat depressed middle aged guy who hates his job does not need someone running circles around him. By using some restraint and doing your pacing, they will not get into an unconscious passive-aggressive reaction to you. They will not have a need to take you down a notch. You can rein in your vocabulary, the grace of your body, and the erectness of your posture. People buy from friends. What qualities would make you more of a model friend for this unique individual?

ATTRACTION WORKOUT

Here are some things that can help you maintain (or develop) youthful, attractive qualities at any age:

- Tooth whitening strips

- Regular exercise that builds stamina and posture

- Yoga or stretching to maintain flexibility

- Sports or dance classes that maintain and build your graceful movement in the world

- Massage therapy or at least using body tools to lower your stress levels and maintain your pain-free physical condition.

- Taking in comedy shows to get some laughter therapy.

- Getting social stimulation from intelligent, involved people. This is also a known source of longevity and prevents Alzheimer's.

- Playing brain teaser games on your computer.

- Singing in the shower or in your car to build your voice and pitch-control.

Turning on a good comic or news caster on television and imitating their vocal style and body movement to build your voice and ability to present, as well as your flexibility, by trying on a different personality style for a while. This is surprisingly valuable, especially when you pick performers who have qualities that you want to bring out in yourself. Try the echo technique: echo everything they say, and do the same changes of pitch. This really expands your personality and switches on your verbal abilities.

Relaxing to stress management recordings such as guided visualization. Regular relaxation or meditation are known to enhance longevity and overall happiness. People will pick up on that. This is a practice that will serve you throughout your life.

A diet that emphasizes your health is very important. It will help you maintain an attractive complexion, a sharp mind, and a long life with which to contribute to your family and society, and to enjoy the fruits of your labors. The research is very clear now, and only adds to our knowledge. Keep learning about this as a life-long side interest.

Maintain a positive vision for your life, work, relationships, and contributions. This will align your efforts and give meaning to even your most tedious activities. This produces a youthful quality that is unmistakable.

MYO WHAT?

While I'm at it, I must share with you a secret. Very few people really understand how important this is in maintaining a youthful quality. This is about staying free of pain, maintaining your flexibility, and keeping up your energy and positive attitude as you age. And it's really good for you at any age. The secret is your myofascial system. It's the way your muscle cells and fibers (myo for muscle and fascia for fibers) work together. A happy myofascial system a true secret weapon. It regulates (or harms) your posture, too!

Many people think that they have ruined a joint or muscle when the real problem is in the tissues surrounding the area. And the good news is that many of these problems are much easier to rehabilitate that you would think. But you have to know enough about this system to understand how to take care of it and how to heal it.

A good massage therapist can tell you a lot while you get a massage. There are good books by people like *Pete Egoscue* and *Bonnie Prudden*. But I can give you a quick idea of it. When fibers and muscle cells get stuck together or into a non-aligned layout, they can cause pain in several ways. But often, it's possible to straighten them out and flush out accumulated junk that adds to the pain. This is different from what we usually think of as healing. There doesn't have to be a tear to heal or wound to close. It's more like a conditioning process. It may take a while, or it may not. Either way, it's well worth it.

You can prevent problems and take care of some problems by learning at least the basics. You can use tools to apply some acupressure in the right spots to keep the kinks out, for example. Yoga is a nice preventive approach, but it doesn't always get rid of painful points. Think of acupressure as laser-focused Yoga that fixes painful points. Of course, I'm not a doctor and I don't know your body, so this information is not for every pain or stiffness.

ATTRACTIVE POSTURE WORKOUT

Here's a great idea for improving your posture. When you exercise or stretch, be sure to emphasize moves that expand your chest, strengthen your upper back, and that lengthen the back of your neck. You can learn more about how to do that from a good trainer and Yoga teacher. These two changes make you taller and more statuesque. That's attractive. It also prevents painful postural problems down the road.

You can enhance this further by keeping your lower back flexible and doing sit ups. Sit ups create more support for your lower back and protect it from injury as well as contributing to your good posture. In addition, exercise that specifically strengthen your upper back will help not only your posture, but your ability to handle a lot of phone or desk time, where your upper back gets some ongoing stress and effort.

That's a tight summary, but it's the core myofascial info that can get you on track for a far, far better life. Too bad every elderly person did not have this knowledge throughout their lives. Many of them would be much more youthful and happy.

THE ULTIMATE COMPLIMENT

While were discussing being a pleasure anchor, and putting ointment to reduce their distracting pain, let's go over how to provide a really smooth, enjoyable compliment. If you follow these steps, you will avoid seeming stiff, insincere, sniveling, keening, or cloying.

1. Say the compliment in positive terms. It must be true. *"That's' a great new doo!"*

2. Briefly justify it with a because. *"It's so sophisticated and hip."*

3. Ask them something about it, like how they did it. *"You must have a really intuitive hairdresser. Do they have room for another client?"*

Be sure to avoid sounding like you're just looking for free advice, unless it makes since in that situation.

Always be on the lookout for compliments that they don't expect, and compliments that they would like. If someone has a ring that appears unusual, it probably means a lot to them. If it's an unusual tattoo, they may regret it. A ring you can remove. A tattoo, not so easy.

Stay away from complimenting their body, no matter how attractive it is. You just don't want to raise questions about what other boundaries you might cross. **This is about building trust.**

SMILE WORKOUT

You don't need me to tell you that smiling makes you more attractive. But smiling is a real art form. Watch any movie, any group of people, any comedian for the smiles, and you'll see that there are many kinds of smiles, and quite an assortment of body language to go with them.

I want you to do something every time you find yourself in front of a mirror, and there's nobody else around. Give your typical forced smile. Then generate a mood in yourself, like smiling when something sad happens but you want to show you care. Then generate a mood that is congratulatory. What kind of smile and body language emerge then? How about when you do something embarrassing and have to admit that it was amusing?

Do this for your mirror time until you have dozens of smiles that you can flash with the emotional tone of the conversation. An important reason for this exercise is that you don't know quite what your smiles look like. With the feedback of the mirror, you can improve your smiles so that they better reflect how you feel.

I learned when I had to get publicity photos that my smile looked a lot better when I use a little more effort on the left side of my face. It's hard to say exactly why, but the improvement was unmistakable. I never would have known, if not for my experimenting in the mirror in advance.

You can do this with more facial expressions, and I encourage you to, but start with your many smiles. You can't lose.

FIRST IMPRESSION WORKOUT

First impressions really do have an impact on what people think of you, despite your subsequent behavior. However, the most striking thing that you do, even though it is an exception to your normal behavior, can end up being the most lasting impression. If you're having a bad day, an outburst can color how people perceive you for months or years, requiring you to slowly earn another perspective of you.

Let's look at the first impression you create with your prospects. If there is a way to get that first impression started before they meet you, you should. For example, have the receptionist say, your appointment is with Stephen, good, he's a very nice guy. There's your first impression. Make sure any words that introduce you are generally warm. Words like nice, warm, helpful, and friendly are good. Words like cool, precise, exacting, and *perfectionistic*, should be saved for later, when the relationship has begun. If there was an emotional interaction with a previous agent, it would be better if they described you as calm and supportive, than objective and cool-headed.

Make sure that all the elements of your first impression are strong. This includes your smile, tone of voice, handshake, clothing, posture, your first words, and how you direct the person physically to wherever your meeting (or how you accept direction when on a call).

To make sure your first words work well, you should have canned phrases that you can use without having to think or risk a fumble. Then your mind will be free to think ahead and size-up your new prospect. I really believe in having canned phrases. Not for everything, just for the pivot points in the sales process, such as your first interaction.

From Pacing to Leading

I want you to experiment with what you do after you have established rapport with pacing. It's called leading. First you pace, then you lead. Think about some customers who weren't in quite the right attitude for your sales process. They just weren't getting into the groove. Perhaps they were stuck on Slow, or they were jumping from topic to topic, or they were staying too reserved and skeptical.

When you have been pacing for a while, and you feel that you have established a basic connection, begin to shift your body language, voice, and so forth just a little in the direction that you want to go in. See if they begin to match you after a little time has passed. Maybe a minute or two. Many prospects will make that shift. That's because, as I mentioned, we all have an automatic tendency to pace, at least to some degree. The more rapport you have, the more your customer will tend to pace you. Watch and see.

Try getting a very dominant prospect to redirect their dominance or control efforts toward the sales process or product, instead of toward you. Try getting a glum prospect to show a glimmer of positive energy. Try getting a sluggish prospect to pick up the tempo a bit. If they are easily confused, and unfocused, see if you can get them into more of a flow through the process and a focus on the end result.

Science is telling us some really interesting things about how our brains create empathy and how we respond to the body language, facial expressions, and movement of other people. We generate impulses that match them, in a way that is kind of similar to our own body doing what they are doing. No wonder you can pace *and* lead.

MORE RAPPORT

Parallel play: Get people involved in the process. Get your customers to help measuring, picking features, customizing, and problem solving. What opportunities are there in your sales process?

Admit it! Acknowledge a weakness to your argument, or anything that might be embarrassing. Do this any time that you can preempt them thinking that you are untrustworthy, inaccurate, or egotistical. Do it with light-hearted humor.

Common enemy: What or who do they hate or resent. People really bond around a common enemy. You don't have to rant or be a bigot. Just get aligned. Let your conscience be your guide, but never take a higher ground than your customer, unless you care more about being right than making the sale. The enemy can be a thing or a trend.

Common cause: Abraham Lincoln said, *"If you would win a man to your cause, first convince him that you are his sincere friend."*

Help the customer buy "*you*." Many customers will buy the product when they buy you.

Listen: Listen so well that they think you are a great conversationalist.

Speak their language: This, too, makes you a great conversationalist. A trusted friend.

People like them: Show your customers that people just like them use your product. Hand them a list. Show them a video. Put up posters. Have a notebook of letters from satisfied customers.

Motives connected: Think of what your customer wants, needs, and values. Then, when you ask about their motives, make sure to phrase it in a way that shows your concern for their wants, needs, and values. "In order to get (need), it looks like you'll want to consider these models. Are you looking for something that (fills the need this way) or (fills it that way)?"

BELIEFS FOR RAPPORT

These basic beliefs will help you build rapport.

"In order to have rapport with another person, it is essential to respect their model of the world."

"The meaning of the communication is the response you get"

"There is no failure, only feedback"

"Resistance in an audience is a sign of lack of rapport."

"There are no resistant audiences, only inflexible presenters."

"In business, you get results, or you get reasons."

If you act "as if" these are true, they will serve you well. Some of them feel awkward at first. *Those* are the ones that you most need now.

Remember that you must notice whether or not you are getting the results you want with people. Then you must modify your behavior until you get those results.

The beliefs in this piece help you do that. They will make you a better manager, because you can help people understand them through your own experience and success.

JUST BEFORE THEY SIGN

As the sale comes to a close, you and your customer will typically have a pretty strong sense of rapport. Even after difficult negotiation, there is an interesting combination of respect and rapport.

Because of that high level, and because of your burgeoning power as a sales professional, I need to suggest that you do something that might sound a little counter-intuitive.

Just before your customer signs the contract, interrupt your rapport connection.

This is not a tool to get the sale. But it is a tool to keep the sale, and to keep community good will.

This technique makes sure that the customer is committed to signing the contract. It makes sure they are not doing it out of friendship or because you are so good at manipulating people. This gives you less likelihood of buyer's remorse. They will not connect making the purchase with a sense of feeling manipulated. They will also have a more solid sense of commitment to the sale, because of how they felt when they signed. In the very rare case that they decide not to sign, you may have gone to far. This could save you more trouble than missing a single sale.

HOW TO INTERRUPT RAPPORT FOR SIGNING

Do something normal that interrupts rapport. You can say you have to make a quick phone call or get something. You can simply direct your attention to something else, withdrawing from the closeness or intensity of your connection with the prospect. Do it smoothly, not in an abrupt manner.

If this doesn't make 100% sense now, it will after you learn more about automatic behavior and how our subconscious minds create meaning retroactively. Those are very intriguing parts of this book.

INFLUENCE POWER TOOLS: WORD MAGIC

WORKING WITH THE UNCONSCIOUS

Isn't it amazing how big our unconscious minds are in comparison to our conscious minds? You go through your day with various ideas popping into your head about what to do. You go through conversations and presentations with things popping into your head to say. You have all sorts of activity in your brain arranging for all of this, and mostly what you're conscious of is merely guiding the process a bit before it pops out of your mouth or into your behavior. To me, it's like comparing the captain of a ship to the ocean and the weather. That ocean and weather are full of powerful dynamics that the captain is responding to. The captain knows that she is not the whole picture, and makes her decisions accordingly. In contrast, the conscious mind wants to think that it's in charge of the ship, the ocean, and the weather.

Since our conscious minds are so busy, most people never stop to think about what this really means. And if they do, they tend to get side tracked by someone else telling them what it means. Perhaps they become occupied with meditating so that they can become enlightened in another lifetime, or they take philosophy classes. They might even study psychology and learn the latest scientific insights and theories. They might even learn to do something practical with it.

THE UNCONSCIOUS CONNECTION

But I think it's just fascinating how an experienced salesperson intuitively understands that they are navigating; that they are working with other people's conscious and unconscious dynamics. They are kind of like a ringmaster for a circus, or master of ceremonies for a talent night. They are not the show, the circus, or the ocean and weather; but they are managing the outcome.

Creative people develop a more intimate relationship with their subconscious than most people. That's because they have to in order to get creative results. The recognize the hidden intelligence there, and they cultivate a relationship with it. It's kind of like the relationship we have with magnetism.

You can't see it, but you use it on your refrigerator door, and your refrigerator door uses it to stay shut. You may not understand it, but you use it all the time.

Creativity, however, is not limited to the arts, unless you understand that sales is an art. **Your unconscious mind can be a tremendous ally.** The better you understand how it works, the better you can establish that alliance. The more you practice working with it, the better results you can experience.

So the unconscious mind isn't simply a place to store your information and reflexes. It's incredibly busy with calculations, decisions, and the challenge of managing all sorts of powerful and sometimes conflicting drives. That's a lot!

Did you know that, by the time you decide to do something, your brain was revved up to do it a bit before you were conscious of deciding to do it? That sounds backwards, doesn't it? But it's true! Instead of having free will, it's usually more like free won't. That is, deciding *not* to do what you *were* about to do, or *not* to say what you *were* about to say.

Now that we have some amazing ideas about the conscious and unconscious, we're ready to influence our customers (and ourselves) with framing.

INTRODUCING THE FRAME

Framing very useful. Like air is useful. You will see framing going on in most all sales techniques is some way. That's because sales depends on people's conscious minds going along with what their unconscious minds want, and their unconscious minds getting fired up about a portion of the many things it wants. That portion, of course, is what you are selling them today.

That really helps to write your job description! Your job is largely to harmonize the conscious and subconscious minds. In order to do that, you have to manage what is in the conscious mind. That's because it's a little like a cow's mouth. It can only hold a little bit of material, compared to the size of the cow, but the cow lives or dies by what is in its mouth.

Since the conscious mind can hold so little at one time, and the subconscious is so vast in all it's workings, you need to be very good at managing what goes *into* and what *leaves* the conscious mind.

The first part of the definition:

Framing is about what the conscious mind has in it, and not in it.

Does that sound like too much to expect from you? Well I'd like you to realize that you already do a great deal of that. This book simply continues your learning and fine-tuning of the process so that you can multiply your income with your existing abilities.

And I forgot to mention this, but as you develop unconscious mastery of these skills, you have more and more fun and satisfaction. And that's not counting the joy of learning really good stuff.

Oh, and then there's the pleasure of experimenting.

And the secure feeling that you are doing it in increments so as to be sure-footed as you progress along, improving your abilities step by step.

I'm so fortunate to be with you on this wonderful learning journey. I am honored that you chose me and my book as part of your growing success! Thank you.

START FRAMING NOW. YES, RIGHT NOW.

"As your and your customer discuss their purchase, how does your role help them efficiently complete the transaction, and what can you learn to make it even more profitable?"

Please imagine a square frame, with the above question inside it. What is really inside that frame? Whatever is inside it, it certainly generated a really good question! Here's what's in that frame: *desired outcomes, solutions, possibilities, useful feedback, and the assumption that you are creative and resourceful.* If you don't feel that way yet, we could call that one the "as if" part of the frame.

So let's see what this question sounds like when we use different framing. Let's switch from a desired outcome frame to a problem frame:

"How can you overcome the terrible resistance customers have to parting with their money?"

Or how about swapping the solution frame for a stuck-with-the-status-quo frame. "What will it take for you to be able to stomach spending day after day with people who don't know what they want?"

Or we could eliminate the feedback aspect and have failure. "How will you keep from getting fired when you have too many chintzy customers that week?"

Those three questions took turns at being in a frame of *problems, status quo, and failure.* Each of them assumed you were resourceful in some way. But they were so limiting, that they directed your resources in a limited way. They turned you into an active agent with inactive success.

So let's push those out, and bring desired outcomes, solutions, possibilities, useful feedback, and your resourcefulness, and look at that question again, to reset the tone of this entire book! *"As your and your customer discuss their purchase, how does your role help them efficiently complete the transaction, and what can you learn to make it even more profitable?"*

Think about your role in the sales process, and how you think about yourself, your employer, your customers, the market, and any other important factor. Ask yourself how you might switch any of your thinking as follows:

- Problems to desired outcomes.

- Failure to useful feedback.

- Status quo to possibilities.

- Lack of resources to your creativity and resourcefulness.

- Sales stuck to sales flow.

DON'T DO FALSE PREEMPTION

You want to connect your prospect with positives and green lights. Anything that would take them in another direction is taboo. So what do you help get into their frame, and what do you work to filter out? Here's a big mistake that I see a lot of salespeople make, especially if they're a bit green, but even some experienced folks trip up on this one. They are concerned that the prospect will think something negative, and they bring it up in an attempt to defuse it. That would work if they were really using the preemption technique, but they haven't thought it through well enough or it really wasn't necessary, because they could have created more positive momentum in other ways.

TIP: So don't bring up anything that can gum up the sales process unless you are absolutely confidant that you are using an effective technique AND you have really thought it through, AND it really jibes with your customer's frame of mind. Direct them toward what you want them to think and feel, not what you don't. This does not prevent you from using negatives, as when you want them to think or feel badly about not having the product.

Frames Workout

Your product or service is designed to prevent bad things and cause good things. You could easily make a list of those outcomes. An automobile has safety features that prevent injury and death. Or you could say that the vehicle has advanced features to protect your loved ones.

Which of the two statements do you think most people will respond to best?

Most likely, the positive one, even though they both say the same thing. But sometimes you should land squarely on the negative. You do this to expose the customer to the potential or current pain of not having the product.

Let's try a couple more.

Now take some of your company's sales literature, or jot down some of they things you typically say to prospects, and underline anything that is phrased in a negative way. Come up with one or more ways to say it in positive terms.

See if perhaps you should start saying it that way. And remember what we said about warmth. Can you use warm words instead of cold, harsh, or impersonal words?

When you feel that you must tell a prospect no, do you really have to frame it as a take away? Must you say, "No, we can't do that." How about, "Ah! Take a look and see if this isn't even better. We have had really positive reviews on this in Industry Perspectives."

All this is in service of framing. In this piece, we focused on the positive frame. That is, having positive material in the customer's conscious mind. What is inside the frame is directed to the customer's conscious mind, what is outside the frame, is filtered from the customer's mind, or is re-framed. Ah! I can't wait to tell you about re-framing.

REFRAMING

You aren't just stuck with a frame. If you can ask questions you can change a frame. You change the topic that's in the frame by changing the frame. Here's an example for your sales practice.

Let's say something got into your customer's frame that was not supposed to be in there. Maybe they saw a commercial about a web service that can connect them to the perfect insurance agent for them. As you know all too well, directly confronting a belief can really backfire. But what really is the belief. They have knowledge of the resource, but knowledge is not a belief. Let's tease that out just a bit so we really know what we're dealing with here.

Is their belief that a web site can actually find the perfect agent? If so, what would make the agent perfect? Lower prices? Better consultation? Better location? You'd want to know that.

If they say they think they can get better prices, you can reframe that in several ways.

1. *"Trimming a little off the price can cost you a great deal in the long run, and here's why..."* This frame added the long-term cost element.

2. *"Having the wrong policy at a slightly lower price is to be avoided. That's why my customers appreciate my expertise."* This frame added the risk of the wrong policy.

You can also reframe the larger experience of using that online service.

"My personal, individualized approach gives you much more than someone who is mass marketing something that cuts prices a little at the expense of providing the right services to the people trying to use it." This frame added the value of my expertise, and the corrupt and dishonest nature of the web approach.

All of the *reframes* made light of the savings by asserting that it would be small, especially in comparison to working with me. This comparison technique is very handy.

MAKE IT PRACTICAL, IN PLAIN ENGLISH

Spin is a kind of framing, but spin is a bad word, because it means *falsely* framing so that people will not really get what's going on. So spin is the dark side of framing. Popular phrases for *reframing* include changing your assumptions, looking on the bright side, getting a change in perspective, having an attitude adjustment, expanding your mind, looking from a different point of view, and walking in someone else's moccasins. Have I beaten that to death yet?

The magic you do with what gets inside of the frame gives it the power of motivation. When I worked to *reframe* that website that competed with my business, I added information without removing any. But when I added the information, I did it in a way that is meaningful; a way that changed how the prospect looked at the topic. You can be sure that when I told the prospect the new information, I used my voice and body language in a way that influenced the significance of the information. Now, when the customer thinks about the web service, it will seem cheap and impersonal, costly and misleading, and most importantly, *effortful* and worthless.

Reframing is at the heart of all of the techniques in this book that deal with the conscious mind. Knowing that they have this in common will help you master them all.

CONTROLS FOR REFRAMING

As you can see, from the earlier examples *reframing* is, among other things, the dividing line between what information is in and out of the customer's mind.

This means it's your job to manage that. I also showed you that you should change the frame when it isn't optimal. When you change the frame, the topic inside it looks very different to the customer.

Note that in the examples, we never removed anything from the customer's frame, although we might have wanted to. We went

100% with the customers values. If the customer wants to save money, that can stay in the frame. What we do about their perspective on the topic is what matters. And we don't just decide what else gets into the frame. We can adjust the contents of the frame.

We can make something seem larger or smaller, we can color it with what else we bring into the frame, making it seem better or worse. We can distract from it or focus on it.

I show people that working with me saves money in the long run. Remember that example? In another, I highlighted my expertise as proving that the prospect was getting the perfect rep. That helped eliminate the option of a web service.

Think about how you can *reframe* the things in your prospect's minds that challenge the sales process.

And think of what you may be accidentally inserting into their minds that can create a problem frame. How might you change that?

Remember that *reframing* changes the way the look at something. This can mean turning a deficit into a benefit.

THE FLIPPER REFRAME

You can create a question out of an objection. Ask what is more important about the objection about a potential new home. It's a bit of a commute to work. Ask which is *more important*, the time it takes to get there or the miles traveled. If they say the time, then show them that the time *difference* (rather than the total time), is *only* 20 minutes.

Then you can flip things around.

Ask which would be *better*, having 20 minutes more on the freeway (with no traffic, lights, etc.) and getting this lovely, clean, save environment, getting the city and all its pollution, noise, congestion, child unfriendliness, and other problems?

Now that's turning a deficit into an asset. You started with which is *worse*, and ended up with which would be *better*. Did you know that most objection handling techniques are *reframes*?

Keep practicing those *reframes* and get good at them. Because the way people feel about things always depends on their perspective, that is, their frame. Their point of view starts with what is included or excluded, and goes on to include the color, priority, value, and every other qualification you can think of.

De-frame

De-framing happens when you don't just change the frame of reference, you destroy it. You save this move for those special times when you are very clear about what your prospect needs and you see that what is stopping them is just fear. Since this is a sensitive move, it helps if you are a really competent closer.

In my life insurance practice, my prospects sometimes dig in their heels for reasons that ring hollow. I'm pretty sure that they are just fearful because of the commitment. They've never had life insurance before, and so they have vague feelings about it. Maybe if they held out they would find out there's some secret angle that "*They*" don't want you to know about. Or maybe the prospect has vague money fears because they aren't used to having a consistent income and a family. In a way, for those folks, life insurance is kind of a coming-of-age ritual. Who doesn't get nervous about those?

Don't those prospects sound like good candidates for the deframe? Let's give it a whirl. One had a lame excuse about needing to see more options from some other outfit, like maybe a boutique shop. I think he got the word boutique shop from small specialized groups like certain advertising firms.

Now that was a real reach. I told him:

"Actually, I don't want you to take this wrong, but you have about the most straightforward, textbook, demographically average needs that I can think of. I'm afraid that I've let you talk me into showing you too many options. This is the right policy for you, right here. Not because it's popular, but because it fits your budget, will take care of your projected needs, and is backed by a solid company and a competitively priced no-frills broker. It really is that simple, unless you're the guy that owns the boutique shop."

I might have been able to do something more in line with my usual objection process, but my instincts screamed *"deframe!"* So I did. And it worked.

At the time, I thought, *"Maybe I'm being too confrontive, because I'm kind of taking him down a notch."* But I realized that when I referred to the guy that owns the boutique shop, I was implying that he would be making too much money from the wrong people, because my prospect seemed to relax knowing that there was really just one policy that was right for him, and he would get it from a no-frills company with competitive pricing.

The Bigger Picture to Framing: Finishing the Definition

Other authors will tell you that framing is something like this: *"A psychological 'frame' refers to a general focus or direction that provides an overall guidance for thoughts and actions during an interaction."* (Robert Dilts).

If you boil this down a bit, you could say that the frame affects what people think and do. Ok, then that is saying what the frame does.

But what is it? To rephrase a bit, it's when you *change* the focus or direction of a person's thinking so that it makes *even broader* changes in their thinking and behavior.

Okay, we know what it is and what it does. *How* does framing do that? The way it changes thinking and behavior is via *"overall guidance."*

That's a pretty good point, really, because when I did a negative reframe on that online service that competes with my business, the prospect lost interest in it. I changed what the online service meant to her, by bringing negative aspects into the foreground of her thinking. And I made sure those negative aspects contrasted sharply with my positive aspects, making my positive aspects look very desirable. So there you have it, a change in focus or direction that caused an *overall* change in thinking and buying behavior. And I didn't have to eliminate or argue with any information. The frame changed *around* the information. I changed how it looked to her.

Whew! When we started out, that definition seemed pretty tough-shelled.

So remember the first part of the definition of framing was what gets into the conscious mind. The second part of the definition is that the *frame itself* affects what gets inside it!

CONJUGATE FOR FRAMING

I do this one a lot. You don't need to know grammar to conjugate. You just need to think about time. Everything sits in some *time frame* in our minds. If your prospect is not so sure about doing business with your company because of a customer service gaffe, it must still be stinging. That places it more or less in their present frame of reference. You might even hear them slip it into the present in some way, like, *"I have having to deal with lousy customer service from somebody that can barely speak English."* Of course, since the problem is not resolved in their mind, it has happened and could happen again. That crosses right through the present moment. It's hurting them now.

If I can tell them about great changes taking place with our customer service in a convincing way, that's good. But I goose the process by putting the problem squarely in the past. We are very fortunate to have a strong customer base that holds us accountable. They are very involved in our development and take a very strong interest in the outcome. When they told us about this outsourcing that we had tried, it became obvious pretty quickly that we needed to use our own expertise. Since we've been keeping it in-house, we are getting fabulous feedback on every dimension of customer service. We are now very invested in this, and we will continue to provide customer service this way from now on.

Did you watch the time frame. The problem is, *"outsourcing that we had tried."* Everything else is about the strong, involved customer base, of which your customer is a member, our expertise, and fabulous feedback. I really buried the objection in addition to putting it in the past.

Note that I used something called past perfect. That's the "had been" kind of language. It seals the problem off into the past by indicating that it is no longer happening. It *had been,* then, but it *isn't,* now. But if it *was,* then, it *might still be,* now.

You'll also see my use of the future in other pieces. That future frame is great for creating a future where the prospect already has the product.

You can use the now for aligning with what the prospect is thinking now. *"As you consider the features available, you are choosing from the best materials available in the world."* This can help with rapport, and help create a fluid, open-minded state, because you are stating what is true now. It establishes a "truth set" that can lower defenses about what you say next.

Negatives Need Love, Too

Negatives are important. You have lots of opportunities to use negatively phrased statements and questions. You can embed statements and ideas pretty easily in *negative phrasings*, and it sort of makes it seem less coercive. For example, "You may not have time right now to *prove to your satisfaction that these are the best features in the industry,* and..." The embedded command is in italics. I love these. I do them without even realizing it any more.

Sometimes you'll need them to make people feel competitive or like they need to qualify. *"I can't tell you if you'll qualify for the loan..."*

People are so used to hearing things put in the negative, that it doesn't really stand out. It's a way to align with a customer who has a negative perspective, and then pull things in a more positive direction. You can also nest your statements to get a more open-minded prospect. *"I would hate to say that you can't make this dream come true just because credit is so conservative right now".*

Let's have me run this by our loan people and see if we can make this go for you, because you'll have no obligation. You might say this with people who already have some motivation but feel insecure about their credit.

You could easily lose them without careful wording and creating a little hypnotic relaxation and engagement.

And if you deconstruct this phrasing, you'll see that a variety of goodies are packed into it. Consider the momentum-building wordings:

"make this a reality in your lives"

"we can make this happen for you."

And the "padding" that makes it go down easier, as in:

"would never want to say that you can't"

"our loan people are cautious"

"see if we can"

"there's no obligation."

Imagine having wordings like this come to you with no effort. It's just a matter of practice. Know that you have the ability. People with far less talent than you can master this.

Here's a good tip. Be sure to get back to a positive frame after using a negative one. This way, you make sure that the negative aspect does not contaminate your presentation outside of its intended effect. You want your negatives to be fairly precise or localized.

Parallel Universes

When a prospect turns their nose up at a sale because they foresee a negative outcome, how can you proceed without trying to take that negative prediction away? Try this. Point out both possible futures. Start with the negative one. Acknowledge the basis for it. Bring up the positive possible future. You must end with the positive one. State a basis for that which is based on their values and beliefs. If you aren't clear on their values and beliefs, see if you can make a little conversation with them. Find out how they dealt with their bad experience, how they made a major decision related to the product, and anything else that might be helpful. Then bring things back to the positive future. If you over hype it, if is too positive, you will lose them, so use some restraint as you do that.

"Yes, our profession has been heatedly discussing the bankruptcy of (insert large insurer here). That was disturbing news, until cooler heads pointed out the overall strength of the industry. I was already aware of that because I stay very well informed of the indicators. There are also safety factors that I tell my customers about, since it is a well-regulated business. I see continued payouts on all policies."

Neural Recruitment, Smooth and Easy

For a negative person who is short on time, you can still splash out a little sales energy. This demonstrates the integrative approach of 1) recruiting their attention, 2) slipping in an embedded instruction, and 3) adding graphics for sensory recruitment (a poster), among other things.

"You may not have the time right now to **fully consider all of these fine features,** *but I can tell you right now that the top features our customers rave about are right on this poster."*

I acknowledged the customer's desire to walk away and go to another experience, showing that I would not fight for their time. However, I slipped in a comment directing their attention to the poster to see if they would engage. Note that I used, as a transitional phrase from the prospect's time urgency, the words "I can tell you right now," which imply immediacy within a limited time. Note also, that I transitioned from my words, to the poster, which included words and images, which would recruit more of the prospect's neurology into the sales process. From there, I might point to the top product, pick it up, and point out a feature, inviting the prospect to see how it feels to operate it. Now I have moved from verbal to visual to kinesthetic very smoothly and rapidly.

Negative phrasing can also be useful because they are negative. You may want to stir up longing or the negative consequences of not buying. You may want to bring up the negative associations of a competing product. The *double negative* of *bad reasons for not acting* translate into a positive impetus to a purchase.

BACK MASKING

Back masking is a little technique I use to help cover mistakes, or distract from something that might trigger some additional resistance. You'll see other examples in this book. It sounds like an audio technique in which words are run backwards to hide them in a recording. But this is not that one. Here is an example.

When I *mis-speak,* I use it to reduce the impact of an error. I correct myself and then emphasize one or two words immediately after that. The emphasized words should have some quality that uses some of the person's attention or processing power. That might be a very positive or striking word, or a big word. Just don't emphasize the newly corrected word.

For example, "I have three options that are freak, that are *absolutely* free for the taking today with your purchase."

You can also mask the part of the close that you feel is the most resistance-triggering potential by adding distracting material immediately after it. For example, when you say what kind of payments you can accept, you might give the person the product and congratulate them in a balanced but very positive way.

Persuasive Questions

Ask questions that lead your prospects in the right direction. When you feel the urge to tell them what to think, translate it into a question. Instead of creating resistance, you will help your prospect feel that you want to understand.

The question can be hypothetical, as in, *"Which model would be the kind you would be most likely to want in an emergency?"*

They can be more direct, as when you are nearer the close.

"If you decide to do this today, how many will you want?"

Notice I changed the tense from and uncertain present (if you decide to) to a definite future (how many will you want).

It's similar to an if/then sentence, and that's no accident. That structure is so familiar as a statement of a reliable connection (if you drop it, then it will break) that some of that rubs off onto this question structure.

In the earliest phase with the prospect, they can be about generating initial interest.

"Would you like to know about a new, proven technology that can cut your fuel costs 100%?"

THE "F" WORDS

This is another response to a customer who is stuck on a belief that is getting in the way of the sale. It's been around for a long time, but it's a good one. It gives the customer permission to change their mind because you invoked the principle of the surprising new fact.

1. Align by expressing understanding of their position.

"I know how you feel..."

"I can understand why you would look at it that way..."

2. Bring up other who have felt the same way.

"Many of my customers used to have the same sense of it."

"I felt that way for a long time."

"I wouldn't have believed in a million years that I..."

3. Say how they changed with they learned more and found out the truth about your fine product, service, or company.

"But on taking a closer look, they discovered..."

"But when I actually tried it for a month..."

Here is simple, **feel, felt, found** one all put together.

I understand how you *feel.* Many of my customers *felt* that way, until they tried it and *found* that it was better than they though possible.

Here's a more complicated one.

The *feel, felt, found* is mapped over to *you're saying, lost customers, began returning* so you can see the function better, instead of just the formula:

"I know exactly what you're saying. The older models had a bad track record, and parts were still scarce. I heard a lot of complaints and the company lost customers. But when they try the new model and learn about the systems we now have in place, they began returning in large numbers."

One Two Three Truth

Confer the halo of truth to an idea that you would prefer your prospect not argue about or feel uncomfortable with. To do this, use the principle of following your new fact with indisputable facts or principles. To maximize the suspension of the prospect in that moment, offer three. Four or more may disrupt the prospect too much.

"You know that for many people, sales can be a tough job. They don't really have the personality or commitment. I'm glad to see that you are seeing this book through."

How was that. Notice that the third statement does not even appear to be disputable, because it seems that I'm expressing my opinion. But look at the presupposition hiding in there: *"you are seeing this book through."* We snuck in a little four into the pattern. That is a common variation, and it works.

Sales people learn a lot of techniques for their craft. But their experience can be even more valuable. You should be proud of your willingness to practice so diligently.

Oh! There I go again.

Create some of these for your sales process. Start with ideas that you would like to turn into presuppositions. Then precede them with two true statements that create a nice set up for the statement. Add the "little fourth" for some added texture.

Volume Control for Authority

I guess this section doesn't just have to be about words. It can be about what you do with them. In this case, it's the volume. Next time you need to convey your authority, credibility, and confidence about a point, drop your volume at the moment you hit that point. (And now in a low volume: You really must try this to experience the impact.)

You'll want to practice it a bit to really get it down. Try doing it with internal pressure in your torso. It's a trick that ventriloquists use in lowering their voice. Once perfected, it helps you control the level of *breathiness* and pitch. The dummy is optional. Practice in your car or wherever they won't think you're too crazy. One skill is recognizing those moments when a power boost is just what you need.

The other is deciding what method of lowering your voice sounds best. Some people sound best with some *breathiness* or softness, others do well maintaining some hardness to their voice. You might want to record it and also get feedback from others.

Good points at which to do this include points that differentiate you from the competition, points where you give an amazing secret, and when you tell the customer that you're about to give them your rock-bottom price.

THE VAGUENESS CONTROL

Have you ever thought of yourself as constantly working your vagueness control? You are always being vague. I can prove it. Find a really irritating person who will ask why or how after each thing you say. It will take a while to get so specific that there aren't any more why or how questions left.

You might not make it there before you can't stand it any more. It's like justice. Everybody wants justice. But then, why are there attorneys? It's like the shore line.

You can say how long it is. But it's much longer if you walk it and follow it's every contour.

But think of the advantages of doing your vagueness control more consciously. In public speaking, you could say things that everyone agrees on.

You could even become a politician. In sales, you could avoid saying something that would trip the prospect's defenses, while amplifying their motivation.

"I know you believe in security for your family, and I'm against anything that threatens that. We have the right to that."

But do you sell home security systems, body guard services, anti-anxiety medication, or family firearms? In any case, you established a bond with your prospect around a vague general principle. Now you can link it to your sales point.

"The Family Security Association offers these amazing benefits."

More Language Patterns

Linkage: Take an established fact, and link it to another fact that is closer to the sale. "Now that you realize that this model fits your needs best, you're ready to experience it at home in our new free trial offer."

Agree and reframe and redirect: When someone makes a general statement that goes in the anti-sale direction, agree and tell how you think of this particular thing as something else.

"I understand why you dislike life insurance agents. Honestly, I think of myself more as being a consultant because I make sure people do NOT over buy and DO buy what is exactly on target for their family."

Notice that you direct their attention to the important matter; that they are doing it for their family.

DECISIONS ON FIRE

WHOLE MOTIVATION

The previous section has moved us parsecs toward the gift of influence mastery. Let's put a bow on it by creating decisions on fire; let's fire up the buying decision. You'll see that the items we cover in automatic behavior give you a good foundation for intuitively deploying this section. There once was a sergeant who learned that his troops were surrounded by the enemy. He told his soldiers, *"Good news, we can attack in any direction!"* For this section, however, I'll be telling you to attack in every direction. We will learn to create a holistic kind of motivation.

There's no need for suspense, so here are the components of a *"decision on fire."*

Your customer has the following Four Big Beliefs:

Your product will resolve their pain in not having it.

Your product will fulfill their desire. They can anticipate the pleasure of acquiring it, having it, displaying it, using it, whatever.

Your product is worth it. Worth what? Whatever the cost!

People important to them will view their buying decision positively and benefit from it. This means they will fulfill social roles important to their identity, and be seen in a good light.

The art of this lies in the weave. At various points you connect your customer with each of these points. In order to do this, you have to know enough about your customer to customize this strategy. This means that your early questions uncover things. As you go along, you say things that make it clear, without insulting your prospects intelligence, how your offering deserves the Three Big Beliefs for a decision on fire.

But you don't stop there. In order to really fire things up, you launch beyond mere understanding, you generate a state of *belief.* That means that the beliefs must be *rooted in feelings.* And those feelings are going to come from the experiences that you elicit and that you *connect with the product.* You'll see how this works in the examples of this section.

PUNCH UP THE PAIN

Help the person experience the pain of not having your product! What is the pain? It is the unfulfilled craving, the emptiness where it belongs, what people think of you if you don't have it, the bad future consequences of not having it, etc. You could go on for miles, right? No? Well start a list! Make it long.

Here's an example of activating the pain. It's from the challenging industry of life insurance sales. Here's how I bring up the matter of their future, which is Death. As you can imagine, I don't set them down and say, *"Look buddy, you're gonna die. It could happen at any moment, hurry up and sign NOW, before it's too late. Do you want to screw your family out of their financial security? Here's the pen."*

I guess that would be a pretty direct and honest approach, but I've never heard of it making anybody rich, either.

Instead, I simply make a comment or two about the purpose of life insurance. I amplify that painful feeling of need that comes from not wanting their family to remember them as the one who left them in the lurch, without financial security. These touchy comments are not an "in your face" style because that would work against you. It certainly isn't necessary.

PAIN WORKOUT

It's common knowledge that people should have life insurance. The reason so many people go without it is that it is easy to put off, and that death is an unpleasant subject that people would rather be in denial about, at least they would until they gain sufficient wisdom through age and adjustment to the fact of their mortality. Oh yes, and the money. You set yourself up for that monthly or annual payment, and you don't even get premium channels. There is no palpable benefit, and the person with the life insurance policy will never experience the ultimate benefit of the whole thing at all.

Oh, really? **Stop the presses. Reframe!** Think again. The benefits to them are numerous. And the pain of not having them are just as numerous. So how does one just "drop in" a comment that incites that pain? How do you make it a nonchalant mention; a cameo, if you will? Like this. *"I'm so glad you were prepared to see me so soon. Some people put off their life insurance until it's too late. I see too many families left in the lurch. As I recall, you said you were most interested in..."*

I also find an opportunity here and there to work in comments that activate the pain in the course of the presentation. It depends on what the customer says, because I am improvising based on everything I know about them, like what their values are and how they think.

DE-FUSE THE RESISTANCES

People have all sorts of resistances to buying things, as I have mentioned. And I'm not talking about "objections," which are conscious concerns that a person can put into words. A resistance is something that subtly holds a person back. You might be able to put it into words, but they usually don't sound very rational when you do. Take, for example, this resistance to life insurance: the feeling that it isn't worth it. Well, of course it isn't worth it... *usually*. And isn't that right to the point. No matter what kind of insurance we're talking about, you are, in a sense, betting against yourself. Insurance isn't SUPPOSED to be worth it. I mean, when super-model Heidi Klum insured her legs for two million dollars, I'm sure nobody thought she was hoping to cash in! You don't WANT insurance to be worth it.

But this resistance thing is a feeling that you don't want to argue with. It's best to de-fuse it with a sort of remote control, indirect effect. It can be as simple as dropping one of those little off-the-cuff comments. For example, in response to a customer's comment about hoping he doesn't need his life insurance anytime soon, I might say, *"Yes, ha ha, the longer you go without needing your life insurance, the better for you and your family."*

Well, look at that, you're providing a nice compliment by implying that his family wants him more than the money. And isn't that the kind of family you'd want to reward with some additional security? But look what else you implied. You said the magic word, "your." **It's "your life insurance,"** as if the customer already bought it. It's best to use that word in situations where it doesn't really stand out, but instead sounds very natural, like any turn of a phrase. That way the customer won't feel pushed or pulled.

YOU CAN DO IT

Think about your offering. List a *bazillion* ways that your offering *deserves* **The Four Big Beliefs**. Remember to include how they experience pain without it, and pleasure with it. Include the value. Include how people will view them.

1. How is it painful not to have it? Bad consequences? A gap or missing piece of life? Hurt to self esteem?

2. How will it be pleasurable to have it? Short term? Long term? Feeling rich or special? Reaffirms that you are practical, rational, smart, savvy, hip, tough, a real humanist, devout, cunning? Getting luxury, high tech, connected, delighted?

3. How will others think they are amazing, helpful, responsible, frugal, generous, popular, promotable, saintly, family-oriented, good, better, best, disco-liscious, or God-fearing?

I want you to brainstorm. You know what that means. Just write frantically, and worry about what's worth acting on later. Go for volume, not quality. Give yourself a good ten minutes or more. Really step out of your own shoes to get into the customer perspective. But not just one customer. Go through your memories of customers and think about a good diversity of personalities and motivations. Think of some really plain ones and quirky ones, too.

This is one of the most important exercises you could possibly do, because all the techniques can use this as their foundation, especially the conscious ones. They rely on framing. Framing is about perspective. This exercise creates perspective. You aren't simply generating information or ad copy, you are creating many statements that you can improvise with as you manage your customer's experience. This is big. If this was the only exercise you did, I would feel that I had made a very special contribution to your career. And I would love to be a fly on the wall, and see how you deployed those frames with your customers.

DISTILL TO TALKING POINTS

I know you like to read, but did you start that list from the last piece? Go ahead, jot down a few ideas to get your subconscious cooking. More will come to you later because you created the "file" in your mind. Putting a question-based project like that in your head gets answers; sometimes when you least expect them.

Take what you have come up with so far and try this little process. It's very interesting, because it gives you talking points that help you improvise with your customers. Actually, you can do this with pretty much any personal issue as well, when you need to communicate with someone.

1. Look at all the points.

2. In your mind, or on paper, say them after discarding anything that isn't absolutely necessary. (*You aren't really discarding it. You'll see what this does, shortly.*)

3. Keep boiling them down like that until you end up with a slogan.

In order to go to such an extreme you'll need to do two things. You'll have to throw out things that are important, but that you can somehow capture with a slogan. You'll also have to jump beyond really making a lot of sense. Instead, you must be willing to put forward a very general impression.

Consider Apple's **"Think different"** slogan. Imagine all the things that you could say about Apple Computer's history, vision, and products that this simple two-word phrase conveys. If you wanted to talk about the company, but merely kept that phrase in your mind, it would organize your presentation and generate a lot of ideas. (Assuming you knew the information in the first place.) Well, I want you to do that with your product. This is a very powerful way to generate improvisation abilities that will pop out of you and actually surprise you. As in, *"Wow! That was smooth. How did I do that?"*

PRACTICE POINTERS

I want to make sure you really get this business about "connecting" and "weaving." These are natural communication methods. They never look like technique, they never come off as artificial, and they never make the customer feel pushed or pulled. There's nothing cloying, annoying, toying about it. My grandmother used to say, "I never manipulate anyone. Unless it's for their own good, of course." Well, that's fine for grandma, but this is all about flow and feeling.

Keep these core "connecting" ideas in mind: Connecting the prospect with the pleasure of the product does not mean shoving some preconceived notion down their throat. It means triggering their own pleasure buttons, whatever they are. You'll know you're hitting the right buttons by their response.

With practice, you'll do it so naturally, that you won't even need to give it much thought. Connecting the prospect with the pleasure of the product means using their body and mind as a multi-media presentation.

Whatever media you have at your disposal, it will never be as powerful as your customer's body and mind. You trigger those connections with simple acts like asking a question, or taking the discussion in a certain direction, or dropping in a comment or story.

A question as simple as, *"what would that increase in sales mean to the future of your company?"* or *"It's amazing how a kind of stress lifts off of a couple when they know they have their life-insurance needs covered."* I feel a little lighter just saying it.

Think about the effect it has on someone on the verge of making a buying decision, who hasn't fully realized that the stress was weighing on them, but who, when they think of it being off of them, suddenly has a good body-feeling connected with that buying decision. That life insurance just went up in value! The buying motivation just crossed the line. Here's the pen!

THE WEAVE

As for the *"weave,"* it's about how you orchestrate the prospect's experience. Think of the nightly television news. Each topic usually could have been any number of different events, but they have time for one. They often pick the news item because it really is the biggest news, but often, they just pick it because it fits the particular string of feelings they want to produce in order to promote viewership. It's kind of like putting together a musical work.

There is a series of feelings with different tones and moods. When it's a good point to have something shocking, they pick one of dozens of shocking stories. There are shocking things going on all over the world all the time. So I'm asking you to think a little like a composer.

First your musicians tinkle some keys, then there's a wash of brass with drums, etc. Look at your list of the things that can trigger The Four Big Beliefs. As you discuss matters with your customers, even as you get to know your customers and ask questions, your job for the next month is to make your main job to orchestrate strings of different feelings through those items. You word them into questions, comments, and stories that trigger the feelings that support the beliefs.

If you want to break this down into some homework before you take this into the field, you can write a script of an imaginary conversation. For each thing you say, start by choosing an appropriate belief you want to support.

Then pick one of the things from your list that supports the belief. Then find a way to drop it into the script so that it is very natural and mainly triggers a feeling. That's because you want feelings to support the belief, not information to make the person believe. The feelings are more powerful nearly every time.

To Summarize:

1. The most appropriate belief to support;

2. The item that will trigger the feeling;

3. The wording of the item that will trigger the feeling best for the given point in the discussion.

PERSUASION WITHOUT PRODUCTS

DIRECTION STRATEGIES

This section is about direction strategies. These strategies go from telling the customer what to do, to creating an imprint for what to do in their minds. I hope that has punched up your curiosity, because telling customers what to do sounds like something for a cult leader, not a polished sales professional. Be assured that this will be very appropriate, showing you exactly where these instructions go. This material is based on a great deal of research.

These techniques team up beautifully with framing to add to your core abilities.

Understanding these direction strategies will put the many of the techniques you are learning into perspective. They are like the stitching that holds everything together. They also do a lot to resolve the resistance that people have to persuasion.

You are learning many techniques, such as activating reciprocity to trigger automatic behavior. They will make you more intuitive as to when and how to use your sales techniques. I will talk about identifying the optimal point in your sales process for using them. This is very valuable.

Start by thinking about when you do give prospects specific action instructions of any kind. Where does this occur in the process? What is it supposed to accomplish? Most importantly, how well does it work, and when does it go wrong in some way? Also, think about how your efforts to get the prospect thinking about having the product can create a sort of subtle instruction set in their mind. Imagination is very powerful, but you won't have to take them on a hypnotic journey to activate their imaginations.

Specific Instructions

Some salespeople are uncomfortable about giving specific instructions to people. Salespeople don't want to trigger any sales stereotypes, so they try not to look too pushy. They like indirect subconscious techniques. I am too, but there are many opportunities for using specific instructions. Salespeople want to focus on building motivation and creating an environment and presentation that compels people to buy. That's all fine, too, but you must have specific instructions, or the cake will fall flat. And if specific instructions are provided in the wrong manner or at the wrong point, the recipe still won't get the results you want. That happens so often, that it makes salespeople afraid to provide such instructions. Don't be fooled. We need to learn the art, so that those bad outcomes will not happen and the sales will roll in.

The fact is that there is a mountain of research telling us about how important specific instructions are. A key trick is that you are not trying to put anyone under your command and tell them to buy anything. Your instructions will be at key points in the sales process; key points that take them through the process, build momentum toward the sale, and prepare them to buy. You need to know what those points are.

Anticipated Regret Plus Instructions

This piece is about one of those key points at which specific instructions work best. It is also about an ingredient that gives power to those instructions. Anticipated regret gives power to your instructions, but your instructions help the person choose which possible regret to avoid. People have many conflicting drives. Specific instructions help to sort them out by creating a sort of release valve for their pent up energies.

In actual practice, this is sort of a matching exercise. You think of regrets that the customer needs to prevent. Then you think of specific actions the customer needs to take. Finally, you see which ones go together.

For example, *"I know that you want to prevent your wife and kids from losing your home, and you don't want your children to be prevented from having a good college education. Since we can scale this coverage back as your needs change, you can scale this policy to where you are now, and with the freedom to adjust it at any time. From what you've provided, I can tell you that families like yours really like this one."*

Did the instructions sneak by? Basically, I said, *"Get enough insurance to cover your needs if you were to die before your kids got through college. Buy this policy here."* The anticipated regret that is linked in is that if he doesn't get this policy, his kids will not get through college, and his wife and kids will lose their house.

IMAGE SCRIPTING

Image scripting is a great way to provide specific instructions. This is an indirect method. You do it by getting your prospect to describe what they will do with your product. It can come in the form of a wistful discussion. You can indulge in a conversation like that quite spontaneously in the course of learning about their needs.

Real estate agents do this by getting their customers talking about how they will decorate and use various rooms, how easy the drive to work will be, what it will be like to have the great neighbors in this area, etc.

"Do you like barbecue? Well good, because there is a community barbecue on Sundays all summer. You can relax with the neighbors while the kids run through the sprinklers."

I use this image scripting method in my own sales work. I do it in the course of talking to a customer how their family would use the money if they were to pass away. I get them imagining the behavior of their family. This gets their imagination going on how people will think of them after they have gone. Most people are really motivated by this. This is even more indirect that the previous example. And note that the actual act of purchasing the insurance is not the point. Making the purchase come to be essential by creating the future that the must have. The must-have future makes the must-have product.

But you can also do image scripting on the actual purchase, by finding something pleasurable about it and working it in. That would be a nice little homework assignment for you, for extra credit.

MAKE THAT IMAGINARY EXPERIENCE WORK

When it comes to image scripting, quantity is at least as important as quality. The more times the person imagines themselves involved in the activity, the better. That means you can work this gambit into your approach as often as you like. You are usually best off doing this more times than for longer duration. It makes it more memorable and *impactful* to have more incidences of this experience, because of how our memories work.

Make sure that the customer is the person in the imaginary experience. Don't have it be someone similar to that person. It should be them imagining their own experience.

The effect from these imaginary experiences has some durability to it. This means that if your customer makes several visits, you can keep the impact going and even building up. The general rule is that these imaginary experiences have some effect for around three days. You know how I like to do integration, putting multiple techniques together.

You can make these imaginary experiences more powerful by adding statements of commitment, and working the law of consistency.

THE BEST POINT OF VIEW FOR IMAGINARY WORK

Here's a really helpful insight. Research tells us that most people benefit from seeing themselves doing the behavior rather than looking from the perspective of their own eyes during a fantasy like this. Try this out on yourself when you are doing some kind of mental rehearsal or motivation-building exercise.

It may be that this works because it is more like evidence. They see themselves, so it seems truer. Plus, they see their reaction, which is happy or satisfied in some way. This adds a state management dynamic. They are happy for themselves. Their mind is less occupied with constructing a narrow, moving, first-person perspective, and has the more positive feeling that comes from seeing the big picture. A bigger view tends to promote bigger thinking. Even a higher ceiling in a room tends to do that. Imagine the possibilities! That phrase is for big-picture, high-ceiling people.

SALES PROCESS CHECKLIST

These pieces are helping you warm up and align your thinking for learning and practicing my sales process. In this piece, you can self-audit for persuasion components that you need in your sales process. Go through my checklist and ask whether you have all these items covered in your current sales approach. How can you improve each of these?

Have you set the stage in your mind? Get a good idea as to what you expect to accomplish and what your prospect is all about. Psych yourself to project a fully professional attitude and process.

Do you master the room? Make sure that there are no distractions. Request things like turning the television off. You can do this respectfully. Manage the situation from the outset.

Do you have a seamless approach? You need to have your words ready so that you can maintain a sense of continuity. By having your presentation well practiced, you can keep your mind on how your prospect is responding to it, and you can think a couple steps ahead.

Are you sincere? Do you feel it? The power to influence flows from your sincerity, your conviction, your certainty. Get in touch with how you are doing this in their interests.

Are you enthusiastic? Do you feel it? If you aren't, how can you expect them to be? Use what you are learning in this book about self care for energy and motivation, and about state management to get into the right state at will. These are the two most important things a salesperson can learn, because they are your foundation.

SALES CLOSING QUESTIONS

Finish your self audit with closing components. The preceding components set you up for these two closing components.

Do you get commitments? Remember, commitments range from those little ones that build overall commitment, to the big one that clinches the sale. Remember that commitments can be used to help shift identity, as discussed in this book. Commitments are what connect influence to results.

People have a drive to be consistent, so they tend to abide by commitments. They experience an inner pressure to do so. They have learned, life long, to be trustworthy as a member of their family and society. Get repeated commitments of various kinds, and your prospect will develop momentum in the buying process. Some sales professionals make it a point to get many yes answers to their questions before they even start the sale.

Personally, I find this to be rude the way most salespeople do it. But this does work with many people. Just watch their body language to see how you are doing. See how far you can go. Can you get 100 yes's?

Do you close? I mean really close? The pieces on asking in this book will take you miles ahead. My sales process will too. You must ask for the money. You may not do it as directly as it sounds, but you have to get the money.

Either the prospect is selling you on their limitations, or you are selling them on the value of the product and their freedom to benefit. Make sure that you both win. Then, they get benefits that are in excess of their investment, and you have made a sale, earned their goodwill and referrals, made a friend, and expanded as a professional and even as a person.

ACTIVATING CORE NEEDS AND VALUES

Uncovering the Sales Drivers

We have been talking about how beliefs can drive sales, as well as your own personal development personally and professionally. Let's get better at finding the fuse that will really light up the prospect.

First, you need to know the basic human needs, so that you can easily identify them and appeal to them with the tools you are learning from this book.

Then, you need to learn to identify the most needy needs for the prospect at this point in their life, not just the needs that your product most obviously appeals to.

We'll start by going over the basic human needs. Psychology has given us various lists of human needs. But we need to sell, not pass a psychology test, so we'll make sure that our view of basic human needs passes the sales test, making you into a master of persuasion.

Is There a Hierarchy of Needs?

Have you come across this idea before? Psychologist *Abraham Maslow* came up with a hierarchy of needs that helps us identify how our product appeals to people. I promise not to turn the hierarchy of needs material into some kind of academic lecture. I have hand-picked a few of the more useful ideas. I think they are important because they help us learn which need or needs our prospect most wants to satisfy.

The key idea is that when the most basic needs are not satisfied, people put their energy into those needs. The more those basic needs are satisfied, the more energy they are willing and able to put into those higher needs. On its face, this makes sense. Hungry children don't learn as well in school. A person who is being threatened by a mugger is less likely to do highly spiritual practices, unless you think handing your wallet over at knife point is spiritual.

Nonetheless, there is criticism of the idea of a hierarchy of needs. But these concerns come from complications like the human ability to override the hierarchy at times, or that fact that products that seem to fulfill high order needs can also fulfill more basic ones. We don't need to fuss with this. You can access and activate your prospects' needs better with a few key ideas from this.

So, to answer the question, as far as sales go, yes, there is a hierarchy of needs, and you can use it. Think over some of your recent sales, and think about whether the person was driven by a really basic need, like survival, or a high-order need, like improving their social skills.

WATCH FOR THESE NEEDS

Here is that hierarchy of needs I mentioned. Think about how your product meets one or more of these needs. Don't be fooled. Even food meets higher needs, not because of what it is, but because of what it symbolizes. Some foods confer social status. Celebrations after the election of *Barak Obama* as a U.S. president excluded caviar from the available foods, because the country had plunged into an economic crisis. Since caviar is thought of as rich people's food, it would have given a bad impression.

Okay, here we go, from the more basic needs to the higher ones.

Maslow's Hierarchy of Needs

1. Physiological: Food, water, and shelter are necessary for your most basic survival.

2. Safety/security: You will mobilize to maintain safety and respond to threats.

3. Belonginess and Love: Everyone needs social support and activity.

4. Esteem: We want to be recognized for our achievements and contributions. We gain support and security as well as motivation from feeling better about ourselves as our identity is enhanced.

5. Cognitive: to know, to understand, and explore;

6. Aesthetic: symmetry, order, and beauty;

7. Self-actualization: to find self-fulfillment and realize one's potential; and

8. Self-transcendence: to connect to something beyond the ego or to help others find self-fulfillment and realize their potential.

When you size up a prospect, think about which of these needs may be most frustrated. This is a bit different from looking for their strongest value, or their beliefs, as we have been prior to this. It's more like figuring out where you need to release pressure in some kind of system.

But don't get carried away. People going bankrupt often keep their cable. Hungry people have cell phones. You can appeal to higher order needs even though there are lower *unmet* ones. But bring the lower, *unmet* ones into your sales process when they are *unmet*.

BRING OUT THE SALES SIDE OF THE NEEDS

Since *Tony Robbins'* version of basic human needs is so popular, and so relevant to the sales process, let's have a look at them. What people like about this is that it is very easy to translate into the appeal of products and services, as well as to boost motivation in any other area.

But this time, let's throw out the idea of a hierarchy. Instead, we'll go back to the idea that people have dominant drivers for their decisions. In this collection of needs, remember that everyone has one or more favorites among them. As a master of persuasion, you want to know which ones to appeal to any given prospect. That will really fire up their desire and motivation to buy.

Approach each prospect as someone who has a primary need or drive. Understand that you can enhance their motivation by getting them to experience the connection between your product and that drive. Also, show them that not buying will create a hurt that has that drive in its cross hairs.

As you read about each of the drives, think about how this applies to your business as well as your life.

THE POWER OF CERTAINTY

Certainty is about basic needs like security, but it embraces much more. Remember what we were learning about how powerful certainty is? A belief drives people when they have certainty. But you can go farther. Certainty *itself* is a highly desirable feeling. That's why people have opinions whether they have good reasons for them or not. Remember, opinions are like belly buttons, everybody has one.

You have met people with a lot of certainty. Some of them are very successful, and you know that they earned their certainty. But their certainty goes beyond knowing their own strengths, even the power of knowing their own weaknesses, but they have a special kind of certainty that is a blend of certainty and commitment. This is the kind of certainty that they have learned to generate in order to maximize their ability to achieve seemingly impossible goals. You might say that it seems like a false kind of certainty, since there really isn't a guarantee that they will succeed. That's uncertainty, technically speaking. But they have learned to use their certainty-generating abilities wisely, or they wouldn't be so successful. They have learned when certainty can be a self-fulfilling prophecy.

And then there are people who are certain about how bad things are going to turn out. For some reason, these folks seem to like to lecture other people about this certainty. Remember the phrase I just used, self-fulfilling prophecy? These folks may be right, sometimes, and have been in a position to say, *"I told you so,"* but they are stuck in one mode, they don't have the flexibility to use their certainty wisely, otherwise, they would be enjoying more success.

UNCERTAINTY

Now hold on. Why do we need uncertainty? Doesn't that make people, well, *uncertain?* Yes, but where would the spice of life be without variety, risk, and challenges? Don't you want any adventure in life? Have you never felt the bracing sensation of going after a goal that there is a significant risk of not meeting? No? Well remember this: many people do have this as a very dominant need.

The most obvious people are the thrill seekers; the ones who get involved in extreme sports or otherwise take chances in life. They are experiencing a challenge. For some, the elixir may be the heady mix of physical sensations and adrenaline, for others, it may be the edge-of-your-seat effect of going for the highest prize in intense competition, for others, it may be much more mental. These mental uncertainty lovers may be playing a game of corporate intrigue, with stakes in the millions or trillions. In relationships, your ability to enjoy uncertainty can be vital. After all, if you can appreciate uncertainty, it means you're willing to try a new way of communicating, or to expose something about yourself that others would not have the nerve to reveal.

SIGNIFICANCE

You need to feel important and needed. Feeling that you count, that you matter to people is very important, not just for networking, but to survival; especially many moons ago as tribal societies.

Significance is a nice side benefit for those who make meaningful contributions. Who wouldn't like to have a children's burn unit named after them? But we're supposed to be talking about people who have significance as one of their top needs. This is the person who donates millions mostly *because* it will get their name on the burn unit.

When you encounter someone with high significance needs, you need to find out what kind of significance they're after. Since identity is so important (and we'll be learning a lot about that), and it's so tied to significance, that's a good place to start. What kind of identity are they creating for themselves. And who are they trying to be (or succeeding at being) significant to? Since we're talking about dominant needs now, we don't need to be so concerned with whether the need is fulfilled or not. This kind of need is more of a way of being than it is a thirst that is easily quenched.

Some people prefer a narrow scope, like being really significant to their family. Think about who you want to be most significant to. I'll bet you have a sort of bean counter that lives somewhere in your head, keeping a balance sheet on what you've done to be significant. Have you noticed how you feel when you have been letting that slip, and things are getting out of balance? Don't you feel compelled to put that significance issue on the front burner when that happens?

LOVE AND CONNECTION

Even Scrooge himself finally had to admit that he needed to connect with people and experience love. Of course, it took three good, disembodied sales professionals to do it. Some people are a real challenge!

Unlike Scrooge, there are plenty of people who experience love and connection as primary driving needs. For them, the contributions they make are a way to connect and share the love. If they go after certainty, it is to secure the situation for love. If they gain significance, they are humble when they receive the award or other recognition.

In fact, they are too preoccupied with thanking the people who helped, and lauding their contributions to be distracted by their own role in getting the award. If they talk about their role, it's because they wish they could put what they know and do into pill form and give it freely to everyone so they, too, could experience the joy of love and connection.

When you talk to them, you'll notice that they make a very direct and clear connection with you. This is not just because they are paying attention, they have spent their lives consciously or, more likely, unconsciously practicing the art of rapport building and making other people feel significant. In fact, if you aren't used to it, you may come away from the meeting wishing you had said what you meant to say, because you were sort of overwhelmed by the experience.

GROWTH

Many people have said that learning is the greatest feeling that you can experience in life. Well, I guess we know how to approach them, don't we? You can fine tune your growth-dar. Do they primarily value learning, spiritual growth, personal/psychological growth, or some other kind of development?

You can recognize these growth-oriented people by the way they describe the big experience of their lives. When another person would have been focusing on how much money they made or lost, or how important they were able to be to others' lives, or what a tremendous connection they felt with the people involved, the growth-lovers will talk about how it expanded them as a person, what they learned from the experience, or how it improved their ability to handle similar situations now.

Sales pros are taught to recognize benefits in terms of to have, to be, or do. Growth junkies definitely want to hear about what they can be. Words like become, transform, expand, learn, and develop help them connect to the benefit. But what if it is an activity? Translate the doing into the becoming. Connect them with how the experience will enrich them with information, spirit, personal expansion, or skills.

CONTRIBUTION

Contribution sounds a lot like significance, but it's different. To understand, you really have to look through a different lens. Contribution is that great feeling that you get when you know you are giving beyond yourself, even in private moments when no one else will necessarily know.

Since these givers don't tend to make a big deal out of what they do, you may not have any that jump to mind right away. Instead, the significance-mongers catbird their way into your mind. After a lot of giving, they would feel bad if they didn't get recognized for it.

When you realize you have someone whose contribution need is in the lead, you have to adjust your approach to emphasize just that. That is the kind of choice that this list of needs is all about; finding the one that will really drive the sale.

And this imbalance means that you should make an extra effort to pull out the contribution need and see how much it factors into their drives. Just get them talking a little bit about how they spend their time, and the contributor will tell you, because, after all, that is how they spend their time. And they aren't likely to totally hold back, since they probably do appreciate some recognition, but only because it encourages and energizes them to contribute more.

And I really didn't mean to be hard on significance people a minute ago. I just want you to be very clear on the difference, and to realize that these contributors really do exist.

NOW ACTIVATE THE NEED

I would be committing a serious omission if I didn't remind you to activate the hurt. Each of the six basic human needs has a pain side. As you'll recall, pain is often the most powerful sales force. The positives attract, the pain drives, and some logic helps seal the deal right at the end point of closing. That's a key formula to sales.

In the following pieces, you will gain insight into this pain aspect of the sales process. I'll give a large number of examples, each of them focused on one of the six core human needs.

By knowing what need they lead with, you know what pain to activate, because you will pick the pain that the need contains. That is the most persuasive pain. The emotional pain of a lead need not being fulfilled stands out as an intense and motivating pain.

Remember that people will do more to avoid hurt than the equivalent gain or pleasure. Consider someone whose lead need is Connecting and Love. They will go pretty far to avoid rejection (pain that is in the Connecting and Love need). If efficiency and convenience is important to them, they will, nonetheless, endure it to avoid rejection when their lead need is connecting and love.

You can imagine how knowing this about someone will shape your sales process. And, as you now know, you are not actually creating those values, needs, or hurts, you are connecting them with them so that they will act and improve their lives.

When to Activate Buried Needs?

This brings up an interesting question. *What about people who might have a very strong need, but have buried it*? Let's take *Scrooge*. His leading need was certainty. He kept his bookkeepers working slavishly, and saw Christmas as an inconvenience. His focus on money and control was obsessive. He even turned off his affection for a beautiful woman who wanted him to court her when they were both young. With *Scrooge*, as in real life, when a buried need sees the light of day, it can power their lives like a race horse fresh out of the gate.

When you see that a primary drive is taking the prospect away from the sale, and another drive could turn things around, that is a good time to see if you can activate it. This is easiest to do when their spouse or other family members are present, because you can make an educated guess that the buried need is causing hurt in the family, and deep inside, the prospect feels their pain and wants to have more significance and contribution in that way.

NEED ACTIVATION IN PRACTICE

I had a fellow who derived so much of his sense of contribution, certainty, and significance from being a good negotiator, that he was fouling up his opportunities to take care of his life insurance. These kinds of things are priced with such care and in such a competitive environment, that there isn't much in the way of negotiation of price, unless you're working with very big numbers, it's more a matter of negotiation how much of which kind of policy. That's where my professional talent and objectivity come in and help to close.

I recognized that this customer would not be satisfied without a realignment in his driving needs. Luckily, I picked up on this very early in the discussion So I took a little detour into talking about his wife, and how he wouldn't have settled for any other woman, and how there was probably competition for her, and how he must have had a special edge, even though all the guys at that age pretty much make the same kinds of overtures.

His wife brought up that she sensed a special commitment in him that made him stand out, and that she was very family-oriented. I activated some pain by saying she must make sure that he eats right and exercises, since she values him so much. (This brings subconscious linkage with illness and death.)

Then, I did something called *"mapping across."* I took the idea of competitiveness, and applied it to the sales situation. I said, "With life insurance being such a competitive industry, the products have to compete so much based on price that they are at a competitive level just to get people in the door. But my customers really appreciate working with me because I do add value by my intense commitment to staying on top of economic and financial knowledge, as well as the insurance industry. I can guarantee you that the package I offer you will be the best arrangement, not because I can slash prices like a car dealership, but because of the care I take. And I do this because I don't want anyone to postpone a decision that can mean so much to their family."

This was my pivot point, and it worked. From a sales point of view, my job was basically over at that point. Here, I put significance and contribution out ahead of certainty, and I shifted certainty from the "I'm a good provider because I'm such a hard-nosed negotiator," to "...because I'm taking action now to protect my family."

CONFUSION AND INSECURITY

This is the hurt within the Certainty need. Feelings of confusion and insecurity will drive a person toward certainty. Whatever it is that will bring them into certainty becomes very important. It's your job to connect not having the product with confusion and insecurity, and show how your product is the cure.

You already know how to recognize people who lead with the certainty need. So let's look at how you can bring the pain of absence into the foreground. Allow me to create an example phrase for a few products.

Life insurance: I know that we can never predict what life will throw our way (that's confusing and makes me insecure). But life insurance brings the certainty that your family's needs are covered (I want certainty).

Cars: I know that all the modern features and considerations can be mind boggling (They're confusing, I hate that.) But our company has a total commitment (total sounds pretty certain, especially when it's commitment) to bringing together the features that matter (not extra confusing stuff), and making them very useable. (I'm certain I could use them if it's only the ones that matter.) You can experience exactly how that feels right now, in this model. (Direct experience makes me certain. Let's try it and see.)

Education: I know parents are very concerned about sending their children away, I see the same news headlines that everyone else does, and I am very involved on committees that expose me to very disturbing information. That's why I make it a point to show parents our innovative programs that take responsibility for providing the structure that college kids really need.

BOREDOM AND UNCERTAINTY

Too much consistency can really drain away our energy and motivation. There is a *Twilight Zone* episode from the classic *Rod Serling* television series, in which a big criminal thinks he is in heaven. But everything always goes exactly as he wishes. He even wins whenever he gambles. When he asks for some unpredictability, saying that since he's in heaven he should get what he wants, his guide starts laughing. *"What makes you think you're in heaven?"* he asks.

Also, this need is tied to our sense of achievement. If we lack challenging goals, there is a part of us that really wants that special kick in the pants that gets us going. When motivation returns because of goals coming into focus, it is a very refreshing feeling.

I'll try applying this to some products.

Life insurance: (Extra ideas are in parentheses, I wouldn't say them out loud.) I know that the ins and outs (notice the physical, animated language) of life insurance can be deadly (attention-getting word) boring (oh no, not boredom!), and only a bean counter like me (you aren't me but you need me to do what you hate) wants to indulge (action) in all the details (yuck, details), so I can tell you right now what policy you can get (action!) immediately (action!), so you can get your focus (intensity) back on living and enjoying your life (exactly what he wants, he can fill in what that means to him).

Vacations: This is not your typical vacation. There are no families with special needs, everything isn't programmed. Most people really need a lot more, uh, maintenance (yuck, those high maintenance people, keep them away from me) than this vacation affords. I'm sure you know how that feels. It can be worse than staying at home because you got your hopes up. (Feel the hurt!) But this endeavor places you directly (no screwing around, let's go) into the settings where you can experience these diverse sports adventures (yes, adventure!) with experts that absolutely love them and think they've died and gone to heaven because we only connect them with people who are on the same wavelength (no lightweights, yes!)

NOT MATTERING

Ouch! That's a really painful one. Being insignificant, trivial, getting kicked to the curb. What would you do to avoid that. Some people are driven to leave their mark on the world for generations, but all of us would like to at least matter to someone. There is the hurt within the drive for Significance. When people or some animals lose their social status, they actually experience an uncomfortable change in their chemistry that really alters their behavior. And much of the destructive behavior that you see in relationships, is simply an attempt to get rid of the hurt of not mattering. It comes out in a destructive way, because those folks lack constructive ways to do it. That means that domestic violence counselors have to be among the greatest salespeople of all.

Okay, now for some phrases.

Life insurance: Spouses sometimes confide in me that it weighs on them that something could happen and their spouse hasn't taken care of key things like life insurance (but I need to matter to my spouse!)

Activity coupon books: I hate to see the look in children's eyes when their parents have to say they can't do something because they can't afford it. And every week they are antsy and need to do something that will stimulate them and expand their world. (I won't matter if I don't provide that.) With this book, you won't need any excuses ever again, it makes your children's dreams totally affordable for the parents.

LONELINESS

Remember how Scrooge had his big epiphany? His ghostly masters of influence activated a lot of pain in order to do their job. They brought him to Love and Connection, but it was painful. Yet this work by Dickens is one of the most famous pieces of literature ever produced. Apparently everyone resonates to this hurt.

Life insurance: I can't imagine anything worse than being in a hospital and knowing that I might die, failing to leave my family secure. Even when they arrived, I would feel like there was a wall between their eyes and mine. (Pretty graphic; a wall, their eyes. Ouch.)

Surfboards: Welcome to Hawaii. I moved out here for a new job, myself, ten years ago last week (so he's credible and similar to me). I haven't regretted it once (nice positive feeling; gee, I'd like to feel like that, too, ten years from now). But I'm a little introverted (I'm new in town, I feel like that), and it was hard to make friends at first (boy howdy). I mean, people are pretty friendly here, but they're already pretty busy and so they'd say let's get together and things wouldn't happen (how sad). So I spent a lot of lonely nights feeling like, Hawaii's paradise, why am I being left out (how very sad). It was surfing that really tapped me into a network of people (the cure). Even just taking lessons got me connected with great people (heal me, I'll take the blue one).

STUCKNESS

The need for Growth, unfulfilled, equals stasis, stagnation, the doldrums, not getting anywhere, being passed up by your peers, becoming irrelevant. Ew! Stop there. I can't take it any more! *What can I do to experience some growth?*

Life insurance: When I have something hanging over me like that, I feel like I can't fully invest myself in the other things I'm doing, as if they were just procrastination.

Toys: I meet so many parents these days who feel disconnected from their children, and like their children are being parented by their computer and by their friends. Their relationships with their children are kind of in limbo (now that's stuckness; limbo). Our toy line was designed with this in mind, to bring parents and children together, not just to pass the time (that's kind of stuck), but to revitalize the parent-child relationship (that's for me). For example, the communication track builds not only the child's communication and interpersonal problem solving, but also gives the parents more tools for connecting with and influencing their children. (I get to grow as a parent? Wow!)

CUT OFF FROM CONTRIBUTING

This is a special example of the pain within a need. Because, as you'll recall, not every person is strongly driven by all of these needs. Some people feel very good about keeping it all for themselves; stingy is great--for them. They will even express some pretty negative attitudes about helping other people. They flatter themselves by invoking social Darwinism. Survival of the fittest, and all that. But Darwin himself actually was against the idea of social Darwinism. He wasn't the one who came up with that idea, not in terms of society neglecting people being a good thing. So think of the times you have felt the need to contribute.

For the moment, forget all about the needs for significance or love and connection, just the need to contribute all by itself. Some people feel like there is a pressure building up inside of them when they are unable to contribute for a period of their life. They will go out of their way to find some means to contribute. Even if they are in jail! They will think about the welfare of the other inmates and start some kind of activity or class if they are permitted to.

The reason I didn't call this one "Being Stingy" is because that would imply that this need is about not being *perceived* as stingy. But this is about an inner drive, more or less independent of how you are perceived.

Life insurance: What's worse than being injured and knowing that the clock is ticking while their family's needs have to slip, sometimes with disastrous consequences (horrible, I can't contribute, I'm going to explode). Especially these days (It could happen to me). I can hardly watch the news any more (It could really happen to me). This product takes care of people when they are disabled, so that they can know that they are going to take care of their family no matter what. (I can take care of my family no matter what if I sign up. I'm signing up.) It brings people a lot of satisfaction to know that their money is really working for them in this package. I know that people really want to know that they are bringing in the best financial outcome. (So I'm contributing with financial management as well, by getting a more comprehensive product. Great!)

MEMORY MAGIC AND BELIEF

Memory Magic

Do you know what two plus two is? You do? Well of course you do. But do you remember the day that you learned it? Do you recall exactly what you were doing and what the teacher said that got through to you and convinced you? No? Well of course not.

The first kind of memory I call sticky memory. You know the fact, but you don't remember learning it. It just is. It is truth. (Psychologists call it semantic memory.) The second kind of memory, where you remember a specific thing that happened is called situational memory. You are going to learn how to use sticky memory, and how to avoid getting tripped up by it as well.

People tend to believe things that aren't really true, for reasons that they don't know.

These untrue things that people believe tend to seem true or believable, or feel desirable to believe, or were part of their lives from an early age. These untrue things came along at times when the person was open to believing them, and they stuck. Of course, a lot of people stay open to these kinds of beliefs most of the time. It's pretty funny how strongly they assert these false beliefs. There's no little circuit in their thinking that stops them and says, "How do I know that this is true? How good is the source?"

One of Countless Examples

I had to research an issue for a business of mine. It involved a federal agency. I needed to know exactly how to be in compliance. I communicated with two representatives from the agency. I read their regulations, which were in three very fat books I had to sift through. I even consulted an attorney who had worked for that agency, and who had helped businesses successfully get products approved by that agency. Then, I occasionally had conversations with people who told me with absolute certainty, that my conclusions about what to do was wrong. I told them what I had done to make my decision, and everything about their tone, face, and body language told me that they just couldn't let that information in. They were too attached to what they believed. When I asked them how they knew *they* were right, they didn't know. Even that didn't not wrest their grip from their opinion.

After that experience, I started betting people money that I was right about things that could be verified. But a strange thing happened. So far, not one person has failed to back down from their beliefs when I offered to bet on it, even when they insisted that they were certain. Apparently, there is some part of their subconscious that actually knows that they are wrong, and jumps in at the last minute to prevent them from losing money. Try it and see if you get the same results. It's amazing. And it's pretty disappointing. I was hoping to win some big money from these incredibly confident people!

CHANGE THEIR MIND WITHOUT CHANGING THEIR OPINION

It is very difficult to change beliefs, by attacking them head on. Emotion, facts, statistics, logic; all are feeble. Once a belief has become ingrained enough, it is very sticky.

Scientists call this *"semantic memory."* That means that you probably don't even remember when you learned it. It's like one plus one equals two. It's just true, and that's all there is to it. I like to call it *"sticky memory,"* because it's so, well, you know, sticky! It's so sticky, that once a memory gets sticky, the person that gave them the memory may not be able to convince them that it isn't true.

That's what researchers found out, much to their surprise. As a human being, I find this kind of embarrassing. Don't you?

But as professional salespeople, we have our ways to make end runs around those sticky opinions that get in the way of the sale. Well, once you have absorbed this section, you'll multiply your ability to deal with sticky opinions. The tools tend to be indirect, like the one about using the imagination. You should probably combine several at once, out of respect for the true nature of stickiness.

We won't be resorting to the authority of statistics. Except for people who are used to statistics, they are no good for persuasion. If they were, people wouldn't go to psychic readers. We'll also forgo comparisons, like you having 20% more technical support staff FTE's than the competition on a per-customer basis.

Some people are absolutely data proof. Their beliefs are completely impervious to all reason. But there are some scientifically-trained or otherwise open-minded types who may be impressed by quality of information. But don't be surprised when even the more scientific or analytical types hang onto an unfounded opinion.

Also, when dealing with a belief that is in your way, keep in mind the difference between a truly sticky memory, and one in which the person can actually be reasoned with. The less sticky memories are the ones that the person can actually remember forming. This means that it is more recent, or that it is less networked into their mind. That is, it has less reinforcement, like a loose thread. Scientists call the less-sticky memories, where the person knows how they formed them, "situational memory."

EXAMPLES AS REASONS

But even situational memory that comes from situations that we actually remember, can be pretty strong. Some people just need to see one example of something, and it becomes a general opinion; it somehow moves straight into situational memory. This is especially true for examples that have emotional impact. That's why people think that they bad things they see on the news happen way more often than they actually do. And since the news broadcasters are hungry for ratings, they bombard the public with so much salacious and horrifying news that there is much more fear and prejudice than need be.

So use example reasons. Those aren't really reasons, but they fill the same purpose because of how people think. Tell them the story of the elderly lady who couldn't make sense of her computer, and how your young tech expert drove to her house in the driving snow so she could send her Christmas cards out, and how she told her family and they thanked him and invited him to her funeral. It meant so much to them that they all bought laptops from you that year for their college-age kids.

But I'm not just talking about full-blown stories. People are better convinced by a good number of examples than a good quality of information. Those lotto winners are incredibly rare from a statistical point of view. In fact, if people really were basing their decision to gamble on statistics, they would never get into a car. Yet they drive to gamble. Bigger odds of getting hurt, in exchange for far, far smaller odds of hitting it big. Examples are gold.

BELIEFS CREATE OPINIONS AND AFFECT MEMORIES

This is really amazing. Once a person has a sticky belief, it can act like a secret agent to sneak around in the person's conscious mind and re-engineer their opinions and memories. Consider the person who is addicted to alcohol. If they are still stuck on the opinion that they are a social drinker, all the facts and memories in their minds magically arrange themselves to get in line with that opinion.

A medical doctor tells the story of his own addiction to alcohol. At one point, he decided that he didn't like feeling so bad in the morning, but he wasn't able to call it a hangover. Social drinkers don't have hangovers. He came to believe that he must have had a problem digesting the alcohol. He even gave his problem a name: alcohol metabolization disorder. Fortunately, he didn't try to get it into a medical journal. But he did run a catheter down his throat one night to empty out the extra alcohol before he went to bed. This was such an extreme move, that it broke through his denial. He thought, *"This is what we do to drunks in the drunk tank!"* Finally, his entire reality made a shift, and he was able to seek help, no longer stuck with seeing himself as a social drinker.

THE BELIEF NETWORK AND HIDDEN TRAPS

A key lesson for salespeople is that they have to think bigger than just the single opinion that is in their way. Sales professionals must consider how that belief is one signal of a possible network of opinions or beliefs. This means that you will see it coming before you find your self conflicting with some other belief. This will make for a smoother flow through the sales process.

If your customer is super suspicious of salespeople, you can predict that this will play out in various ways. Just telling a story may have little impact, compared to a story that was published by a legitimate publisher, or a video of someone who clearly is not an actor.

A salesperson I know thought that a customer was conservative and so he made a conservative political comment related to being a "law and order guy." He saw the negative reaction from the customer and the customer's wife. He said, as a law and order guy, I really want to see (and he named an uncouth conservative politician) brought to justice and the constitution respected. This got a laugh and really softened things up. And he didn't have to betray his true beliefs.

THE MEMORY-STATE CONNECTION

You want your customer to disconnect from the competition and buy from you. Let me introduce you to an ally in that quest. It is the negative memories they have of buying from the competition. Or at least negative memories of buying something that could remind them of the competition. They must have negative memories you could activate for this purpose. First, it's strong memories that have the most recall power. Second, they *are* coming to see you for some reason. Is it because they weren't entirely satisfied with another source?

Be sure to activate useful negative memories, and help them frame them in terms of the competition and not the product line or related companies in general. We'll be talking more about how to do that as we go along.

When you move into the positive points about your product, focus on their best experiences with the product or anything like it. Bring up any related memories that might put a positive aura around your product. You can do this in the course of getting to know why they want the product and how they intend to use it. This also helps activate the ingredient of imaginary action. It helps to connect them with the product.

In life insurance, I may have a conversation with a prospect about their other insurance experiences. It could be that they know someone who got a large insurance settlement. Perhaps they feel good about having the coverage they need. I tap into the good feelings connected with insurance in any way I can. Think about the kinds of use positive memories that your prospect may have. Cast a wide enough net that you include things that may be a few steps removed from the actual product. Just look for meaningful connections, like in the examples I gave. Neither of them were experiences with life insurance. But either of them can get the prospect into a positive state that is *connected* with life insurance. That's because the mind works by connecting similar things together.

INOCULATE

You already know there will be resistance in a lot of your prospects. Inoculate your prospects against it before it comes up. You can even do this when you are close to closing. You need to. Different resistances get activated at different points in the sales process.

Let's say you have gotten good agreement with your prospect and it looks like they will go ahead with the purchase. You set up the inoculation something like this: *"We know all the facts now, and you and I understand that this is the right decision for you. But you know how people like to debate things and make you doubt what you believe. Have you thought about what you'll say to people try to change your mind?"*

With this question, you have reminded your prospect that you are both on the same team. You also used the magic word "because" that generates some automatic pressure to agree. You have also moved the prospect from the emotions of the decision toward the identity of a person who does things logically.

This is a preferred identity for most people. You'll learn plenty more about how to use identity shifts and logic as a part of closes later in this book. When your prospect tells you what they will say, you are doing more than preparing them for nay-sayers. You are getting them to make a commitment that will create an inner pressure for them to be consistent from that point forward. You are shifting their identity and anchoring it to a new point. They are now a customer.

The best time to use this technique is when you feel like there is some potential for buyer's remorse. You wouldn't sell the product if there was a legitimate reason for buyer's remorse. You are concerned because they have some hesitation in their voice that tells you there is an emotional resistance of some kind.

Or you know that your product is one that people try to talk people into not appreciating. I see people try to make people feel bad about buying things all the time. Maybe it's some kind of social protective thing that people do to try to keep each other from getting carried away. Maybe that's not such a bad thing, in general. But you don't want it to make your customer feel bad about doing something good.

Figure out how to work this into your sales process. How might it apply to your products and customers? Try it out and see how powerful it is.

BECAUSE REASONS

Tell HOW something does or doesn't happen. Don't use statistics except to augment something that is already very compelling. Use because reasons. This is because of that; causal reasons. Our customers love us because we always have enough tech support people scheduled that at least two are expected to have nothing to do except other kinds of work. If there are any extra calls, they get pulled away from whatever they're doing immediately. We have the happiest tech staff you're likely to see. One of them brought in a treadmill and tells the callers how many blocks he walked while he walked them through their problem. The customers love it.

In this example, the customers are learning how they will NOT have to wait a long time. Pretty much everyone expects that they will have to wait too long for tech support. Instead of giving the average wait time, or where you stand compared to the industry average, you offered this charming, engaging story.

Remember the idea of integration; using more than one source of persuasion at one time. This story was engaging because it really created images in the person's mind, and it was kind of humorous. It appealed to multiple senses, and not just the visual. It also brought up good feelings, because people like to hear about people being industrious, committed, and creative. That's people like to hear stories about Benjamin Franklin.

UNPLUGGING STICKY BELIEFS

Sometimes a sticky belief can really get in the way. This is especially galling, since they are usually untrue. If they are actually true, then you would use reframing to get them in touch with other true things that are conducive to the sale. This way, you are not fighting the truth. That's what bad guys in comic books do, anyway, isn't it?

So let's talk about how to reduce the power of a sticky belief. I call this "unplugging" the belief. It may still be there, but it isn't plugged into a power source. The best way to unplug a sticky belief is through action. But not necessarily action in the real world. Imaginary action can work quite well.

And I'm talking about doing something, not saying something. This means that the action must help them unplug the belief. That explains why image scripting is so powerful. So far, you have learned to use image scripting to produce more motivation to buy. But that motivation came from giving them imaginary experiences of enjoying the product. These experiences involved not just the senses, but action.

To use this technique in unplugging sticky beliefs, you do not directly confront the belief. You create actions that involve things that take them beyond the belief. Not contrary; beyond.

Unplugging Workout

Here's an example from my business. I was talking with a family, but the father was kind of superstitious. They had to drag him into my office, and he was really just there to get them off his back. He had a sticky belief that, "What will be will be." He has a vague notion that fate dictates what happens, and you shouldn't mess with it.

People with this belief never have a detailed understanding of it. They even have a tendency to believe it sometimes and not other times. Since they aren't very deep, they don't notice this. That means that they haven't really even thought through questions like, *"Where, exactly, do I draw the line between interfering with fate, and doing what I do in life?"* and *"What bad thing would happen if I intervened in fate?"*

Without these answers, these people live in a vague world with a shadowy bogeyman and an undefined threat. You'd think they'd be pretty nervous not having clear instructions as to how to avoid this ever-present and powerful threat, wouldn't you? But no. They just bring it up when their subconscious mind isn't ready to do something.

In the case of this gentleman, his family was ready and he wasn't. So I tried using imaginal action to unplug this belief. I expressed my understanding and appreciation for his respect for fate, and his desire for fate to smile on him and his family.

I told him about a widow who did not know that her husband had life insurance, and how she was so depressed at losing him that she temporarily lost her mind and was about to jump from a very high bridge. Just before she started walking, she got a call from her mother-in-law and learned that her husband had life insurance.

Somehow, fate had intervened to prevent her from ending her own life by a margin of a few seconds. She thanks God every day that her husband cared about her fate enough to make this small investment that saved her life.

This story sounds silly, doesn't it? That's because the man's belief in fate was silly. I took a true story, and framed it in terms of fate, so that he could respect fate and still buy life insurance. That's all there is to it. But what about the imaginary behavior? I told the story in a way that would remind him of his own wife, who had some trouble with depression. That caused the story to really strike a nerve. I guessed that, at some level, he fears that his wife might suicide. There's enough about this on the news, and concerns about medications contributing to suicide. He had to have this somewhere in his mind.

My ending of the story was really about the husband's behavior, giving him an experience of being the one who saved her, being the one who bought the insurance, and being the one who fulfilled his wife's fate. That last piece is a very important reframe for this example.

MOMENTUM MAGIC

BELIEF PREQUELS AND SEQUELS

Remember how we learned that people's beliefs actually engineer their opinions and memories? Like the alcohol doctor. Everything that his mind had access to confirmed that he was a social drinker. But this goes farther. People will even change their memories retroactively! In research, people who were told they did poorly on a test actually came to believe that they knew in advance that they would do poorly.

This means that you need to manage perceptions throughout the sales process. If your customer is very involved in calculations that help them decide how much they can buy, you would want to drop a comment about their skill. You know that people are more likely to buy a better model if they feel secure in their job. So wouldn't you want to reinforce a comment they make about how the math was no big deal, because they do it all the time at work. "Oh, how long have you been doing that?" "Twelve years." "Oh, so they really know how fast you get the job done, then." Look what you did, taking away time pressure and reinforcing their job security at the same time. You are becoming more of a sales genius by the minute. What a brilliant move, getting this book! Okay, I know, I'm going overboard, but how could I help it, basking in the radiance of your mastery?

And this dynamic is so powerful, that even a single word can alter the person's memory of what happened. This means that you must train yourself to have every word hit the right tone, like a very polished musician that gets every note right. Of course, this is a life-long quest, so think of it as something you always practice, not something you expect to get immediately. Experienced musicians practice. Doctors call their practices *practices*.

Why not you?

BELIEF SEQUELS

So the term prequel is kind of the opposite of sequel, because it refers to those movies that show what happened prior to the movie you already saw, like that Star Wars series, where the last two episodes were really the first two.

A belief prequel, as you saw in the previous piece works because, by managing the customer's perceptions of the process, you will help them alter their beliefs about the intentions and opinions that they came into the process with. Think of the possibilities! This really deserves some thought. Your sales process probably affords you numerous points at which your creativity and genius could produce useful imaginary memories from the future, and fresh opinions from the past.

But this also works in the opposite direction. So we'll call this the belief sequel. If you liked King Kong, you gotta see Son of King Kong. Well, if you get people to make a commitment or decision or statement of belief more memorable, then it will be more memorable--and more motivational. Getting something put down in writing, even non-binding writing, will increase the customer's commitment.

It doesn't have to be a formal process, though. It could be as innocent as jotting down some ideas about how you would use a product. The military has gotten young people to sign a statement of commitment to consider enlisting. Later, this would be used to encourage them to enlist.

Now, remember when we learned about how memories changed. Some of the staff got carried away and told some of the young people that they had enlisted and would be in big trouble if they didn't cooperate.

I guess that was a pre-sequel belief when it worked. I'm glad that you are an ethical person and would not lie like that.

Using Up Skepticism

Did you know that many people have a limited supply of skepticism? It's true. The more gullible someone is, the shorter their supply. This means that you should get people to exercise their critical thinking abilities early in the sales process. Many will become more open-minded as they go along.

Get them thinking about the numbers involved or the options involved, figuring out what they can do without, or figuring out how to get the best per unit price, or following your explanation as to how other companies will scam customers like them.

But this flies in the face of all the talk you hear about creating a positive state of mind. You're supposed to emphasize the value and getting relaxed and into rapport all to create a buying situation. Well that is true, but when you do a recipe, you can't do the steps at random. And you can't just pick a few of your favorite ingredients and hope for the best. You need all the ingredients that particular recipe calls for, and you must know when to do what.

When it comes to being critical of things, you want them to criticize things other than you and your product. You want them to wear out their criticizing muscles before they regard your product.

Think about ways you can do that in your sales process.

Unsticking for Momentum

Stuck on Not You: It's an unfortunate fact that when people make a choice, the option that they eliminated can take on a certain wistful value. It's not quite the same as the grass being greener on the other side of the road, because of there being a sense of loss. Maybe you can recall some feelings like that about potential spouses that you bypassed for someone else? If you had chosen them, then your current mate would probably seem even more valuable than now.

Slow Equals No Go: The stuck on not you principal can become so powerful that it actually kills the sale *before* it takes place. This is not remorse. This is prevention! People have had plenty of experiences of Stuck on Not You. They develop some fear of giving up an option. If they have to think to hard and long about a decision, they can end up holding off in order to prevent the loss of their other options. One or more other options can actually begin to seem more valuable before they even have the chance to buy and regret it afterwards!

Speed Thrills: This is a great example of turning a disadvantage into an advantage. Deliberation can work against you. The more the prospect thinks, the more they can experience fear of losing options. Find ways to create efficiency, momentum, and outright speed. Get the customer moving through and involved in the sales process. Keep the deliberation time to a minimum. This will prevent the potential loss of their other options from kindling into a drive to prevent that sense of loss.

Teflon for Momentum

Seamless Credibility: Remember to harmonize with the prospect's opinions or perspectives before you move near the close. Does that mean to pretend to have their opinions and perspectives. No, find the closest things in yourself and bring them to the foreground.

Absorb and deploy: Sales professionals have countless ways to get the customer absorbed in the sales process. These ways usually serve multiple purposes at once. I really want you to think in terms of integration. That is, making your sales ingredients serve several purposes at once. for example, in a timeshare presentation, you might absorb the customer in thoughts about the perfect vacation, complete with a beautiful video in stunning colors. This not only absorbs the customer into the process, it activates the feelings and values that can drive the buying decision.

Motion unsticks: What if your prospect just doesn't seem to get unstuck. They are in some kind of stuck state and it's starting to look like there's nothing you can do about it. It could be their energy level and mood. They aren't getting jazzed about the product. It could be their perspective and opinion. They just aren't moving toward a close. Get them moving. Physically. Get them into a different location. Get them to take a potty break. Offer them a snack in the lunch room. Show them around. So SOMETHING to get them moving. Moving changes the physical and mental state.

Undo the Loss Factor

Harness the Loss Factor: If your prospect is absorbed in deciding which option to eliminate, but both options are from you, their regret will not prevent them from buying one of your products, unless they become unable to choose at all. Since you are there, shepherding them through the process, you can help frame their decision, so that doesn't happen. Create choices that absorb their attention and choosing activity.

Shepherd That Loss: Here's a good way to prevent the prospect from experiencing a sense of loss of options. You want to frame their decision so they don't dig in their heels, feeling like they have to prevent a loss. Get there be highlighting the values that drive them forward in life. Those values can drive them to the sale. You know some things about their driving values, because you have gotten to know them. You have been very observant, watching for signs. Translate their emerging decision to NOT do an option as a clear exercise of their values and beliefs.

Let's say your customer is looking at water heaters and she is considering the top of the line model. On the conscious level (what she tells you) is that frugality is their driving value. But you are making an educated guess that status is her more primitive value, and status is getting activated by this better model. You can talk about being able to be certain there will be hot water for a luxurious bath. You can mention how funny it is that people like to see what kind of water heater you have, you show yours off.

But don't forget to prevent that sense of loss of the frugal option! Point out that the cheaper water heaters really aren't the best buy in the long run, because the one she's looking at is so energy efficient. People are very concerned about having greener homes these days. Now her frugal conscious mind can win by making the cost-effective purchase.

MOVE FROM NEGATIVE TO POSITIVE

Your customer should always start with the choice that they are least likely to end up wanting. That enables you to move them from negative to positive. This creates buying momentum. Make sure that they see that the wrong choice is the wrong choice very quickly, so that they do not develop any sense of attachment to it. Do not explore it in any way that can create ties in their mind. You are not analyzing an engineering problem or performing psychotherapy.

I must admit, I once purchased an overpriced mountain bike, in part, because the dealer had purposely de-tuned a cheaper mountain bike in order to make the superior one quite obviously superior. The gap in value was so great, that it seemed to justify the high price of the better model. Had I done my homework, I would have gotten a better deal, but I had not had time prior to a vacation that was very important to my, so I made a rash decision in a situation that was set up to take advantage or naïve consumers.

I'm not recommending that you create a false negative choice. But if you ponder your sales situation a while, I'll bet you can think of plenty of ways to create negative contrasts that will boost sales by allowing you to move the customer from a negative choice to a positive one. At the very least, move them from less desirable to more desirable.

Beyond the Puppy Close

I suppose you've already heard of the puppy close. Take the puppy home and see how you like him. You won't give him back! Take that car for a test drive. You gotta have it! But not every business lends itself to the puppy close. Or doesn't it?

Put on your brainstorming cap. While you do, keep in mind that the customer doesn't have to take anything home, and doesn't have to be in reality. That means they can get involved in their imagination, and they can get involved in more ways.

My interior decorator had me look at computer-generated images of what my rooms would look like after the kinds of treatments I was talking about. She made sure that the interior images were very realistic, except that everything was neat and organized. This made the need to use her services even more compelling. And my involvement in holding the pictures and looking from various angles was playing right into her hands.

Life insurance might seem like an even harder one for this approach. But I always work in comments about the outcomes of their buying decision. I make sure those comments are driven by their values and are from their perspective. I do my best to get them talking about how this is valuable. Again, this is one of those integrative approaches. I'm getting them involved as well as making verbal quasi-commitments at the same time.

It's a Shocking Fact!

This is a shocking fact, that few people know.

If you disclose to someone a shocking fact that few people know, they are more likely to agree with you that they should buy your product. Just make that shocking fact (even a surprising one will do) support their understanding of the product in some way. If the shocking fact is an amazing-but-true claim, then that's even better.

A special secret can do this as well. That might be a way to get more out of the product that isn't in the manual, or a way to save money that most salespeople won't tell you.

It's a good idea to hold back an amazing-but-true claim, or shocking fact for one of two points in the sales process.

1. You have gotten stuck and want to really shift the customer's state.

2. You are nearing the close and want a boost.

Especially at point #2, you have nothing to lose. It isn't a concession, it's a fact. But be ready to verify the fact or claim.

It's easier for people to make the purchase when their logical mind opens the gate to let the emotions do their thing. The amazing claim does that in spades.

CAPTURING REBOUND

Have you ever achieved a milestone of some kind, like losing weight or getting into shape, and then taken permission to turn around and do something that goes against that goal? People who have achieved a level of savings suddenly do some excess spending, for example. This appears to be a rebound reaction, and it seems to be driven by the unconscious. No one I've ever met has been able to describe some kind of rational, conscious deliberation or forethought prior to this kind of action.

As a sales person, you may wish to amplify the warm glow that people have about an accomplishment or milestone. It may help them get into a celebratory mood that encourages spending on what you have to offer. This is another reason for asking questions and doing some chit chat. You never know what useful information they will offer.

CHOICE PARALYSIS

Have you ever offered too many choices to a customer and felt the momentum drain out of the sales process? I used to experience this. I was so excited about my customers making informed decisions that I'd inform them out of the sale.

Now I know to watch them for signs. And I observe those signs before we ever get anywhere near making any choices. The same signs that people show when they start to get choice paralysis are the signs they begin to show if you share too many ideas, talk too fast, or get them analyzing too much.

They may look a little overwhelmed. Their eyes may seem to dial out a little bit. That's an odd expression, but people seem to know what it means. It's the look people get when they don't connect with you as much visually, because they are trying to keep their brains from losing the information they are trying to piece together. Their color may darken a bit and their posture may collapse a little as if they are drawing in protectively.

They may seem sort of fatigued. Their face may go a little flat. But some people get a little edgy and tense. Their speech may be a little more jittery, as they try to talk and assemble their thoughts at the same time.

Where people who are very good at juggling details and choices may be hungry for more, everybody else will tend to show those stress signs if given a lot of details to sort out.

The answer is to get a feel for their processing power and style very early on. At least you should if you have to decide how much leeway to give them in sorting out choices. In some businesses, the choices are limited enough that it doesn't matter.

In paint, people expect thousands of choices. It doesn't seem to keep them from buying paint, though. It just slows down the process. In my case, it caused me to buy more paint. I had to repaint because I realized what a terrible choice I'd made from just looking at a swatch.

If you have a lot of potential choice scenarios, really look at your sales process. See how you can match a very limited number of choices to specific types of prospects. And remember, whenever possible, show them the best choice after the worst choice, and make it last choice of two.

MOTIVATIONAL SCULPTING

I learned a very useful skill that you find among drug counselors, and I've been really appreciating what it does for sales momentum. No, I wasn't in rehab. I just have a good board of advisors and collection of friends and contacts chock full of ideas.

The pint of this skill is to get people to make more sense, and to do it without any kind of pushiness. In drug counseling, you can imagine how important it is to stay out of the way of any struggle. Many people recovering from drug addiction are trying to catch up with themselves emotionally.

That means they may be at the level of a fifteen year old or so when it comes to relationships and authority figures.

I adapted this for sales some time ago, and I find myself doing it in very subtle ways, and sometimes more dramatic ways, but it's always working itself into my discussions. I use it at times in my personal life as well. Enough suspense. Let's have a look.

The technique has two sides to it. One side is for encouraging and rewarding statements that make sense. The other side is for punishing and eliminating statements that don't make sense. Punishing is a strong word. I'm using it to mean merely that there is some discomfort in the interaction.

This tends to reduce the behavior, as any punishment does. Even work is a punishment, apparently, since you have to pay people so much to get them to do it unless they're hungry.

Did you know that in one research study, teenagers who had to peddle in order to keep the TV on ended up only watching half an hour per week. I think I want one of those TV's for my family.

The Motivational Interviewing Technique

The technique goes like this. When your prospect says something that is not very supportive of the sales process, if you respond to it, tweak your feedback to highlight what is least appropriate about it. When they say something supportive of the process, highlight what is really smart about it. Much of the time, you may have something else to do that will support your sales flow, but I find this to be pretty handy.

If a prospect says that they want to wait on life insurance, I may say, *"So you're feeling lucky, then?"* or *"So you're okay with leaving your family exposed?"*

As you can see, these responses can be subtle or more confrontive. But either way, they're a far cry from, *"Now that's the stupidest idea I've ever heard."*

If the prospect says they would like to have enough coverage for their family's needs and college for their kids, I might say, *"Oh, yes, I'm always glad when people think that far ahead,"* or *"Yes, education is so important, especially these days."*

Note that there's nothing forced or school marmish about it. I didn't say, *"That's very good. You are a true family man."*

Who am I to judge him?

The complete version of this method, for counselors, is called *Motivational Interviewing.* This is just my adaptation of a part of it for sales people.

MECHANICS OF MOTIVATIONAL SCULPTING

The negative responses have a mild behavior modification effect, acting as mild punishments, in that they are a little unpleasant. But they also make the position seem less desirable, because I highlighted something that is bad in the position.

Notice that I didn't add anything that wasn't there. It was unspoken, but it was, in fact, a direct conclusion that any reasonable person could take from the statement.

Similarly, the positive response not only rewards the statement, but also propels the sales process by highlighting what is in favor of it. This also helps to confirm a positive identity shift.

But what about the negative statement and identity shifting? It appears to have the effect of causing most people to want to self-correct. I believe I know why. Because what I highlight is contrary to their more established identity and values. It's as if they are saying, "Well, since you put it that way, I can't really live with what I just said."

The trick to avoiding lowering the bar in a negative response is to quickly provide an opportunity for them to rehabilitate themselves in my and their own eyes. I like to do that in the form of a soft test close with the Hypnotic Language Pressure method. You'll be learning that in the Advanced Skills and Knowledge section. This is a really good sequence for people with bad ideas.

STEPHEN'S SALES PROCESS: FROM CONTACT TO CLOSE

CONTACT PHASE

UNDERSTANDING SALES FLOW

When you carry out your sales process, you want every phase to work perfectly. That means planning it in detail. Of course, you'll have plenty of room to improvise. In fact, I think it's essential to improvise, because every prospect is unique, even the ones that seem exactly the same. However, this improvising happens in a well-designed structure, like a jazz musician improvising to a great piece of music.

With that in mind, we will start with the initial contact that you make, and even this phase will be broken up into a good number of pieces so we can get this process working beautifully for you.

The section after that will be about the actual sales presentation, and it will be very detailed. I want you to come away with some scripted things to say, pretty much word for word. This is because there are certain points in the sales process, where it's really good to know exactly what to say. I call these the pivot points of the sales process. The pivot points are so crucial that I want you to do them smoothly and confidently while keeping your mind one step ahead.

Once you are finished with this section, you will be ready for the presentation. Here's what you will have before your presentation even begins:

1. An appointment,

2. A prospect who is really interested in what you have to present,

3. Enough time so that there is no pressure to convince the prospect of anything in a short period of time.

To achieve that, I will explain how to defeat the two fangs that poison the sales process: too little interest, and too little time to present. I will explain why it is so important to get face time with prospects (for businesses that aren't fully appropriate for telemarketing). I will explain the keys to getting appointments by phone, right down to using physiology that you thought you could only do in person. I'll cover the biggest telephone mistakes and exactly how to avoid them. I'll tell you precisely how to get past the gate keepers who think it's their job to keep you from contacting your prospects. I'll cover exactly how to handle your contact with the prospect, including how to make a real connection and generate interest in your offering so you can get that appointment.

Let's get started!

This is not just about getting to the sales presentation, it's about doing it so efficiently that you not only have a high success rate in getting through to decision makers, but also a high rate of productivity in setting appointments in the first place. That means being fully psyched up for the process and having an efficient method that allows you to track your productivity.

This will enable you to reach the goals that are necessary for you to have the success and income that you desire. Many salespeople have failed because they did not keep themselves honest about what was really necessary for success. They did not do the right tracking to ensure full productivity.

PRIMING YOUR PROSPECT

Remember that things change. Your rejected effort one month may result in acceptance six months later. Have a tickler that recycles your contacts. You may find that someone more open-minded has replaced the person who rejected your latest overture. Maybe this time upper management wants your contact to look into the very product you're selling.

It often takes multiple "hits" to get enough "mind share" to get a yes. The more contact your prospect has with your product and business (and you), the more they are "primed" to buy.

Television commercials and product placements in movies rely on priming. They are not usually intended to provoke a purchase or even a conscious memory of a product. More likely, they are meant to create a sense of familiarity with the product. That familiarity in turn produces a positive feeling about the product when the consumer encounters it. This can affect how you feel when you see a car on the lot or a can of peas on the supermarket shelf.

Priming is a type of memory. It is in your subconscious. You don't know why you have a more positive feeling about the product when priming is causing you to feel that way. You can prime your prospects to feel good about you by priming their memory banks. Send an occasional piece of news about your product. Announce a new feature, price reduction, or favorable review by an industry rag.

CORE PHONE SKILLS

The telephone is truly a power tool for making contacts. But you have to use it properly to get the most out of it. Sales professionals waste a great deal of valuable time misusing their phone time. To maximize your phone skills, you must start by getting into the right state of mind. After all, you are the most important part of the sales process.

Unlike a face-to-face contact, you must keep in mind that the phone filters out a lot of what makes you a great salesperson. There is no body language, of course. This is more important than it seems, however, because we communicate much more with our bodies than most people realize. Especially the elements of communication that influence people: establishing trust, building rapport, and bonding. Even your voice is filtered by the phone. It cuts out come of the timbre of your voice. You need to maximize the power of the phone by developing a good phone voice. You can add some physiology back into this communication channel by doing two things. 1) Learn to put a smile into your voice. You can do this by smiling while you talk, and by listening to voice mails that you leave for yourself, experimenting with your voice. Explore pitch, timbre (quality), tempo, and volume. 2) Stand or at least move and gesture while you speak. This sets up subtle dynamics in your voice that may not be so much consciously audible as they are subliminal sales forces. Also, perhaps more importantly, this helps you generate and maintain the state you need to be in to be persuasive and energizing. Never underestimate the power of state, and the value of doing things, no matter how silly they might seem, to generate a dynamic state!

PHONE SECRET: WHAT IS IT REALLY FOR?

Consider the strengths and weaknesses of the phone. On the plus side, it saves time, taking you nearly anywhere in the world instantly to do your sales magic. On the down side, it takes away much of the sales magic that you can provide in person. Unless you are in a business in which the benefit of many rapid contacts outweighs the loss from not being there, this is a very important incentive for personal contact.

Let's talk about sales that rely on personal contact for now. If you really get what this means, if you really accept what I just said about the pro and con of the telephone, then the conclusion is clear: you must use the phone to get the personal contact, but NOT use the phone to prevent it. This is easier said than done, though, because sales professionals often shoot themselves in the foot by not taking this to heart. They try to do some of the personal, face-to-face part of the sales process over the phone, the very time that it is much easier to *lose* the sale.

I'm going to do you a big favor right now, and make the whole thing easier. Unless you are a telemarketer, forget about selling the product over the phone. What you are selling is time with you. By the time you get through my contact process, you will have your prospect very interested in having time with you. Here's why: it's free, you have information that they are very interested in, if not downright excited about, and they trust you to be respectful of their time and their needs. Besides, the decision to see you was a minor decision in the life of a person who has many appointments and considers many products and services without making any up front commitment.

But how did your prospect get so interested in your offer? Largely because you, in your best state of positive caring, described benefits that you knew with bone-deep conviction will improve your prospect's life.

Conviction? Yes! Conviction that the prospect would have to be crazy not to see you. That kind of conviction generates sales performance and really moves people.

Now, let's break this topic out into the keys to phone success.

THE STATE FOR PHONE SUCCESS:

I'm going to be telling you the biggest mistakes that sales professionals make in using the telephone, and exactly what to do instead. I'm even going to give you very precise strategies and scripting. Let's start with your foundation, your state.

For many of us, the phone is an automatic state trigger. And what is that state? A recipe: Boredom with a pinch of mediocrity. You have to "see" through that phone into the heart of your prospect.

Experience the value of your offer and the fundamental beauty of your prospect's humanity at the same time, then psych yourself with your success goals, and you are in the right state of mind to call a prospect. Anything less is, well, less!

You want your intensity to come across to your prospect in a way that generates interest. By now I'm sure you know that I'm not talking about extreme acting or intense energy. I'm talking about a very positive state that is grounded in your certainty of your offering's value and your desire to create value for your prospect.

INTERRUPTION ANTIDOTE

First, the bad news. You are interrupting someone with your call. And it's a busy person, to boot. Not to mention the fact that your prospect rejects so many unwanted calls and other intrusions that they will be in an automatic rejection mode when they pick up the phone. They are not curious, they are thinking about whether to be nice or not when they reject your offer, depending on whether they think you're too pushy, fake, or rude.

Now, the good news. You will learn so much about automatic behavior in this book, that you will come to feel it is your friend. You will become a master of ceremonies for automatic behavior. But you will have to get out far enough ahead of that automatic behavior to buy just enough time to generate some interest. The main ingredients for that are a) being unique, b) being in state (we've already beaten that to death, no we haven't, you can't stress it enough, but I'll give it a rest anyway, for now), c) being respectful, d) dropping in a big value bomb, and e) getting a teeny-weeny concession for a little bit more attention. My contact system, coming up, pronto, will tell you how to do all of this.

PREEMPT THE REJECTION

This one is almost a copy of the previous one. Remember that your prospect, in their automatic rejection mode, are also assuming that you will be too greedy for their time. They are used to pushy wannabe salespeople.

You need to pre-empt that one as well, just as in the item above. That's why I talk about being respectful. I don't mean tentative, squeamish, wavering, or uncertain. I mean directly expressing respect for their time.

You should strongly show your respect for their time in the way that you elicit small concessions such as permission to ask a question. This, too, is in my contact process coming up.

It is possible to be very grounded and confident, while being very respectful. A good psychological trick for this is to imagine that you are getting next to them, looking at the same priorities as they are. Then you make sure to express that alignment with the same kind of passion or intensity that comes from them, or that you can imagine they feel. It really makes you unique and interesting when you do that.

MAP ACROSS TO BRIDGE THE GAP: HANDLING AGGRESSIVENESS

Here's an extreme phone contact that I love to respond to.

The prospect booms something aggressive like, *"I'm under a lot of pressure, get to the point!"* To which you boom back, *"I can do better than that, let's not even talk, let's just set a time when I can show you how we can really save you 20% on your energy costs!"*

This pattern has won me converts. At first, it surprised me, because these people sound so hostile and threatening. Just remember that there is someone in there who wants to be understood, and who thrives on alliance. Most people don't know how to do that for them, because of their personalities. Most of them love it when you step up, as long as you are aggressive about *their* desire or *their* enemy. You must share it with them. Look at my example from that point of view, and it will make total sense.

Here's how it works in exact detail. This is important, because it really is a formula that anyone can do.

Notice how that sentence was structured to "map across" to a similar statement that would normally be very confrontive. It would be, "Oh yeah, I can do *better* than that, you wanna talk *tough?* Meet me behind the church and I'll *really* kick your arse." This is absolutely what I do.

1. I take in the way the aggressive person sounds.

2. Then I think of the kind of response that he arouses in people.

3. Then I make my problem attacking response (and the problem I attack is a problem of his) take on the general quality of that negative reaction.

It always grabs their attention and creates a suspended state, because they have to process the "map across" to the actual thing being said. They are ready to let me have it for talking back. But then they have to do something else with the energy I stirred up. They almost always agree to what I am requesting. I never tire of this, because it feels so surprising.

CONTACT SYSTEM FOCUS: RESOLVING REJECTION

This piece is a special focus on your prospect's automatic rejection behavior. Start by improving your own state with a simple *reframe*. Remember that your prospect is not rejecting you or your offering, they are rejecting the time of the appointment. Other than that, they really don't know what they are rejecting. By re-connecting your prospect with their need to see you, and offering a different time choice, you can resolve a lot of these rejections.

Here's how to do that re-connection: be compelling. For example, say, "*I have a unique life insurance product that can reduce your lifetime costs by 20%, while improving your family's security by 30%. I'd like to know if we could get together on Monday or Tuesday so I could briefly go over the product for you.*" (Note the use of the word "could" which makes the offer a little easier to swallow by throwing it into a tentative kind of conjugation.) I have provided this for over 1,000 families so far, and Family Insurance has the highest rating of satisfaction among families who have lost a covered family member.

CONTACT SYSTEM FOCUS: RESOLVING INTENSE REJECTION

What if the prospect rejects your idea out of hand? For goodness sake, do NOT try to explain them into accepting. That kills the energy. Remember, the meeting is for selling the product. The phone is for selling time with you. You know that they are in automatic rejection mode, and you don't want them making a big decision in that state, so you are sticking with the much smaller decision to receive a little time with you.

So try responding like this, *"Of course, I realize that you're busy, so I called for a brief appointment where I can come to you, so that's why I wonder if Wednesday or Thursday might be better for you."*

Ah, but things aren't usually so easy, are they? If your prospect is still a rejection-bot, remind them of their need with this, *"You realize, Mr. Jenkins, if you could have the benefit I described, of saving 20% while giving your family this 30% improvement in their security, I imagine it would certainly be worth a brief time out to find out the key information you need to know, you'd certainly want to hear about it, wouldn't you?"*

"Well, I dunno..."

"Especially with no up-front costs of any kind involved."

"Yeah, I guess, I'll be around Thursday afternoon."

By this point, you should have a good rate of acceptance.

Notice how this is hardly a strong close. It's respectful, not pushy. You have a caring tone, and are showing respect for their time. Your wording has a certain elegance, in emphasizing the benefit to them, and making the offer of your time feel harmless.

Contact System Focus: Maximizing the Super-Calling State

Now that you have this system for avoiding rejection, or, to put it more nicely, maximizing appointments, we are ready to build on this. In this section, well take that foundation, and focus on maximizing your desire and behavior of making calls.

Let's start with the questions that you are asking yourself. Do you pay attention to them? You probably have questions in mind much of the day. Your questions have a lot to do with your mental focus and the state that you get from that. If you find yourself asking negative or unresourceful questions like, *"Why am I making calls on such a sunny day?"* or, *"How am I going to get through all these cold calls?"* or *"Why do I get so much rejection?"* try questions that create a mental set of maximal opportunity. *"What fresh thing can I do get kick my productivity up toward my goal?"* or *"What new ways can I create a unique, attention-grabbing presence so they won't lump me in with all the other salespeople?"* or, *"What great questions could I ask that would increase my creativity and my positive state?"*

Definitely come up with new ideas for making the process more enjoyable. The more you enjoy your calls, the more driven you will be to achieve your goals and make serious money. Cover the other side of this by taking away the negative associations that you have, that is, the negative feelings that are connected with your calls.

Condition your feelings by eliminating negative associations and building a positive state in connection with your calls. If you ever feel like you "need" the appointment, you must banish that feeling right away. This makes you project the wrong vibe. Focus on amping up your belief in the value of your offering, and the importance of sharing it with the world. That vibe helps the prospect really get who you are, and sense that you are unique. That helps grab attention and dissolve automatic rejection patterns. After all, those patterns are protective. If there is no threat and no neediness, there is no need for automatic rejection, is there?

CONTACT SYSTEM FOCUS: MAXIMIZING NUMBERS

No matter how much you refine your sales skills, not matter how much you love your product, there is a bottom line factor that no sales pro can ignore: Productivity. I'm not talking about your pay check, at least not directly. I'm talking about how many contacts you make and what your success rate with those calls is. You have to have a way of keeping yourself honest about your call volume, and motivated to achieve the volume you need. If you're operating in the dark, you are likely to slack off and miss the mark. You need numbers.

It doesn't have to be a fancy system. You need to look at how much you make, on average per sale, how many appointments you do for each sale (your closing ratio), and how many calls you typically make to get an appointment.

From this, you can create goals for productivity, especially the number of calls you need to make in order to reach your target income.

Let's say that you knew that you could make $100,000.00 per year by making 22 calls a day, three days per week, and you could have six weeks of per year, plus two days off per week. And that is not counting bonuses.

Now think of starting your day, getting psyched to make 22 calls, knowing that they were worth $100,000.00. How does that feel?

Let's punch it up even more. Think about the goals that you have that that income will allow you to experience. What do you value most that is connected with that? Add to that motivation your ability to bring value to your customers and to the employees of your organization, who enjoy their jobs and salaries because of the sales team of which you are a member. Put all those feelings into your body and savor them. That is the state that I'm talking about for your phone calls. Always produce that state prior to making your calls.

$100,000 WORKOUT: CREATE YOUR PRODUCTIVITY GOALS NOW

I'm going to show you the simple formula to use for producing your call and appointment goals.

Let's use a guy named Salesman Joe for our example. Let's say Salesman Joe wants to make $100,000.00 per year, and that he makes, on average, $500.00 per successful appointment. And let's say he makes a sale from one out of three appointments. He makes an appointment from one out of five calls.

How many calls must Salesman Joe make per day, three days per week, to make $100,000.00 per year? This is starting to sound like high school math. Thank goodness it's only high school math. (That was a pre-emptive reframe, by the way, but you noticed that.)

Okay, here goes, 100,000 dollars per year, Salesman Joe's income goal, divided by 500 dollars per sale gives us the number of sales we need to make that income goal. The result is 200 sales to make $100,000.00

200 sales times three appointments per sale (a 1:3 closing ratio), gets us the goal of 600 appointments.

600 appointments times five calls per appointment (a 1:5 appointment-setting ratio), tells us that 3,000 calls are worth $100,000.00.

52 weeks per year, minus six weeks for vacation and sick time, gets us 46 weeks per year of work. Salesman Joe has three days set aside for calls each week, so we have 138 days per year for calls.

3,000 calls divided by 138 days equals 22 calls per day for an annual income of $100,000.00.

Now if you didn't know that 22 calls equal $100,000, it might seem like drudgery. But if you *think of each day as a $100,000 day,* because doing that each call day adds up to that, you can *think of each call as being worth over $4,500.00.* That's true in the sense that Salesman Joe will be duplicating that day three days a week, with *six weeks off per year,* for his $100,000.00. It's a motivator!

Now that Salesman Joe is excited about his calls. His inspired productivity will net him about 13 appointments per week (600 appointments divided by 46 weeks) that he can see on his two free days and parts of his other three, leaving him with weekends (and six weeks off per year) to recharge with some rest and relaxation.

Play around with this formula for your own sales, and see what you come up with for goals.

ACHIEVE YOUR PRODUCTIVITY GOALS: REJECTION QUOTA

So far, you have your positive state and your income goal as inspiration for achieving your productivity goals, such as daily calls. I'm going to tell you some other things you can do to pump up the volume on your inspired productivity.

This may sound a little odd, but I want you to have a rejection quota, too. For each contact you reach, I want you to get a yes, or get at least seven no's. When we go over my contact system, you'll have some scripted ways to make multiple attempts for getting your yes from your prospect or gatekeeper. But that means getting some no's along the way to your yes's. In fact, if Salesman Joe gets an average of three no's per call, then he gets about fifteen no's for every yes.

And if Salesman Joe could get callers to hang up on him less often, he might get even more no's, but he'd be getting more appointments, too. I guess he needs to learn my contact system. Good thing that's coming up soon.

As you'll recall, Salesman Joe got five calls per appointment, so that's three no's per call times five calls per yes, means fifteen no's per yes.

MORE PRODUCTIVITY GOAL TIPS

Hours Quota: Help yourself reach your call quota by setting a quota of hours for calling. Make this a solid commitment. You will schedule time, but that time will sometimes be violated. If you track the hours, it will help you get motivated to take time away from something else when necessary. Plus, you will see how many hours you typically get in per hour. This will allow you to refine your quota of hours. You can use a timer for this and do the equivalent of punching in and out when you start and stop for things like breaks.

Reframe rejection: I suppose that's sales 101, but many sales professionals experience creeping demoralization when they let this one slip, especially when they hit a dry spell. Remember that you're playing a numbers game.

Create protected time: Block out time for prospecting. You have already seen how valuable your time is in my earlier pieces. Educate your people. Manage their expectations. Make sure you have protected time for doing what really matters.

THE ADD SOLUTIONS

More action: Do what people with ADD do. If there's anything I know about salespeople, it's that most of them would rather be seeing live people, or doing something active, rather than sitting at a phone. Even though you have tools to get psyched for the calls, I know many of my readers will begin to suffer from the law of diminishing returns if they flog themselves. So I advocate that you take a productivity tip from the pages of self help for people with attention deficit disorder.

More breaks: Have more breaks. But when you *are* working, make it a sprint to see how much you can get done before that next break. In many work environments, a break comes after about two hours of work or longer. For sales on the phone, I suggest one hour.

Move: The break needn't be long, but it should involve some physical exercise, like taking the stairs to another floor where your potential fiancé works, and getting a drink of fresh water.

Stand: And there's nothing keeping you glued to your chair while you make your calls. By standing, at least some of the time, you'll help yourself stay upbeat, and put more pizzazz in your pitch.

Work with the Gatekeeper

If you do corporate sales, you will deal with gatekeepers. They occupy various positions and levels in the corporate bee hive, but they all have a mission. They must prevent salespeople from wasting your prospect's time. I almost said, *"salespeople like you."* But they aren't like you. They are pushy and they don't respect your prospect's time. They may not even be as sincerely excited about their products as you are about yours. But, worst of all, they aren't as fun or interesting as you will be after reading this and giving it some thought.

Become their best friend: Learn their name before you call them. Yes, I'm talking about the gate keeper. It will help. One way to do this is to ask the operator. You can say, *"I'm going to be speaking with Mr. Schmeckly's office, but can you remind me of his assistant's name?"* If you don't have an easy option like that, is it worth it to do some research? Depends on your industry.

Get into state: Have you mastered the state of enjoying your fellow human beings? It will make you more attractive and interesting. It will get you through more gatekeepers. They need more charismatic, likeable people in their lives.

It's creative: When they ask what your call is regarding, have a creative response that is appropriate, but not too appropriate, for your industry. One sales professional says, *"It's personal."* I suppose you could justify that in your mind because you are personable, you have a personal interest in improving Mr. Schmeckley's life, and you want to make a personal connection with him, in person. Some people would find that offensive, though. I'll let you explore your options here. But whatever you say, when they ask you to elaborate, be firm in your unique approach, and always end with, "will you put me through to him, please," or some variation of that. Be firm about it, because the assistant doesn't have the authority to buy, and the assistant won't know how to recognize that Mr. Schmeckly needs some face time with you. Since you're in a very personable state, your friendly purity will pour right through the phone, and they might put you right through.

Work the Phone

Wait on hold: Don't play phone tag if you can avoid it. Do paperwork or something while you're on hold. Even though the assistant tries to convince you not to hold, insist on holding. Tell them that you are at your desk and it's just fine. This may actually cause the gatekeeper to put a little extra umph into connecting you, since they tend to be programmed to clear the lines.

Creative messages: You're very likely to leave a lot of voicemails, since many of your prospects do not have assistants who handle phones. Take time to experiment with variations so that you can craft messages that get a call back. Find out, if you can, whether calling back repeatedly can ever actually get to the prospect or to a gatekeeper when they are in. If not, then you should message them according to your tickler system and according to their priority to you.

They are out: If you learn that you can reach them, but they are out, learn when they will be open to calls and call then. This is better than leaving a message, because it means that you have not established a history with them of them not returning your calls. You can't exactly be a pest that way. At least not to the prospect.

WORK THE PROSPECT

You have reached the prospect!

Say their name: This is such a big deal, it gets it's own little heading. Work their name in several times early in your contact with them. Show them how important they are to you.

Ask questions: Their mind is probably somewhere else, so get them grounded in the call by asking them some questions. Your fresh approach, friendly demeanor, and use of their name has probably bought you enough time to do this. You are changing their focus and their state. They are collecting thoughts that are relevant to conversing with you now. Coming from a more resourceful state of mind, they will respond to you more favorably.

"Hello, is this Helmut Schmeckly? This is so-and-so with Acme, Incorporated. How are you doing today?"

Take the temperature and ask to talk: I've asked him two questions already. His responses are very important for gauging his mood. Remember not to ask a question that is easy to respond badly to, such as a "no" question. "Can we talk?" is definitely a "no" question.

If your prospect is in an unpleasant mood, you might want to show some sensitivity and even surprise him a little with, *"would you rather I call you back? It will just take a minute or so."*

If Mr. Schmeckly sounds receptive, but says something like, *"I'm surviving,"* you should align briefly with an acknowledgment, like, *"Oh, you're having a day like that, too."*

You want to know how he reacts to your company. By asking for his reaction, you kind of imply that it's one he should have or might have heard of. *"Have you heard of us?"*

His reaction will tell you whether or not you're starting from scratch, or whether or not you have some image improvement to do.

Continue with, *"We do xyz and we are a abc."* This explains your company in very, very brief terms.

GET HOOK IN

Make a major claim: Immediately make a major claim that is relevant to his company and that you can back up. Like so: "we've been visiting companies like yours because we do (insert major claim here).

Qualify: But Helmut, I'm calling now because I understand your company is (get confirmation of qualification standards such as size). Asking either or questions helps create engagement and does not alienate them by asking them to tell you precise numbers that they may not know or may feel private about for some reason. Ask nothing that would create an answer that seems to eliminate them, unless it really should.

You are building investment and engagement: Investment in time, and engagement in attention and connection. If your prospect corrects any mistakes, that is increasing their engagement and investment. Since this is your most vulnerable point for being clicked into oblivion, you want to keep things moving along.

GET THE APPOINTMENT

Ask and Process: Once you're done, ask for the appointment by offering some dates and times for them to choose from.

You may have to go through some objections, much as you would an actual sale. Really, this is a sale. You're selling time with you, and the cost is whatever they'd rather be doing than talking to a sales rep that they don't really know.

What if your prospect says, *"I'm not really interested, why don't you give me your web address..."* You need to turn this around by citing your major claim as an irresistible question. *"You are interested in reducing your energy costs by 12%, aren't you?"* If he responds favorably, then go for the appointment again.

As you go through the actual sales process, you'll be learning more ways to process objections. But remember for now that you want to minimize any objections. You don't do that by fighting with the objection.

You may loop through this any number of times. The more ways you have to stress benefits, the more engaged your resistant prospect may become.

If he says, *"Good lord, you're persistent!"* You could say, *"If you could save companies like mine over $30,000.00 per year and make a living at it, you'd be persistent to, wouldn't you? And which day do you prefer, Thursday or Friday?"*

I just can't seem to stop turning objections into statements about the value of your product and it's perfect fit with his company, can I. And there's no harm in using a little humor to make the call feel lighter and more personal.

Creatively hook: Always think about creative ways that you can get appointments and meaningful connections with qualified prospects. Brainstorm. Think up wild ideas. Sooner or later, you'll reel in a winner. A surprised prospect that also feels flattered and senses that they can trust you, is very likely to want you to provide your presentation. What can you do that nobody else is trying?

I want you to think of yourself as calling for an appointment, not calling to see if they are interested. And I want you to understand that you are a solution as soon as they talk to you. You can make their boring lives more interesting.

MOMENTUM PHASE

A SUPER BRIEF OVERVIEW FROM PRESENTATION TO CLOSE

This section, Stephen's Sales Process, will take you from the first moments of your presentation to the closing of the sale. You will prepare your solid foundation with an attuned approach to assessing the situation. You will prepare yourself with a powerful psychological catapult into intensity. Finally, you will complete the sale with a very special kind of close. Let's start with a big picture view of this. Because these steps span four entire sections of this book, they just give a very brief overview.

A Super Brief Overview from Presentation to Close

1. Prepare by learning who are you dealing with, what some of their personal needs may be, knowing what you will need to know about your product AND the competition, and by having a well-tuned plan.

2. Tune your SELF to deliver your presentation with a special kind of intensity.

3. Use an attention-getting approach to make contact and generate interest.

4. Make a friend of your prospect, such that they feel connected with you, knowing that their best interest is your total priority. You have given them good reason to trust you.

5. Make and back up a major and attention-getting claim, engage your prospect, who becomes eager to hear your presentation.

6. Use various professional selling techniques to create momentum in the sales process. That means that the negatives of not buying are greater than the negatives of buying, and the positives of buying are greater than the positives of not buying. It also means that the customer is fully aligned consciously and unconsciously to buy.

7. Bring out objections and perform test closes that get you to the one true final objection.

8. Overwhelm the objection with reasons to buy.

9. Close the sale.

Get Started with Questions

Transition

You are now at a transition point. You have made your appointment. Now you will go from making contact to making a real connection. You have created enough interest to be heard, now you must generate enough interest to begin building momentum in your sales process.

Questions are Innocuous

Your first step in that direction is to create some initial curiosity. Contrary to your first impulse, the way to do that is to start asking questions. Your prospect will be more interested in your presentation if they feel that you are interested in them. They will also be more open-minded if they feel secure.

Feeling in control helps people feel secure. Your questions help them feel in control. You aren't talking *at* them.

You are also helping them focus on their interests. But isn't everyone focused on their interests. Sure, but you are pulling their brain power into focus on the interests that will build momentum in the sales process. When you first encounter your prospect, they are pulled in multiple directions. Your job now is to take care of that.

This questioning helps take some pressure off you as well. You aren't trying to compress everything that you know and feel into a solid presentation. You are getting input that will guide and shape your presentation. You will feel like you have more of a map to navigate by. Each answer will help you tailor your presentation and your actual offering to your prospect. But you knew that.

THE QUESTION WEAVE

In the course of asking questions, you can increasingly weave in your other sales techniques. You gradually go from asking a few questions to the more advanced phases of the sales process.

You shift their perspective with comments about the reasons to buy and the negatives of not buying. There is so much else imbedded in a person's response. Your questions are engineered to do this perspective shifting as well. The prospects answers tell you more than the obvious information. You begin very gentle test closes. This will make the process go faster. More dollars per hour!

If you ask a prospect how long they've been considering owning this product, and their answer is, "Well, honestly, I was curious about it I didn't know these even existed," then you got some really helpful information. You might want to tell some stories about how people have benefited, and what it is like to own one.

If you ask, *"What kind of experiences have you had with these?"* and they say, *"I have had a model for a long time, but it's given me a lot of trouble,"* then you really need to get them up to speed about the new models and customer satisfaction. And you will want to know the main reason they got one before.

QUESTION FOR MOMENTUM

You don't want to just assume that you can launch into your questions. You want to convey respect and you don't want to test your early connection too much. You can introduce your need to ask questions like this, *"Mr. Prospect, my goal at this point is that I would really like to get your answers to a few questions. Do you mind?"*

Notice that I'm not getting carried away, like I'm just *dying* to convey that it will only take a moment, *please,* I'll be really, really fast and brief! Instead, be very grounded and comfortable with what you are asking for. I know that you want to preempt customer concerns as much as possible, but if you go too far, you will feel and appear off-balance.

Remember the power of the commitment. Each tiny commitment of the customer moves their investment and their identity closer to that of *customer*. Their permission to you for asking some questions is one of those small, customer-creating commitments. Again, you are building momentum in many small, initial ways.

To maintain this bit of additional momentum, you must respect that permission. The prospect must develop the certainty that they will get what they need from having given that permission. That means that your questions will not slide into any pedantic discourse. Your questions will not feel like an interrogation. Your questions will never show that you failed to do your homework. You can show your commitment to integrity by making sure that you are correct, though.

"I understand that you have won a major account. It looks like you'll be needed an outfit like ours that can really provide for that kind of build out. Am I on target so far?"

ENGAGEMENT INTO MEANING

Engagement

From there, you engage your prospect with your presentations. Here are the key elements of that:

Make you major claim and provide enough information to show that, when challenged, you will be able to back it up. This is not the time to get into a data groove; do not stifle your first bit of momentum with analysis. Right now, your job is to convey the power of your basis, not the details. The Question-Answer Matrix piece will be very helpful for conveying the power of you basis. You'll be offering information such as, *"We have provided this to 20 new companies this year alone, and we still have tremendous additional capacity, as you can see here."* or *"We have consulted with thousands of Fortune 500 companies."* (Just kidding on that last one.)

Meaning

Directly state what your sales points "really mean" to your prospect. Instead those "really means" pivot points directly into the benefit statements. "We do xyz, and what that really means to you is abc.) Do some brain storming and come up with more than just one layer of meaning. Doesn't everything have multiple layers of meaning?

MEANING WORKOUT

Here is an example of layering meaning with "really means" pivots.

"Mr. Prospect, we have the trust of over 800 companies and the competition just can't seem to take them away from us. What that means to you is that we have a track record of fulfilling needs just like yours. And what that really means to you is that you will have a stress-free way to get this fulfilled. That really means for you is that we are good for your bottom line." That was four layers.

In short, those layers were: Book of business equals track record equals low maintenance equals money.

Notice that the last point is the most core. The last point appeals to the prospect's strongest drive for completing the purchase. Whatever topic you are on, wherever you start, your "what this means" pivots can always come back to the driving motive. That's because your every sales point is somehow connected to it. Otherwise, it wouldn't be a sales point.

Try this with your key sales points. Do some of these meaning pivots until you get to a typical core drive. What are the core drives in your prospects and industry? If you think it's only money, think more. Because the prospect is not the company. The prospect must fulfill the company's bottom line interests, but the prospect is driven by things like job security, brownie points, being perceived as competitive, being known as a hard bargainer, etc. And what if the prospect has a health condition that is magnified by stress. Wouldn't that make one of your key points the stress-reducing nature of your offering?

MOBILIZE MEANING

Your questions, claims, and conversion into meaning are all generating early sales momentum through interest, trust, and satisfaction.

Tip the balance: They also afford you constant opportunities to activate the negative experience of not having the product, and the positive anticipation of having the product. I'll go into this in plenty of useful detail shortly. This is that "tipping the balance" aspect that makes or breaks the sale. Your early move into this dynamic is setting the tone for closing the sale. The sooner and more persistently you do that, the more momentum you build. This dynamic is possible because you built your foundation of *interest, trust and satisfaction.*

Every element: Think of every element of the presentation as mobilizing meaning around your prospect's driving needs. For each element, you are shifting the balance toward the purchase decision. You shift the balance with the negatives of not buying, and the positives of buying.

Don't allow any element of your presentation to escape this analysis. When you demonstrate, using visual aids of some kind, this helps to eliminate uncertainty. It tends to generate belief. But is it belief in facts you want? Only up to a point. How do the facts *is presented in that medium* tip the scales in terms of core drivers?

Future scenario: When you create a future scenario as to how it will be to have and use your offering, how does it tip the scales? It feels good, but how relevant is that good feeling to the core drivers?

This is like that: *When you make this-is-like-that comparisons, how is your that connected to the forces that generate momentum and drive the sale?*

Stories and metaphors: *Your stories support your sales points, but how well do they provide metaphors for the core needs? How well to you link those outcomes to driving needs?*

PASSION PLUS FACTS

Every fact that you state should be infused with a feeling of some kind. Even the most boring, raw fact. For every fact in your presentation, I'd like you to track it backwards to it's reason for being in your presentation. This isn't school for prospects. It's sales. When you find the most core reasons for that fact, connect with the values that drive that reason. Find those values in yourself. Not as thoughts. As feelings. Physical feelings and emotions.

Now, someplace that nobody can hear you, well up that emotion into a peak state of that emotions. Then express all the feeling of that emotion as you say the fact. Nobody's listening, so really go for it.

Now, say it again, just letting that feeling color your tone and body language.

Now that's nice. That's what I want to see and hear when you're presenting that fact. Imagine all your facts being colored with the appropriate emotion! Every time you are about to state a fact, look for your emotion and value connection to that fact. The reason you are saying it. I mean the real deep reason you are saying it.

This is not an act, it is not dramatic. It is the subtle shading that boosts your close rate and wins friends. It shows that you are connected to meaning.

That is the mark of a true professional. It is very attractive. It is compelling. It means you are compelling, professional, and attractive. We want to do business with *you*.

You have been cautioned not to get people analytical or it will kill the momentum. Yet you know that there are many facts that people want to or need to know in order to make their choice. Think how much momentum you will be able to maintain with this technique.

People respect that kind of connection. It imparts credibility. This is balanced emotion. It is not so strong that anyone would raise an eyebrow. You aren't screaming at them during an infomercial. This is live, one-on-one charisma.

THE QUESTION-ANSWER MATRIX

I mentioned that you must get across the power of your ability to back up your major claim. I have a really good way of doing that.

First, I bring up the major claim. Then I say several topics that would help me back up the claim. Then I touch on one of the topics by brining up several topics that support it. I can continue with additional layers, depending on how important it is to show depth, and on the sophistication of the prospect.

I'd better provide an example.

"Mr. Prospect, our services provide (major claim). We are able to do this because (briefly state topics a, b, c, and d). Take (topic a) for example. We have perfected this through (briefly state topic a1, a2, a3, and a4)."

You have just created a projection in the prospect's mind. You have strongly implied that you can go into detail on each of the four main topics. Then you conveyed that there were four topics supporting *each* of the other topics.

You did that by using only *one* of them as an example. But the implication is that you can *actually* go into detail on *sixteen* topics to support your major claim. And the impression is that you're *just getting started.*

THE POWER OF THE QUESTION-ANSWER MATRIX

With the Question-Answer Matrix, you have conveyed several very valuable dynamics.

1. Respect: You showed your respect your prospect's time and intelligence, because you didn't launch into a deadly, linear exposition on all this material.

2. Professionalism: You have shown that you have the judgment and knowledge expected of a true professional.

3. Trust: Finally, and this is very important to build your prospect's trust and comfort with you. Your prospect will have a big picture sense of what you have to say. This alone builds trust, but it also means that you have created a *question-generating matrix* in *their* mind.

4. Engagement and Interest: This question-generating matrix creates engagement and interest. You have inserted a powerful engine of sales momentum into the prospect's mind.

When this causes questions to pop into mind, their interest level increases. And when you answer their question using this technique *yet again* you are not just satisfying their curiosity. You are building an even more intricate question-generating matrix, even *more* engagement and curiosity, and even *more* trust and respect.

5. Satisfaction with the Purchase Decision: Ultimately, what you create is satisfaction that your product *is the one for them.* And that stems, of course, from the answers that you provided. You tailored those answers to all that you have learned about the prospect and their needs up to that time.

6. Prepare and deploy: This is a very powerful method. It's pretty easy to do, so long as you already have those topics in mind. You could even write it out and memorize it. But if your prospects have diverse needs or the situation changes quite a bit over time, it is very important that you learn to improvise this. Especially since this enables you to respond very powerfully to your prospects challenging questions.

DON'T YOUR WAY TO THE SALE

People tend to know more about what they don't want than what they do. The less familiar they are with the product or service, the more what they don't want is in the foreground. It is so in the foreground, that it can kindle, strengthening their automatic rejection behavior.

If you help them reject those things that would take them away from the sale, they will "don't" their way into the sale, or at least a lot closer to it. Think of all the ways that a choice toward the sale could be seen as a choice away from something else.

The more negative a person is, the more you should ask them about their negative experiences with things that are different from your product. You should ask about negative consequences that would occur without your product. They don't have to know just yet that these negatives point toward your product. They may be too busy "don'ting."

In life insurance, I've had whole conversations with people about the state of the world. Seeing the world through their eyes is pretty negative. I focus the conversation on the negatives that life insurance avoids, like destitute families, *homelessness*, single parents, and so on. I focus on people who are irresponsible. I focus it on less appropriate savings, investment, and insurance products and everything that is wrong with them.

If any negativity comes up about my products, I use the methods spelled out in this book to turn those around without confronting them. It's amazing, though, how good my products look during a conversation like that. It even affects me. My image of the other products is dark and poorly defined. When I think of my products, my mind creates an image of the forms and brochures in very bright light so I can see them clearly. They look like they're ready to be signed. They seem fresh and pure. It seems that my prospects begin experiencing the same thing, because I can sell to negative people. Part of the reason may be that they don't get a good listen very often. I don't think they find a lot of light-hearted people who want to have very long conversations with them.

Whatever the reasons, help your negative prospects "don't" their way toward your product.

CREATE MOMENTUM TO THE SALE

This piece takes a big picture view of the sales process. It gives you steps that create momentum in your sales relationship. This will move you directly toward the final sale. The steps in this piece give you an overview of the entire sales process, but it is only a very bare skeleton of what is to come. By the way, all the steps do not have to be performed in the order I show. Many of them recur and feed into each other based on how the process is going for that individual situation.

The Momentum Phase of the Sales Process

1. Complete the aspect of your first phase by learning more about your prospect first hand. Who is this person, really?

2. Learn about their values, especially those related to their buying decision and related needs.

3. Get small agreements and concessions in line with the direction to the sale. Don't worry, I'll be helping you with this in some detail.

4. Get clear on their logical AND ESPECIALLY emotional reasons to buy now.

5. Begin bringing out, in small pieces, from them, their reasons to avoid buying now.

6. Convey to them, in bits and pieces as well as according to your sales program, what positive feelings they will get by buying, and what negative feelings they will avoid by buying.

7. Work in "test closes" at various points in order to get your prospect's real objections. I'll provide some great tips on test closes and their role in your sales process.

Steps five and six bring us to an important piece: handling objections. We'll drill down into that process, in the form of steps in a coming piece in this section.

GET TO THE PIVOTAL OBJECTION WITHOUT KILLING THE SALE

When prospects voice their objections, some of us are tempted to prove them wrong, make bigger and bigger promises, debate, or simply give up. My approach is to work with their objections and build the relationship *at the same time*. People buy from friends. Objections test your friendship with your prospect. If you pass the objections test, then you will have someone who is considering buying from a real friend.

The way to do this is to get to the pivotal objection. That is, the objection that will break the sale if it is not addressed. The trick, however, is that the person may not know what it is, simply because they haven't really thought about it. You can bring it into focus with these steps. A side benefit is that you will also make your process efficient by letting the unimportant objections fade out. Remember, as you build motivation, non-pivotal objections will either disappear, or get worked out in a normal sales discussion. Putting the wrong kind of energy into them will either build them into sticky objections that didn't need to be sticky, create new objections, or create an even stronger, but vague, unwillingness or loss of interest. This process helps you avoid shooting yourself in the foot that way.

STEPS TO GET THE PIVOTAL OBJECTION

These steps come into play when you have already identified what you are selling, and the core benefits that the product represents to them.

1. Pass the objection by, maintaining the momentum of your presentation. Does this sound crazy. Then think of it as postponing dealing with the objection. Remember, your work to build motivation may vaporize it without any loss of time or momentum. As you'll recall, time can kill the sale, and momentum saves it. This step serves both of those purposes!

2. See if the objection is brought out by additional test closes.

3. If so, then *listen* to the objection attentively. Resume the momentum of your presentation. Can you believe this? You still are not actually saying anything about the objection. Remember that attention tends to cause more of a behavior. That is not metaphysics, it's the science of behavior modification. The last thing you want to do is create more objection behavior because the person responds well to attention from you!

4. See if the objection is brought yet *again* by additional test closes.

5. If so, show that you understand by *stating* it. Just saying the objection yourself, in a pleasant tone. Resume the momentum of your presentation. Keep your resolve! Continue!

6. See if the objection *again* emerges from your test closes. That's the third time. Let's talk about it a little.

7. If so, show your understanding that they have their *reasons* for the objection, and ask what they are. This objection has shown that it has enough staying power to deserve your involvement. In fact, you now know that it *holds the key* to the sale.

8. Find out if they would buy *if you were able to handle the objection.* This turns the objection into a *commitment point.*

9. Make sure that this is really the pivotal objection by bringing things into focus even more. Find out if the prospect would like you to help them get the True Benefits (the core, felt benefits that you identified in the sales process) in a way that would outweigh their concerns. More to the point; *if you could take care of their objection, would they buy?*

10. If not, then this is a false pivot. Go back to your test closes to find the deeper, truer objection.

As we continue through the sales process, I'll provide good, detailed information about where to go from here. That includes more on handling objections.

THE SMOOTHEST WAY TO HANDLE OBJECTIONS

Good news. You have already done the hardest part of handling the objection, by setting it up for this smooth move. You got the pivotal objection, and now you're ready to deal with it.

1. Find out why they are bringing up the objection, considering how great the benefits of the product are. You are experiencing some disbelief at this point. But you're being nice about it. This means that you are framing the situation with your quality of disbelief. And your disbelief is sincere, because you are fully in touch with the value of your product. You also work your language to make the act of objection a form of work. Your customer is "bringing up" the objection. This language also distances them from the objection so that you are both looking at it. It almost makes the objection sound like it is coming from some place and maybe you shouldn't touch it without putting on some rubber gloves.

2. Explain why their reason may be the very reason why they *should* buy. Are they concerned about spending time on this? "That's why I have a sense of urgency about this. This financial product will position you well, but the sooner you act, the more value you will receive."

3. Provide more reasons to buy now.

4. Make the objection seem *smaller* in some way. Take care to not make their feelings seem small.

5. Your sales program may specify what kind of concessions you can make in order to lubricate the sale. This is a likely spot for that to happen.

6. Nail down the solution that handles their pivotal objection as well as you can. First, frame their objection as a question that needs an answer, then spell out the answer.

7. *Test close* by asking if your solution or response answers the question. Don't let anybody change the subject before you get a clear answer. If not, work with them to fine-tune your response or solution until their objection is sufficiently resolved. Remember, they have already told you that this objection is all that stands between them and the decision to buy.

8. As quickly as possible, move from getting that you have resolved their concern, to the final transition, which is to ask them, if they are going ahead, what choice they would make in some aspect (color, delivery mode, extras, etc.) You have saved this choice especially for the close, because it moves them out of the sales process, and into the purchase process.

Smoother than Smooth Objection Handling

Now that you have gone through my sales process, you have a bird's eye view of selling. You also have a process that helps to put every technique of this book into perspective. As you saw, a great deal of attention went into handling objections. I hope you agree that the whole process, including handling objections, was very integrative.

For example, if a customer was really not going to buy, the way we handle objections would keep you from getting into some kind of endless loop or prolonged fishing expedition. At the same time, it is industrious and systematic enough to close many sales that would not have otherwise survived the customer's objections.

This is the perfect time to beef up the objection handling process with more phrases and techniques that fit the structure we have learned. We learned about framing. We'll put it into practice with a special "as if" close. Then we will take what we have learned about the pain pleasure balance, and take that to another level with a tipping point technique. We are at a special point now in the training, where integration really comes into play. That is a sign that you are ready for what I think of as mastery. It's where you start improvising with methods and perspectives that are stored in your subconscious. As you master these, you will be in an even better position than ever to surprise yourself with your ability to move the sales process along.

What is this piece about, other than an introduction? It is more than that. This piece is about some things you can do to boost your excitement level and motivation through the roof.

I want you to really notice how you can combine techniques. I want you to start watching yourself, to catch yourself doing unconscious mastery, integration, and improvisation with your customers. Most of all, I want you to watch how this flows the sales process forward and closes sales. Better yet, I want you to experience your income soaring.

The "As If" Frame in Objection Handling

Do you remember the "as if" frame, from our discussion of framing. With the "as if" frame, you think about success as if it were already true. That frame helps bring success into focus.

Have you ever gone after a goal, and then bumped into problems from lack of foresight as you were just about to take the final steps? I'm talking about problems such as recognizing obstacles kind of late in the game, or realizing that there would be problems with actually achieving the goal that you wish you had thought of sooner. Sometimes goals like that shouldn't have been pursued in the first place. Or maybe it was as simple as realizing late in the game that there were things you should have gotten out of the way before you got so close to the goal, because you might not get them done in time.

To prevent situations like this, you need to think with the "as if" frame. In my sales process, I use an "as if" close to get similar benefits. It helps the prospect bring up any remaining objections with you, and do it efficiently. Remember, getting through to the sale swiftly helps to prevent the problem of the customer becoming attached to options that they must surrender in order to choose.

Being efficient at this point in the process is very important, because that kind of emotional response can create more objections out of the blue, as the emotions of the subconscious push the conscious mind to justify them with ideas that aren't necessarily rational.

THE "AS IF" TEST CLOSE

The "as if" frame is good for test closes after you believe you have handled the pivotal objection, or when significant objections have not emerged. Here's an "as if" test close: "So if we could handle this problem, then do you feel right about taking this package?"

Notice how I phrased that. I'm so concerned about creating any emotional resistance to the sale, that I make it sound more tentative. The "as if" frame, in itself, is soft and tentative. But so is the language. I ask if the customer feels right rather than saying, "would you."

Maybe more people would get married if the preacher said *"do you feel right about taking this man/woman"* than *"do you take this man/woman."* Or it would backfire when people realized that they had been overriding their feelings or they were very nervous!

"Well, since you put it that way, I don't really feel right about it. Maybe I should pass on this and consider more options before I pin myself down to a final marriage decision."

That sounds pretty funny, but isn't it what customers do all the time? They may not say it quite that way, but they feel it. So if they don't feel right, and that feeling is strong enough to prevent the purchase, then you can bring the remaining objection into focus and process it.

That is, after all, what test closes are for. They help to bring unspoken objections and resistances into the light of the sales process, so they will not gum up the works from the shadows of the customer's mind.

If the "as if" close gets a "no, I'm not ready," then go back to the point in your process where you start handling pivotal objections.

CHANGING THE BALANCE

I have a wonderful little verbal device for when the customer is not tipping toward the sale, but really wants the product and recognizes the value. This is for when they just aren't getting that the value outweighs the sacrifice.

I'm going to show you how to use a special kind of wording to massage the customer's mind a little bit. It helps them get to the heart of the matter, which is their motivation to get the value. That motivation comes from the value being greater than the sacrifice. This wording helps to crystallize that in their mind. That often rearranges their frame of reference enough to get the sale.

First, I want to put something into perspective. You know that there is a balancing act in sales. The pain pleasure balance. If the prospect is not moving to the close with you, somehow, they associate more pain with the sale than they do pleasure. Or the associate more pleasure with holding off than they do pain with not buying. Those two may sound like the same thing; like rephrasing, but they are not.

That's because the pain of not buying and the pleasure of buying are two very different sales resources. Same for the pain of buying and the pleasure of not buying. Now you have two resources, and two potential obstacles.

Think about the things that you currently say to try to tip the scale. So far, we've talked about activating the pain of not having the product. That can be things like the anticipated problems of not having the product. We have talked about increasing their appreciation of the pleasure of the product. Now ask yourself how you might directly get them to override a concern that is not as big as the value of the sale, but is keeping them stuck. Say, a person who runs their own business, but is hesitant to commit to monthly payments because of the ups and downs the business is currently experiencing. What would you say. After you think about that, go to the next piece and see what you think of my answer.

THE TIPPING POINT TEST CLOSE

Your "as if" test close didn't quite cut it. There is a lingering concern. Let's add power to the process with another move. We start this on the right foot by aligning with your prospect. Become connected with the objection. Say something like:

"Oh, yes, I know that committing to monthly payments are a legitimate concern when you own a business that has ups and downs, you never feel quite like you can lock on to the things that the people with regular jobs take for granted. Many business owners have told me exactly that. It's almost like they're jealous of people with nine-to-five jobs. I've been there, too. And that brings up something. I have a question about that. In spite of this concern, is there a way we can get you more of the benefits of life insurance that you want, than the concerns."

What? The person may not get it at first. But you have put a special kind of bookmark into the conversation, because at this point you seem to be trying to work something out or make some kind of concession or something. What could it be?

You might explain, *"Well, what I mean is, we know that the value of life insurance is very great and that you really have said that you want it as soon as possible. So I'm wondering if there is a way we can make that value more valuable than the concern you have about the monthly commitment. I mean, isn't the question really, how can we get what you want without any delay, right now?"*

You may have some ideas ready to go as a normal part of your sales process, such as a discount for paying a year in advance or some other kind of payment arrangement. The customer may get a bright idea, like thinking, *"Well, you know, I just need to make the commitment (ah he resonated to your commitment word that you just used!) and I think I should pull it from another budget item that I've been hanging onto. This just needs to be in place."* Well, that was easy.

Align with the prospect: I know that x is a legitimate concern. It *is* inconvenient. Lots of other people have told me that. I have felt that way myself, AND that brings up a question. The question is, in spite of these concerns, can we get you much more of the benefit that you want by doing this, than the concerns

AGREEMENT PHASE

THE AGREEMENT CYCLE

In this section, about the agreement phase of the sales presentation, we are going to focus on the process of getting up to the close. If you thought the last section was about that, you were almost right. The last section was about building momentum.

That's why I spent plenty of time on test closes. I know a couple of those closes sounded like final closes, but they really weren't.

You'll see the final close in the Closing Phase. In this phase, we focus more on the tipping aspect that a couple of those test closes brought up. But we'll get deeper into it. This is super important, and definitely deserves that depth.

In this phase, when I talk about your presentation, it's about sitting down with your prospect to work toward closing the sale. We definitely aren't talking about showing a video while everyone sits back and takes it in, or giving a presentation to a room full of people that you expect to sit and listen.

I'm not even talking about you cracking open the presentation binder. Here, we are talking about the interaction that you have with the prospect in working toward really getting the sale.

As a result of doing that tipping point work that I referred do, you get to a real agreement. It is not until you have that agreement that you nail down the final specifics and do the final close.

We call this a cycle for very good reasons, as you'll see. It is a process that seasoned sales pros have used to dramatically improve their sales success.

Vitamins for Agreement

I'd like for you to warm up your focus for this section. I'm going to ask you to start thinking about how the elements of this section play out now in your sales practice. First, here are the main topics of this section.

Congruency:

How well do your insides and outsides (how you feel and what you express through your voice and body language) line up? How well do you feel and show that you have your prospect's interests at heart; that you are a giver instead of a taker? How conscious are you of the real value you are providing? How well to you exude conviction that the time to buy is now? How much balanced, grounded intensity to you emote?

Convincing Power:

How many features and benefits can you muster to tip the scales toward the purchase? How well can you connect them to your prospects' driving needs? Are you intimately connected to their best reasons to buy now? How much certainty can you produce in your prospect?

Tipping Power:

Can you take something that seems negative about your offering and flip that into a reason to buy now? Do you constantly reframe the prospect's perspective toward the negatives of not buying and the positives of buying? Instead of leaving meaning up to the prospect, are you continuously shaping the meaning of all aspects as needed? Do you make it easy for them to discover and express even more motives to buy now? To you run with that momentum, spinning those new reasons into the sales flow?

Monitoring:

Do you continuously monitory your prospect's response to your role in the presentation? Do you constantly adjust your approach based on this feedback? Are you watching for subtle changes such as facial expression, posture, and even skin color? Are you watching for the tipping point at which you know the power of your presentation is moving you to the close?

Are you adjusting your presentation for efficiency, so that no fraction of your sales momentum is ever lost?

KEYS TO AGREEMENT

The essence of the agreement phase is to create the conviction that your product and company can truly meet their needs. To move into this phase, you must already have a couple of things on board. They must be *interested* in what you are presenting, and they must *trust* you. *You* must really understand them and their needs.

Without these conditions, the only sale that will proceed is one that only needed you to function as a clerk in the first place. Not that I mind those. They are still sales. And they don't take much time, either.

You know that you have won over the prospect's mind when they feel 100% certain that they are justified in buying. They have enough reasons. But reasons are not certainty. Certainty tips the balance. The certainty you must generate is that *the benefits outweigh the sacrifices, and there is no reason to wait.*

You have done some test closes to bring out any lingering agreements. And when you think you have gotten certainty, you also test close. At this point, your test closes are to bring out any lingering objections that are hiding and could kill the sale.

Doing this phase smoothly will maintain the momentum you built in the previous phase.

Create Congruence

To complete the Agreement Phase, you must create that conviction we were talking about. The conviction that the purchase is *right*, right now.

You must resist the temptation to be too wordy or provide too much additional information, because you must not lose momentum. You must also have *congruency*. You have gained trust prior to this phase. Your *congruency preserves that trust*. As you'll recall, congruency is the match between what you mouth and body are saying. As a personal experience, it is the match between your outsides and your insides.

You also have congruence between the customer, product, and presentation. They are all aligned. The presentation flows from what the customer needs in the product. That's why you got to know the customer so well. You are not selling a product at this point, *you are selling a deep match to values, motivations, needs, and the customer's communication style.* Your way of putting it across matches the customer's way of hearing it. That's congruence across every dimension.

Inner Congruity and Conviction

Your congruence will help give them the experience of conviction. Your tone, body language, and facial expressions will seem to transfer your conviction to them. Your congruence will sharpen your instincts. You will instinctively know not to focus too much on facts. You will have that barometer that tells you precisely how well each subtle change in you and your presentation is moving toward the close, and what subtle changes need to happen in order to maintain your momentum.

To get that inner congruity, the personal experience of congruity, YOU have to be sold long before you come across the customer. Your conviction must be so strong that you stay connected to everything that you know as to why the product is right for your customers. That way, a negative customer will not throw you. You will, instead, have an exciting and interesting challenge. Times when the company disappoints a customer will not throw you. You will not allow yourself to fall into boredom and taking things for granted. Each day will be fresh. Once you realize the sales value of your inner congruence, you will take it so seriously that you will do whatever is necessary to create an intense connection with the value of your offering.

That means you need to get to know yourself well enough to know what pushes your conviction buttons. Does it mean not taking the fundamentals for granted? Does it mean listening to motivational and educational seminars? Does it mean stirring your interest in what makes people tick? Is it recalling the great feedback you've gotten on the product? The ones that work best for you are your personal conviction strategies. They are very valuable for you. Think of this as a conditioning process. Athletes condition themselves in terms of motivation as well.

If the customer has some amount of conviction that tells them they don't absolutely need to purchase the product now, then the power of your conviction must be stronger than that.

FOUNDATION FOR MOVING ON

Now I'm going to lay your foundation for closing. This is the time. We're going to look at tipping the balance toward the sale. You will use this for responding to objections, for test closes, and for your final close. You'll even be using it to generate the proper perspective for sales momentum.

Your prospect's are mostly dynamic people with busy lives. Those that aren't might be largely stationary objects that have somehow gotten mobilized enough to communicate with you about a need. Either type needs to make a decision. Either type, in absence of that decision will continue with the status quo.

Though most people think of sales as the art of getting people to buy things, let's look at it as the art of getting people *mobilized to make a decision.*

Whether they spend too much time on the couch, or have too much on their minds to focus on the needs you are there to fill, *you need to mobilize them.*

Your most important mobilization vehicle is *"big reasons to buy now."* The most important status quo maintainer is *"big reasons stopping buying now."* Obviously the second one is not helpful.

Notice that these aren't just lists of benefits or reasons stopping buying. That's because of the word *now*. That tells you we're talking about dynamics. Dynamics are the interplay of changing forces. That's why your professional skill is so important. Otherwise, someone else could get paid a lot less to hand out leaflets.

Think about this in your sales practice. What do you do to identify and bring forward the big reasons to buy now. What is so "now" about them? How is what you do dynamic so that you bring the right reasons into the foreground of the prospect's mind? How do you diminish the reasons stopping buying now?

BUILD THE BUZZ

Dynamic situations are about changing balances. In your sales practice, you are tipping the balance toward the sale. You are getting people mobilized to make decisions. They start in one balance, you change the balance, they move and find their new balance in a new place; the place where the big reasons to buy now have overwhelmed the (previously) big reasons (that were) stopping buying.

To shift that balance and mobilize, let's start by thinking about the big reasons stopping buying. You could say that they are the pain of buying. Remember that we are talking about two kinds of reasons.

1. Those irrational, feeling-based, reasons that the prospect may or may not ever be able to put into words.

2. The irrational, feeling, and rational reasons that the prospect *can* put into words.

Let's make a little more sense out of that. The first collection of reasons are unconscious. The prospect may be helped to put them into words, but right now, they can't be put into words. They aren't even in the prospects awareness. That makes them no less powerful. If anything, it makes them more powerful, because they drive the prospect from a place the prospect has little, of any, control over. That's a very good reason not to expect logic to move them to buy now.

The second collection of reasons stopping buying are those that you can handle as objections, because you know about them. The prospect told you about them.

But there is something funny about this. Wouldn't you tend to think that the irrational and feeling objections would be the unconscious ones, and the rational ones would be conscious. Not so. And this is very important to you because it gives you more power in dealing with objections. That what that means to you is more sales done faster.

Liberating Your Sales Power

What you just learned in the previous piece frees you from trying to use logic to handle reasons that don't make sense (irrational objections), and rationality to handle objections that are really feelings. You can liberate yourself from logic, when logic is not stopping the sale.

Adjust your priorities: Use this knowledge to recognize the value of the pieces in this book that share feeling-based, unconscious, and creative (illogical) strategies. When an objection is logical, don't let it surprise you. Have logic ready. But don't be fooled by reasons disguised as logic. And don't be fooled by a logical reason that is really there to hide an illogical or feeling one. People have a lot invested in appearing consistent and rational. The last thing they want to be seen as is inconsistent or untrustworthy, or rash and irrational.

Re-define your job: This really helps to define your job right there! If you defeat a logical objection with logic, and this puts your prospect face to face with their underlying irrationality, how much do you think they will like you? And, since our subconscious minds tend to work in the blink of an eye, you can usually count on them coming up with another more or less rational-sounding objection, or to just fade away. This puts you into the battle zone. Fighting for logic or fighting for attention. That is not where any professional salesperson wants to be, is it? You can avoid that battle zone by remembering this:

OBJECTION LIBERATION

The majority of the objections you handle are really feelings and irrationality.

Liberate yourself: Use the objection handling process you will be learning in this book.

When I tell you about ignoring objections, take that part seriously. It will sound crazy to anyone who has not read this piece. But there is a method to my objection-ignoring madness.

When you appear to ignore an objection, you are actually busy working on its irrational and feeling-based underpinnings.

The *objections that survive that process* are the ones you can handle more directly. And you'll see how this works in the sales process flow. Each phase is more direct about getting to the sales close.

Each phase is more direct in doing test closes. Each phase gets more direct in overwhelming the objections with reasons to buy now and reasons to avoid the negatives of not buying now.

GET CLARITY ON UNCONSCIOUS OBJECTIONS

Here is the beauty of the objection and test close processes. When you learn them, you will be able to do some real magic. You will help your prospects to two things with their *unconscious* objections.

1. Put them out into the light of day. Help your prospects put those objections into words. Help the product benefits overwhelm those now-conscious reasons.

Wait! You may not need to lift a finger! Sometimes, the reasons are so obviously irrational, that your prospect doesn't even have to say them. They pop into the prospect's mind, and they dissolve as soon as they become conscious. That was easy. There's one less objection between the prospect and the product.

2. The rest, the ones spoken aloud, you can handle with your objection handling process. We'll get into that in good detail.

Before we get into handling objections, let's get clear about these unconscious, unspoken objections. They will not defeat you if they continue to reside in the prospect's unconscious.

You don't have the burden of unearthing each one of them so you can undo them. Unconscious objections tend to disappear on their own because of the things that you do with your prospect's unconscious.

In other words, you are defeating objections without you or your prospect ever knowing what they were. You can tell you are defeating them by the changes in your prospects physical signs, like body language.

THE CERTAINTY CYCLE

It's time for me to share a powerful tool. You have been gaining a lot of perspective in the last pieces. You have been getting a map that tells you a lot about where things belong. You have been getting a dynamic understanding of the sales flow and how we build momentum.

This tool is the **Certainty Cycle.** You use it to build certainty about the benefits of the product. This certainty will dissolve a lot of objections before they even make themselves known. It can also be a good part of how you handle objections. And it will even come in handy when you do your final overwhelming close.

This is the perfect spot to learn this, because we are in the Agreement Phase of my sales process, and the *Certainty Cycle* is a systematic way to get agreements on key selling points without arousing defenses.

The *Certainty Cycle* exists because the sale is not a collection of facts and features. It is more of a compelling set of benefits that really *mobilize* the prospect buy now.

The *Certainty Cycle* gets the prospect to consciously and verbally acknowledge that there are good reasons to buy now. Done right, this is no begrudging admission. It is a recognition and an increase in interest, or, better yet, excitement.

The flow of the *Certainty Cycle* is this: You state a claim based on a feature or fact, then you back it up with two benefits, the second of which really touches on a core driver. You end with questions that help to propel the sale forward.

Here is a list of the pieces. The following pieces will give you exact language you can begin using immediately. You will see it function in the example coming up. This is not some academic rote learning. This will make so much sense, that you will be able to begin using the *Certainty Cycle* with you very next prospect.

CERTAINTY CYCLE STEPS

First, you need the basic outline, or skeleton of the Certainty Cycle. These are not just pieces, they are a well-engineered flow that gets you to an agreement or an important objection. Set up right, you are almost certain to get to an agreement. You can scale this. Going for a little, incremental agreement might be best at first. Later, as you near the close, you might go for a much bigger agreement. In the example you'll be seeing, we will show you how, in the Agreement Phase, you can go for a little agreement. We will merely be asking the decision maker if perhaps the service is worth looking into. That's about as tiny as they get. But it's bigger than your first request. That was when you merely asked for an upgrade to a warm call from a cold call. Then you got an appointment. Now you go for agreement to consider your offering. What's next? Asking them to buy something? Could be!

Here are the steps:

1. The claim

2. A fact to back up that claim

3. A benefit

4. A secondary benefit. Make sure that it affects them personally and emotionally as much as possible. It needs to hit close to their driving needs.

5. Some evidence that backs up what you have said

6. Permission from the prospect to ask some questions

7. Questions that get the prospect to acknowledge that they need the product; that there is a reason to buy. Remember how important small commitments are in adding up to a sale. Also, the permission and question steps act to "seal in" the claim and evidence, helping to move it into the kind of memory that is less vulnerable to doubts and questions. This is called priming. It is where assumptions live, and it is why it is so hard to see past assumptions. They are like water to a fish.

8. Ask an agreement question. You'll see this in action in the Workout piece below. This is what the Agreement Phase is about, getting to agreements that build momentum and certainty about the purchase being right.

9. Go from there. You will use your judgment, but your main intent now is to cover material that will give you the knowledge, relationship, and prospect certainty to get you moving through the Nailing Down Phase, where you begin doing your test closes.

WORKING THE CERTAINTY CYCLE

A great thing about working this cycle is that it makes a lot out of each selling point. That's important, because your sales points are only clear in your mind. If you rattle them off, the customer may not connect with them. They will be a blur. But if you repeat yourself a lot, the customer will get the idea that you aren't going anywhere. It's just brow beating at that point. The Certainty Cycle is the antidote. It creates intimacy AND a small commitment for every one. This is really leveraging your sales points into more than sales points. Each one is an increment of commitment. That one technique is worth bazillions.

Let's say you have a seesaw. The kids have allowed me to borrow it for a demonstration. One side of the seesaw is completely loaded down with a stack of reasons not to buy now. There is pain connected with buying. There is happiness from the status quo of not buying. There are plenty of reasons for pain from buying. There are various money problems, insecurities about the product, discomfort about giving up control, and goodness knows what else. And there are plenty of reasons for being happy with how things are now. The prospect has their habits, their adaptations, their sense of the familiar, and their security in knowing what people think of them as they are. I'm sure I haven't even scratched the surface. You know how deep subconscious minds can get.

There's nothing on the other side of the seesaw. If I put one of those children on it, they would be stuck up in the air and think I was a big bully. Well, I'd better keep the children away from the seesaw a bit longer, because I'm about to dump a big stack on that side of the seesaw.

I'm so glad I have my Certainty Cycle, because it has a very special "certainty trebuchet" feature made of the finest material in the known universe, your prospects mind. It allows me to catapult certainty up onto that seesaw.

Take a collection of sales points about your product. You can pull them from your sales brochure if you are new to the product line. Create a Certainty Cycle for each one, based on a typical prospect situation. Experiment with doing it for small agreements and for bigger ones. Try it for creating test and final closes. That will build up your chops.

If you're still mulling this over, I have good news. The next piece gives you a good example, with plenty of details as to how it works.

CERTAINTY CYCLE WORKOUT

Let's take this cycle for a spin. Your prospect is concerned about the budget. But your service will save them big bucks on energy costs. You made your major claim about that. You don't want to argue. Try the Certainty Cycle.

The claim: *"Acme Industries is so experienced with installing these systems in plants like yours that we can do this with very little disruption of operations, and in a very short time, compared with anyone currently out there."*

Fact to back up the claim: *"Our extensive, documented success in government contracting with universities and military facilities has honed our skills from materials acquisition to logistics to a fine point."*

A benefit: *"Which really means to you that you will not have anything resembling the headaches that you have come to expect with contracts like this. You will have a very efficient upgrade."*

A secondary benefit that hits a nerve: *"And what that really means to you is your customers will have no service interruptions, and your employees will remain productive and have minimum complaints."*

That's hitting a nerve, because the company you're selling to is in a very competitive situation that tends to make companies very conservative about changing anything that could possibly threaten their reputation. They are in a no excuse situation. Going greener or saving money means nothing if they shoot themselves in the foot by having a change as big as the one you're proposing go off half-cocked.

Permission to ask some questions: *"I really appreciate you hearing me out about this. For now, though, my objective is to understand your situation better. Would you do that for me?"* or *"Right now, I want to get a couple answers from you, if that's okay with you."*

Ask an agreement question: *"From your perspective, do you feel like saving that much money with so little disruption could be worth learning a little more about?"* (Or, "worth looking into," or "worth considering?").

BUT THEN WHAT?

Once you have completed the Certainty Cycle you must make a judgment call as to where to go from that agreement. You want to transition from the Agreement Phase to the Nailing Down Phase.

Let's say that you want to cover material that you know will be necessary in order to get bigger agreements. You want to preempt an objection that you are anticipating. The company is very sensitive about making major changes. They have good reasons for that. You won't try to take them away, but you want to provide helpful information and reframe the situation.

You anticipate that they will have concern about potential disruption to the assembly area of their largest plant.

"Would you mind if I asked a couple questions to make sure I'm on track about something."

"Okay."

"Because I've been wondering about your assembly area, where much of the work would take place..."

Nice phrasing. You didn't make this a future scenario by saying "will take place" because that would be a little cheeky this early in the process. But you are asking about the potential future scenario so as to continue garnering the prospect's mental focus. You have done your homework. You are fully prepared to help them see how you can minimize disruption.

NAILING DOWN PHASE

NAIL IT DOWN

Finally, we have arrived at the last phase before the close. The Nailing Down Phase is about the final moves to ensure that you are ready to close. But why wouldn't the Agreement Phase do that? Didn't we do the ultimate close to get the last little nuance of objection out of the customer? What more could we possibly need to do besides dip their quill? Maybe nothing.

This phase is kind of specialized. It's your last chance to get to the close with a difficult presentation. It's where you take some risks that could lose your momentum. You're willing to risk losing your momentum, because this is your last dance with a prospect you seem to be losing.

Every phase has it's own style. In each phase you do your test closes with a distinct style. You must master the nailing down style in order to capture the more difficult sales. And, if this phase doesn't nail the sale, then you can at least walk away with a clear conscience, and hopefully a learning experience to absorb.

Do you have a superstitious streak? Do you think that perhaps I just jinxed your entire career by brining up the possibility of losing a sale. I hope not. Because the best salespeople I know have very clear ideas about how to approach a difficult sale, and how to avoid wasting time on a lost sale. They are focused on the bottom line, and that means that throwing away time is not an option.

Every business person should have an exit plan, and every salesperson needs a sales exit plan.

INTELLIGENCE FOR DUMMIES

I want to add another point here. But I'm afraid to. I mean, it might sound perhaps insensitive. I really would hate it if you thought that I was being judgmental. But I need to say that some people just aren't very bright. The test closes in the previous phases *might just be too subtle* for some of those people.

If you think your customer is a wee bit thick, then you might feel like your test close kind of drops to the floor with a clatter. If that happens, consider moving directly to these more black and white test closes as well as to more concrete statements about the product.

Let's make sure we're on the same page about concrete benefits. That means very solid, palpable, straightforward, easily understood benefits. It means benefits that are more like actual things than ideas. You need to be able to do that because many people's thinking is limited to concrete thoughts.

For example, they can understand that, "Life insurance gives your family money when you die. They will need it because your checks will stop coming and they will need to pay the rent and buy food. You never know when you might get killed in an accident. This is like you are renting a big, giant bank account, and they let the money out of the safe if you die and give it to your family."

But they might not understand, *"...and I know that your family will appreciate the security that you create for them by taking care of your life insurance."* That is abstract.

Abstract thinkers can take in a big sweep of ideas in a few words. They think in bigger symbols. They're just smart that way. I once told a fellow that a concept is abstract, but a chair is concrete. He said, *"No it isn't, a chair is wood."* He was a concrete thinker. That didn't really happen. But did you know that only about half of adults achieve the ability to think in abstract terms? Surprising, but true.

Be very careful about how you phrase your sales pitches, and take care to figure out who is abstract and who is concrete. If you are more concrete, learn abstract ways to say things to those abstract people. Your abstract colleagues will have ideas about that for your particular industry. Same thing for you abstract folk. Pay attention to your concrete colleagues and learn to speak as they do. Watch a televangelist. You have been missing out on sales!

Test Closes for Nailing

With these test closes for nailing down the sale, you will be working a little more directly to tip the balance. In fact, I'm not sure I should put it that way. Maybe more like carry the ball into the end zone, because these are more direct; more of a do or die approach. These test closes do everything you've come to expect from a test close, including taking the customer's temperature and ferreting out remaining objections. But there is definitely more emphasis on getting permission to close, and there is a more direct sense of terminating the remaining objections. But I think you'll find that to be pretty obvious, so let's dig in.

Start by thinking about what you currently do with those more difficult sales situations. The ones where your customer really just isn't making the move to the close. Think about what you are trying to do with their motivations, framing, and pain/pleasure balance.

The Opinion Test Close

For nailing with a close, this one might just be your best buddy. You will ask an opinion-getting question. Your goal is to get a small concession and identity shift. You start the opinion close with a question about their opinion. You make it kind of soft and non-committal for starters.

Start with these magic words: *"In your opinion,"* or *"Do you feel,"* or *"Would you say that..."*

Hook those words up to the most valuable benefit to the customer, according to your best assessment of the customer's values. For example, *"Would you say that you could make more money if you were able to consistently apply the techniques in this book?"*

Now, you can use contrast to see if you can pin them down to a value that is well in excess of the cost of this book.

"How much would you expect that it might be worth? From what you've seen so far, would it be more than $1,000.00 in the first year?" And your customer might reply, *"Uh, well, sure."* "So," you say, *"this book is worth at least a grand, then? And that's just in the first year, while you get started perfecting the techniques, and then get even more into your practice the following year?"*

Now tell the customer the actual price, with the attitude that this is a no-brainer and you fully expect to move right into the close.

You can use this with far more complicated things than a book. And it's easier, since you can get a value and then say, *"...and then there are all these additional features, think what they're worth,"* or some variation on that theme.

I'll bet you can think of variations on this close, too. What else could you ask your customer's opinion about that could turn things around? Just remember that you use this to create some kind of stark contrast that shows just how crazy a person would have to be not to see that this is a no-brainer.

THE PROGRESSIVE TEST CLOSE

What do you do with prospects that seem to be bogged down. Things seem to be stuck and you're running out of ideas. The progressive test close comes to the rescue. They tend to be vague, otherwise you'd probably be handling an objection.

This close is an **"if/would"** question. "If this happened, would you do that." It starts with a hypothetical about moving forward in some way, or being satisfied in some way. Then it asks the prospect to pin themselves down to something that they would do *if that were so.* You can do sophisticated progressive test closes, or you can do the bonehead version.

Let's start simple, with, "If you were to move forward with this, would you want the spa package for all your employees, or just management?" The obvious answer is that they aren't really thinking about moving forward with it. But if they don't say that, then they must have some lingering curiosity. There's some hope. If she says that she was thinking of this as a possible management perk as part of a meeting package because of a good year, that is really useful information. That will shape your approach. There's money, there's a target population, and there's interest.

A nice feature of this close is that it's framed as you asking for their opinion. You're able to test the water at the same time.

A SMARTER PROGRESSIVE

Let's make this test close a little more sophisticated this time. "If you were to get some kind of package of extras like this for your employees, would you be thinking about it just for your management staff?"

Look at the improvements. You took greater care to avoid setting off commitment alarm bells. You only said, "some kind of package of extras like this," rather than, "this," and, "the spa package." Another benefit here is that you are showing respect implicitly for the fact that this person is a decision maker who is considering various options. And, it creates less of a conflict in her mind if she isn't considering a spa package but *is* considering a similar kind of option. You are casting a wider net. You can winnow the discussion down to what you are really offering soon enough.

A MORE DIRECT PROGRESSIVE

Let's construct one that is more of a test close. That previous example was really tentative. Really, it was more for data gathering and commitment building than test closing.

"If we were able to provide the high-end gift certificates and a package of home spa items for each staff person to create more excitement about what you're doing for them when you unveil the gift, you'd want us to put that together for you, wouldn't you?"

That was more direct. It ended with a yes or no question.

You can adjust these any which way, of course. Let's say your decision maker is still a little too touchy for a yes no question. You could end it with, *"...would you want to see what our home spa gift package looks like, it's really beautiful and generous."*

There you go. That's just a commitment to keep the possibility open. *No it isn't!* Did you catch the "puppy dog close" element? If she sees that home spa package, maybe she'll develop some excitement. After all, she is trying to impress her management staff with how valued they are for a great year.

Come to think of it, why not invoke some reciprocity pressure and give her one of those lovely home spa package to take home. She'll see it, smell it, and feel the heft. While she's looking forward to luxuriating, you can move to your next test close. See if you can tempt her to stick her big toe in the water and negotiate.

EXTRACT MORE FROM THE PROGRESSIVE

What happens next? In our previous progressive test close example, you add some detail and make a special offer to her. If she says no, she'll feel obliged to give you some information about that. Maybe she is going to move into negotiating with you.

Maybe she wants to explore another option, since you put the home spa idea in her mind. Maybe she'll voice a concern that you can handle as an objection, or mitigate somehow. *"We have several men on the team that might not think highly of the home spa package."* or, *"I wonder if the men would feel funny about asking for a particular gender of massage therapist?"*

You have answers for all these things. Questions like this would be very encouraging. Aren't you glad you weren't psyched out by her earlier stuckness. I'm glad you tried the progressive test close!

Back to the Certainty: But what if this test close doesn't seem to resonate so well for your prospect? Then your next move is into the Certainty Cycle. Use these doldrums as an opportunity to build more awareness of the offering, more conviction about its value, and more of the little commitments that can get some momentum into the process, however small.

Concession or Lure? By the way, about that home spa offer you made. You didn't shoot yourself in the foot. It wasn't really an early concession that would harm your negotiations. This move is actually one that you were prepared to do. You industry is in a competitive environment. Besides this offer works well when the sales process gets tenuous. It could save the sale.

THE TIPPING CONTRAST TEST CLOSE

You could call this one the Tipping Point Test Close Revisited, because it is very similar. But it reflects the change in style that the Nailing Down Phase is all about. In this one, you go for a starker contrast, and try to push that tipping point over more directly.

In this test close, you take a benefit that you know they really want, and you contrast it with their reason for not buying. The message you are setting them up to get is simple: The customer's reasons for not buying are not as good as the customer's reasons for buying. There are not as many, they are not as powerful. So buy, already.

To do this, you must have amassed in your mind a good collection of reasons why *this* customer wants to buy. Values of the product that *this* customer is aware of.

You will also want to punch up the customer's conviction level as much as you can. You did this every time you got the customer to acknowledge that there was a value to the product. You got those admissions when you asked your questions to size up the customer's interest early in the sales process.

This way, when you do this close, you will be able to offer up the evidence of the reasons to buy. The evidence will be that the customer said this, not you.

Let's have a look at an example. *"Would you feel it was worth making the small investment of $100.00 in order to earn over $1,000.00 in just the first year alone?"* or, *"Would you invest a hundred bucks for a guaranteed ten-fold return on investment? Because no mutual fund does that."*

You will put something in front of this kind of question: the objection. Try it like this, *"I understand you're concerned about the price, but if I could guarantee you a ten fold return on a $100.00 investment, would you make the investment?"*

TIPPING CONTRAST, RELOADED

If they say no, then what could possibly entice them to buy the book? Either they are crazy, or you have somehow missed the selling point that would move them. But what could it be? Could the entertainment value move them? Could it be showing off what they know? Could it be impressing their boss.

Hmmm. Well, you could simply keep running things like this by them. It wouldn't take long.

"Well, that leaves me with a question. If you knew that you could impress your boss with an encyclopedic knowledge of sales, would you invest $100.00 for that kind of job security and pride at work?"

"Well, since you put it that way, I guess you have a point."

What do you know. I had the wrong idea about my customer the whole time. Maybe he thought he should be showing me that he is money motivated for some reason, when, really, it's more a matter of security and pride. I admit, the example is a little unlikely. That's because you should already know enough about your customer at this point to really nail it. Hence, the name of this phase. But, still, now you see how this close can be quickly reloaded and aimed at a new benefit. That's nice insurance.

A TIPPING CONTRAST CHALLENGE

Since we're talking now about your toughest customers, let's do more with the person who says no, they wouldn't do the no-brainer, the thing they'd have to be crazy not to do.

First, you have some law of reciprocity on your side at this moment. That's because, when people say no to you like that, they feel a little bit bad, like maybe they should throw you a bone. Down inside, they want to say yes to something. They'd really love to spend some money. They'd like to walk away knowing that they didn't waste their time. Better, they'd love to have a dream come true.

And their "no" doesn't simply mean, *"No, I'm not purchasing that."* Really? Yes, really. Because you didn't set them up to say no to the purchase! Look at that test close. It's phrased so they can say no to the **"what if"** contrast. *"No, I wouldn't invest $100.00 for a ten-fold return."* Did I hear anybody say, *"No, I absolutely will not buy that book."* You have allowed the word "no" to be a normal aspect of selling; part of the flow.

Lucky us. The sales process is still alive. That means we can leverage that "no" into some fresh momentum. I just *love* fresh momentum.

Here's a tip before our more detailed example. If you have a very clear goal or desire from them, you can put it in front, using a slightly different style for variety and keeping their interest. For example, if they had mentioned being bored in their sales job:

"If you knew that you could turn your job into an exciting learning experience, in which every customer that walked through the door became a fascinating way to learn how to make even more money than the last one, would you invest $100.00 for that?"

"Heck yeah!"

RELOAD WORKOUT

So let's try a reload, in a little more detail than in the earlier piece.

1. Start with alignment

2. Get permission to ask a question

3. Learn what the objection is

Like so: *"I imagine you have perfectly good reasons for saying that. Would you mind if I ask about that? Why wouldn't that be the way to invest $100.00?"* Their answer will give you another idea on how to sell your product.

What if they said, *"I'm up to here with expenses. I have a new baby, and I'm paying off student loans. My sales job isn't really paying off so well..."* This is a gold mine of reasons to buy. They need money. The book will provide it. They aren't selling enough. This book will get them going. It will even get them the confidence they need to get into a higher-paying sales position. It will even give them techniques to help them get hired or negotiate a higher salary.

By aligning yourself with their beliefs, you put yourself into a position to show them how to get what they want. You can help them eliminate their fears. With your influence, they will reach for success.

I'm sure you have good reasons for saying that. Do you mind if I ask? Why are you saying it's not worth it? They will share their relevant beliefs. You say that so that you can get an answer that allows you to do your job as a salesperson, which is your goal is to align what you are sharing with their beliefs to show them how they can get what they really want, change some of their fears, by aligning with their beliefs, saying I know this is true for you, and, let's look at it this way.

Another test close:

In order to achieve your x goal, would it be worth a one time investment of $x?

LIMITING EMOTION WORKOUT

What if you have someone who just doesn't' know why they don't want to buy. They just have what they experience as pure emotional resistance. These customers usually have problems in their lives from emotional limitations. And, without having to become a therapist, you can actually do a test close and a *reframe* around that. Check this out.

When you ask why they wouldn't invest $100.00 for a ten fold return, etc., they say, *"I don't know, I just don't feel right. I don't like to spend money."* (Or something like that.)

Your response can be a kind of understanding reframe. *"Oh, of course. I know what that feels like all to well. It's like knowing that taking the jet across the country is far safer than driving, but being afraid to fly, even when you feel fine driving. The fear or whatever it is can really control a person."*

He says, *"Well, I suppose I'm following that."*

And you add, *"I'm starting to wonder if I wouldn't be doing you a favor by getting this book into your hands so you can surpass your limits that are getting in between you and multiplying your income. Especially since the benefit goes way beyond $1,000.00. Far more money, and a lot more satisfaction. Even how it plays out in your personal relationships. Real improvements with people there."*

Then look at him with a gentle expectation for an answer.

Only look for half a second. Then look down and to the side like your mind is wandering for a moment. He will probably say something at that point that serves as your next cue. If not, you can ask what he thinks of that.

ANALYZE THAT LIMITING EMOTION WORKOUT

Now look at that language. You know you are talking to a person whose emotional limitations can really stop them, and they surrender to their emotions that way. They endure painful limitations because of that. You have to guess that they have relationship issues stemming directly from the very thing they have revealed.

So you do several things. You talk in impressionistic language: partial sentences, allusions to things that you don't need to really explain, emotional impressions.

You refer to their personal relationships, but in a way that gets them thinking since there's nothing very specific to argue with. It works really well for psychic readers, doesn't it? And you punch up the pain of the limiting aspect.

You're hoping that they will get some bile up and want to bypass the limitation. Especially after you used that air flight example. They don't want to come off as being too irrational.

You also amplified the benefit. You were saving that just in case you got a "no." It's like the fireworks displays. They fire off almost as many fireworks in the last few seconds as the whole show. It makes for a memorable show, and it makes for an impressive escalation of your sales process just when you need it. Now that's an integrative approach.

And look at what you *didn't* do. You didn't try to pin them down for a reason. You sized up the situation and said, this person says they don't know.

Stephen says don't argue, *align* with their objection. I guess that means you can even align with them not knowing. Yes, that's exactly right. Sometimes, an answer is so obvious, it's hiding in plain sight.

R.E.A.C.T.

When we were talking about tipping the scale during the Nailing Down Phase, I talked about how important certainty was. You can punch up certainty throughout the process, but you may really need to rev up the certainty engine to get that final push over into the Closing Phase.

What better time, then, to cover the various ways that you can amplify certainty? You want to give you customers ways to feel that this purchase will bring the benefits and stave off the pain. Here are great ways to do that. I call it the REACT collection. Get them to react!

R is for Reality. What verifiable situation or tend can you produce that will improve their certainty?

E is for Evidence. Are there experts or other evidence?

A is for Accolades. What wonderful things are people saying? Are they celebrities? Important people? People you customer can directly relate to, because they are like your customer?

C is for comparison. What can you compare your product to that will help them understand it, or create a favorable impression?

T is for test, as in see for yourself, as in "show me." Can you do a test drive, walk through, hands on, puppy dog close, or other experience that proves your point and establishes more desire?

CLOSING PHASE

READY TO CLOSE

The Closing Phase is here at last. Don't worry. It'll be fun! But before we go there, keep your eyes peeled. You want to see how your prospect is reacting on every level as you maneuver for the close. You want to make all the right moves as you shoot for the hoop. The subtle feedback from your prospect is telling you every step of the way. Use it to adjust and perfect.

Here's a quick review of the dynamics that you have put into the process in order to get to the Closing Phase:

You realized that the contact process is a numbers game, and you have been working to quotas and goals.

You have become so good at establishing rapport, that objections melt away.

You gave things that create reciprocity.

You learned to preempt objections by taking their power away up front with pre-framing, like bragging about the high price in connection with high quality.

You learned ways to work with objections, never fighting them.

You got into the spirit of enjoying the objections, like a lot of folks enjoy video games.

You use principles like contrast to make objections seem puny and irrelevant.

You manage what you put emotional attention into, so as not to cause objections to increase in importance. That means that, until the right time, you let them go by.

You know objection behavior can be automatic, so you break their state and pattern by connecting them with a different state of mind and focus of attention that is engaging.

You are processing objections so that they move you into step-wise commitments and test closes.

Your objection process gets you to the final, true objection.

I APOLOGIZE TO THE READER

Closers wanted! Have you seen these ads for salespeople? It sounds like some kind of macho challenge. As if through the sheer force of your personality you could close people against their will. You almost expect them to give you pictures to blackmail your prospects with.

There is a kind of mystical aura around closing techniques. But closing techniques do not exist in a vacuum. They work when they work because of how things are set up before you ever do the closing. Yes, the closing technique has to be the right one, done right. Yes, the closing technique has to have the right attitude behind it. Yes, the closing technique must fit the prospect. But monster closers are monster closers because they do monster prospecting, monster marketing, and monster relationship development.

Remember this, whenever you learn a close. Don't depend on *it,* have it depend on what you have done to set it up. Have it depend on the look and body language that tell you it's the right one. Have it depend on the spirit that you bring to the sale.

And this brings me to my apology.

How many times have I used the word "excitement?" Not very many. I keep talking about watching for those signs that tell you your prospect is becoming more relaxed, interested, and trusting. Those are such weak word, compared to what you ultimately want.

You want excitement. You want your prospect to be thrilled at the opportunity to buy such a fine product from such a fine company. That isn't expecting too much. Shoot for the moon! What's the worst thing that could happen. The prospect will *only* buy the product because it makes sense?

I just couldn't sleep at night if you finished this section expecting nothing more than interest, acknowledgment, engagement, and other tepid states of mind. Go for excitement. Now that you know so much about creating the buying context through the relationship, the subconscious, and momentum, I totally trust you to create excitement without forcing it or overacting. You were a professional when you cracked this book, and you have even more professional skills and perspectives just from what you've read so far. Expect excitement, create excitement, engineer excitement.

THE FINAL TRUE OBJECTION

Here, you will process the final true objection. The one that the customer has acknowledged is the ONLY thing standing between them and the satisfaction of having your product. The objection that this entire sales process has been leading to. Whether it took six minutes or six hours, you have arrived.

Start addressing the objection as you would any objection that you are responding to. Align with your customer, putting them at ease, and making them feel respected. You might use a phrase such as, *"I often hear that from my customers, I mean, it's a large investment, as you say."* Notice that no "but" shows it's face anywhere around here. We aren't here to attack or fix their beliefs, and we don't want to see anyone's "buts" here.

Work in your agreement aspect. You can start that with words like, *"I really appreciate that, and,"* or, *"I certainly agree, and,"* or, *"I truly respect that, and..."*

Next, turn their objection into your shared question, for example, *"That brings a question up for me, because I'm wondering, despite the cost, isn't the key question about whether it's possible that you can get enough value to be worth moving ahead?"*

They might respond with a simple, "We don't have that kind of money in the budget."

To which you could respond with a brief alignment statement, such as, "That's sounding like a tough one to move through, isn't it?"

The time has come to create the closing question.

THE CLOSING QUESTION

The closing question is the gateway to the close. Here we go.

"As you can imagine, I hear that from a lot of the companies I work with. They have already allocated their budget, but they still want the product, and I really appreciate that it makes them feel like they're out of options. I think they're real question is, not so much what their budget is, but how we can secure the benefits of the product for them in spite of that. *Isn't that really the core question?*"

If it's no, you are still seeking the final true objection.

If they need you to clarify, since you're taking some chances with vague, somewhat eccentric language, then you rephrase for them, trying to create an agreement that they want the value of the product, and the real question is how to get it.

If you get a yes, then the focus is on figuring out how to fund it or otherwise arrange it. Sometimes they just need to get more in touch with the value and find a way to do it without working with you on that problem at all. For some sales processes, you will have a card up your sleeve in the form of payment options, negotiating room, bundling, leasing, or whatever your industry lends itself to.

If your instincts (or, better yet, your business intelligence) tell you that you should focus on motivating them to find the money, you might word this question close like this: "How can we take care of this to give you the benefits of the product so you don't have to continue on, stuck with the current situation." That's good, you're punching up their discomfort with not having the product. In your earlier interaction, you found out exactly what that was so you can improvise as needed.

You continue with their rapt attention, "Wouldn't it be important for us to determine how you can accomplish that so you don't have to continue without the product with this awful situation?"

Depending on your industry and offers, this point may lead you into an agreement to negotiate, or into a close. If they were just softening you up all this time so you would negotiate from a weak position, they didn't exactly succeed. You winnowed their objections down to "the budget" with several statements from them along the way. That will be part of the power of your negotiations. You may not have sealed the deal, but getting an agreement to negotiate puts you in position to work on closing the sale. That's great progress compared to not even being sure that you were getting through to them!

Whether it took negotiation, or you moved right through settling their objections, you are now ready for the close. I hope you feel that the close itself is *anticlimactic*. Well, it *should* be! You wouldn't want anything that could possible trigger any kind of resistance, do you? With all the care you take prior to the close, the close itself should be a piece of cake.

The Close: Assume the Sale

The is the moment at which you know that it's time to close the sale. You may realize that the prospect is ready to proceed before they do.

With all that work you've done to understand them, and all of your sensitivity to their needs, and your intimate knowledge of the objection process, give yourself some credit here. Do enough sales and you have to grow some intuition as to when to do the close.

When you feel that the point has arrived, conduct the sale. You don't need a yes; you don't need to be told to pull out the contract. You've done all you can do, this is the next step.

Congratulate your customer for their great choice, wise decision, smart buy, or whatever you call it in your world. No, don't thank them for doing something smart for themselves, congratulate them in a grounded, solid, confident way. Practice this in front of a mirror if you practice anything. Practice doing the congratulation, because that will align your entire sales process. Your subconscious mind needs to know that everything is flowing to this moment, and this moment needs to be a smooth, well rehearsed reflex of an act.

Now, let the buyer know they bought your product. Take out the form or whatever you have there and complete the transaction.

Good for you, you have completed a sale.

WHAT IT THEY STILL DON'T SIGN?

Wait, are you telling me you want me to address the customer who throws up an objection at this point? You're really going to make me work, aren't you. Well okay. The customer says, *"Hey, wait a minute, buddy. I didn't say I was going to buy it."*

"Well," you say in shock and disbelief, "you do what the benefits of this product, don't you?" and move right back into completing the form. If your instincts tell you otherwise, then go back to the objection process and into another attempt at closing by moving into the transaction again.

Remember, much of what I have described is for that extra margin of sales that will boost your income. *Much of what we have covered will not be necessary for most sales, depending on your industry, of course. But any part of it could be the part that saves any sale.*

I'm looking forward to hearing your success stories. Please email them in!

WORKING THE
SALES PROCESS

ZEN ARCHERY: ACTING IN THE OPTIMAL MOMENT

When You Have Only Moments

You must have some lingering doubts about my sales process. Most likely, they have to do with those situations where you are cold calling, or otherwise have very little time to develop the relationship. What about those products that don't have a reputation yet? More than any other sales situation, these deserve to be analyzed like an exploded diagram. You've seen those. They are the diagrams where a device is completely taken apart, and all the pieces moved away from the center, as if the thing was exploding into all it's component parts. You can do this with processes, not just hardware.

You can take a knee-jerk reaction you have, one that happens in an instant, and deconstruct it that way. This helps you reconstruct it into a better response. You can take a very brief sales process, and deconstruct it into its nuances, moments, and opportunities. This helps you discover how to enhance it.

This section is dedicated to situations where you have limited time or a close to the close.

Exploded Diagram Example

One of the first things you'll notice about the first moments of contact is that they aren't so much about the sale as they are about getting attention; getting the *additional* moments that you need. As brief as it is, this moment can be exploded into intentions and opportunities, strategies and ideas.

You have a wealth of choices in how you approach cold calls. What do you pick up from their voice in that first moment? Maybe there's a hint of boredom in their voice, and you should try something a little cute, like, "Hi Fred." "Who is this?" "Stephen." (It sounds like he should know you. Who is Stephen?) "I'm the one you almost got to talk to about cutting your fuel costs by 30% last week, but I missed you."

Would you do that with everyone? No. This is just one example of endless varieties of things you can do based on your first impression of the person. Even a word or two contains a lot of information that you learn to pick up from vocal stress, attitude, approximate age, gender, cultural background, and so forth. Yes, just from a couple words.

So you see now what I mean by exploding the process into its parts. I just did that with the first words over the phone from a prospect that you have never seen or met. Then, intuitively, you approach them with the attitude and technique that you feel is most likely to buy you enough time to generate interest in your actual sales presentation.

JUST ASK

I want to share with you a sales technique that is hiding in plain sight. It is so basic and obvious that it's almost embarrassing to put in a psychology of sales book. I want to spell it out, separate from the other techniques. I want it to stand there naked in the light of day.

Ask. Ask for the sale. Ask for the appointment. Ask for the signature. Ask for the time.

Many experienced salespeople manage not to do this at key moments. Somewhere inside them, there is this hesitation or awkwardness. Or there is something about the direction of the chit chat or the customer's body that tells them not now. And then it's too late. You must understand that intuition is not always right. Part of your work as a sales professional is to fine tune your ability to discern in an instant whether your intuition is coming from your professional experience and training, or from some old hang up about being pushy; a misplaced sense of etiquette, perhaps.

While we're at it, apply this business about asking to your own industry and practice. Think of several different things you could ask for, ranging from a small move to the sale itself. Think about all the points along the way that you could ask for one of these things. Commit yourself to making a habit of asking. You will develop a whole new level of intuition that will serve you well. And, you will develop such a smooth style through practice, people will hardly feel that anything is being asked of them at all.

The next pieces will get us even deeper with this.

Perfect vs. Optimal Moments

While it is important to set things up so you have the best possible odds of getting a yes response, you must also develop the smooth spontaneity to ask, even sometimes when conditions are not quite right. *The reason:* often, conditions won't quite be right, but that point in time is the best you'll get with that person. You must practice recognizing those moments that are optimal. You must understand that optimal is not perfect.

If you grab a rope to swing out over the river and drop in, the optimal moment is when it has gone as far as it will go. You then let go, and enjoy your swim with your friends. If you hesitate, and miss that chance, the next swing out will not be quite as far. That first swing may not have been perfect. Let's say you had some fear about it, because you hadn't been on that particular rope swing before. Feeling anxious is not perfect. But that moment on the rope swinging out over the river *was optimal.* **Not perfect. Optimal.**

By practicing improvising, and by practicing your intuition, you will capture more and more optimal moments. You will become a well-to-do, imperfect person. Wonderful! Keep practicing.

THE ART OF ASKING

In seeking your optimal moments for sales actions, you are playing a kind of game of chicken. If you delay, you may lose the person. If you ask too soon, you may get a no. To prevent the problem of too much delay, here is what you can do.

Engineer into your sales process several different things that you can ask for that will move toward a sale. The more time you have, the more you can ask for things that will move things along in a richer way.

If you are on a car lot, and a prospect is antsy, your instincts will tell you that they are a bad prospect. But will your instincts tell you to ask for something? Not unless you have been developing the *practice* and *habit* of asking.

But what would you ask for? Not to have a look around, that's too time-consuming. Not to consider some models, that's too unfocused for an antsy person. You want to ask for something that will quicken the pace. But you don't know what she wants. Is she looking for a mini van or a something sporty?

How about saying, *"I'm free to accompany you on a test drive right now. What looks interesting?"* or, *"Oh, you're looking at our finest sports sedan. They're a dream. Have a test drive."*

There you go. You got on the scene, you took in a lot of information in a short amount of time, you sized things up, you got an intuitive hunch, you pulled one of your many different arrows from your quiver, and you took your best shot.

Now you're as precise as Cupid, and she'll soon be falling in love with your product.

Integrating Your Asking on a Cold Call

Let me draw your attention to a technique I have shared with you that might sound like it contradicts what I've been telling you. In that technique, when you do a cold call and the person is gruff, you apologize and say they obviously don't want to talk. Then, however, you also briefly state a grand promise and ask when they will have time to talk to you.

At first glance this might look like a weak move. But consider the integration here. First, you align with your prospect by providing an apology. This buys you a moment so they don't just automatically hang up their fifth sales call of the day. Then you slip in your grand promise. That will perk their interest or at least surprise them, and buy you another moment or two. Then, when you ask for a time when you can talk to them, that request isn't just out of the blue. You aren't just any other salesperson. You have connected, promised, and asked for something small; a time to meet.

And by placing it out into the future, you have made the time to talk seem less onerous. Now your prospect is less likely to default to "auto reject." You are not demanding their time *right now.* Not only are you asking for a time later, but you are leaving the time and day up to them. This frames the choice not as, *"Will you talk to me,"* but, *"When in your schedule would be the best time."*

If your request is granted, you will have kicked your call up a notch from a cold call to a warm call. And that's if they don't let you see them in person. That reminds me, if they'll offer a time, you can offer to see them in person, so you can show them some useful materials. You can even offer to bring something that they will like. In your industry, what might that be? Samples?

Considering their gruff attitude when they picked up the phone, just moving your call up to the status of a warm call is pretty darn good! And to think that, at first blush, this approach looked like a wimpy way to give up.

It just goes to show how important this "exploded diagram" perspective is to perfecting your approach and increasing your income.

DEEP INTO OBJECTIONS

Get Deeper with Objections

This is a really good time to take another look at how I handle objections. That sales process section gave you a lot to digest. I'd like to do a bird's eye view of handling objections as a single fly by, so you can see it all put together as a single example in one place. And then, there are some very important aspects to drill into, exploded diagram style. I think you'll find this very interesting and useful.

As you'll recall, there is a different style of handling objections for each phase of my sales process. Since this section has been getting into the theme of how you can handle limited-time and limited-contact situations, I'll lean in that direction with this example. That means it will demonstrate kind of objection handling that you might do later in the process, closer to the close. One notable difference is that there is much less focus on alignment. This presupposes that you have already done what you can to create rapport and you're moving forward more directly.

Objection handling is so useful in so many situations that this book has even used it to deal with someone who is adverse to discussing their financial situation or budget. Objection handling is very important to practice extensively and perfect.

To make this example more of a training experience, and not just a rehash, I have broken it into phases. I think you'll enjoy how this makes the learning more bite-sized and colorful. Take a look!

Phase I for Handling an Objection: Getting to Overwhelm

Remember, this is for situations that call for a more direct, time-sensitive, momentum-using style: where time is running out, where you had limited time to begin with, where you have so much rapport that you can move swiftly, or where you are just about in a position to close toward the end of your sales process.

Let's do phase one, now. These are the very general steps:

1. Get the basis for their objection.

2. Turn that basis against the objection itself.

3. Take that dynamic and make it overwhelming by appealing to their pain, needs and values.

And here are the details.

Reason Plus Attitude

Respond to the objection by asking as to their reason for objecting. Plus, display your attitude about this. Your convictions about the product should make you have feelings about the objection. Are you surprised or confused? Show it. You need to disrupt their sense that their behavior makes sense. It doesn't.

Reversal

Reverse their reason by showing how it is a reason to buy. In fact, show that it is a really *compelling reason* to buy. To do this, make sure that you connect this to their highest values and drives in at least one way.

For example, *"Money? That looks like the most important reason for you to go ahead with this. You're concerned about money, and you have recognized how much money this will make for you. Every day that you wait is **costing** you money. And with prices going up soon, waiting will just make the money problem more of a problem."*

I prefer to say *"you recognized"* instead of "you admitted" because if feels like less to of a thing resist, and if creates less of an impression that I'm trying to lord over them somehow. I'm not. I'm showing them a valuable perspective.

Tip the Balance

Now that you have gotten the basis for the objection and turned it against the objection, tip the balance. Do that by *overwhelming* the objection with their existing needs and values. Go for the strongest needs and values that you know of. If you are in a situation that didn't give you much time to learn about them, take what you know and give it your best guess. Make a judgment call. That's part of what makes you a good improviser. You, *"Do what you can with what you got."*

Phase II for Objection Handling: Getting the Agreement

Now that you've done Aikido to the objection, you're ready to move to a test close. You will *shrink the objection* down into insignificance. Then you will get your prospect to *agree* with you that *your solution is more important than the objection.* Finally, you will do your test close and maybe even complete the transaction right then and there.

Shrink

Shrink the objection using one of your many techniques for this purpose. You might use the reduction to absurdity technique.

"You're right, $100.00 is a lot of money for someone new in their career, but I have a question for you. You remember how we figured that in just the first year it was a really conservative estimate that this book would be worth $1,000.00 to you? You'll use this book for many years, but even if we just consider the cost, are you going to allow something like 27 cents a day stand between you and the life you want? That's about one cappuccino a week. Isn't your career and life satisfaction worth more than a glorified cup of coffee?"

Agree

You are *not* done until they agree that your solution handles it. Your solution is the product, but it is, *at this moment,* your perspective. You are asking them if their career and life satisfaction is worth a glorified cup of coffee. They'll almost certainly agree.

If they don't agree, they will most likely provide some interesting information that you can use to continue your objection handling. Maybe they'll cough up a deeper objection. That means you were chasing down a red herring. That's fine, because that's progress, since it means you'll be closer to the one true final objection, from which you'll close.

So, if they say "no," then harmonize and get the reason, as shown at the beginning of this formula. *"I'm sure you have a good reason for not being fully satisfied with that idea. What is that, exactly?"*

PHASE III FOR OBJECTION HANDLING: CLOSE OR TEST

Let's say that the objection that you just resolved *is* their final true objection. That means that their agreement with you (that your solution resolves their objection) is an *agreement to buy.* This means you should now do the kind of test close that is directly linked to the close. You'll see that the language I'll be using isn't quite as tentative as other test closes from this book.

Test Close

"Now, based on your needs, do you think you should look at my offering that includes this book and audio programs to really boost your abilities, or just start off with one copy of this book?"

Hey, did you catch that little integration thing? I added some contrast to help goose the sale. Just before my final mention of the book, I offered a more expensive package. That made the book's cost seem even smaller than it did when I did the earlier minimizing step. This also helps continue the force of that minimizing step. How could he say no?

Also, I provided the test close as a two-choice question. His answer should serve as a step toward the final close.

Let's say he says that, since money's tight, he'd better just get the book, for now. That's an excellent choice. And look at that! He used his earlier objection (money) as a basis for picking one of the choices! That's a big improvement from saying money was a reason not to buy. Now, it's a reason not to buy the bigger offering!

At this point, you're ready to close. You hand him the book, again minimize the sacrifice, reaffirm the value of the book, and congratulate him. *"When you start making money from this book, (reaffirmation of value, future frame) I'm sure you'll have no problem getting these other trainings (minimize the sacrifice by comparison) to continue your quest (boost self image in connection with the purchase, reaffirming the value and your positive relationship). I'm fine with cash, check or credit card (initiating the transaction) And congratulations on a fine purchase (congratulate and minimize the transaction)."*

And look at that. I didn't even say the word "pay." At the very last moment, initiating the transaction, I sidestepped a word that can trigger his negative feelings about parting with money.

CLOSING LANGUAGE, REVISITED

Let's look at that language one more time. Now we're really putting this under the microscope! We're about to explore an exploded diagram of the closing language, from within the exploded diagram of the objection handling process, which, in turn, is from my sales process. Think how smooth you're going to be as you go from objection to closing with such detailed understanding. Remember to practice!

First, here are the steps from the example in the previous piece. In actual practice, you might do these in another order, but the first and last steps are best to leave in position.

1. Symbolically initiate the transaction by handing him the book.

2. Reaffirm the value of the product.

3. Create a future frame.

4. Minimize the sacrifice (again, using contrast).

5. Make the purchase even more positive, by boosting your customer's self image.

6. Reaffirm the positive nature of your relationship around the sale, with a 360 degree wraparound.

7. Initiate the purchase.

8. Congratulate your prospect.

Okay, let's feed the text back into this structure.

Here's the language without any interruption, so you can get a better real-life feel for it:

"When you start making money from this book, I'm sure you'll have no problem getting these other trainings to continue your quest. I'm fine with cash, check or credit card. And congratulations on a fine purchase."

Wow! Did you realize how short that would turn out to be? Three short sentences! And there's so much sales know-how packed into it. I can hardly believe it myself. No wonder salespeople can make so much money.

CLOSING LANGUAGE, VIEWED IN THE STEPS

Finally, let's have a look at that closing language when it's plugged into each step, and with some comments. And I'd like you to take these steps, and plug in *your own* language, based on typical transactions that you conduct. Would you do that for me? This will really get your mind fully wrapped around this. Then practice in the mirror or on video until it's smooth as glass. That piece of self training will be worth thousands, I assure you. And you'll find yourself using variations of it in so many personal situations that it may well transform your entire life. I could tell you such stories! I'm not exaggerating at all.

1. Symbolically initiate the transaction: Hand him the book. In another situation, you might turn the presentation binder back to its first, extra beautiful image or do some other symbolic gesture.

2. Reaffirm the value of the product: "When you start making money from this book..." Making money is the key promise. It was used to handle the objection.

3. Create a future frame: You already did that with the previous words! And we'll continue that through the next steps. With the future frame, you place the customer in the future, where they already have the product, and they are benefiting from it in that future scenario. *It's as if they already bought it.*

4. Minimize the sacrifice: *"...I'm sure you'll have no problem getting these other trainings..."* This tells him all he is buying is a book. It's nothing compared to all the other training he might have purchased. He's being thrifty, while getting something that will make a big difference. He's making a small sacrifice for a big benefit.

5. Make the purchase even more positive: *"...to continue your quest."* In this case, you are boosting your customer's self image. At the same time, you are tying the purchase, again, to its career benefits. You are also continuing with that future time frame, where he already has the book.

6. Reaffirm the relationship: Your positive regard and expectation is expressed in the previous words. You are also reaffirming the relationship around the sale. In other words, you're on his team, you're a fan, you're rooting for him, and you're coaching him all at the same time. This 360 degree wraparound really helps reduce objections and inspire the customer to purchase from you.

7. Initiate the payment: *"I'm fine with cash, check, or credit card."*

8. Congratulate your prospect and shrink the payment experience: *"And congratulations on a fine purchase."* Notice how initiating the payment is NOT the final step. That is actually a very important psychological technique that I call back masking. You psychologically "seal in" the transaction, as well as diminish it, so that it won't stand out in the prospect's mind as a transition point or decision. You did this by immediately stating something that confirms the transaction and creates a positive psychological reaction *at the same time.* Have you noticed how it's practically a reflex to shake an outstretched hand? How about accepting congratulations during a high level of rapport?

That Tip the Balance Step for an Objection

This step from phase one of the objection handling process is a really good one to put under the microscope. Here are the steps for this:

1. Frame the basis: Bring up the problem that is the reason for the basis. The problem must be that which your offering solves. Frame this problem as the source of pain and need.

"You have mentioned how you are dissatisfied with your job, and really need to have more pride and fulfillment from what you do."

2. Amplify the pain: Amplify the pain of that situation.

"I know this is really a shadow over your life right now."

3. Bring in the Solution: Tell them that your product is that solution.

"Your purchase of this book directly solves that problem for you."

4. Overwhelm the Basis: Don't stop there. Kick it up a notch. Directly connect the pain of buying with the pain of not buying, and make the pain of not buying OVERWHELM the pain of buying. Start with the pain of buying. Frame it as a question, where the best answer is, basically, *"Yes, the purchase would solve my problem and make the most sense."*

"I know you mentioned that spending money seems like a sacrifice for you at this point in your career, but isn't that feeling of being so limited a reason to do something that will take away that limitation and get you to the life you really want?"

I'll bet this will really help with tipping the balance. But I'd like to help a little more. This time, I'll provide what I said without interruption, and then add some valuable comments that are about the wording. I want you to know some subtle, yet important, things about the wording.

Tip the Balance, With Brilliant Commentary

This time, we'll look at Tipping the Balance wording straight through. I'll add some ideas about it at the end.

"You have mentioned how you are dissatisfied with your work, and really need to have more pride and fulfillment from what you do. I know this is really a shadow over your life right now. Your purchase of this book directly solves that problem for you.

"I know you mentioned that spending money seems like a sacrifice for you at this point in your career, but isn't that feeling of being so limited a reason to do something that will take away that limitation and get you to the life you really want?"

Notice that I soften the pain of buying with words like "mentioned," "seems like," and "at this point."

Notice also that I *connect the pain to his career.* That's because this book is there to help him with his career AND because the pain of not easily buying a book results from the current state of his career. That's what I meant when I instructed you to link the pain of not buying with the pain of buying.

Then, the final blow, to *overwhelm the objection* with the pain of not buying, took the form of, *"...that feeling of being so limited..."* I also threw in the desire factor, in, *"this book directly solves that problem for you."*

Finally, I issue the *call to action*, which is framed as stopping the pain, saying *"...do something that will take away that limitation."*

Now I'm sure you're ready to take this out into the world.

OBJECTIONS, MIND MASSAGE STYLE

MOVE PAST OBJECTIONS WITH A MIND MASSAGE

This is one of those sales techniques that takes a little practice, because it involves six steps, and a couple of them involve a bit of a mind stretch to do, because you'll need to match your sales points up with the prospects objection in a creative way. I'll give very specific guidance on how to do it, though, so I think you'll come to enjoy this and use it without even needing to think about it.

The benefit of this is that it helps you hold your prospect's interest and get them into a more open-minded frame of mind. At the same time, you present selling points that increase the perceived value of your offering.

Example

Here's an example from a friend of mine, Stephanie, who sells a well-known weight loss program. In this example, my friend is talking to a prospect that she has approached on a warm call. Early in the discussion, before the prospect has shown real interest, Stephanie says, *"I just don't the discipline for something like that."*

This is a good time to use the Mind Massage, because you will want to use more pointed objection handling as you get closer to the close. But in this example you have hardly gotten started. You want to generate interest and rapport, and get this person who is showing early, knee-jerk resistance to be more open-minded.

I'm going to provide plenty of detail on how this works. But first, let's just have a look at what Stephanie said to her prospect.

"I have **good news**. People actually *enjoy* the program's meals because they taste so good. It means *not* having that nagging feeling that they have to use their will power all the time. And you actually get to eat *more*, because of how we plan out the calories. We are disciplined *for* you so you can do what you *enjoy*. And we *totally guarantee* that you will enjoy these meals, and the ***freedom from discipline*** that they create for you."

ANALYZE IT A LITTLE, WHAT ARE THE ALTERNATIVES?

Look at the basic purpose of the preceding quote. You can see it pretty well from the bold print. The basic message of the mind massage is that the prospect needn't worry about not having discipline. And why? Because the program creates freedom from discipline.

How does it do that? By planning out the meals for you, and making them delicious so you will want to eat them. What might a salesperson present that information if they *weren't* doing the Mind Massage style? How well would it work *at this point*?

Direct Confrontation Probably Won't Work

Let's say Stephanie simply said that to *"disprove"* her prospect's objection. It would sound something like this:

"I have good news. You don't have to have any discipline to do the program, because the meals taste so good and we plan out the meals so you get to actually eat more without getting too many calories."

This would be fine if you were talking to a highly analytical and somewhat open-minded person, I suppose. But a highly analytical and open-minded person wouldn't automatically say they didn't have the discipline for the program before they knew anything about it, would they?

That's why I began using this approach to early, automatic rejection behavior. One of the things that makes this technique relevant to automatic behavior, is that it usually expresses some kind of impossibility that exists in the prospect or in the prospect's life. It can be money, time, discipline, stress tolerance, or countless other things.

Continuing the Presentation Might be a Problem at This Point

There is another way you might normally handle this objection, and that is to *ignore* the objection and *continue* with your presentation. You'd keep the objection in mind and tailor your presentation accordingly, but you certainly would not directly try to take it away, fight with it, debate, or disprove it.

The problem with taking that tack right now is that most people who throw up automatic objections so early just won't respond well to you expecting them to listen to a presentation. They may get into kind of a loop of doing more automatic reactions, kindling their resistance. Or they may just not feel like spending the time.

When people have either of these experiences, you can see them physically change. They tend to look more physically compressed, and may show some characteristic changes in color and facial expressions that are good signs that you must help them unwind before you can really hope to get anywhere.

But if you try to continue with your presentation it and they *actually do* continue to listen to you, then you will *not* have to directly confront the objection. This focus away from their objection may allow it to dissipate because of the good feelings your presentation creates. If the objection returns in a test close, you will have built up enough momentum to use the regular objection handling approach.

How to Start the Mind Massage

Here are the steps I used to create the Mind Massage set up. This phase gets you to a selling point that helps to soften the resistance without directly confronting it. You know it is working if the prospect begins to look less defensive. If not, keep practicing. You will become intuitive with it.

1. Find an example that includes proof of, plus an exception to, the objection

Television watching comes to mind. Stephanie's prospect probably watches her favorite show regularly. It requires no real discipline for her to watch her favorite show, because she enjoys it so much and it's a passive activity. Real discipline would be to refrain from watching it in order to do something productive such as to study. But television watching is okay to use because doing something consistently is an important aspect of discipline, even though it doesn't require much will power because it's fun for her.

You can say this out loud, because it may help distract the prospect from her resistance, arouse some curiosity, and even break the resistant state. You could start with a conversational style, saying, *"This program is kind of reminds me of watching my favorite television show."* Notice that she made it personal, about her own TV watching. There is no confrontation, and it sounds conversational.

Or you could start with a "free association" style, like something just occurred to you and you don't really know why you're saying it, as in, *"This reminds me of television watching, of watching a favorite show. I just thought of that, because people watch their favorite show like clockwork, every time it comes on."* Notice that you are even pulling the prospect's attention away from herself. Now it's about "people."

2. Sales point that mirrors the example from step one

Think of a sales point that mirrors this in the sense that it is enjoyable and passive, but can be related to the "undisciplined" discipline of consistently doing something you like. The meals are very enjoyable, so they don't take discipline to eat. The pre-planning, done by the program makes them even easier to enjoy.

You could say it this way, "I have good news. People actually enjoy the program's meals because they taste so good. That way, they find themselves losing weight almost by accident." If you said your television show idea out loud in step one, you can say it with a segue. That's kind of like the good news about our program, because people actually enjoy the program's meals; they taste really good. Then they just keep losing weight without really even expecting it."

3. What is the prospect "disowning?"

Take the aspect of the objection in which the prospect has disowned something. In this case, it is her own capacity for discipline.

4. Place the "disowned" aspect of the objection under an external force.

Place that disowned aspect under the control of an external force, and express this as a sales point. In this case, the external force you chose to use is the program. It tells you what to eat and prevents you from eating too many calories, but you can say it in a more attractive way, of course. You could say, *"It means not having that nagging feeling that they have to use their will power all the time. And you actually get to eat more, because of how we plan out the calories."*

COMPLETE THE MIND MASSAGE

Now we'll complete the mind massage producing an additional selling point that works to overwhelm the objection with the value of the product. It eliminates the core of the objection by juxtaposing it with the external force, and follows up with strong verification for the value of the product.

5. Provide the mind massage by combining the external force and the disowned aspect.

Provide the mind massage, in which you combine the two elements of the external force and the disowned aspect. That will be the program and discipline. Express it in a way that carries the sales point you got in step two. That was that you lose weight without experiencing any need for discipline ("...they just keep losing weight without really even expecting it.") *"We are disciplined for you so you can do what you enjoy."*

6. Do strong verification for the positive feeling just produced.

Watch your prospect and see if you get signs that she is feeling more relaxed, interested, or positive. Hopefully, you'll get all three states at once. Now create a sense of strong verification for the positive feeling that you produced. You can do this by echoing the key selling points that you already offered, of enjoying the meals and not needing discipline. Add some punch to that point with something that makes it more credible, in this case, a guarantee that the program offers. Add the fulfillment of a secret desire (those tend to be special) at the end.

"And we totally guarantee that you will enjoy these meals, and the freedom from discipline that they create for you. But I warn you, you'll have to decide if any of your friends can handle you giving them plus-size clothes that you won't be needing."

I call this a mind massage, because it tends to produce an open-minded flow that can buy you the time you need to move forward into more of the presentation without creating a sense of coercion or time being taken.

LOOK AT THE MIND MASSAGE TEXT

As you'll recall, Stephanie's prospect said, *"I just don't have the discipline for something like that."*

Now that we've gone through the six steps, let's take a final look at what Stephanie said, and without any annotation. First, here is the shorter version.

"I have good news. People actually enjoy the program's meals because they taste so good. It means not having that nagging feeling that they have to use their will power all the time. And you actually get to eat more, because of how we plan out the calories. We are disciplined for you so you can do what you enjoy. And we totally guarantee that you will enjoy these meals, and the freedom from discipline that they create for you."

Now, here is the version with the television idea included, using the "free association" style.

"This reminds me of television watching, of watching a favorite show. I just thought of that because people watch their favorite show like clockwork, every time it comes on. That's kind of like the good news about our program, because people actually enjoy the program's meals; they taste really good. It means not having that nagging feeling that they have to use their will power all the time. And you actually get to eat more, because of how we plan out the calories. We are disciplined for you so you can do what you enjoy. And we totally guarantee that you will enjoy these meals, and the freedom from discipline that they create for you."

YOUR MIND MASSAGE, PHASE I

I'm going to go through the steps one more time, with a little more and different explaining. I want you to think of an early knee-jerk objection that you are likely to hear from *your* prospects, and come up with mind massage text using these steps. This could take some getting used to, but the mind stretch will increase you sales intuition.

1. Find an example that includes proof of, plus an exception to, the objection

Think of some activity or situation that the prospect can relate to, and that contains proof that the objection is reasonable or true. It must also contain an exception to the objection, showing that it is not always reasonable or true.

The prospect says she doesn't have the discipline for the program, so think of something what involves some kind of discipline or at least consistency. However, it that example must also contain some exception to discipline.

You can keep this to yourself and move to step two, or you can express it in a special way. Tell the prospect how the situation kind of reminds you of that example in some way. It might sound like, "This reminds me of y, and..." If you have enough rapport, you could ask them about their experience of it, as in, "You know how it feels like x when you y?"

2. Sales point that mirrors the example from step one

Of all the sales points for your product or service, come up with one that has very similar qualities. Present the point as good news about your offering.

3. What is the prospect "disowning?"

When a prospect offers an objection, read between the lines to see what they have "disowned." For example, if they can't afford it, they are disowning their ability to save, make, or budget money. Which stands out the most, based on what you know about them so far. In our example, the prospect was pretty straightforward about disowning something. She denied outright having enough discipline.

4. Place the "disowned" aspect of the objection under an external force.

Now, place that disowned aspect under some kind of external control. Express it as a benefit

YOUR MIND MASSAGE, PHASE II

Now you complete the Mind Massage by eliminating the core of the objection by juxtaposing it with the external force, and following up with strong verification for the value of the product.

5. Provide the mind massage by combining the external force and the disowned aspect.

Take the disowned aspect and combine it with the external force in a way that it expresses a selling point. Keep the selling point in mind from step two. That may help. In the weight loss program example, we had the program absorb the "disowned" aspect of personal discipline. In effect, Stephanie said, "You don't need discipline," but in a mind massage style. If the issue is money, and the prospect seems to "disown" their ability to budget, how can you connect that with your product? Other disowned aspects can be time, interest, motivation, intelligence, or mood.

6. Do strong verification for the positive feeling just produced.

The mind massage, done right, usually produces a positive feeling. It is intended to bring home a sales point with conscious and subconscious impact. The statement also helps reverse mask the previous statement, which you prefer to go by without really being analyzed.

The person may be inclined to think about it, but you don't want a detour like that to disrupt the momentum of the sales process unless there really is a new objection that you are certain is worth processing. But remember, in the sales process, you normally don't deal with them directly the first time around during the body of your sales presentation. That's a good section to review and practice, because it's hard to believe.

You do the strong verification with three things. First, repeat the key selling point that you already offered in this sequence. Second, add some punch to that point with something that makes it more credible. Third, add the fulfillment of a secret desire (those tend to be special).

I call this the mind massage because it creates an open-minded flow that can buy you the time and open-mindedness that you need to move forward into more of the presentation. This helps you give more information without creating a sense of coercion or time being taken up.

ANOTHER MIND MASSAGE EXAMPLE

Let's go through another mind massage process, to show that the pattern can apply to a variety of products and situations.

Joe's tried out a massage chair at your store, and his wife made a comment about the hot tubs, you overheard and asked if he'd like to take a closer look at your brand. "Yeah, I could use a hot tub for my back, but I'd never get a hoytie toytie luxury like that."

1. Find something that contains both proof of what the objection AND an exception.

A poor person in a tenement would consider having a back yard pretty bourgeois, and having time to exercise when there is work to be done is kind of a luxury.

2. Think of a sales point that mirrors this, in the sense that it is practical, but would look rich to some people.

"Like exercise, seeing the chiropractor if your back goes out, or having a back yard to play with the kids in or have a barbecue, our hot tubs are practical for people who need to decompress from their work day, and get some therapy for their backs. We even have special attachments for your back therapy."

3. Take the aspect of the objection in which the prospect has disowned something. In this case, it is his desire to have a luxury. Place that disowned aspect under the control of an external force. In this case, the external forces are the back pain and the therapy. You could say, "I know that when I'm too stressed or my back demands care, I have no choice but to get what I need so I can stay productive and put food on the table."

4. Provide the mind massage, in which you combine the two elements. "After a bout of back pain, it's a real luxury to get back to work so I can decide what is a luxury and what isn't." Note how this language mirrors that used by many men who are heads of households and don't want to appear too fancy. *"I decide what is and isn't xyz,"* *"Because I said so,"* and so forth. This enhances rapport around that mentality, while inserting the product as a part of that mentality.

The contradiction that helps create the mind massage is the bit about the luxury of getting back to work. The luxury of the hot tub (which Joe had "disowned") is transferred to his job via the therapeutic and stress-reduction values.

5. Add a statement that helps to reverse mask what you just said, and create a sense of strong verification for the positive feeling that you produced. Echo the key selling points that you already offered, of enjoying the meals and not needing discipline. Add some punch to that point with something that makes it more credible. Add the fulfillment of a secret desire at the end. *"And with the top-notch engineering and equipment we use, we offer a five-year guarantee that is beyond the industry standard, no matter how often you need it or just have your friends over to enjoy it."*

THE PSYCHOLOGY OF MONEY AND BUDGETS

WHERE IS THE MONEY?

People have trouble talking about money, and they never have enough. So, as a salesperson, you have trouble getting people to discuss money, but if they do, they tell you there isn't enough. But you must qualify your prospect, or your sales process will be inefficient, with time wasted on the wrong people. Your smooth sales process depends, in part, on presenting options that your prospects feel they can afford.

You need ways to learn about what your prospects can afford, at least you do in many industries. A common problem you face in getting the financial question answered is that your prospects resist the feeling that they are surrendering control; that it will be easier for you to manipulate them somehow.

They more they show they have, the harder it will be to bargain with you, or the less willing you'll be to show money-saving options. However, their automatic behavior of, *"It's none of your business,"* is not impenetrable.

Your ability to gain rapport and manage the emotions in the process will certainly help here. Your clear intention to help them, and your problem-solving focus help to gain trust and information.

The preceding sections on my sales process help a great deal with this, of course. They show you how to refocus onto needs and solutions, and this puts the value of the product above the sacrifices necessary to get it.

You wouldn't have to do that if you were selling insulin, and your prospect had diabetes. But your intense connection to the value of the product helps you convey that they must buy it.

REVEAL THE MONEY WITH OBJECTION HANDLING

There is more that you can do to qualify your prospect. Your wealth of business intelligence and sources can help you. But let's look at the personal side.

You can use what you have learned about handling objections to get more financial information.

You could start an objection-handling style process with these simple words: *"I know people have their reasons for hesitating about discussing their budget, but could I ask about your concern about sharing this piece?"*

You did a little alignment move with the "people have" part. And you avoided making it sound like an obstacle they should be attached to by merely calling it "hesitating," which implies being about to do something, but just hesitating for a moment. If you said they "are hesitant" that would amplify it into a state of being rather than a fleeting feeling, so the wording is very important.

I don't need to pry into all the details of your finances, of course, I would just like to know about your budget for this kind of thing because I can help best when I understand your goals."

In that sentence, you reduced the alarm factor, by showing respect for their privacy with, *"I don't need to pry."* You also used the automatic trigger of a "because" clause, after you asked again for the information. You even avoided saying "but" as in, *"but I would like to know,"* by saying, *"I would just like to know."* That's integration! Keep it up!

From there, you can use any of the objection handling patterns from my sales process.

The Fluid Budget

People shuffle their priorities, mentally taking some money away from one area and shunting it into another as their priorities change. They base their budget on their priorities in the first place, if you don't mind me stating the obvious. That means that the impact of your sales presentation in highlighting the value of your product will recalibrate their budget as you proceed.

This has important implications. One is that you might be making a big mistake if you get the prospect to say how much they intend to spend on that budget area or type of product. Remember that when people verbally commit to something, it tends to fix them to it because they want to be consistent, and because they have set an anchor point. But if your presentation could make them increase it's priority, wouldn't you want it to be very easy for them to shift their priorities without the encumbrance of a commitment, the hob goblin of consistency, and that pesky anchor point?

Additionally, many industries involve seeing prospects who are really vague about their own finances. This is especially true for prospects who are making purchases that do not require much deliberation about their budget. It may be a matter of loosening their psychological grip on their credit card.

All of this is to make the point that you do not want to create an artificial barrier to sales by thinking of budgets and financial objections as being sacrosanct or fixed, because they aren't. You are deploying your sales skills in a much more fluid situation, and so they must be relevant to that dynamic. This book is putting you into a very advantageous mindset for doing just that.

Your skills for focusing on desires (or criteria), and pain (or needs), while managing psychological dynamics like frames and automatic behavior are just what that fluid reality (people) responds to best.

Getting to the Numbers

For the many situations in which budget numbers are helpful, you can usually just go for ball park figures. That's because they want to fudge them in order to negotiate with you, because they don't want to risk manipulation, because the information is private, and because, most importantly, you know that the budget may change as you talk with them.

You can defuse their resistance and start talking money by introducing the subject this way: *"Without making any kind of commitment,"* (this would be a really good point at which to put your pen down and lean back and relax a little, maybe take a nice, full breath along the way...you aren't holding your shoulders up around your ears as you do this, are you?) *"what kind of budget are you thinking of, just ball park?"*

When they give you a number, you can show your interest in a way that conveys a professional, helpful attitude. You might even drop in a comment like, *"Oh, yes, that's very helpful, because there are solutions in that range that I think you'll feel are very effective and thrifty."*

You also want to see if they will give you a clue as to how elastic that is. Not that you don't already know these budgets can be fluid, depending on the company or person. So you might say, *"Is that a broad range or do they have you pretty well pegged to that amount?"* Or, if they give a range, *"Is that closer to $20,000.00 or $25,000.00?"*

Dealing with financial issues up front is often a real sale saver. If money is an issue, resolving concerns about it early on will prevent loss of momentum as you get closer to the close. You want it to be like an asteroid headed for a moon. It accelerates until it hits. It doesn't lose steam anywhere along the way.

GETTING TO THE VALUE

The flip side of the coin is finding out more about the value of the product to them. An ideal place to start is in the *cost* to them of *not* having the product or service. In situations where there is a money cost, you want numbers. Let's say you're selling inventory management software.

"How much would you say you are losing because of the problems your legacy system is causing with inventory management. I know there are issues with unnecessary outlays for warehousing, and inability to meet deadlines competitively."

If they don't know, maybe you can get them to guess. You might even be in an industry where you can create an alliance around that, because your work together in getting a number will help your prospect sell this to upper management. Then you'll really have you foot in the door.

Another phrasing: *"What is it costing you, ultimately, to keep having these problems?"*

"Ultimately" helps them think of the full costs over the long haul, and "keep having" ratchets up the pain factor. Excellent!

ADVANCED SKILLS
AND KNOWLEDGE

AUTOMATIC BEHAVIOR

Don't Deny It

I'm a little worried about how you are going to take to these automatic behavior articles. That's because of a major automatic behavior generators that affects humans. It makes us feel like everything we do is a conscious choice. It can make us *automatically* reject information about automatic behavior. It can even happen when we do automatic behavior and someone points it out. People tend to deny the evidence. A friend of mine asked another one of my friends to prove that he knew hypnosis. He hypnotized her and then, afterwards, told her all the ways she could tell that she was still in light trance. She insisted that she was not hypnotized.

Maybe this is an evolutionary survival mechanism. But this is a powerful sales tool, so you should not be in denial about automatic behavior. But please don't abuse your customers' denial.

The most automatic but complicated behaviors in animals, as you know, are called instincts. Even though we know that animals aren't as aware or thoughtful as we are, it's hard to believe just how true this is. For example, when ants die, they emit a chemical. This triggers the other ants to put them on the dead ant pile. But if a mischievous scientist comes along and puts a little of that chemical on a live ant, the ant's friends will pick the ant up and carry him over to the dead ant pile. His struggles to get loose are not enough to tell his friends that he is alive. Red breasted male robins will fight for territory with other red breasted robins. They will even attack a clump of red feathers. But if you color a male red breasted robin's breast a different color, the other robin will not fight him. In both these examples, there is no thinking, otherwise the behavior would be quite different.

Imagine what it would be like if you could sprinkle some kind of color or magic onto your product and get everyone to buy it automatically! Wait! That's going too far! It might go to your head, causing you to enslave the entire human race and establish a galactic empire... Or not. But I can tell you that there are many ways to use automatic triggers to help the sales process along, to improve your rate of success, and to give you more options for designing your sales processes. That's what this section is about.

A FANTASTIC SALES RESOURCE: AUTOMATIC BEHAVIOR

Many a salesperson has improved sales by capitalizing on prospects' automatic behaviors. I don't mean to say that we're all robots. We certainly aren't as automatic as most animals, but sometimes we all act automatically. This definitely plays a role in many of our buying decisions. It is essential that you use these automatic behaviors in your sales techniques, because they are nearly universal, and they are quite powerful. You may be missing out on many opportunities for sales because of untapped automatic behaviors, because many of these opportunities are hidden.

The articles about automatic behaviors will enlighten you about all the key aspects, so that you can apply this to all aspects of sales. This will also help you better grasp many of the techniques and perspectives that we share, making them easier to learn and apply in an intuitive, holistic way.

There are also two levels of sophistication to automatic behaviors: simple and complex. You'll see that I'll be pushing the envelope a little to call the complex ones automatic, because actually the complex automatic behaviors are kind of in between automatic and conscious. But you'll love the idea, because it adds a powerful tool called behavior priming to your toolbox.

We have three ways into these automatic behaviors, constituting three opportunities. We will start with very direct automatic behavior triggers, then we'll get into a broader idea of automatic behavior generators, and then we'll get into automatic behavior pressure. Each level requires more orchestration and planning than the previous. But the simplest level, that of triggers, is the one that you can most directly treat as a scientific experiment. You provide it, see how a number of customers respond, and you'll know pretty quickly if you have a good trigger.

Your job is to take all this in and think about ways that this factor can be a resource in your sales process. This requires a bit of an open mind, because these opportunities are not always very obvious. In fact, they can be surprisingly counter-intuitive, as we shall see.

SIMPLE TRIGGERS

An automatic behavior is a predictable behavior that takes place because of something that set it of, and that behavior tends to be pretty reliable. In some situations, it's so automatic that you can count on it. The more unconscious the behavior is, the more reliable it is.

The thing that sets off a truly automatic behavior is called a trigger. The connection between an automatic behavior and its trigger is so tight that it's like cause and effect. An automatic behavior trigger does not lead to what you'd call a well-considered decision, by any means.

Consider humans and animals. In one, their automatic behavior can be triggered by a single feature of the situation, and that behavior can be so automatic as to be laughable. And then there's animals. Okay, I'm kidding. This is true for animals *and* humans alike. Scientists debate just how automatic people are in comparison to animals, but humans can be pretty automatic, as we'll see.

Keep in mind that, while automatic behaviors are very predictable in animals, humans are another story. One the one hand, many people have learned from experience or thought deeply enough about something to not be as automatic as other people. On the other hand, automatic behaviors are predictable enough that, statistically speaking, you come out ahead by putting the triggers in place.

I mentioned that you can be very scientific with automatic behavior triggers

THE PRIMITIVE POWER OF AUTOMATIC BEHAVIOR

Pole cats are natural enemies of turkeys. These cats are much larger than house cats, but not as big as tigers. They are big enough to kill people. If you've never thought of a turkey as anything but an awkward bird, watch it turn into a fighter when a pole cat approaches. The crazy thing about turkeys, though, is that they will also turn into fighters if a stuffed pole cat approaches. That's another example of automatic behavior. Especially when you see a turkey attack a cheap imitation of a pole cat. But if you put a recorded sound of a baby turkey in the stuffed pole cat, the turkey won't attack. Now that's a REALLY automatic behavior. Nobody said turkeys were especially bright. I just wonder why pole cats never evolved the ability to make baby turkey sounds.

What we're talking about here, of course, are instincts. Grooming is a great example of an instinct, because it appears that people with obsessive compulsive disorder (OCD) have a brain problem that allows the ancient grooming compulsion to break through. In these folks, urges such as pulling out hair one by one or excessive hand washing are so automatic that the person may not be able to control them, even though the consequences can be devastating. A person can't hold a job if it takes them four hours to run through a series of useless rituals before they can leave the house, not to mention rigid behavior patterns that may make them very inefficient at work.

OCD is an extreme example of automatic behavior in people, but that's why it's a good one; it shows that automatic behavior can be very powerful. But what puts you in the driver's seat as a salesperson are the *triggers* of automatic behaviors. These behaviors are not just animal tricks and mental illnesses. They are a big part of what makes people tick. When you start using the automatic behavior triggers that facilitate sales, you are taking hold of a very powerful force. You will need to stay on top of your ethical guidelines, because you may feel like you're getting away with something.

But, now that we have an appreciation for the irrational power of automatic behavior, we need to move beyond instinct and dysfunction to the real people power that can fill your sails. We are going to start talking very directly about the automatic behaviors that you can trigger as a salesperson, how to trigger them, and how to manage the sales process with this in mind.

AUTOMATIC BEHAVIOR IN SALES

Individuality: As you deploy your many automatic behavior triggers, you'll see something interesting and useful. Some people are much more pressured by these triggers than people are. For example, some people are strongly compelled to complete things. Those folks have trouble resisting the forms close (where you hand them the form to complete and sign).

Pressure: Remember that these automatic behaviors come from more primitive parts of the brain than they appear to. That's why I talk about the "pressure" to act on them. People are not usually aware of that pressure when it occurs. They tend to notice it when they feel pressured to do something that they don't really want to do, like return a favor at a really inconvenient time. Research studies catch people doing things that don't make a lot of sense, until you see the automatic behavior patterns that we all share. Of course they are stronger or weaker in individuals. But statistically, you can count on them.

In the sales process: As a salesperson, you can trigger a lot of automatic behavior for things like incremental commitments that add momentum to the sales process. The more your learn to recognize and use these opportunities, the stronger your sales will be. So part of getting to know your customer is getting to know their individual automatic behavior profile. However, since these behaviors are nearly universal, you should also engineer automatic behavior triggers into your routine sales process including the environment. These methods will not affect everyone the same way, but the *average* effect will increase sales *overall*.

ETHICS AND AUTOMATIC BEHAVIOR

Where automatic behavior is concerned, ethics is a tricky subject. Some people would have you banish it completely from your approach. But that is impossible.

Our automatic behaviors run very deep and are interactive. You could never tease out the full effect of automatic behavior triggers and pressures on our behavior. You could try to never use the triggers consciously. But this seems extreme.

These automatic behavior triggers don't turn people into robots. They create an inner sense of pressure to respond. And it's true that the result can be unconscious compliance. But I'm content to use them, so long as I am not betraying anyone's trust. By that I mean attempting to trick someone into doing something that would be bad for them.

There are drugs that con artists use to get people to give them access to their homes so these bandits can run away with their possessions. Now that is truly compromising a person's free will.

Automatic behavior triggers would only be truly unethical if we were primitive animals. But then, we wouldn't care about ethics if we were primitive animals. That's what sets us apart, except for con artists, of course.

PRESSURES

Now that we have talked about simple triggers in animals and people, let's talk about the broader triggers called pressure triggers. Although pressure triggers are not the simplest, they can look pretty simple. That's because a pressure trigger creates an internal pressure inside the prospect to do a kind of behavior. Not a totally specific behavior, but a kind of behavior. A pressure trigger can generate pressure that the person was not feeling, or it can be used to capture a pressure that already exists. Either way, you are working with a pressure that is inside the person, waiting for a catalyst to turn it into buying behavior. Just to be clear, we aren't talking about using high-pressure sales tactics, although those are a form of pressure trigger. When I had my wallet taken at knife-point, I was pretty sure that the mugger was using a high-pressure sales tactic.

When a tourist wants to save time for fun in the sun, but is taking some time to bargain shop, they are experiencing some efficiency pressure. They don't want to log onto the Internet and spend an hour learning all the ins and outs of jade jewelry. This efficiency pressure can cause them to use a single, simple cue, such as price, in evaluating whether they are making the right purchase. They don't want to get something cheap, and price is usually a good way to tell if something is of good quality. In this example, the vendor raised the price of their jade jewelry and sold it very fast.

GENERATORS

A generator trigger is even less of a simple, see-this-do-that, knee-jerk formula than pressure triggers are. It varies more by individual than other triggers, and it takes a little more orchestration. By orchestration, I mean arranging the elements of the sales process, kind of like a composer deciding what instruments will play what parts for a musical piece.

The automatic behavior of reciprocity is a great example. It's simple enough. If you do something nice for a prospect, they will usually feel driven to give something back, especially if you ask for it, and it is not too much. For example, when you give a free sample, people feel obligated to listen to a brief spiel about the product. Reciprocity is a "generator" because it can generate quite a variety of behaviors in response, and because the prospect has more conscious control over this behavior than a simple trigger, or even a pressure trigger. That's why in generator trigger examples, you're more likely to see direct verbal interaction used to get the response, and why, in pressure triggers, it's easier to get away with indirect verbal behavior. But those are just generalizations.

Table: **Universality in Trigger Design,** showing that triggers can be nearly universal to all people, while others vary much more from person to person.

	Simple Trigger	Generator Trigger
Universal *(Applies to most people)*	Most reliable	Reliable statistically
Individual *(Must be determined what works for who)*	Must be customized	Must be orchestrated

Auto Behavior, the Big Picture

All of your automatic behavior work on your sales process will fall into one of the six boxes in this handy little table. It shows how some triggers are for simple, knee-jerk responses, while others are more broad and general. A good example of a knee-jerk response happens when the forms close (when you pull out the sales form and start filling it out) washes away any remaining objections and the person lets you close the sale. That is in the Complex/Direct Trigger box, nicknamed "Impulse." Anything simpler than that would pretty much requires that the person have a mental disorder or impairment. That is the Simple/Direct Trigger box nicknamed "Primitive." That box is considered off limits because you'd definitely be taking advantage. Only cheesy con artists work that box, and they are despised by true sales professionals.

Of course, this table is a little simplified in order to get the ideas across. For example, you could take the reciprocity strategy out of the Simple/Generators "Drive" box and make a complicated, orchestrated use of it that is very much customized to an individual. That would put it in the Complex/Generators box, nicknamed "Repertoire."

Table: Matrix of Pathways and Levels of Automatic Behavior, with a "nickname" for each of six cells, followed by an example.

Pathways -------------------- Levels	Direct Trigger (Narrowest, Most Internal)	Pressures	Generators (Broadest, Most External)
Simple Try it, and track results statistically	**"Primitive"** (Unethical) Seen in animals or people with certain mental disorders or impairments.	**"Percept"** Ambiguity vs. Efficiency Pressure leads to valuation based on price alone.	**"Drive"** Reciprocity vs. Feeling Obligated leads to concession.
Complex Orchestrate & customize, can also be tracked.	**"Impulse"** To complete things, as in the "forms" close.	**"State"** "Urgency" close leads to buying now (e.g., today-only offer).	**"Repertoire"** Identity shifting brings out more of a type of behavior.

"BECAUSE"

Sometimes a little word will make a huge difference. Just giving a reason for a request, even if it doesn't make sense, may trigger cooperation. But you must use the right word.

This trigger is so simple and easy, I'm almost embarrassed to put it in writing. But once you start using it, you'll find that it deserves to be one of your habits. Research has shown that when people make requests, they are much more likely to get a favorable response if they give a reason. The reason doesn't have to add any new information. In other words, it doesn't have to be a good reason. I'm sure that a bad reason would trigger some skepticism or resistance, but who would think a non-reason would work?

But there's a catch, it seems that the results hinge upon how you give the reason. In the research that first pointed this up, someone would ask a person in line for the copy machine if they could cut in. And, like I mentioned, they would give a non-reason, like, "Because I need to make some copies." Is that lame, or what? But it worked much better than not giving a reason. Now here's the key. In between the request and the reason, you have to insert the magic word, "because." I'm not kidding! Memorize this and start practicing it immediately so it becomes a habit.

"May I use the copy machine, because I have to make copies."

"I'd like to know his secretary's name because then I can leave messages without bothering him directly."

"Please give me your card so I can share any good resources I come across."

"Lemme ask you to turn down the radio because I'd better get some calls out of the way."

"May I have your hand in marriage because I'm a bachelor." Well, maybe not. I mean, you DO have to consider the size of the request. We're talking about smaller requests.

I wonder if this works because the conscious mind wants to think it's in charge and the "because" gives it some feeling of control. Or could it be that this sequence appeals to some primitive syntax that shortcuts the conscious mind altogether? Since the reason doesn't necessarily have to be a good one, maybe it's the latter. There's another funny thing about this. It shortcuts automatic resistance, so I don't know if it's an automatic behavior trigger, or an automatic behavior preventer. Either way, it's a very smooth move!

SOME OF MY FAVORITE TRIGGERS

Here is a quick reference to my favorite triggers for automatic behavior. You've heard me referring to them throughout this book. Let this remind you to master them and use them systematically.

Reciprocity: The strong need people have to return a favor. If you can create this need, you can ask for small things such as the opportunity to do your presentation or to acquire names for warm calls. How can you invoke more reciprocity in your practice? Don't just think about gifts, think about favors or assistance.

Bonding: When a person connects on a deeper level of trust with someone. If only you could bottle it. You almost can! The material on building rapport is very important to bonding. Just add a little *time* and you have bonding. People bond with kidnappers, as in Stockholm syndrome. Surely they can bond with you!

Consistency: The pressure to maintain trust and credibility by continuing opinions and patterns of behavior already established. An important thing about this is that people play trick on themselves. After they have done something, they seem to *recalibrate* their *mental timeline* in order to feel more consistent. After winning a bet, people think that they were more certain than they really were.

PERSUASION MASTERY

THE EFFICIENCY TRIGGER

People have an ongoing pressure to be efficient. This is not just a conscious pressure. It goes all the way from their subconscious minds to their cells. We depend on efficiency, but it isn't obvious. Why do peacocks expend so much biological energy to produce their spectacular plumage? Why do people around the world have complicated, time-consuming rituals, such as half time shows, that take so much time and preparation? The answer is that these larger expenditures of time and energy serve important purposes and have evolved over time.

But if you look on the smaller scale, you will see a tremendous priority put onto efficiency. Even in our muscles, there are triggers that cause a muscle to relax, so that it's opposite muscle can move with minimum energy and maximum speed at the time it is activated. When we create proteins, our cells make an efficiency compromise, transcribing them in sections in order to reduce the likelihood of an error. When we make buying decisions, we must decide how much time to take to make that decision. Often, our efficiency drive gets triggered without our knowledge. This happens when something is priced higher than normal, and we assume that it is of higher value.

You will find many opportunities to use the automatic behavior of efficiency in sales.

VALUATION AND PRIMING: A TEAM

Valuation: We constantly evaluate. If anybody tells you to stop being judgmental, ask them how. I think it probably takes years of meditation on a mountain, and then only if the high altitude kills enough brain cells. Value is very psychological. A product or service can veer wildly up or down in people's estimation depending on subtle cues. Chivas Regal wine dramatically increasing their price in order to capture tremendous market share is a classic example. Not that a price increase will always increase perceived value. People rate the size of requests. If you make a small enough request, you will get a concession that you can use, but it will fly under their radar and not provoke resistance. Are you capturing all the sales that could be promoted by subtle cues about value? You wear clothes that give the right message about the value of your product. Hip clothes tell people you have a product that is of value to hip people. If they are perceived as cool, they got the value they wanted. If you wear an expensive, well-tailored suit, then your clothes connote high quality or prestige.

Priming: Priming is a type of unconscious memory. One of the things it triggers is a sense of familiarity. This in turn makes people prefer what they are familiar with. That's why product placement is so valuable. The advertiser isn't trying to get you to buy. They aren't even trying to get you to consciously remember the product. Their goal is simply to have you feel good about it when you see it. You won't know why you feel good about it, though. Most product placements go unnoticed by our conscious minds. I'll share more with you about this amazing form of memory. It can be a great challenge or asset to sales depending on whether you have the right tools. I'll provide them in this book. It is powerful in a way that led me to call it sticky memory. Primed memory is responsible for much of the valuation we do. That's what makes priming so automatic. This section is not talking about conscious, deliberate valuation. All automatic behavior stems from the unconscious, even if you become conscious of it, even if you are able to short circuit it.

Trigger Weaves

Take a look at some of the ways triggers can work together in ways that are very valuable for sales professionals.

Commitment: Consistency pressure and social pressure team up in our minds to make us lock onto our commitments. Nearly everyone has a strong pressure to stay consistent with their commitments. If you get some commitments during the sales process, you can use them make progress.

Identity: Consistency in identity is important, but commitments and other factors can shift identity. In research studies, people have made really large commitments that they would not normally make. They did it simply because those commitments were in line with a shift in their identity. Just getting them to make a small commitment to the principle of civic duty has caused this kind of identity shift. It greatly increased people's willingness to allow a large public safety billboard to be put on their front lawn! As a salesperson, you can use various methods to get identity shifts that then allow you to get larger commitments or greater appreciation for a feature.

Efficiency vs. Value: This could be titled "Efficiency vs. Whatever" because the drive to efficiency competes with everything else. The less we do our homework before a purchase, the more they have to rely on factors under the salesperson's control. People usually at least have a clue what things are worth, but in some markets, the wrapping matters more than the contents. An investigation into chocolate revealed this.

Social Truth: People have no idea how much they pick up cues from other people about how to act. Try standing facing backward in a crowded elevator. Just the thought sends an odd feeling through the body. That's the pressure to conform. Non-conformists probably have a unique brain configuration that is somewhat immune to social pressure. Even how intensely people experience pain (including their heart rate) is affected by how another person responds to the same pain. Videos of children enjoying dogs or playing have helped children get over shyness and fear of dogs. The video worked so well on the shy kids that they became more social than average. How can you work social truth into your work? Testimonials? Video? Other people getting excited about their purchase?

CONSISTENCY TRICKS PEOPLE

Research shows people doing some odd things to be consistent. They don't realize they're doing it. Here are some examples:

- Disliking someone we have done harm

- Liking someone more after doing something nice to them/ for them

- Affirming that a purchase that we made was a smart, good choice

- Coming up with good-sounding reasons for doing bad things.

This is especially true when the person is in a cultural or social environment that makes the bad behavior into a normal behavior. Drug addiction can be a strike out against the bad authority of the state. Stealing can be a Robin Hood act. A man, now serving time in federal prison in the U.S., evaded taxes with the belief that it was God's money. Why? Because he was teaching that evolution was false and that the earth was 10,000 years old.

Here are the kinds of beliefs that people unconsciously and consciously work to be consistent with:

"I am a good, considerate person."

"I am a hard worker."

"I support justice."

"I deserve a meaningful place in society."

Other beliefs that are not necessarily true or nice. You want to know if they have them:

"Business people are greedy, and we have to do whatever we can to avoid their traps, even tricking them."

"People are basically bad."

"*The world is a dangerous place, and I must be on guard all the time.*"

"*I am all that really matters. The people that matter are the ones that express this to me through their words, attitudes, and behavior.*"

"*Salespeople are greedy tricksters, and they must be overcome, so that there can be justice in the world.*"

I want you to think of ways that your sales approach could harness each of these attitudes.

A CLASSIC CONSISTENCY TRICK

There is a fellow who sells memberships in a buying club. He's gotten into some trouble because of being too greedy. But here's his business. It offers discounts for merchandise that he can get as a retailer. He claims to offer it for less than the department stores. His sales pitch involves getting unsophisticated people to believe that these big stores are spending so much on advertising that they can't beat his price.

This spiel works for people who hold a negative belief about business people being greedy and needing to be tricked, and the one about justice requiring that salespeople be overcome. It also appeals to the belief that they are smart enough to outfox tricksters. In order to do this, the business creates an image of being people who got around the system and will let you join for a price.

The sad fact is that this guy was using their beliefs against them, to do the very things to them that they felt were unjust. This person got in trouble with the law shortly after I heard his pitch, because he couldn't really deliver on his promises. But the fact that he was making money on this corrupt business shows how powerful basic beliefs are in driving our choices. How can you use your prospects' beliefs to help them create value in their lives with your offerings?

Body Language for a Concession

You've probably heard about the importance of body language. You use it to establish rapport, to show confidence, to be non-threatening, to show cooperation and openness, and to trigger positive states in yourself. But what about triggering automatic responses in others. Remember, we aren't just talking about something like rapport or an impression. We're talking about a fairly specific automatic response.

Let's learn about a "yes" trigger. Of course, since we aren't talking about turkeys or red robins, the automatic behavior probably won't be completely stupid, but it will improve your odds of success, AND it may at the very least, help you avoid triggering an automatic resistance. That alone is pretty good!

Learn to do this simple behavior every time you make a request. As you practice it, you'll fine tune it and become intuitive as to when this or another trigger is best for the situation at hand.

1. Make your request.

2. As you complete your request, relax your face, create a very subtle smile, tilt your head a little bit to one side.

That's it. This is another one of those things that are so simple, I'm almost embarrassed. And I'm not so easily embarrassed.

Start practicing this immediately, just like your because trigger. Knock yourself out and do both of them at the same time. This will be fun.

Fighting Fire with Fire: Opposing Efficiency Triggers

You can put a number of simple triggers together to strengthen the effect. Let me share with you a way that I do that.

I consider it a point of pride and of professionalism to not over-sell life insurance. From a selfish point of view, I would say that my reputation depends upon commitments such as this. However, I also know that people can lose their enthusiasm for buying life insurance. Of course, it is a very important obligation, but people find excuses to postpone the decision. You could say that this is an opposing efficiency trigger. There are many demands upon their time, and they have a natural defense against taking on new projects. The more life insurance looks like a project, the lower their motivation tends to be. My sales success depends, in large measure, on making the buying process feel attractive and efficient.

For my product line, my understanding of the customer and my professional judgment as to what and how much they should buy are part of what they are buying. They don't pay me by the hour as a consultant, but I make every effort to show them that I am a professional that they can trust. This triggers their efficiency response. Act now, and this professional consultation will get them where they want to go, with minimum fuss. The alternative is to be back in that disquieting sense of going bare that afflicts people without life insurance. It also means that the need to research the subject will be nagging at them once again.

Here, I have countered their opposing efficiency trigger, and provided favorable ones as well. Of course, I make sure to comment on what they have to look forward to if they postpone the decision: nagging, unfulfilled responsibility.

ACTIVATE THE VALUE METER AND THE EFFICIENCY TRIGGER

Have you ever tried to explain water to a fish? You'd be wasting your time because, for a fish, water is simply a universal; it's the very fabric of reality. Well, how about value? Gauging things for value is a behavior so prevalent that it is almost like the air we breathe. It is constant and everywhere. If you monitor your thoughts for "value assessment" as you go through your day, you'll notice that you have a "value meter" that is switched on pretty much constantly. I don't care if you're a non-materialistic and saintly Buddhist monk, you still have your value meter going.

But, at the same time, we are all ready to do our automatic "efficiency" behavior as well. That means that there is this pressure inside us to make our value meter act efficiently. This can cause us to pick up on value cues and respond to them without thinking. This automatic valuing helps us be efficient, and it fulfills our need to compute value, but it is not always right. That famous example of the dramatic increase in the price of a new wine fits perfectly. It was expensive, therefore, it was valuable. It worked in the wine market for reasons that do not apply to every situation.

That highlights an important point. Triggering the automatic efficiency behavior requires some thought on your part. It is automatic for your customers, but not for you. It isn't a simple formula such as the head tilt or the "because." You must consider the conditions. Think about any automatic behavior that you see in your customers. Ask yourself what conditions contribute to any automatic behavior. Most important, ask yourself if there are any automatic behavior-generating conditions that you can create or take advantage of now.

Combining Your Pressure Triggers

In my business, key efficiency triggers are my professionalism, knowledge, and judgment. Playing this up and fostering my reputation for these traits activate those triggers. As I have shown, the efficiency trigger is a pressure trigger. The prospect has various pressures in this example.

I provide all the triggers I can to intensify this. I dress the part and speak the part. I show confidence, and it is not inflated. After all, I'm experienced. I would expect anyone with my experience to develop confidence. Since people are used to getting the best, most trusted service from people who show these qualities, there is an association made.

I've been talking about my professionalism as a collection of simple pressure triggers that capitalize on the need for efficiency. This shows that you don't need to use them one at a time. But let's also look at how they function as complex pressure triggers. My office, demeanor, clothing, and other presentation elements create a sense of authority and trust. This is quite a combination. People have done very questionable things because of this form of pressure. You may have heard of the psychological experiment in which people thought that they could be electrocuting someone to death, but continued because of the authority of the experimenter. This just goes to show that you must use ethics as a professional. This book is disclosing many very powerful tools of influence.

Think over your business and look for automatic behavior triggers that can work for or may be working against you. Consider the simple, unconscious ones as well as more sophisticated ones. What efficiency triggers can you maximize in your business?

CONDITIONS FOR AUTOMATIC BUYING BEHAVIOR

Since we're on the idea of value and automatic behavior, lets get into more detail to help you in your quest for fine-tuning your sales conditions. You don't want to miss out on any automatic buying or valuing triggers that will work to your advantage.

Let's start with that famous wine-pricing example of Chivas Regal. For wine, the market is still one that many consumers are ill-informed about, it is one where impressions are very important, and it is one in which many consumers do not have a good memory or handle on the labels. They rely on little comments from store clerks, and little signs that the store places here and there about various wines that they want to promote. Since they need your trust, they put some effort into making sure that you aren't disappointed with their advice.

But price? That's a bit different. Consumers rely on it more than they may even realize. In other words, price is a more unconscious cue than an informative sign is. Price has subtext, it conveys information that it does not directly state. More to the point, price can trigger unconscious connections that border on reflexes because of the large number of times that particular kind of trigger has been fired off.

Remember this when you are looking for automatic behavior triggers. Consider your sales process, the site where sales and presentation of your product take place, and the media that exhibit your product as all being the sales environment. Sales environment equals the process, the location, and the media.

So what I want you to do is to ask yourself what things in the sales environment may trigger automatic behavior in your customers. How can you use those cues or triggers to improve the sales process. Don't limit yourself to your customers' perception of value this time. Cast a wide net.

Discover and Use More Automatic Buying Cues

Now ask yourself, what things in the sales environment have "old" associations. By old, I mean long-standing and used many times. I'm sure you won't be surprised to know that this is grounded in neurology. The more you fire a neural pattern in the brain, the stronger that pathway gets. It could be a mental association between two things, it could be a habit, it could be a memory, or it could be a way of responding. Whatever it is, it gets stronger through use.

Our example of this regarding value was that price is used in connection with value throughout our lives. Therefore, it is a strong, automatic association. It is an old association. That's a good thing, so far as our search for automatic behavior triggers goes, anyway.

People are so used to equating price with value that, given enough ambiguity and other conditions (such as those I mentioned in the previous section), that price can easily equal value. It certainly did for that particular wine at that particular moment in wine history. This is not the only example of such a phenomenon, of course, or I would just write it off as an oddity and not even mention it.

Many service providers and retailers in particular have noticed that the impression of value is critical. A survey of chocolate found that the more expensive chocolates were actually cheaper chocolate. But there was a difference between the chocolate situation and the Chivas Regal wine situation. The expensive chocolates were wrapped in a very classy way that screamed VALUE. Here, the issue was not so much an ambiguous market as it was that chocolate is already so wrapped up in our feelings as a classic comfort food, that the wrapping and impression easily fused with consumers' other desires that are triggered by chocolate. I'll wager that the chocolateers had little trouble figuring that one out.

In another example, a woman with a gift shop in a tourist area accidentally doubled the price of some jade jewelry she was having a terrible time selling. Once the price was doubled, the jade items vanished from the racks almost immediately. She was shocked. But she remembered that higher price the next time she offered up jade jewelry! Again, this is a situation where ambiguity and impressions played a big role. You would NOT expect to see this happen on a used car lot.

Go through the ideas that you have been developing during the previous two sections, and ask yourself about the things you've been coming up with. How strong (well-worn, old, frequently used, or typically used) are the associations that trigger the automatic behaviors? What would happen if you prioritized them by this factor. Do the strongest associations look like the ones you should act on first in enhancing the sales experience? Does looking for strong associations give you any new ideas for buying behavior triggers? Again, don't just look for value associations. Anything goes here. We have covered a number of different automatic behaviors. And there are more in the following sections!

EVERY LITTLE SHIFT COUNTS

Identity shifting is a tremendous sales resource. We're going to build upon the automatic behavior triggers of the previous section. For identity shifting, we need to ask questions such as, "What do the prospect's actions do to help define, redefine, or refine who they are in their own or others' eyes IN the direction of being a customer?" This can work for major campaigns that seek life-long customers, as well as one-off sales to people you may never see again. Identity shifting can work in a single encounter, or be a highly-orchestrated series of shifts over a long time period.

The term identity shift is a little strong for some of the identity work that salespeople do. Most of it should probably be called identity focusing, because the point is to bring certain aspects of their identity into focus. The aspects to bring into focus are the ones that help to promote the purchase. In my business, I sell most easily to people who have the following identifications:

- Concerned about family

- Consistent wage earner

- Avoids getting ripped off by the system

- Knows how to score big for their family

- Committed to their kids' education

STRATEGIC IDENTITY SHIFTING

But how do you find out what identifications to bring into focus?

What kinds of values do your best customers have?

What things about the product suggest identification? Thrifty people buy this appliance. Cool people buy this media player. Macho people drink this beer. Powerful people drive this car. All individualists must have this.

What kinds of famous people are associated with the product, whether coincidentally or by design?

What generation most identifies with the product, and what values stand out in that regard?

Think up a list of customer identity factors. Make it well-rounded by thinking of different aspects of the product or service experience. Then, review these automatic behavior sections, and think about ways you can shift (or refocus) your customers in one or more of those directions. *Consider every aspect of every aspect of the product experience.*

Here are some ideas right off the bat:

- What you say about your other customers when you meet your customer?

- What you have your customer write down?

- How do you hand your customer a sample?

- What tiny acknowledgments of shared values would fit? Choose values that few people would deny having. Make the questions feel very natural, not coercive. *"Do you like to save money?" "Do you want to go green, if it won't cost you any more?" "Do you like having ethical ways to increase your sales volume?"*

- Do you have video or posters of people who obviously have the values? Health food costs more. There are lots of images of very healthy and attractive people enjoying healthy products.

Some Large-Scale Examples

Identity shifting has been used on prisoners of war as a non-torture method of promoting ideology, and it has been used by organizations as non-controversial as blood banks. It is certainly an asset to any sales organization. Jet Blue, in fact, went to a great deal of trouble to figure out just "who" a Jet Blue person is, and then to make all of its promotion and features, right down to the upholstery, match that person. But this was not just a matter of conforming to a pre-existing type of person; going after a definite target audience. This involved more than "attracting."

The marketing also worked to shift people into a "JetBlue person" identity; to shift their self perception. As an organization going after the youth market, they created a mobile studio where people could talk about their experiences, creating media that would be included in their national advertising. This helped existing customers solidify their identities as Jet Blue people, and to attract people who identified with them. JetBlue has used youth ambassadors doing various guerilla marketing activities as well. They even offer a realistic taste of their cabin environment and youth-oriented features in an RV. Anyone who enters that environment gets more than a sample, they have moved their identity a notch toward being a JetBlue person. Every little identity shift counts.

In an industry as high-risk and volatile as the airline industry, these bold moves not only captured market share, they also captured a lot of attention. Whatever happens to an airline in the long run, any marketing push that creates a sustained wave of demand deserves notice.

Once you start, you can probably think of many ways a person could make little identity shifts in the direction of being one of your customers.

Inner Pressure, Outer Push

Understand the difference between inner pressure and outer push. Inner pressure is the feeling when an automatic behavior wants to be expressed. If the person has a problem like obsessive compulsive disorder or trichotillomania (compulsive hair pulling) they feel that pressure build until the have to act. That is similar to the inner pressure of a normal automatic behavior, except that the normal behavior is, well, normal.

In either case, a compulsive disorder or a normal automatic behavior. It is possible to resist it (or less impossible, depending on the person) through education.

But let's say you are trying to trigger an automatic behavior in someone and you feel a kind of pressure building in you because it isn't working. That inner pressure is really an outer push. Because your will and effort have absolutely nothing to do with their automatic behavior. This is not a Jedi mind trick.

If you are feeling a sense of effort when you are trying to trigger automatic behavior, you're taking the whole thing far too personally. And you are misunderstanding the phenomenon.

Take a nice, deep breath, relax, tell your ego everything's fine, and focus on building automatic behavior triggers.

The automatic behavior will occur or it will not. The trigger is not there to influence every individual. It is there to get you a statistical benefit. It is there because enough people will respond to it for it to be worth doing. You have a net gain. That's it.

HYPNOTIC LANGUAGE

Embedded Ideas

I don't know how often you'll use embedded ideas, but I know that you are serious about learning every technique that will ethically increase your income. So I wonder how much you have developed curiosity about the nature of embedded ideas, when, with the demands on you, you are very committed to making the best possible use of your time.

No one may have ever told you that *an embedded idea is a phrase that is hidden in a longer statement.* But many sales people say that when you learn to use them, they become a valuable part of your unconscious mastery of persuasion.

In the text above, there three embedded ideas. One is, *"You'll use embedded ideas."* Another is, *"You have developed curiosity about the nature of embedded ideas."*

It is easy to sound corny when using embedded ideas, so I suggest playing around with friends and family, practicing this as a game. See if you can catch each other using embedded ideas.

In one schools of thought, these are called embedded commands. I prefer to call them ideas, because I can't command anyone to buy products. Well, I could, but they would laugh at me.

The point of embedded ideas is that people reject ideas automatically and overcritically. You might say, "But, isn't it up to them how critical to be. My response is that I'd like to be able to bring some ideas in neutrally so they can consider the purchase without rejecting it for false reasons. Good objections will stay. I have closed thousands of sales, and I know that rational, grounded objections stay until they are resolved no matter how persuasive I am. The only exception is very gullible people. A sales person can't always know who is gullible in every situation, but there are ethical methods available to all sales people, such as truly qualifying a prospect.

MARKING EMBEDDED IDEAS

You can add to the effectiveness of an embedded idea by using a slightly different voice quality of some kind when saying them. You must be very good at hiding them in your sentences in order to do this, and you must be very subtle in your vocal changes. You can change any aspect of your voice. I prefer to dip my pitch down on the first syllable and let it come up during the idea, but have the pitch a little lower than normal. However, I fluctuate the pitch in a way that sufficiently resembles normal speech to prevent it from being noticed. My voice is also just a hair softer and more gentle.

This is one of those things that you'll need to practice until you are sure of it. The last thing you want is for prospects to think you're trying to control their minds. Few people understand the real function of embedded ideas.

HYPNOTIC LANGUAGE PRESSURE

There is a hypnotic language pattern that creates something that resembles automatic behavior pressure. But it's really more of a way to get past automatic resistance. It is a gentle method to bypass defenses. Once that is done, the person will have greater likelihood of moving forward.

Hypnotic Language Pressure Steps

1. Begin with a set up phrase.

2. Add an embedded command, such as, "buy life insurance."

3. Do a set up phrase that conveys certainty.

4. Add a true statement that contributes to the sales process. The truer it is for the prospect the better. But most importantly, it should further the process.

HYPNOTIC LANGUAGE PRESSURE EXAMPLE

"I don't know if you will buy life insurance today. But I know that you want to be satisfied that you have all the facts."

1. *"I don't know if you will..."* is the starter phrase. It doesn't really say anything. It's there to set up the next step. It can't be argued against. It's just there. But it does create some interest because it opens a question. What doesn't he know about me? It also creates some suspension, since it promotes some internal mind scanning in the prospect.

2. *"...buy life insurance."* There is the embedded command. It isn't really a command, but it makes the idea more a part of their considerations than it was.

3. *"But I know that..."* This set up phrase conveys certainty, and lends some certainty to the entire statement, despite the "but."

4. *"...you want to be satisfied that you have all the facts."* This is more complicated than it appears. You are aligning with them and goosing the sales process.

TRUE STATEMENT: DECONSTRUCTION

That statement in step four deserves some analysis. It serves many purposes. It is very important for you to understand each one.

The statement was "...you want to be satisfied that you have all the facts."

1. Understanding for rapport: You are showing that you understand them.

2. Credibility through truth: You made a statement that is true about what they want.

3. Sales process momentum: You also picked something that is part of where you want the sales process to go. You want them to be convinced by the facts. You want them to be curious enough to learn more about why now is the time to buy life insurance.

4. Identity shift: You are reinforcing this thing about them, by bringing it up now.

5. Back mask: It also serves as a back mask, because it distracts from the embedded command.

6. Alignment: It also aligns with the prospect, because it shows that you accept their need to get the facts and not be rash in their decision.

SEQUENCE FOR CREATING THE HYPNOTIC LANGUAGE PRESSURE STATEMENT

You can start constructing these with the following sequence. I have no idea exactly how much you will enjoy constructing hypnotic language, even though you have worked very hard in developing your skills in sales.

1. Determine your purpose based on where you are in the sales process. How aggressive or direct should this be? Do you want to do a test close or just propel the mood?

2. Choose the embedded idea. What do you want them to consider doing?

3. Come up with a statement that is true to the prospect, and gives energy to a good next effort for the sales process.

4. Create a set up for the embedded idea.

5. Create a set up for the final statement.

Review the purposes of the components of the statements in the two examples. This will help a great deal. Start constructing a few of these right away. I don't want this opportunity to slip by without you getting this into your brain. You might get busy with other things! (Might?) But if you do this now, you'll start seeing opportunities to use it right away.

EXAMPLE 2

This is a very different example. It is for later in the sales process because it is a test close. It's a mild one, but much farther along than acknowledging that the prospect wants all the facts.

"Don't you feel that if you buy life insurance, your family will be certain that you love them very much."

1. *"Don't you feel that if you..."* is the starter phrase. This time it is about the prospect in stead of the salesperson. It still creates suspension, though. It has "feel" and "if," which appeal to non-logic and the subconscious. "Don't you," arouses curiosity.

2. *"...buy life insurance."* There is the embedded idea again. Same one.

3. *"...your family will be certain that..."* This set up phrase also conveys certainty.

4. *"...you love them very much."* Again, a true statement that serves the same purpose of the one in the prior example. Instead of an appeal to logic, it is a feeling statement, and a strong one. It is irrefutable. And it pushes the sales process toward the close because you are bringing forth the biggest reason for life insurance. You would use this when an appeal to emotion is what you need to move things ahead.

SET UP PHRASES FOR HYPNOTIC LANGUAGE PRESSURE

Here is a collection of phrases that you can use for the initial set up of the hypnotic language pressure recipe. Each is followed by an idea about what you might use it for.

Your prospects will have no idea that you will soon be using this to create sales momentum. They only know that it is easier to buy from you when they feel at ease about new ideas.

- *I wouldn't tell you to... softens resistance.*

- *You don't have to... same.*

- *Don't think that just because people... invokes social pressure.*

- *Have you ever noticed how people who... same.*

- *Don't you feel that if you... creates a hypothetical.*

- *If you chose to... same.*

- *How surprised would you be to... same.*

- *I don't know how you'll make your decision to... implies the purchase.*

- *You might want to know why people... invokes rationality.*

- *You may not know exactly why you should... same.*

- *What would it be like if you were able to... questions ability, is hypothetical.*

- *If you could... same.*

- *What most helps you know whether to... invokes decision making and certainty.*

- *Imagine what would happen if... creates future scenario.*

- *I'm not sure why some people... could be for rationality, or to create contrast (some people fail to, but...)*

- *I don't know if you will... amplifies embedded command.*

- *Some people have to... implies an alternative.*

- *I've been wondering if you were curious about how to... invokes involvement in learning, curiosity, involvement in a process.*

- *If I could show you a special way to... same.*

THE CERTAINTY SET UP PHRASE

Once you have the other components, it's pretty easy to link into the true statement (component #4). But I want to be sure you aren't thinking in too much of a cook book style. So I'll throw in a diverse little collection to show how diverse they can be.

No one can convince you that you have all the creativity you need for this. Everyone who learned to do this is just surprised that they do it without even realizing it after a while.

- *but I know that*

- *even though*

- *because*

- *your family will be certain that*

- *I imagine that*

- *when you have been trying to*

- *even though you are certain that*

- *wouldn't your colleagues realize*

- *but you are even more certain that*

KEYS TO THE PROSPECT: META-PROGRAMS

THE PSYCHOLOGICAL KEYS TO YOU PROSPECTS

Meta-programs are a little like computer programs. They are rules that manage how we do mental things like make decisions. Once you know some of the meta-programs a prospect uses, it will help you work with them. It's best to just go right into examples.

Toward

Consider the toward vs. away from programs. A "toward" person tends to move toward an option. They are attracted to things. When they talk about their decisions, they talk about the incentives. If their will power fails them, they'll say what they indulged in was irresistible.

Away From

The away from type is the opposite. They make decisions based on what they must avoid. They follow rules to avoid breaking them. They talk about the negative consequences of things that must be avoided or not done. What they talk about what they want to do, they talk about what it will prevent.

When you sell to a toward person, you emphasize the benefits they are going toward, and the pain of not having them. With an away from person, you emphasize the negative consequences they are avoiding, and the pain of experiencing those negative consequences.

You can see how this would play out in my business. Toward people want benefits for their family. Away people want to avoid leaving their family impoverished. I know, I know. Those are exactly the same thing, said differently. Well, that's the point. It's how you present it that matters. It's what you emphasize.

Here are a few more

General vs. Detail: Big picture people who are bored by the details vs. detail people.

Past assurances vs. future possibilities: The past is what you can expect vs. the future is full of possibilities.

Convenience or efficiency people: Convenience is most important vs. willingness to invest in creating higher efficiencies or cost savings.

THE CONVINCER STRATEGY

It's called the convincer strategy for a reason. That reason makes it good for sales. It answers the questions, "How does the person come to be convinced?" Listen to how your prospect talks about a problem, something they are sure of, or how the decided to do something, and you'll get all sorts of hints as to their convincer strategy. Listen for things that they refer to:

What they saw, felt, or heard. Which sense mode do they refer to the most?

The number of times they needed to experience a convincing thing.

Whether the had to do it, see other people do it, or learn about it.

Do they assume that something is as it is supposed to be, or must it be proven somehow? How?

How long must they experience the evidence for it to be true?

How much do the tend to have to think about it? Do they always need to sleep on it?

Do they have a consistent belief in what has been shown, or do they need ongoing proof. Do their employees have to keep regaining their trust?

Here is an example of a real life person I know, who has a common convincer strategy:

He is best convinced by what they read, if it's from a professional source. He will postpone decisions until he has more information than most people would ever want.

If he was going to buy a car, he would learn all about the choices he was interested in, and then test drive it. He wouldn't care much about how it looks, but he would care about the impression it gave if it was too far afield. But if it was a steal, he wouldn't care if the body needed some work.

He wouldn't believe anything the salesperson told him, unless it was a commitment that was in writing, or he had read enough to believe that it was true.

He would want to mull the information over until he felt like he had his "head wrapped around it," but he would only need one brief test drive to be convinced it was right, once the data was right. People gain his trust first, and have to violate it in order to lose it, but he is hesitant to actually believe what they say. I'm not sure what that even means, but it works for him. He doesn't need things reproven to him. He errs on the side of believing that things are as agreed until proven otherwise.

Try this on yourself. Go through the elements and find out what kind of convincer strategies you have. You can come up with more factors as well. Then think about how you can appeal to the various types of convincers that people use.

THE MATCHERS

Matchers notice how things match, **mismatchers** notice how they don't.

Matchers: Matchers notice how things match. Most people are in this group. Some are a little, some are extreme. Matchers tend to overgeneralize. Extreme matchers act like things only have to have one trait in common to be all the same. They are impressed with psychic readings. The psychic may rattle off forty possible names, but their customer only remembers the one that matched their deceased grandfather. A famous debunker of psychics, who also happens to be a skilled magician, named The Amazing Randi, has shocked people by showing them the actual numbers from their cold readings. Use comparisons to sell to them, because when you show them that *this* is like *that*, they will see the truth in it.

If a matcher thinks poorly of you, your product, or your company, they are actually thinking badly of your profession (or some other group you're in), other products they have experienced that are like yours (maybe just one that is a little like yours), and the same for the company. Do not argue. Point out similarities with good things. Recruit their neurons until their minds are on what is good about your product, you, and your company. If the matcher tends to be negative, you might resort to comparing the competing products to bad things, and yours to good things. If they tend to be positive in making comparisons, you'll have an easier time.

The Mismatchers

Mismatchers: Mismatchers notice how things don't match. They tend to see every error in what you say. Mismatchers think by counter-example. That can be an effective strategy, because it makes them precise and they catch errors. If you try to sell them by making impressions about feelings, they will find plenty to disagree with. Be exacting when you sell to them. Put extra effort into eliciting their criteria for making decisions. Be very attentive to and use their convincer strategies.

Do not try to argue, just emphasize how things are different. You are so used to telling people what your product is like, that you may have to practice this! I joked about someone who was bad at grammar. He used the singular to refer to plurals, like, "*Look, there's* cows." I said, *"I guess he could have said there's a bunch of cows."* The mismatcher said, *"No, there's a herd of cows."*

Sell to the mismatcher in terms of probabilities, exact numbers, and what distinguishes your offering and company from the others. Just don't generalize about the others, or you may draw the mismatchers attention to the others. They will be finding fault with your generalization. You might want to make a mistake and under-represent something good (or over-represent something bad) about your product. They will correct you. You will have focused their attention on something positive about your product or will have boosted it up. Do not give counter-examples to their counter-examples, though. This will kill the momentum. And with mismatchers it is more challenging to develop momentum.

ATTENTION FOCUS

This meta-program is about what people tend to focus on. What draws their attention first and foremost? This tells you how to get their attention. It is also related to their convincer strategy, since it filters what sensory information gets priority. First you get attention, then you get the convincer strategy.

Here are a few examples:

Data focus: Give these folks the details. Tell them what makes it tick. They are easily bored, even offended, by emotional appeals. They think emotional people are weak-minded. They take pride in noticing any way that someone tries to manipulate them, and they can take a pretty harsh view of manipulative people. Nonetheless, they may view life as a game, and other people as being like video games. The more interesting you are, the more interesting you are.

Process: Process people are really into making the process go well. Their criteria may differ though. For some, it's everyone having a good time. They can be great team players. They don't tend to care passionately about getting the exact, specified outcome. They tend to be content with getting there by successive approximation.

Completion: Completion people are on the judgmental side. are high on judging, and this makes a big difference. Organizations usually need completion people in larger numbers than process people. Their strength is that they are driven by criteria and outcomes. They are not satisfied with vagueness or approximation. They can't understand why anyone would feel any differently. Sell to a completion person by bringing in various processes that need completion and that bring more engagement or other aspects of the sales process. You might frame these completion processes as being necessary to assess their exact needs, and because you have to follow the rules management sets down for you to do your sales process.

ATTENTION FOCUS: SELF

We all pay attention to how things affect us, but for some, this is their sole focus. You sell to this type in terms of "what about them." You don't sell them on the benefits to others, unless it's in terms of how those others will view them or reciprocate. If image doesn't matter a lot, then forget about the issue of how they will be viewed. If image matters, their style and possessions can give you some clues about whose opinion matters the most to them. Who are they appealing to with their clothes, car, etc. Don't be offended if they don't exactly connect with you or care about what you are feeling or experiencing. It's all about them. Unless it's inappropriate, be especially cooperative with their every self-focused request. Take the idea of couching your negotiation tactics in terms of their interests to an extreme.

Keep in mind, though, that self-sorters are not exactly the same as people who lack a conscience. This is because there are plenty of people who do not have much of a conscience, but who naturally pay attention to other people. They can be very successful at being manipulative, because of their acute sense of other people. They are capable of being very concerned about the welfare of people that will get them to the top, get them rich, or get them other things they desire. But when they don't need them, they can easily stop caring. They can be good co-conspirators., and they make sure they are on the boss' good side. The self-sorters tend to just not be very attentive to other people. They are self absorbed from a sense-filtering point of view. A person who is unethical and lacks a conscience is not necessarily so naturally oblivious to others.

SELF SORTERS IN THE WRONG JOBS

One company found that the majority (95%!) of the customer complaints concerned only 5% of their employees. They researched what made these people different from the other 95% of their employees. It turned out that the problem employees had a self focus. This was bad for customer service, because anyone who wasn't them was an inconvenience. They tended to feel offended by other people having needs or feelings. They were so preoccupied with themselves, that they just didn't notice opportunities to prevent negative customer experiences. Once there was a negative experience, they didn't make customers feel understood.

These employees were anything but intuitive about making people feel whole again by responding to a problem that, were they paying attention, would have come to their attention in a timely manner.

They did fire the high-complaint employees, and they changed their hiring process: they had potential employees give a presentation as to why they wanted to work for the airline. But the judges paid attention to the employees when they *weren't* presenting. They looked for how supportive the employees were, and how connected they were to the employees who were presenting. The self-first employees were just preoccupied with what they were going to say.

ATTENTION FOCUS: OTHER

You can guess, from what you read about self focus, what you get with other-focused people. They focus a lot on other people. If they are dedicated to customer service, this trait will help them. If they do not have good values, they will focus on gossip, revenge, and other unseemly preoccupations.

Sell to the other-focused person with attention to who they care about, and who they want to have an effect on. What message or impression do they want to deliver? Know that their development is enriched by their ability to take in more of what is going on with other people.

THE MATRIX

It might help you to come up with sales strategies by putting people in boxes. This helps you simplify things. Pick some key meta programs and make a spreadsheet.

Here's an example. Let's compare people based on the following:

- *Toward vs. away from*
- *Attends more to possibilities vs. necessities*
- *Focuses on pain or pleasure*
- *Here are the categories that result, with some typical personality characteristics. How would you sell to each type?*
- *Toward Possible Pain: Deals with emergencies, courageous*
- *Toward Possible Pleasure: A dreamer, a visionary*
- *Toward Necessary Pain: A soldier, a champion*
- *Toward Necessary Pleasure: Addicted*
- *Away Possible Pain: Fearful, timid*

- *Away Possible Pleasure: Self-rejecting, doctrinaire, prudish*

- *Away Necessary Pain: Avoidant, self-neglectful, procrastinator*

- *Away Necessary Pleasure: Neurotic, confused*

As you work with *meta-programs*, you come to have all the categories working for you automatically. You might want to focus on one meta-program per week.

Once you've dealt with people over a week's time, you will be able to identify a meta-program pretty quickly. Get them talking about decisions and beliefs, focusing on the "how" factor. "How did you decide?" "How did you come to realize that?"

NEURODIVERSITY: DIVERSE PROSPECT CATEGORIES THROUGH SCIENCE

I Can Do It and So Can You!

I can sell to people that most other salespeople can't. I'm talking about people with difficult personalities. It's partly my nature, but it is largely because of what I have learned about human diversity. I got into this subject because of someone I care about very much who has struggled with a mental illness. The more I learned, the more I wanted to learn. There is so much incredible stuff happening in psychology that, for me, it's like following a good drama. I can't wait to see what they'll come up with next.

I guess I just feel like the mind is the ultimate frontier. And I suppose that is one of the reasons I'm a fanatic for learning more about influence at every opportunity. And that, my friends, has a lot to do with my success in sales.

But I wanted to make sure I really nailed this section. I wanted it to be dead on accurate, and I wanted it to be truly useful for sales. So I did some serious consulting to really get it right, and a lot of mulling over my more unusual customers to pull out really useful sales wisdom. And now, I'm very proud of this section.

I hope you really enjoy it and that it makes you lots of money.

I took care to only pick a few categories that I think will be of special interest to salespeople because they are the ones that you can capture the most sales with by understanding them a little better and having some guidelines as to how to relate to them.

WHAT IS NEURODIVERSITY AND WHY SHOULD I CARE?

This section will show you how go get rapport and workable sales flows with people that can be difficult to understand or appreciate. You will learn the key assumptions that can get you past the obstacles that are keeping you from some perfectly good sales. In the process, you'll learn some things that will also help you understand people that you will run across from time to time outside of the sales situation: co-workers, family members, and even friends (or certainly, somewhere along the way, friends of friends).

The main idea of neurodiversity is that people who fall too far outside of the bell curve of what we call normal are often quite functional people who can buy things, sometimes very expensive things, and who can live their lives, sometimes very accomplished lives. That means that you need to know how people lose sales when they come across the more neurodiverse among us, and how to capture those sales. While we're at it, let's cover some ways to enjoy it more, since that's one of the big reasons salespeople lose those sales. They don't know how to enjoy certain unusual, eccentric, or disabled people. And by disabled, I'm talking about invisible disabilities. Those are the disabilities that affect people's brains, causing them to fall outside of what we consider normal. Some of these disabilities only affect a very limited range of the person's thinking or behavior. If you didn't know, you might not have a clue that the word disability would even apply.

SALES NOBODY ELSE COULD MAKE: THE NEURODIVERSITY SECRET

There probably isn't a salesperson alive that hasn't come across some kind of people category system for salespeople to use. These are categories that tell you to use a different sales approach depending on what category the person fits into. There is the Myers Briggs Type Indicator, and there are various personality types such as the impulse buyer or the analytical.

This is all well and good, but we want to go farther than that. We want to take this to the level of neurodiversity. **But what is neurodiversity and why should you care?**

At its most basic, neurodiversity means that people are different from one another, in large measure, because of their brains. That's so painfully obvious that it sounds silly. But it goes farther than that. It's about accepting the fact that there is a really wide variety of people, and that they all count. This is a civil rights issue, but it's also a sales issue. You don't want to lose sales because of outdated knowledge. Some of the quirky people that you weren't sure how to relate to can become your customers when you simply add some knowledge about these types.

This is why you should care; because many sales are missed when salespeople are content with personality categories or even sales intuition that is stuck in the past. There is so much new knowledge about human motivation and variation that has been coming out that it would fry anyone's circuits to learn it all. Fortunately, one of our panel members drinks from the fire hose of neuro-research, getting doesn't of research papers every day. In the following articles, we'll boil down the most important neurodiversity information into practical sales knowledge and technique.

MILD BRAIN DAMAGE

I'm going to share with you what I feel are the top categories worth learning about to help you get more sales. There is one area we won't cover, called personality disorders. It's so deep, it would take forever. But I really think these categories are the most useful for you to know about in sales. I developed this information from my experience and consultations with my well-educated panel, which includes a mental health expert.

Brain damage is a problem that alters people's ability to think as effectively as they'd like. Most of those folks are improving, but it goes slowly. Many of them don't realize what has happened to them, and the people around them don't understand. Most of the people who end up homeless in developed nations are there because of some kind of brain damage.

They may have gotten it during military service, a car accident, sports, or any of many other ways. They deserve better than what they get. Much of this goes unrecognized by the mental health field, and some suffer from problems with judgement that get them in trouble with the law. Instead of treatment, they get jail time.

A big source of brain damage is from blood leaking into the brain, as in a stroke. This can happen on a small scale, so you end up with mild brain problems.

Salespeople need to know that many of their customers have mild thinking problems that can affect how the sales process goes.

AUTISTIC TRAITS

People with autistic traits, but who can manage their finances or who are at least fairly independent. These folks can have very quirky personalities. Many have a diagnosis called Asperger's syndrome. They tend to have trouble reading social cues and facial expressions, and their social skills tend to be kind of out of whack. Many geniuses have some autistic traits. Well get into selling to these folks in the uber nerds pieces.

Salespeople need to know that if they can get in synch with these people, they can capture more sales.

SCHIZOPHRENIA AND SIMILAR PROBLEMS

These folks can be doing just fine, but have some mild brain damage that can make them seem a little off. They may have no symptoms at all, or they may have some things missing, like they may not have many emotions or sense of pleasure. Some have hallucinations or weird ideas and beliefs.

The ones who have hallucinations *plus* too much brain damage tend to believe that the hallucinations are real, and they tend to get into trouble or into treatment. Many of those people are unable to live independently. But the ones who hallucinate, but who are in pretty good shape otherwise, just *ignore* the hallucinations and get on with their lives. You have probably met some of them, and had no idea because they are smart enough not to tell anybody about their hallucinations unless there is a really good reason or high level of trust.

Salespeople need to know that if they can get past things like blank facial expressions or weird ideas, they can sell to the many people with this mental illness who are making money and spending it appropriately.

NEURO-WISDOM FOR SALESPEOPLE

The current revolution in the mental health field is that researchers and clinicians are discovering that the categories they have for mental, emotional, and behavioral problems can be misleading. Different physical problems (whether they are directly in the brain or not) can cause various symptoms that fall across various diagnostic categories. This means that diagnosis, as a practice, is kind of a mess.

But there is some wisdom to pull from this for sales. Whenever someone acts strange, you can safely assume that they are put together differently, they are under serious stress, or there is something physical going on with their brain or hormones or something else that affects how they feel, think, or behave.

Don't take it personally just because you grew up in an environment where people take things personally. Don't assume that when someone is not acting respectful, it is because they are trying to violate your honor and therefore must be punished in some way. Don't assume that because someone is really quirky, that they can't or shouldn't buy something from you. Keep in mind that people with mental issues may have major ups and downs. If they can't work with you one day, they may be much better the next day.

And don't assume that acting normal is the right way to sell to these folks. Sometimes it is best to stay normal, sometimes it's best to pace them in order to establish rapport, and sometimes it's best to get more creative than that. We'll be talking about those three options as we go along. This is going to be interesting, and profitable.

Rapport and Being at Ease

Let's get into the matter of rapport. You already know how critical it is to like people in order to establish rapport with them. Or at least to be comfortable enough with them to act like you like them. That way, even if you're having a bad day, or take a disliking to someone, you can still treat them right. I know that sometimes you just don't like someone, but you don't want to take it out on them, because you know everybody can't like everybody. It just isn't how we're put together.

But it can be more of a challenge with some of the folks who fall far from the center of the bell curve (people who are *way* not average). Let me offer a few philosophical tid bits.

I think that the key to unlocking your affection or appreciation for people who are not very easy to like is the idea that you cannot predict their potential. I hear many stories from people who were told they could not do something, but who broke through those predictions to live a dream.

It's tragic that many people in the mental health field have the delusion that they can predict the future, because those predictions can get people into a lot of trouble.

A Successful "Crazy" Man

I know of a man who had a mental illness, and who ended up in the hospital. He developed the idea to research the ability of people with mental illnesses to recover. He thought that he could do that because he held a Ph.D. in sociology. The staff of the hospital told him that this idea was part of his illness; that it was a "delusion of grandeur." Whenever they called him "doctor," as in, "Well, doctor," he knew that they were actually talking down to him.

But now he is researching mental illness, just as he intended. As of this writing, he works for a very large corporation and provides talks about his research and philosophy to large groups of people. His name is Dr. Ed Knight. So if you meet someone who seems crazy, you're probably right, but there is no reason to lock them into that identity in your mind. Any number of things could happen that could unlock their larger self, and it is probably dying to be released.

Who knows? It could be your kindness and inspiration that unlocks some of these people. It should be no surprise, because you are becoming a master of influence. Even if the only reason you want to become a master of influence is to get rich, you can't help the fact that your skills can be used to connect people with their larger selves. There is a lot of overlap between the skills of psychotherapists and salespeople. Seriously!

Besides, even people who don't have major influence skills, even people who aren't particularly bright sometimes cause other people to transform. Sometimes it's by including them in something and just being kind. So a more sophisticated person could easily do it by accident. Now, do you have any reasons left to take people's attitudes personally? If you do, it will hurt your profession and your humanity, so I encourage you to examine them, and seek opportunities to live large.

PRINCIPLES OF NEURO-DIVERSE SALES

Here are the core ideas that will help you sell to a broader range of people.

Concept #1: It's all around you, you're just missing out.

Abnormal is the new normal. Seriously. The more brain scans the scientists do, the more they are telling us that just about everybody has a quirky brain in some way. Many of them are people that you don't know how to do sales with smoothly. I want to help you capture the sales you've been losing because of these hidden needs. Remember, sales is about filling needs, and those needs are often not the obvious needs that the product most obviously fills.

Concept #2: Quirky people have money to spend.

The mental health field tells that most people have a real mental or emotional problem at some point in their lives. For most, it's a temporary thing, ranging from the mental funk of a hangover, to suicidal depression after the loss of a loved one. For many people, it is an ongoing problem like panic attacks, a serious personality problem or a mental illness. Even people with mental illnesses may have busy lives and money to spend. They usually the smarter ones who know that they can ignore the little voices. I'm serious.

Concept #3: A little flexibility goes a long way for capturing a sale from a neurodiverse person.

People have all sorts of reasons for saying or doing odd things in a sales situation. I recall, after the suicide of someone I loved, I still had to get something in a store. I should have stayed home, but I thought it would be good to get out of the house. I saw that there was a special offer on something I had just gotten in the store at regular price. I told the salesperson that, since it was the same price, I would take the larger item. He told me if I did that, he would call the police. I think he didn't want to fuss with the computer to change the sale. And, he seemed to have his own personality problem as kind of a control freak. But what he didn't count on was the fact that I felt so bad at that moment, that I really didn't care if I spent the night in jail or anywhere else. The weird interaction we had caused another customer to leave the store. There a lost sale right there.

Concept #4: A little respect goes a long way for keeping a customer.

Most people who have some kind of ongoing mental or emotional problem are pretty sensitive about it, even if they don't know what it is. Their self esteem can be on a real roller coaster. If your style is to tease customers a little bit to loosen them up, be careful about those who seem to be slow or awkward in some way. Usually, these problems are pretty narrow. The person may be fine overall, but have some difficulty navigating around objects, or they may lose track of details easily. The best thing that you can to is to make things easy for them.

Don't make a joke out of "invisible disabilities" such as schizophrenia, by using words like "crazy" unless you are absolutely sure that this is how your customer talks, and be careful who else hears you if you do.

UBER NERDS

This is about selling to people with autistic traits who are also very bright. Some of them earn very large incomes in scientific an tech fields. These folks tend to be in very technical areas like engineering or math, some are in medicine, including psychiatry, which, I realize, is a little ironic. I hope none of them find the term "uber nerds" (which means ultra nerds) insulting. Since techy people call themselves nerds, I figure I can't be too far off the mark.

Many of these folks are diagnosed with Asperger's syndrome. Since they aren't real good at reading social signals and facial expressions, they don't interact as effectively as most people. In fact, they can come of in ways that they don't really feel inside. They can seem cold, smug, haughty, or superior. They can seem to really not like you, even if they think you're fine, just because of what they don't do, which is to act normally warm. It can freak people out. And if you have any self esteem issues, you may put them all onto the uber nerd and think they are thinking really bad things about you.

At worst, they probably just know that you aren't as smart as they are. But that doesn't count your street smarts, social skills, and abilities to have a family in ways that many of them are pretty clueless about.

There's a really interesting theory about the uber nerds. At least the ones that actually have autistic traits. Apparently one of the things that gets them marching to the beat of a different drummer is that they don't have a good supply of "mirror neurons." This is the part of the brain that kind of echoes the movements that the people around us make. It helps us create rapport and feel connected with other people. This really influences us.

In fact, it influences us so much that it may explain how people can get into "group think." In group think, people can go along with really bad ideas like witch burning or not intervening in an emergency, just because of what they are seeing around them.

But people with limited mirror neurons may be kind of liberated from some of this. Even though it is a disability, it also may help them think out of the box. This may be part of the reason that they tend to come up with really major innovations, like realizing that electricity and magnetism are part of the same thing. Yes, it looks like Benjamin Franklin was an uber nerd. But there are many examples. If you have time, look at a lecture by Temple Grandin for more on this kind of thing. She's a gifted engineer who happens to be autistic.

SELL TO UBER NERDS

After all the talk about the emotional side of selling, I want to suggest that you break some rules with these people. Go analytical. Get statistical. Focus on features and technical comparisons. If they are mathematically inclined, don't hold back. They may end up helping you put the sale together where that is concerned.

Definitely don't worry about how your nuanced approach to rapport building is falling flat. It just isn't the issue. The issue is what *does* create rapport with them. That is being into what they are into, and respecting their direction in the sales process. If they want stats, analysis, and details, and seem immune to emotion, go with it. You should still seek and push emotional buttons where you can, but don't let it throw you if you have trouble with that.

If they make social missteps or get too wound up about some issue in the sales process, don't take it personally or think that they won't calm down. Just help them calm down. If they seem to space out and withdraw, they may be thinking or needing some kind of mental break. Ask them if they'd like a break, and offer some cold water.

Get them in the most unstimulating environment that you can. Especially where intrusive noise and people milling around are concerned. They can be easily confused or fatigued by distractions. Then they dig in their heels and won't make the purchase because they don't feel that they understand it well enough. They have to feel focused to feel good about a sale. They will easily postpone it if things aren't quite right. Ask them to help you pick the right environment. Ask them if any noise or anything else is bothering them.

If they start to seem to "high maintenance" just be calm about setting some limits with them when you have no choice. But really show that you care about their feelings. You can say, "Oh, yes, I know. I'm really sorry, but the shop is part of our facility, and I can't really cut the noise any more than I have. I don't have any other room where

I can access this information. All I can do is keep the door shut. Will that do for now?"

Too Obsessed to Buy?

Have you ever met someone with a one-track mind? It seems like all they can think about is some conspiracy theory or some other interest. They tend to only have friends with the same obsession, because they drive everyone else away. Some of them can keep enough of a lid on it to have a broader base of support, but push the right button and they really go to town. On the other hand, some of them are very limited, and can even have very destructive ideas about race, religion, or politics that they get really fired up about.

A lot of these folks seem to have some autistic traits, like Asperger's syndrome people. And it's true that people with Asperger's are infamous for having a topic that they are into to the exclusion of everything else. But not all of these folks are smart. They cover the range from very bright to very not bright, to needing caretaking for many of their daily needs.

As a salesperson, you need to know when to sell and when to cut loose. And if you can sell to one of these people, you need to know how to establish rapport and keep them focused. You could easily establish rapport by getting them going about their pet topic, but then what? How could you possibly get to the sale if they get too wound up? Not very easily! Maybe not ever! Your objective is to invest just enough time to tell the difference without spending your afternoon learning about an underground alien civilization, reptiles of South America, or a wacky religion. They can take up your time and have no intention to buy anything, how do you tell?

Invest some time in the situation, do some pleasant state-breaking that appears to be on their topic (bringing in more sense modalities that you can bridge to your sales situation), then make the bridge. The piece on re-directing gives a detailed example of how to do this.

My best sense is that about 50% of these zealous types will become real prospects. It's worth a small investment of time to sort them out. And, by having a smooth way to give the other 50% the heave-ho, you will have left some good feelings. Maybe, as a result of those good feelings, they will come back when they are in a true buying mood, or maybe they will refer someone to your business.

The Art of Re-Directing

These pieces will help you figure out what to do with people who have one track minds or rigid thinking. You will also find it helpful with people who are really easily distracted and who lose track of the time without realizing how much time is passing by. Many of these folks are perfectly able to complete the sale with a little help from their friendly local salesperson.

Here is the kind of thing that I say to people that tend to get off track. I use a bridge statement that aligns with them and then redirects. "This is such an important subject. You've gotten me interested in it, and I'm going to learn more about this, but I have a question for you." And then I plug back into the sales process.

If necessary, I get more direct about the fact that we need to stay focused. If the person is so extreme that you can't finish a sentence, then you can try state breaking, distraction, moving to a different situation, having another person break in, or getting them physically involved with the product in some way. I'll give more details on that in a piece coming up.

If you feel you're spending too much time and not responding to your efforts, then cut them loose. They may just be using you to give their speech, especially if they interrupt your bridge statements and seem to be obsessed.

ESCALATING YOUR RE-DIRECTING

But let's say you are making some last-ditch efforts to get them on track. You should definitely be willing to risk breaking rapport by redirecting and distracting them a bit from their current state.

For example you might say a little louder, with a mild look of amusement and surprise (but friendly), "John, John, please, I can only take in so much at one time, you've given me so much to digest and share, and I also know you're here with your wife, and with the afternoon coming to an end, and these questions you came in with about how life insurance serves you as an investment as well as security for your family. While I'm thinking of it, there is a graph that gives the big picture perfectly right away, I should open this up to."

This is a nice, tight example of breaking their current state, redirecting their attention, setting the agenda, and moving into a presentation. Since our prospect had so much momentum on a different line of thought, such zealous types do, we didn't ask his permission. Instead, the focus was on diverting momentum and maintaining flow. Your first question should not be for permission for anything, rather, it should be for what aspect of the presentation is the most interesting. You need to corral them to focus their choices.

Notice that there was a lot of sensory input there about the wife, the surroundings, and finally, the sales materials. That was a state break followed by redirection toward the sales materials and process.

"This is the portion that shows a typical investment scenario. Is your situation more like this, where you are looking at shifting your existing investments...?"

And, of course, getting mastery of this response means that you will be more energized and positive in your presentation with this prospect and the next one.

Hard-Core Redirecting

Let's look at the example from the last piece, and add some comments that show exactly why this is phrased just so.

"John, John, please, I can only take in so much at one time, you've given me..."

Note how we're using the past tense, putting the prospect's lecture into the past.

"so much to digest and share, "

Ah, share, you're going to help spread the word, your prospect's zealous mission is being accomplished.

"and I also know you're here "

Insert some grounding phrases now, based on what's happening now, such as...

"with your wife, "

Gesture toward her to continue directing his attention outside himself and into the environment, especially to things that may facilitate the sale.

"and with the afternoon coming to an end, "

Time is passing, action is needed, we are building a little sense of urgency, but not too obviously or intensely this early in the transition toward sales activity, but DON'T gesture toward the window or the door, you aren't sending them outside.

"and these questions you came in with about how life insurance serves you "

Present tense now to put this into his immediate reality, and to tell his subconscious mind that he should have this now.

"as an investment "

We chose the word "investment" because of a comment the prospect made when he set the interview that told us something about his motives.

"as well as security for your family. While I'm thinking of it, "

Flat, palm down motion toward the booklet on the desk you will be directing his attention to, hand is loose, not pointy or demanding.

"there is a graph that gives the big picture"

Briefly make a circular pointing gesture to maintain the prospects attention down toward your hand and the presentation booklet.

"perfectly right away."

This sounds like it won't take much time, and like it will give some immediate gratification for an information-oriented person who is maybe feeling like he's lost some control.

"I should "

Should, there is some external authority you are obeying, apparently, and it's vague, which helps create more psychological flow, and maybe it has something to do with your prospect's interests, that must be why you "should" open it.

"open this up to... "

You sound like this is all some kind of afterthought or parenthetical comment, thus creating more of a here-and-now experience to condense psychological time, creating more of a flow so that the prospect does not feel that too much time is passing by.

Let's look at that again without the comments:

"John, John, please, I can only take in so much at one time, you've given me so much to digest and share, and I also know you're here with your wife, and with the afternoon coming to an end, and these questions you came in with about how life insurance serves you as an investment as well as

security for your family. While I'm thinking of it, there is a graph that gives the big picture perfectly right away, I should open this up to..."

Direct Redirecting

After all that redirecting magic in the prior pieces, I want to suggest something very different, and a lot shorter. It is a very directive approach. You may not want to use this approach when you aren't sure enough of their personality or your rapport with them to be really direct. However, you need to know that many of the people that get off track like this are not obsessed, they are just unfocused and lose track of time, not realizing that they are wasting yours. And many of the people that are obsessed are not so touchy that they will be offended by your being very direct. You'll have to decide which approach to use when.

Here is a directive approach example: *"This is fun, but I really need to get focused here because I'm on the clock and I need to keep my boss happy. I'd like to ask you to really keep extra comments down to a minimum now while go over this with you and we see if we can set you up with the right vehicle."*

Yes, you actually should say things like "extra comments" when you are doing the direct redirect. You risk the possibility that they might take offense. But they'd have to be easily offended. You are using nonjudgmental language. What more can you do and still be direct?

Besides, if you are using this with people who don't respond to your more subtle signals, then this is your last chance, anyway. Otherwise, they'll just keep monkeying around, and you have other customers coming up who will not waste so much of your time.

More Details of Direct Redirecting

Here's another example: "Oh, gosh, I had no idea it was three! Can you possibly forgive me for letting myself get out of whack here. I only have a little time here. Can you help me make sure I get through the presentation part quickly so we can decide what would be the best option for you here?"

That involved several good angles. You showed surprise to break state and command attention. You improved rapport by being a space cadet who had no idea what time it had gotten to be. They can relate to that. You created urgency by saying you only had a little time. Urgency can get an ADD person back on track to finish a project. In fact, they use it on purpose to help themselves get focused. Sometimes that works for them, and sometimes it's a disaster, as you can imagine. Also, you asked for help, so now they have the opportunity to be a hero. Remember their hunger to be the hero in a pinch.

Bear in mind that these folks often really want to please and be accepted. Especially the late bloomers. So your willingness to give them very specific instructions in a respectful way may be a very positive and refreshing experience for them, and an opportunity for them to prove themselves. Yes, to prove themselves. I'm serious. So give them the opportunity.

In fact, if you feel that they are not the obsessed type, and tend to be more the distracted type, like you tend to see with folks with ADD, I suggest you use the direct redirect BEFORE you consider the more subtle version. As you use these, you'll become intuitive about it. The conservative thing, of course, is to be subtle first. It's your call.

Some folks who are off track distract you by being very flirtations or getting your attention off the sale in other ways. These folks have unfulfilled needs that are kind of like a tire with a slow leak. If they don't get those needs refilled regularly the go flat or something. You could say these are narcissistic needs. Self absorbed people can generally be redirected using the methods above, but you have to have your own head on straight not to get sucked into their needs. You can try getting their tire pressure up to the right level though by providing comments that they seem to need. You just have to be very careful about the implications. A very flirtation person shouldn't pull you so far out of shape that you end up accused of sexual harassment or something. But you can certainly be very complimentary about his or her stylishness. You can ask questions about where they get their hair done or where they shop, even where they work out and how they obviously keep in great shape.

ABOUT GESTURES AND RE-DIRECTING

I'd like to share some useful thoughts about using gestures when you redirect people, especially people who get distracting. I'll provide an example gesture to learn.

Keep in mind that gestures help you as you break their state. Part of the power is that it is a sensory-rich experience because it adds the visual element with movement and significance to your redirect. They aren't just looking at your arm or hand, they are seeing movement and arm and hand movements are meaningful. But you knew that.

There is also neural recruitment. That is, getting more of their brain involved in what you want it involved in, which is the sales process. And we really are talking about the numbers of neurons involved.

Be sure to use hand motions and expressions that do *not* show agitation. You might be feeling some agitation because of their behavior that feels like they are controlling you in a negative way, and because of time slipping by, so you'll have to practice this so the wrong impression doesn't come out of you. You want to use smooth motions.

Don't push with your palms. If your palms are facing them, it's like you're rejecting them and pushing them away. Don't give them anything to "push" against on an emotional level. If anything, draw them in so they will initiate their own stability.

Here's a great example to use with people that are caught up too much in distracting thoughts that are taking them out of the sales process. Learn to use this one for redirecting attention to what you are saying and to your face so they will see your facial expressions:

Move as if you are bringing the person's energy toward your chest and gently swooping it up toward your face. This hand motion will help both of you stay positive, too.

A key feature of this hand motion is that it redirects your prospect's attention more to your face, where there is a lot of information that can help draw them out of their inner world and get them into a more interactive state of mind.

WHAT ABOUT PEOPLE WHO ARE EASILY OFFENDED OR UPSET?

Since you focus on rapport building and have very good social skills and etiquette, it must feel especially strange when someone seems so easily offended that they almost seem to want to be offended. Some people seem so fragile that you almost feel like you can't do anything right. In the structure of a sales situation, you aren't likely to have trouble with them they way you might in personal situations. Nonetheless, it happens. They may take offense and try to get you in trouble with your boss or talk about you behind your back to other people in the community. The one thing you do have on your side, at least, is that most people can tell that the person complaining is the kind of person who has all sorts of offensive things happening to them, but doesn't notice that other people don't have this problem. They never seem to figure out that they are the common denominator, and they should be doing some introspecting or getting some good therapy.

Odds are that, if you follow the steps in the next piece, you will be able to get things back on track and close the sale. This personality type has difficulty feeling okay, and is easily thrown, but with soothing from an outside source, they can usually stay on track long enough to make it through a sales process.

BACK ON TRACK WITH A SUPER-SENSITIVE PERSON

You can get back on track with these people with a simple two-step maneuver. First, you recognize what their sore spot is and make a mental note to avoid it. Most likely is not so much a spot as a style. It is a kind of thing that gets them going, like a tone of voice, a look, or anything that has to do with their behavior when they are being distracting or intrusive. Since these people feel like victims, they are not very capable of recognizing that they can victimize other people. To them, they are always David, and everyone else is always Goliath. They need rescuing. They tend to want people to ally with them against a bad guy, so the may split other people against each other. A favorite game of theirs is, "Let's you and him fight," to borrow from the late Eric Berne.

Your second step, which you should do immediately, is to issue a profound apology. What do you have to lose? Your dignity? I'd rather have the sale. I'm not married to the person. Try something like this: "Oh, I really owe you an apology. I didn't realize I sounded like that, and I apologize from the bottom of my heart." Then add something that you think, feel, or respect about them that helps put a salve on the hurt. Then make a comment that bridges to your intention to make the process positive. Then bridge to the sale as soon as things seem to be sufficiently on track.

When you start, be sufficiently surprised, chagrined, and horrified, that they know they had an impact, and then become more positive in increments. Don't, under any circumstance, display that you are overwhelmed by their feelings, or resentful that they don't see you as a good person. Do not be defensive. Do not become agitated. Do not accuse them of being unrealistic, irrational, over-sensitive, high-maintenance, shrill, or any other negative trait, no matter how true it is and how much they need to know about it.

Borderline Personality Disorder, an Oversensitive Type

To help you think about this issue, I'll cover a couple of the oversensitive types that you are most likely to come across. These can overlap with each other, or yet other problems, or all occur in the same person:

Borderline Personality Disorder

These folks have a terrible time staying steady with their emotions. Once they get upset, it can be hard for them to get back on track. Worse, their "reality" tends to shift with their feelings. That's whey you can suddenly find that, in their eyes, you are the bad guy. Their level of feeling justified about their temporarily warped perspective can be really jarring. These folks often use drugs or alcohol to medicate their own feelings, which can make for an even wilder ride if they're under the influence when they are in the sales process. You wouldn't necessarily no it unless they're very impaired or smell like alcohol.

They can get a lot of help from psychotherapy if it involves enough of a specialized educational approach, and from medication, but that isn't your problem. Your goal is to provide enough understanding and guidance to get them through the sale. Your inner goal is to override your normal instincts to be defensive, patronizing, angry, frustrated, insulting, or hurt. It isn't your fault they have this serious personality problem. It isn't exactly their fault either.

Trauma and Abuse History, Varied Needs

Some people with trauma and abuse in their childhoods can seem like people with borderline personality disorder, but the problems are rather different. These folks may have some very specific buttons, but most of them are living their lives and do fine in a sales situation. Some of them have immature social skills, but you can work with that. Some of them have trouble thinking because their trauma is interfering with their sleep, or it included physical trauma that caused one or more brain injuries. They may self-medicate with drugs or alcohol.

You may notice that there are some topics or situations that begin to arouse anxiety or some other emotional reaction that seems out of proportion to what's going on. You can usually see it coming if you're sensitive to their emotional state. They can usually tell you what they need, such as not to be in a confined area or for you not to stand too close.

If the person has enough psychological trauma affecting them that their sleep is troubled, they may really be coming apart at the seams. This can mean becoming hot-headed and otherwise really reactive. In this case, it's best to show understanding, but mostly be very neutral with a pleasantly positive, grounded demeanor.

There is excellent therapy for these folks. Medication is sometimes helpful if things are getting bad. But your job is to watch for signs that people are becoming reactive, and explore how to modify the situation so they can stay comfortable and focused on the sales presentation. Soliciting their desires and how they want things to go is usually fine, because they usually can get to the point and de-escalate without a lot of help, other than you being understanding. Some of them will need extra help because they have trouble with focus or details.

What about People Who Escalate?

This is possible with some mental illnesses and mood disorders, and maybe with some rare versions of trauma. You could go through your whole career without seeing it in a sales situation, though.

In Trauma

In the case of people with trauma, if they shift into seeing you as the bad guy, it's likely to be because they feel coerced or that you are unfair in some way. Give them the sense that you are backing off and letting them vent about what they want to see happen. This is not the same as borderline personality disorder.

If they seem to be escalating, and this is really rare to see in a sales situation, then you might want to get into a spot where you can't be cornered. Ask them what they would like to see happen, what they want to do, and what they think would help the situation. Do this whenever they get off that subject and begin escalating again, such as by becoming accusatory. Let me say again, this is only something you'll see in a very small subgroup of people with trauma histories. I don't want to create a stereotype or unnecessary alarm. I've seen it once, and that was a street person who was off the hook when he came in looking for a bathroom.

In the unlikely event that the person were to become threatening, someone in your office would probably have called the police by then. You would certainly want to forget all about your dignity and get out of there and into a safe situation, even if it meant sprinting. Do not fight, even if you know how, unless you have no options.

With Psychosis

The problem with escalation and possible violence in mental illnesses is that it may involve psychosis, in which the person is not responding to reality. They may think that violence is justified for very bizarre reasons, such as you being in a conspiracy involving the CIA and using mind control. If you get the sense that there is escalation and psychosis, then you do not want to focus on calming them down as much as getting in a safe place and getting the authorities to see what this person needs. That's because it is unpredictable. It isn't that mentally ill are typically violent, even the ones with delusions (bizarre beliefs). It's that you want to play it safe. You don't want to try to sell to people who are actively psychotic (in the middle of a false reality), anyway. They are impaired. It would be unethical in most sales situations, except for routine purchases such as for food, and for small items. But you aren't a clerk.

Sell to People with Thinking Glitches

As I said early in this section there are countless ways to get brain injuries. That means that many of the people you sell to are recovering from brain injuries. It also means that they are all over the map in terms of what they can and can't do, and how steady their emotions are.

Here are the key things to know. The brain has different parts that do different things. That means that one brain injury can make it really hard to remember details, and another brain injury can throw people into an emotional roller coaster.

However, if the damage is widespread enough, they can become disabled across many areas. Consequently, they may and need a lot of help just living independently. You see this with elderly people who are developing Alzheimer's syndrome, a disease that tends to just keep getting worse.

Also, brain damage can range from being a vegetable, to just having a little trouble staying organized.

For salespeople, you could almost say that this adds up to a lot of nothing. The category "brain damage" is kind of useless, because it could mean any ability is affected, and it could mean that it is affected to any degree. Maybe the person is lousy at math. Maybe they can't remember the details and are really depending on you to keep the facts straight. Maybe they think they can make a purchase they can't, because their relatives haven't realized that they need a whole lot of shepherding to stay out of trouble. In that case, you have an ethical responsibility to refrain from taking advantage. Any so-called salesperson who can sleep at night after taking advantage of a mentally impaired person is really no better than a common thug.

Responding to Thinking Limitations

Many, many medical problems, including psychiatric ones, cause brain injuries, just like a good hit to the head. Depression, bipolar disorder, schizophrenia, and mild strokes can all create thinking problems that need to be healed. And the healing is in two phases. First, the brain has to heal, just like you might have to heal an athletic injury such as a pulled tendon. Then, information that got scrambled has to get put back in. That's basically relearning or reconnecting. Like any learning, that phase can take a while.

There was a very talented professional photographer who made very good money at his craft, but who had some kind of stroke that made him forget who he was. When he was first shown his apartment after the stroke, he didn't know that the photographs hanging on the wall were his. He first thought that perhaps he was a collector. He had no idea that he was a photographer. Part of his rehabilitation was to go to school and relearn photography. He learned very fast, because the connections weren't completely gone. But he still had to go back to school. It's hard to believe, but it's true.

So I think the take away message about thinking limits is to be very alert to what your customers can and can't do, and to refrain from being judgmental. Someday, it could easily be you, as common as problems like brain injury and Alzheimer's are. All it takes is a good smack in the head from your head rest when your car gets rear ended, and you could be recovering from serious thinking difficulties for months or years, depending on how bad it is. Honest!

Keep in mind that everybody has some mental slowing, and it starts in our thirties! Sorry to deliver the bad news. But look at the bright side, there's a lot we can do to preserve our wits. That information is readily available to you online and elsewhere.

We've all met quick-witted elderly people, but even they normally have some difficulties with mental inefficiency including memory glitches and slower thinking in some ways.

When you talk too fast to someone who doesn't think as fast as you do, it makes your words kind of blurry, like a fast-moving object. It makes the ideas kind of dance around in a way that's hard to get a grip on. This is unsettling to customers who are less efficient, because they want to understand. You don't want to trigger feelings of insecurity and confusion by getting out of step with these customers.

Practice pacing your slower customer so you can get good rapport with them. Take a walk in the park and find an elderly person to chat with. Or go visit an elderly relative. Sit down with an elderly person and notice how you can adjust your pace more to their liking. You might notice that this throws off your natural style, though. You can practice bringing more warmth and presence to your style while you converse with slower or elderly people. If you get a real quick-witted elderly person, notice any ways that they miss the beat so that you can understand how these mental inefficiencies are not across-the-board, instead, they can be very specific difficulties.

Saving the Sale and Maybe a Loved One

If you can pick up the slack as needed when your customer has a brain injury, you can save the sale. If you can talk slower and not get impatient going over the details repeatedly, you can save the sale. If you can be understanding and warm, even though they are slow or easily confused, you can save the sale. If you can keep from taking it personally if they misunderstand agreements or think they are entitled to something they aren't, you can save the sale. If you can educate or remind instead of lecture or get angry, you can save the sale. And if they are too impaired to go through the sales process, perhaps you can get them to connect you with a relative. That person might help them through the process by taking charge. Or that relative might explain that they really shouldn't be buying what you have to sell. Well that's good to know. That will save you some time and keep your conscience clear.

And here's some valuable, possibly life-saving advice. If one of your friends or relatives starts doing something like getting disorganized, not following through, forgetting stuff, or hoarding (which is basically not being able to decide what is important), then really look into it. Those are all common characteristics of brain injuries, whether they are from a smack in the head, a concussion from an explosion, a small and undiagnosed bleed in the brain, or a serious condition that is just getting started. Homelessness is not the only problem caused by brain injury. These folks have a high suicide rate, largely because they go undiagnosed and just take the social stigma to heart. This leads them to carry out the ultimate form of self criticism. But it doesn't have to be like that if everyone would just get a little better educated and be more responsive about pulling some help together.

Late-Bloomers Need to Be Heroes

Have you ever noticed how comic books usually have a hero who is kind of nerdy, and who has to keep his identity a secret. Doesn't that sound like the inner world of a kid who is a little (or a lot) marginalized.

Why do you think techies have a reputation for being into fantasy?

Why do late bloomers and underachievers seem to have big comic book collections or a fascination with online identities and role playing games?

It isn't just because they have fertile minds. Many of them resort to fantasy worlds because they are not satisfied socially, and don't get the kind of positive feedback that they need for good, balanced self esteem.

I'm not saying every person who is into games has a brain challenge, I'm just saying that there are reasons for these stereotypes. One of the most prevalent diagnoses for the people this piece is about is attention deficit disorder (ADD). A lot of salespeople have that! Same for actors, emergency medical technicians, fire people, counselors, and people who are into extreme sports. I can't tell you the percentages, just that they are likely to end up in work that doesn't require the kind of mental organization that being an administrative assistant or major event organizer does.

ADD lends itself more to situations that don't cover too much of a span of time, unless there is enough support for staying organized, like the owner of a large business who has a good assistant.

RAPPORT WITH THE LATE BLOOMER

The thing about this for salespeople is that many of the people who have brain challenges have not overcome some fantasies, and they have not fulfilled some important social needs. This means that you can do two things to improve your rapport with them.

One is to help them feel like a hero, because they tend to have a real hunger for that. They may even have a bit of a false identity around *that* that you don't want to interfere with.

They may have developed a real identity around that, being a hero over and over as an emergency medical technician or fire person. That's a pretty good outlet for a need like that, don't you agree? I respect that. If you're heroic, maybe it shouldn't matter how you got that way!

To feed the hero hunger, you should stress that aspect of the purchase. The aspect of how others will perceive them. Of course, this is a general rule. Don't let this advice override your instincts if you are getting the sense that you should handle a late bloomer differently.

To avoid stepping on their sometimes fragile sense of self, don't take any chances with joking around or bringing attention to any mistakes in any but the most gentle way. Never show frustration with them. It won't fix their neurological problem. It will only risk breaking your rapport.

Learn and focus on anything you can that is about the heroism or sacrifice in their struggles or contributions, whether it's sports, family, career, or anything else. If they need the attention for that, you'll have no trouble getting them to respond to questions like, *"Great weekend, wasn't it? What did you do?"*

MORE IDEAS FOR ABSOLUTE FANATICS

ANCHORING

Anchoring sets you up to trigger a state of mind or an emotion in yourself or a prospect. The anchor is whatever you do to promote that state. It comes from the science of behavior modification that animal trainers use. It works on people, too! You'll learn how to do it in the Anchoring Workout. Do NOT underestimate the value of anchoring! It works unconsciously, so nobody has to believe in it for it to work. The animals don't believe in it, either.

One way to anchor is to get positive feelings anchored to your product. It's easy. Every time the prospect is in a positive state, expose them to something about the product.

That could be the product itself, an image of it, a thought about it, or a thought about using it or benefiting from it. So if the prospect comments on the drive they took up a beautiful highway, you mention that the car your selling is create for road trips, because (insert reason here).

You have many opportunities throughout the sales process to help your prospect get into a state of mind or feelings that are good for the sale. "You don't have to wait for a positive feeling to flit through your prospect. In life insurance sales, I will drop in a story with a good feeling connected to life insurance. My last customer mentioned that he was having some marital problems.

Later, he told me that when he went home and told his wife about buying the life insurance policy, her estimation of him went up a lot." This is a great one to tell a customer who is married. You don't have to be as obvious about it as in this story. I'll leave it to you to create the kind of subtle moves appropriate for your customers.

USING ANCHORS STRATEGICALLY

The power of the anchor does not just lie in creating a positive connection to the product. You can activate an anchor at a strategic moment. You can goose the sales process with it, help process an objection with it, and do your closes with it. This is called "triggering" the anchor. You trigger the anchor by doing whatever it was that you did each time the prospect was in that positive state of mind. You might anchor for any positive state, or a particular kind of positive state.

So let's say every time your prospect shows a positive feeling or thought, you work in a word and gesture combination into your immediate response. It could be as simple a saying "yes" in a warm voice with a gently positive emotional feel to it. At the same time, make a little thumbs-up gesture. Not a big one, just one that is almost unconscious-looking. Work that in as many times as you can. Then, when you need to activate a positive sense, do that same word/emotion/gesture combination.

When you're close to closing, work your trigger into the test close. Considering everything we've talked about, wouldn't you say, yes (do your emotion/gesture with that, that's your anchor), this is the right model? When you get a positive response, hand them the contract.

By the way, you are getting yourself positive and focused as you anchor your prospects. This creates the double whammy of your own positive alignment moving the sales process forward, fueled by charisma.

ANCHORING WORKOUT

You have learned that you can anchor a state by providing the anchor each time the person experiences the desired state. Once you have anchored that state, you can quickly activate it by triggering it with the anchor.

Here, I have broken the process into steps to help you practice. You can practice on yourself by anchoring confidence.

Step #1. Pick the state.

Based on your sales process, pick a state that would promote the buying decision in a typical prospect.

Step #2. When and how will you elicit the state?

Think of various ways that you get your prospect in touch with that quality during a typical sales process. For example, if quality is a key selling point, think of ways that you get the prospect in touch with quality. At those points, you would probably be using words like quality, top notch, excellence, fine workmanship, and so forth.

Step #3. Decide on the trigger.

As you'll recall, this can be a gesture, sound, key word, or any number of other things. I like to combine the first three. It might be straightening your posture just a bit, with a flash of pride on your face, and making a little smack sound with your hand on the desk or your thigh. I'm still surprise at how much anchoring I can do with no one noticing. I caught myself doing it during a sales training and explained what I was doing. Then the students pointed out that the person I was working with changed their own posture for the better when I fired the anchor.

Step #4. Anchor the state in a prospect.

Get with a prospect, and apply the trigger each time you believe that the prospect is responding with the desired state. For example, any time they give you a look that they are in touch with having quality in their life, apply the trigger. Remember, it doesn't have to be the quality of the product. It good be any experience of owning or being in contact with quality. Make the state as strong as you can. Remember not to use the trigger when the prospect is in any other state so that you will not dilute the power of the trigger.

Step #5. Elicit the state during the close.

When you feel that the prospect can respond to a close, make firing that trigger a part of the close. For example, "Having this fine workmanship (fire trigger) in your home is an excellent (fire trigger) choice, this form will get our people over to your home to install it perfectly (fire trigger) within 48 hours. By the way, to add to the effect, hand the customer a very high-quality pen for completing the form.

PROFOUND IFS

How many of the limitations you have regarding your current sales situation are conscious? Probably a small minority. In this piece, I'm suggesting that you make a lifestyle discipline out of uncovering the unexplored beliefs that are costing you sales, satisfaction, and inspiration.

When inventor Dean Kamen (the guy that came up with the Segway mobility device) made his fortune by re-inventing health care devices, he did it by revisiting and trashing assumptions that we had about these devices. He did not make an amazing new discovery, he just re-applied known laws of physics, but with a limit-breaking, profound-if question: what if these things could be smaller?

Now he has patents for much smaller versions of filtration devices and other things that allow people to have health care at a lower cost, and without spending a lot of time in a hospital or outpatient treatment setting.

I want you to list as many limits as you can think of; things that limit your income or sales. Include things that are obvious, and seek things that are unspoken assumptions.

Then stash them in places where you'll find them. Put a few on your desk at work. Put some by the toilet at home. Put some on the counter and your desk at home. Lay a few on the floor in your car.

Each time you come across them, look at one and think about it on and off while you engage in an activity that gives you some room to think, like driving. See how many ideas you can come up with that might be breakthroughs. As you know, when you're brainstorming, go for quantity, not quality. It's most likely that you'll get your best breakthrough ideas because your mind has been thinking in that way, rather than because you're in a breakthrough thinking session. Instead of in the session, it could be in the shower.

Here are examples of limits that people have come up with:

- *There are some personalities that I just can't sell to.*

- *Our reputation for customer service has taken too many hits, and it's costing us x% of sales.*

- *The economy is harming our sales figures.*

- *The new media is killing us.*

- *Cultural changes are making us less relevant.*

- *Burnout is hurting my productivity.*

- *Our location is bringing in the wrong kind of people.*

- *Young (or old) customers are taking up my time for small purchases.*

- *Management is getting in the way of real progress around here.*

- *I'm so bored with this pitch I could scream.*

- *I have to work around the clock to make what I used to. This lack of exercise is killing me.*

- *The other sales reps are out-foxing me, and it isn't fair.*

- *The competition has a better offer, and people are voting with their feet--against us.*

- *The manufacturer just isn't in step with the times.*

- *My face (hair, disability, voice, speech impediment, dyslexia) is not helping me with sales.*

WHAT ABOUT ANOTHER LANGUAGE

Hmmm. How useful would it be for you to be able to talk to several million (or many millions) more people? Are you already too busy? Consider the possibilities.

Would you like to try working in other countries? How about combining business with pleasure (and a tax write off) by selling while travelling?

How about being able to make and pick up calls that the other agents can't? You get the idea. If you want to become basically conversational in another language, we recommend starting with an audio program.

The *Pimsleur* programs are the best to get started with. Then the ones that go a bit faster and do drills, such as Barrons are good. Then we think you should join a language club and sell to all the members while you learn, or find a way to work in a country that speaks the language.

Well, we did say this section was for absolute fanatics. I'm not going to hold back now.

You can put your audio language lessons on a player and practice while you drive, walk, do the dishes, you name it. You can watch movies with subtitles. You can subscribe to a word of the day from a service such as *Dictionary.com*. There are many ways to infuse yourself with another language.

What language would be most useful to you in your preferred industry? If it's an Asian language and you're sued to a western alphabet, you'll have a bigger challenge, because it will be like reading all over again, only worse. Arabic? Not quite so hard, but hard.

But then, you are a glutton for challenges. I guess I shouldn't try to talk you out of it.

Succeed in School

I can hear some of you saying, "I'm not going back to school. I'm not the school type. I've gone as far as I can. Besides, I don't have the energy I used to." ...or something like that. Ah, you can do even better than that. You know plenty of examples of entrepreneurs and sales successes who dropped out of grammar school to turn tricks on urban streets in the snow while on heroin, but who are worth millions now.

Well, this article can't take such things into consideration. This, after all, is one of the ideas for Absolute Fanatics, and it's about the benefits of going back to school, or, more to the point, succeeding in school, since that's the point of going, for most of us, anyway. With that in mind, let's start with the reasons. Since you already know all about turning selling points into feelings, I'm going to take it easy for a moment and share some logical ideas. If you think they're true for you, please turn them into emotional motivators based on the Four Big Beliefs.

Okay, here are some really good reasons to go back to school:

- Your Career relevance, as in, being a choice candidate;

- Keeping up with changing times, as in, your ability to maintain mastery of your profession with demands that are changing with technology, culture, economics, business models, etc.;

- Being more interesting, as in, well, just being more interesting...wouldn't you like to be more interesting?

- Your career arc, as in, higher, longer, and more profitable;

- Sales engineering or other career moves, as in, your ability to make a semi-lateral move into a more lucrative area of sales such as sales engineering;

- Being competitive, as in, being the one who gets hired;

- Relating better to certain target markets, as in, people who are more educated and, generally, have more money to spend on higher-ticket items. You know that rapport supports sales. You know that like attracts like. So if you are better educated... you do the math.

- The security and buying power of the two-career, highly-paid couple. Your higher education could net you a classier mate, if you're looking. Hey now, don't judge me for being materialistic. It's just part of life. It's as easy to fall in love with a rich person as a poor one, but it's easier to get a highly-paid, educated person to fall in love with you if you are also such a person. Okay, I was just pointing out something I've observed. Don't shoot the messenger!

GROUP PRESENTATIONS AND SALES

GROUP PRESENTATIONS AND SALES PSYCHOLOGY

PRESENTATION PSYCHOLOGY

A lot of you, dear readers, are old hands at presenting. But even experienced presenters will find some very useful items here. At the minimum, they will come across some things that will make them say, "Oh, yeah, I should really practice that. I don't really do it as much as I could." I won't go into much about stage fright. There are so many books on public speaking that go into that, there's no point in me reinventing the wheel. But I do want to remind you that the best presenters find ways to just be themselves in a powerful way.

Much of this section is based on the idea that you continuously communicate with your participants' subconscious minds. I want to show you how to turn that to your advantage. Think about your current presentation abilities. What do you do to choose and elicit the optimal state in your participants? How many ways do you have to manage their state of mind and emotion? How well are you getting your audience into an open-minded, patient state? Do you have plenty of ways to create a sense of rapport between you and the audience?

Think about that, and the pieces to follow will be easier to use and remember.

THEIR STATE, FOR STARTERS

At the beginning of a presentation, you want to get your participants into the best state for the presentation. But many participants will have arrived in a state that is not ideal for your presentation. This means that you need to direct them, in subtle or indirect ways, to be present, and to build momentum toward the sale, no matter what happened prior to their arrival.

I'll take a crack at it. *"Because of our wonderful reputation, I know that many of you are here for the coffee and cookies. (Laughter) And some of you were referred by customers who have experienced our Acme Vacation Experiences. How many of you are out there? (Raised hands.) Great!"*

You started by breaking their state, whatever it was, by getting a chuckle. This took their minds off things and warmed them up to you a little. Then you directed their attention to the product in the context of customer satisfaction. To that end, you even fired the social truth trigger we talked about, by having the participants who were referred raise their hands.

You will want to kindle this state by adding elements and triggering desire. For example, *"Certainly, many of your best memories are vacation experiences, because that is a special time for adventure or for bringing families together. And I know that you were drawn here tonight by the possibility of having truly great vacations. Of course, you have had to limit your vacations in order to be responsible when it comes to your budget. I'm not sure what kinds of sacrifices you have had to make when it comes to time with your family away from the daily grind. But I know that you would do just about anything to make it a reality, so long as you could do it in a responsible way."*

As you might have guessed, the demographic for this presentation is heads of households who feel that they are on tight budgets, and who take some pride in making responsible decisions. They also value their families and dream of having more togetherness, as well as getting away from it all to have special memories.

At this point, their minds are on their needs, I have stirred up some of the pain they feel in wanting more togetherness and away time. From here, I would go for the attractiveness factors. But the point is that, for beginning the presentation, I shifted their state in the right direction, and brought them into the presentation as full listeners.

Ways to Elicit States in a Group

Here are some ways that you can get your audience into an optimal state, whatever that might be for your particular presentation.

Go into the state and model it. The more rapport you have with the group, the better they will match your state. If you go there in stages you will keep more people with you. It prevents losing people.

Rely on group mood: Moods are infectious. Even if only a couple people are beginning to follow you into the desired state, that's a good start. You can do something with them to get other people to feel like that is the group direction. For example, if you see someone getting excited about the product, you could briefly get them to interact with you about how they will use it. Existing customers can offer a positive comment.

Refer to memories that generate the state: You don't know what specific memories every person in your audience has, but you can still refer to them. Speak in general terms and let them fill in the details. *"What things from your vacations create the memories that you most enjoy recalling or retelling?"* This works when you refer to common experiences like going on a vacation. Most likely, at least 75% of the audience has experienced it. Most of the remaining 25% have experienced something like, so they can still relate to it.

Scale the experience for the state: You can use major experiences, such as receiving a gift or having a success, or experiences fragments, like planning something that was going to work out well. Do you need to goose the state along, or do you want to be more dramatic? Which choice best fits that point in the presentation, that audience, and your subject?

Avoiding Problems with Group States

Caution: Never assume that you know what state you will get when you refer to a common experience. The larger the group is, the less of a concern this is. In a smaller group, one person having negative memories about what you bring up could throw things off. But even in a larger group, if you are insensitive to a cultural issue, you could throw the entire group. How many people in your audience would feel left out or uncomfortable if you appealed to their memories of Christmas. Especially if you were speaking to the Anti-Defamation League. Not everyone has experienced the birth of their first child, and if they did, the experience may not have been joyous.

Your experience: If you talk about your own experiences, people can better appreciate what you're feeling. Also, your experiences help you generate and model the desired state.

You can go for a wide reference, like being in a hurry, or a micro reference like wishing a line would go faster

Looking forward to it: Can you refer to something most of them are looking forward to? Audience members are likely to have an idealized version that is not contaminated as much by past negative memories. On the other hand, it may not be as compelling as an actual past experience in eliciting a state.

Mix it up: Don't depend on a single thing to generate a state. Have a whole grab bag of things that you throw in, all promoting the same state.

ACCESSING PERSONAL REASONS WITHOUT BEING PSYCHIC

Your audience's personal and professional reasons for being in front of you are keys to a useful state. You can't walk up to each one and interrogate them, but you can use general language that will activate the individual listeners interpretation. Consider using a sequence like this:

- *Why you're (the audience) here.*

- *Dissatisfaction with prior experience (for which you will have solutions).*

- *Present desires and the opportunities that they are aware of now.*

- *Future possibilities.*

- *Urgency (while this opportunity lasts).*

Consider these phrases that you could work into the presentation to activate their reasons for being here.

As you read this, imagine any profession that provides a service. You could rewrite this, inserting text about any profession with which there has been some dissatisfaction. Business consulting, psychotherapy, debt consolidation, debt collection, advertising... And any product, for that matter.

"The reasons that brought you here tonight may be that some of you have experienced a service like this, but it did not go as well as you had hoped. You may have already thought of ways that it could be improved upon. You may have doubts about the entire profession because of other things people have told you about their experience. Many of you feel that you have lost a great deal because this service was not available or not providing what you wanted. But you decided to see what was offered during this presentation because we promised that there would be fresh insights about new ways of doing things so you can have a better result. Maybe, from the advertising, you are holding out some hope that you can do some things that had seemed impossible before. Others of you are looking forward to doing the things this service makes possible."

Notice that this speech begins with a general reference to "reasons" and continues through to negativity. Using what "you decided" (reinforcing their commitment to being here, to help with a useful identity shift) we transition into the positives: what is offered, what we promised, fresh insights, new ways, better result. That's a lot! We move into future possibilities of hope, can do, had seemed impossible (contrasting with past perfect tense), looking forward, makes possible.

That's a lot of triggers. Putting in some profession specifics would not dilute that very much, it would only make it more meaningful.

From there, you will have an easier time creating more interest and acceptance. You will be leveraging their enhanced connection with their reasons for being there. You will use the many methods you are learning to do a compelling presentation that sells your product.

CREATING A SUSPENDED STATE

A suspended state is a light trance. People experience suspended states on and off every day. Some do more than others, of course. A suspended state is useful for sales presentations because it promotes a more open-minded and patient state in the audience. I'll show you ways to promote that state in this section. These states are also used a great deal in one on one sales, but I'm offering it here because it goes so well with the group topics in this section.

I encourage you to learn more about hypnotic communication for sales. It is not a hokey way to do robotic mind control, although you may run across some scheisters who promote these skills in that way. They make pretty big promises. But it is true that those skills are very valuable.

This book includes many of these skills, but not all in one section with a title saying "Hypnosis Here." Hypnotic communication can go on without actually trying to create a significant trance. They don't require you to act spooky or speak in a slow monotone. Some speakers that use a lot of hypnotic methods speak very fast and with a lot of emotion. They get the conscious mind very occupied. But they are speaking on two levels. They are talking to the conscious and unconscious minds at the same time. When we learn about metaphors, you will be learning an important hypnotic communication method.

A lot of the language you are learning in this book is based on what I call "hypnotic grammar." It produces a mild suspended state because of the way the mind has to sort of scan for meaning in order to process it. Hypnotic grammar is a very important part of the art of persuasion.

I believe that using language for influence goes far back into pre-history. Still, that's no excuse not to think about the ethics of such powerful methods as hypnotic communication. Throughout the ages, ethical principles have prohibited abusing people with powerful methods. This is interesting to me as a salesperson, because I know that hypnotic communication training got a lot of its knowledge from medical and psychotherapeutic hypnosis. I think this obligates me to consider their ethics. I may not be helping someone stop smoking, but I shouldn't help throw away their money, either. If you have any concerns about the ethics of your business, make every effort to clean it up or move on to a better situation.

IDENTITY FOR RAPPORT WITH A GROUP

It is important for you to have rapport with your audience. Obviously, much of what you have learned about gaining rapport with an individual does not apply to a group, because you can't match the body language and other aspects of a group. There is plenty you can do, however. Remember that the majority of rapport-building has to do with the unconscious and more-or-less automatic behavior.

Part of your rapport depends on your ability to influences how your audience sees you. What is your identity in their eyes? How you do that will depend on the group, the effect you need to create, and your own natural strengths.

Here are some typical aspects of your identity that you the presenter needs to boost.

An alpha person, an attractive leader to be watched. Your introduction can reinforce that. You can describe your accomplishments, but packaged as inspiration or instruction.

An interesting person. One who has very important or provocative material, or who arouses curiosity as to what they'll do next. Come up with unique or humorous ways to convey your points.

A very likeable person that the audience really wants to see succeed and have a good time. Self-deprecating humor and stories that show you are one of them will help you do this.

This work occurs on both a conscious and unconscious level. If your material is very important to the audience, that will create enough arousal that you will hold the audience even if you are not all that interesting. But you don't want to be satisfied with that, because you want a strong buying response to what you are selling.

RAPPORT: MATCH THEM, MATCH EXPECTATIONS, OR BREAK EXPECTATIONS?

When you work to gain rapport with a group, is it better to match them, match their expectations of you, or break out of their expectations?

Maybe all three!

Match: You can't match every member of the group as you would one-on-one, but you can demonstrate that you are one of them, if that is appropriate. Even when you are supposed to be different in some way, you should still find as much overlap as possible. Even if you are from Mars. Especially if you are from Mars!

Different: But if they expect you to be different somehow, how do you generate rapport? If they expect you to be the expert, a comic, a leader, a brilliant business person or anything else that they don't think they are, that is no reason not to be fundamentally like them.

That is your foundation for rapport. The rest is fulfilling their desire for instruction or inspiration.

Break out: And when would you want to break out of their expectations? If they have stereotypes or preconceptions about you, your cultural identity, your business, your career, your company, or anything else.

Subvert prejudice: It's okay to draw their attention to the preconception in order to preempt it. Humor is very good for this. Stories that show your commonalities can help. Having a person they relate to and respect do your glowing introduction is a strong prejudice breaker.

Gender stereotypes are alive and flourishing in some groups. If you are a very feminine woman presenting to a group of technical, mostly male, specialists, your feminine charm might hold their interest. If you can prove your competence, you might subvert their bimbo stereotypes, preventing them from assuming that you lack expertise. They may not want to be biased, but it's pretty easy for people to maintain unconscious (or even conscious) stereotypes in an environment where they are not exposed to enough exceptions to their stereotype. So a group of male techies that don't see a lot of competent women, may not even realize it, but may feel less motivated to take the presentation seriously.

Genuineness Injection for Rapport

There's a sure-fire way to let people know who you are in a truly genuine way. It does not require embarrassing yourself! I'm sure you're relieved. Simply tell a story of how you dealt with an awkward situation and got out of it. Note that I said awkward. Not tragic, difficult, or stupid. Those can be good. But awkward is special. It has a certain balance of light-heartedness and seriousness.

People are very curious about an embarrassing, or potentially embarrassing situation. They want to see you get out of it, because they can imagine themselves in it. And they are pleased to learn of whatever wiles, wit, or other resources you brought to bear.

I heard a psychologist once talk about having realized that he was in the ladies bathroom when he saw the woman's shoes going by. He described pulling his feet up out of view and having to wait through several rounds of ladies coming through before he could escape the embarrassing situation. He had the audiences full attention, and got some good chuckles from a serious audience that he was going to talk about some serious things to. I don't even know if the story was true. But it was a good way to connect with the audience.

THE ALPHA FACTOR

To achieve an alpha status as a presenter, you must either have it transferred to you, conferred upon you, or you must build it with your content and attitude.

Starting off with a strong, well-rehearsed beginning is important. But you don't have to try to act bigger than life. In fact, you don't need to act at all. You need to bring out your own voice, and your own conviction, so that you come through to people. A common misconception about alpha behavior is that it is commandeering or aggressive. In fact, in most situations, trust, good judgment, and predictability in a command situation have more to do with building up an alpha identity.

If an alpha presenter precedes you, then their handshake with you in passing the speaker role to you can transfer that alpha status for your presentation. You can generate some of that status by using some of the mannerisms or other aspects of a presentation by an alpha presenter or other alpha person that everyone knows, such as the CEO of their company or minister of their church.

You can gain alpha status by getting the group to all do something. This can also help get them into a good, energized, attentive state. For example, some presentation situations will allow you to get everyone moving in some way. Tony Robbins has gotten everyone up on desks, dancing to Wipe Out, a 60's surfer song. He has also gotten everyone to stretch.

You can get the group moving by saying, "I know you have been in your seats for a while now, and bodies need to move, so let's stand up for a minute and do a couple very good stretches I like to share with people." Doing a very obvious upward sweep of some kind with your own body language will help the group get up without hesitating. Notice the wording. There was warmth in, "for a while," and "for a minute," and, "I like to share with people." There were some alpha qualities in, "I know," "bodies need to move," and "very good stretches." In these, the speaker knows what's best, invokes what bodies need, and has something very good for you.

MOVE IT, CHANGE IT

Use these techniques to maintain interest. These are little skills that make a big difference.

Maintain interest by changing position, direction that you face, and posture every few seconds.

Maintain asymmetry. Do not say in a symmetrical (forward facing, limbs the same on each side) position for long without a really good reason.

Gesture consistently, expressing the mood you want to convey.

Change the mood you express. Make abrupt and significant changes in mood and tone periodically. Engineer your talk so that it makes sense for this to happen.

Change volume substantially along with mood changes, or changes in the material.

Walk to different parts of the stage. You can use connecting with different parts of the audience as your apparent motive. Actually that is your motive. Just not your only motive.

THE INTEREST FACTOR: ANIMATION WORKOUT

Watch a major comic or talk show host, and you'll see that they do not stay in the same position for more than a few seconds at a time, except for special circumstances. Perhaps these seem like extreme examples to use, but you don't have to imitate their comedy or intensity to take advantage of this animation factor.

Try this experiment. Give a five-minute talk in front of a mirror, and set an alarm to go off every five seconds while you give your talk.

Every time the alarm goes off, change your physical orientation in a significant way. Turn your body to the side, then to the other side, cock your head, face directly forward, change the angle of your body, crouch. Do this exercise again, significantly changing your facial expression with each shift as well. Do it again, adding a significant change in your position on your pretend stage. Do it again, adding a significant change in your tone of voice, speed, or pitch.

Finally, do the exercise with those changes happening with each sentence, so that your voice, facial expression, and body position somehow highlight or help to express that sentence. Keep this important guideline in mind: Do not make your movements or gestures extreme.

Until you have gotten mastery of this skill, keep your gestures within an imaginary egg-shaped boundary that is only a few inches beyond your skin. For now, you must have a very good reason before you move your hands outside of that boundary, because it is the silly boundary. Without a good reason, any hand motions outside of that boundary will probably look silly. Try it and see.

Once you have made animation into a habit, you will be able to generate more interest and hold people's attention. You will also make your material have much more impact, because so much more meaning will be coming from your body and voice.

THE FRIEND FACTOR

This factor is the one that depends the most on the rapport skills that you use with individuals. But, since you can't mimic traits you observe in all the individuals in a group, you have to imitate the group, sort of. Although there is diversity in every group, get to know the demographics of your audience. Are they conservative, all business all the time, easily bored, highly educated, technical...? The essence of the friendship factor is that you blend in with the group by how you dress and speak, and how you express your values.

If you have people from a general population coming to you, get to know what kind of people your offer tends to attract. If you do the presentation in different locations, then you want to learn about the people in those locations. You can learn a lot about the demographics of a location from a librarian or online. If you weren't able to do that, take notice of the body language and clothing of your group. Do they have money? Do they seem stiff?

It is easier if you are brought in to an organization, because the coordinator will be able to tell you a lot about the group well in advance. The coordinator or other organization contact wants things to go well, and knows their group.

They will be motivated and informative. If you have other contacts in the organization, give them a call and see what they can add. You can always learn more about an organization online, taking a look at news, discussion, and their own site. News well help you know what to be sensitive about. Most organization have certain topics that are sore spots.

A comedian did a bit for a group of sex therapists, and thought they were kind of cold, so she said, *"I guess they just like to watch."* If you encounter a group that is not very responsive, don't let it throw you. Just make sure that you aren't offending them, and keep going. If you are in front of a clinical or technical group that doesn't seem very responsive, emphasize information and know that they just aren't very expressive people. But afterwards, get some opinions or have them write comments, so that you can see if there really was anything wrong.

But what about if you are supposed to be the expert, and you do that by dressing very well and carrying a very expensive briefcase. You can have your cake and eat it, too, by dressing well, but knowing your audience so well that you will still be able to come across as one of them in numerous ways. Here's a good example. Some presentations benefit by the presenter being one of the people that came from a poor or working class neighborhood and made it good. If that applies to you and your group would resonate to that, then make sure they know a little about where you came from.

MIND MULTIMEDIA: SENSORY RICHNESS

I think there are two kinds of multimedia. One is from physical things like projectors; things you see and hear. The other is the movie in your mind. You can create quite a multimedia presentation with nothing more than a listener.

Sensory Richness: The most well-known way to do this is to create sensory-rich presentations. That is, you include all the senses. You include language describing what you're describing in terms of sight, sound, feelings, and maybe even taste and smell. You can give a glimpse into your own thoughts or the thoughts of the person you're talking about as well. And remember that feelings aren't just what you can touch, like heat or cold. You can create very strong identification with a character in a story by including some of their internal feelings. When you do, don't just say "upset" or "relaxed." Come up with something a little more descriptive like, *"as the situation began to resolve, I could feel my shoulders coming down from ear level and I took a deep breath."* Weave the senses together for what you are describing.

MIND MULTIMEDIA: 4MAT

There are dimensions other than senses that you can include. You'll find various systems and categories. Here is an example that is popular, called **4MAT**. It is known more among educators than presenters, but I think you'll see it's value for certain sales presentations. The purpose is to involve the participants, regardless of how their brain works. As you know, people have different ways of being sold, different profiles of strengths and weaknesses in their intelligence, and different learning styles. Research has been very supportive of 4MAT for education. In sales, I use it to get clear on my primary role in doing a presentation. I also make sure that I include each style in every presentation I do. I even use different body language and a different tone for each one. This variety helps to hold interest.

1. Why? Give the why to the point, Reinforce it with discussion, if possible. People understand why best when they are involved. A demonstration discussion can create a sense of participation. Even bandying about the perspectives on your own can accomplish this. It also shows your ability to understand other people's perspectives.

2. What? Tell the what. This puts you more in the position of teaching. Your job is to make it interesting.

3. How? Explain the how. You are now coaching. Not one-on-one, but you can use a coaching style. People like to know how to do things and how things work. Especially how to improve their circumstances. When it comes to how, they trust the person who knows how, whose been there, and who is a kind, nonjudgmental teacher.

4. What if? The magic of "what if" helps open people's minds to possibilities. With "what-ifs," you can break the ice with some humor. You can promote self discovery. You can build vision.

"What if your company was the global leader in using green technology in your industry?"

"What if you could break records for production in your unit?"

It's good to start with what they call a "little what" to frame the presentation. *"this is what we'll do for you today,"* or *"this is the experience we have for you this hour."*

Think about this when you see the section on meta-programs. You can appeal to more people in your audience by using making your talk reach out to the different meta-program types.

Think about one of your presentations. How can you tweak the material to include the senses and the 4MAT categories.

MIND MULTIMEDIA: HAVE, BE, AND DO

Here's one more. Does your presentation tell people what they can have, do, and be as a result of purchasing your product? If you start making a list on that, you'll realize that those three words each mean a lot of different things! As you look at the examples below, note that you could say the same thing three different ways. This is so you can appeal to different people in the same group. It also helps you appeal to different aspects of the individual. Take your product for example. Try expressing two points about it in all three ways.

Have: You can have the product, have an experience, have an insight, or have a belief, and I'm just getting warmed up. Your prospects can have an experience of having the product, which can be a real insight that gives them a strong belief in the product. What can you say about each of those things for your product? Is the insight that they can have a cut in energy costs with minimal disruption?

Be: You can be a better person, be confident, be accomplished, be a better, confident, accomplished salesperson... You can be frugal by buying this product, but confident in it's long-lasting quality. And you'll accomplish more, making you a better, more accomplished person.

Do: You can do a project, do something with your life, do something in a new style, do more with less... As you consider the many things you can do with this product, like slicing, dicing, and even julienning, you will be able to do so much more in just a half hour in the kitchen! And you'll cook more new dishes from around the world with this free cookbook, designed especially for this fine product.

TAKE THE PULSE: POLL AS YOU GO

You may think you should always give exactly the same presentation, but... We'll maybe you don't think that. Anyway, whether you do or not, your audience will never be exactly the same from presentation to presentation. I like to have modules that I can insert to my talk depending on the general make up of the audience and how they respond to the presentation.

To help me do this, I ask the audience some questions as I go. I ask for a show of hands. I have found that audiences are very cooperative, because they are all used to raising their hands from grammar school on. This also helps me work with the audience a little bit to improve sales. When people see how many hands are raised, it acts as social proof. Also, getting people involved and moving is good for breaking their current state. Breaking state is a good way to get started generating a new state.

Here's an example. I need to know whether I need to explain basics in detail or gloss over them.

"To make sure I give you the best possible talk, I'd like to take a quick poll. How many of you know someone who has benefited from a life insurance policy? Well, it isn't surprising that few of you have raised your

hands. *Now how many of you know someone who needed to benefit from a life insurance policy? Wow. This really speaks volumes, doesn't it? But how many of you are really confident that you understand the different types of policies? Right. Most people don't. Well, it's pretty easy to understand the basic types..."*

In this example, I introduced the poll with a good reason. I brought out that people need life insurance. I established a good reason to go into the basics. I even introduced that it would be easy to understand. Notice that I didn't say explain or teach, I said understand. That is active and positive. It's what you want.

AUDIENCE RESPONSE

As you take in the response of your audience, you'll get a sense of how you are doing. If the response is poor, that's a good sign that you should make adjustments to your presentation.

But which adjustments? If you're getting disinterest or boredom, I'll guess that you were blind-sided by getting an audience with different demographics than you prepared for, or you are simply new at presenting and need to develop a compelling presentation.

It's good to get some laughter from your audience, but don't allow this reinforcement to have a behavior mod effect on you, causing you to lose the sales power of your presentation by providing too many humorous antics.

On the other hand, if your audience is not laughing as you expected, you should completely change or eliminate your humor in a conservative manner. It is very easy to lose an audience with the wrong humor. People tend to underestimate how challenging it is to create comedy, and how much practice it takes to develop comedic skills. It's one thing to get your friends laughing, and quite another to get an audience laughing.

A common error is to be so caught up in trying to do your presentation perfectly, that you don't catch the subtleties of the audience response. Scan the audience as you speak. This also creates the illusion of eye contact with the audience, because everyone in the general direction of your gaze will feel that you are looking at them. Use what you observe to fine-tune your presentation on the fly.

Whenever possible, especially when you are developing a new presentation, have an associate watch the audience response and take notes. You can even have a camera trained on the audience and watch their response the way football players review their game on video.

STRUCTURE A STORY OR POINT JUST SO

You make many points in the course of delivering a presentation. You probably throw in some examples or stories as well. You can make more impact by presenting your points, examples, and stories with some structure.

Here is a good structure, and I'll bet you've heard this one. But are you using it?

1. Tell them what you're going to tell them. "I want to tell you about a feature that will save a lot of time."

2. Tell them. "This feature can do..."

3. Tell them what you told them. "As you can see, our customers save a lot of time with the xyz feature."

You can use with structure with any point you'd care to make.

Here's another structure.

1. Fact or story: "At Acme Industries, they have saved this many FTE's in just their first year of utilization."

2. Point: "Your company has the same needs and can get the same benefit. You need this."

3. Benefit: Our analysis suggests that you can save this many FTE's, adding up to this much money.

Think about your points, and make a reflex out of delivering them with a structure that brings out the point and the benefit. Elsewhere in this book we will provide more structures based on the core needs that drive the prospect.

STORIES, METAPHOR, AND SLEIGHT OF BRAIN

Metaphor, What's it Good For?

A metaphor is a way to get something across to people without saying it directly. It is an indirect way of talking about something where a symbol takes the place of what you're talking about. For example, William Shakespeare's line, *"All the world's a stage,"* introduces the stage as a metaphor for the drama of our lives. A story full of metaphors is an allegory. Some economists think that The Wonderful Wizard of Oz was an allegory for U.S. monetary policy in the late nineteenth century. All I knew when I was a little kid was that it was too scary to watch!

In sales, you can use metaphors to help bring a good meaning of one thing over to your product. You can help to put a perspective on the purchase or use of the product. The examples to come will show you that very powerful people use metaphor in sales and politics very successfully.

People absorb metaphors best in a suspended state. And you are now learning how to get people into a suspended state. Not only do they benefit from a suspended state, but a metaphoric story helps to produce or reinforce a suspended state.

One on one situations do not lend themselves to lengthy stories, but you can drop smaller metaphors into your sales process. But in presentations, you would be remiss if you didn't think up at least one metaphor to work in as a story.

You can increase the power of metaphor even more by nesting stories, where the multiple stories are embedded into layers. I'll show you exactly how to do that and provide a good example.

As you go through this section, see what kind of metaphors you can think of for your sales process.

METAPHOR EXAMPLE: GOOD RETIREMENT

Here is an example of a practical metaphor: After he retired, General Colin Power was doing speaking engagements. He told a story to a very large audience. The story was meant to help Americans feel good about American products and ways of life, and to get them prepped for a brief sales presentation that was to follow his talk.

He described his pride in buying a Corvette, and getting to drive a Corvette as a pace car before an Indy 500 race. He told this in the context of his retirement, making people want to have a good retirement. This just happened to be a promise of the sales presentation that was to follow. He was, in effect, an alpha male transferring his dreams onto the product that was coming up. His retirement was a metaphor for everyone's desire for financial security and their own retirement. I'm sure most people had no idea that they were listening to a metaphor for selling a product. But Powell was paid a lot to be there. He wasn't promoting a foreign policy or political candidate. He reason given for the speakers was to provide inspiration and motivation for success. And the speakers did offer that. But the business model for the talks was based on making money from sales. Most of the people who came paid little or nothing to get in. They had free tickets that had big prices on them, implying that everyone else paid a lot to be there. This gave even more imputed value to the experience and the products. Metaphor works in many interesting ways.

METAPHOR EXAMPLE: ECONOMIC RESILIENCE

At the same event where Powell presented, Rudolph Giuliani told a story as well. It was about a situation in which he was with George Bush. It sounded like a photo op that involved meeting the fireman and rescue workers involved in 9/11 when a fireman who was very angry about 9/11 was talking to then-president Bush. In the story, the fireman was much bigger then Bush, and angrily told Bush to just, "Tell us Americans what to do and we'll do it!"

The objective of the story were to 1) Elicit the pride that the audience felt about being Americans. The story held the audiences attention. This was in the wake of 9/11, so it built upon the bonding everyone was experiencing. At that time, the media was working very concertedly to give the feeling that the public was facing a common enemy. 2) Make them feel good about Giuliani by reminding them of his role in helping New York post 9/11, by referring to Giuliani and Bush being together with the workers. 3) To generate faith in America and it's economic resilience.

But these were metaphors and states. The political and commercial purposes of these were this (in my opinion, based on what I know about the funding of these events. 1) To boost Giuliani's bid for president that was to come. He was working hard to transfer as much of the heroism associated with the twin towers, and the power of Bush, and good feelings about being blue collar (this audience was largely blue collar) to himself. 2) This was to build, through metaphor, interest in a stock analysis software product that was to be presented and sold there. The evidence of the economy being resilient supported the feeling that stocks would be a good investment vehicle. 3) To promote buying behavior. By increasing the bond that the audience felt, the audience members would be more likely to go to the purchasing area when they saw a lot of other people doing that. He was enhancing the power of social proof. We'll learn more about that in the section on automatic behavior in sales.

NESTING

You can get your audience's attention fixed on your story, and help them experience a suspended state, by nesting your stories. You can put several stories together into layers. You do this by starting your first story, and then interrupting it to begin the second story. You can go several layers deep if you like. When you end the deepest layer story, go on to finish the next to last. Continue until you finish the first story. If that's hard to picture, it will be clearer when you see the example.

Each story that is left open is a piece of unsatisfied curiosity for the audience; some unfinished business. This helps to hold their attention. You don't have to do anything special to interrupt your story and begin the next. It can be a simple as, "Oh, that reminds me." when you close off the story you could say, "oh, yes, I was saying..." You can use more sophisticated connections for a smooth and meaningful transition if it serves your purpose. As you gain experience, you will come up with transitions that fit your topic, audience, and the mood you are creating.

Nesting is a good way to get people back into the state they were in before they took a break. You can leave one or more stories open and promise to continue when they return. This regenerates their attention. It also resolves the unfinished story, creating a desire for more of these kinds of payoffs. It tells them that they can trust you to present well. Payoffs show people that they can trust their attention to you. This is an unconscious payoff, as opposed to the ones where you tell them directly what they are getting. You do that when you follow the advice to, "Tell 'em what you're going to tell 'em. Tell 'em. And tell 'em what you told 'em."

You can build your skill in nesting by writing out the topics in an outline style. This way, you will be able to keep your place, beginning and ending them in the right order.

STORY NESTING: FULL EXAMPLE

Here is an example story that goes four levels deep. If you didn't know it was going to be an embedded story, you might not even notice the technique, because each level holds interest on its own. It is a metaphor for the audiences fears and needs pertaining to life insurance. It is very direct, and could almost be considered an example, rather than a metaphor, except that there are symbolic elements that go beyond being examples, such as the staff person taking people under his wing, which represents the feeling of having life insurance ready to take care of you.

(Start 1, drawing interest from current disastrous event.) The very sad news about that freeway accident last night...

(Start 2, drawing interest because the audience can relate to the industry described, and it arouses curiosity about what will happen.) ...reminds me of a time when I was presenting to a group of very fun-loving people, in a very fun-loving industry, and you could tell they were people who wanted to be where the action was, they didn't settle into the talk very well at first, because they wanted to finish the conversations they were excitedly having as things were beginning,

(Start 3, drawing interest from a serious incident that affected the staff that they are already identified with.) ...but I noticed how somber they all got when the boss made an announcement about one of their crew who was lost to an avalanche. His name was Dale, and he was in critical care and they all hoped he would pull through, I felt bad about the atmosphere being so sad and me coming in to talk about another serious subject like life insurance, so when I was called up for my presentation,

(Start 4, draw interest from me deciding what to do with the group.) ...I thought about how groups like this respond best when I talk about being able to take care of their insurance needs and then, since it's all taken care of, get back to enjoying life.

(Start 5, drawing interest from what staff had to say about Dale.) Prior to the presentation, I had been talking to the staff about Dale, so I knew some things about him; so I talked about what his life was like, and how staff had told me that he was always contributing to the fun, and was very giving, He taught several of the other staffers how to ski, and even did volunteer work with disabled skiers on the weekends. I talked about how the desire to have fun, work hard, and give can make life into an exciting blur that makes people skip right past taking care of an important need like life insurance.

(Start 6, drawing interest from more intimate details.) One of the staff told a story about him, saying that he actually was a very organized guy, and that he was the type who would take people under his wing. He would even bring up life insurance when he went to a baby shower, and somehow could get away with that without seeming intrusive, I guess because he had earned everyone's trust.

Well this staff person told other things about Dale,

(End 6.) ...and I kind of didn't present my full presentation because I saw that they needed to talk,

(End 5.) ...so I made it really brief,

(End 4.) ...but several of the staffers who had been putting off their life insurance signed up because they had him on their mind.

(End 3.) I left the meeting with a strong reminder that often people have to be moved by a profound experience to take care of something that many of us take for granted.

(End 2.) I suppose that accident will affect some people that way, but for the victims that did not have life insurance, it is too late.

(End 1.) Whatever your motivations are for creating the security that life insurance affords, you can be sure that there is a product that matches your needs...

Packaging Your Nested Metaphors

If the audience is pretty well engaged, then you don't really need to explain yourself when you launch into a story. But some situations call for some set up. The more suspended and interested the audience is, the less set up you need. But for professional audiences that have very distinct expectations, you may need justification. They will be more impatient with a story, unless they expect some entertainment because of the situation.

You can make the what and why of your story a part of the flow, like this. "You know, the accident last night reminded me of..." and it seems to make sense that you would bring up what it reminds you of. You aren't really giving a reason that appeals to anything other than their curiosity. To give a more meaningful why, you might say, "The accident last night really reminded me of just how life can happen after we've made our plans. I have to wonder how many people postpone things like their life insurance and have their families regret it. I want to tell you this story so you will be more motivated to protect your family."

But is it really necessary to say all that, given the power of the metaphors? I think this would make people feel coerced and cause the story to feel tedious because they already know exactly why you're telling it. A little suspense is good for a story. My advice is to make the metaphor convey the meaning, and save the more direct messages for the instructions to the audience to visit your booth or whatever it is they're supposed to do during or after your presentation.

METAPHOR NESTING WORKOUT

What metaphors might help your sales process? It's okay to use obvious metaphors, like the ones in the life insurance example above. But it's a good idea to make them subtle enough not to make people feel manipulated. The body language feedback you get from people and the results will help you dial in your technique. As you work with metaphoric stories and comments, you find ways elaborate and lengthen them. Find ways to make them more sensory-rich and natural. Remember, adding senses makes what you say more engaging, like they way a good movie fills the senses and gets the audience involved. The movie you create pushes out things that distract from the sales process, and builds a world in which they can easily buy. You decide what is and is not in the movie.

Pick a metaphor. Think of a story that fits the metaphor. It's okay for it to be brief.

Come up with more metaphors as you get used to thinking this way. Once you rack up some metaphors, think about how you could take a few of them and nest them into a nested story.

YOUR "INSTRUMENT" FOR TOP-NOTCH PRESENTATIONS

Speech Level Singing Technique for Presenters

There is another very popular trick that is part of a system called Speech Level Singing⬚. It offers so much vocal quality and control, that it is used to meet the special demands of today's popular vocal styles. A vocal trainer named Seth Riggs designed Speech Level Singing to meet this challenge. Even public speakers find that they experience greater ease of speaking with this method.

By avoiding too much pressure or vocal distortion, Speech Level Singing allows your voice to do a "zip" effect, in which the vocal cords narrow when you raise the pitch (frequency) of your voice, and to open easily as you drop down into your bass (low) range. This effect is mechanically like a violin or guitar string. With this technique, you can glide through your full vocal range with no breaks in your voice. You can also increase your pitch range and accuracy without creating strain that can damage or tire your voice. It also supports your full use of your body's resonance, making you into a higher quality sound instrument with a very adaptable voice.

When Speech Level Singing was being developed, they used stroboscopes to perfect it. Vocal cords vibrate so fast, that you can't see them. However, with a stroboscope, you can tell exactly how fast they are vibrating, and how far apart or how tight they are. This is an excellent way to measure vocal stress scientifically.

Key to Good Vocal Mechanics

Your vocal cords, also referred to as vocal folds are fairly soft and vulnerable to damage. They are two folds of tissue that join at the front of the structure in your throat called the larynx. The technique I'm going to share with you is popular because it respects the vulnerability of the vocal cords, preserving them despite the demands of a heavy presentation schedule.

This technique differs from the untrained speaker or singer in that they tend to force their vocal cords to fight against their air pressure. They are tightening their vocal cords against the pressure. They constrict their vocal cords and then use a lot of pressure to force them apart in order to create high pitches or special effects. They think this is normal, but it can harm or exhaust their voice. By using this technique, you will learn to relax your vocal cords and get maximum voice quality.

This technique has helped some performers maintain very demanding schedules while maintaining vocal luster. You can tell the presenters and vocalists who use this kind of method by the way they run through the range of their voice without sounding effortful or distorted.

The basic idea of this technique is to keep the larynx in the proper position as your vocal cords stay together no matter how high or low you take your voice. This gives you a rich, even vocal quality. If you like to use different voices or vocal effects because you do more of a performance than the typical presenter, then this technique offers some advantages. One is that you will be spending less time distorting your voice in ways that can wear it out. Another is that you will be more conscious of when and how you are doing it, so you can maximize the effect while minimizing the stress to your vocal chords. Finally, you will have added control that can help you discover more ways that you can manipulate your voice that are not stressful.

Vocal Method Workout: De-Stress Your Voice

To get the full advantage of this method, we recommend that you consult a Speech Level Singing coach. However, I have enough comfort with the technique and have used it long enough, that I can offer you a key to the method that can get you well along to the benefits of the technique.

1. Get to know your larynx. That bump in the front of your neck that everybody calls the Adam's apple is the cartilage around your vocal chords, and it's called the larynx. When your Adam's apple moves upward, your larynx is changing shape to tighten your vocal chords.

2. Shift your voice up and down while you are touching it or looking in the mirror and you can see for yourself. In fact, I want you to do this for a while, whenever you practice speaking or singing. This will really build your intimacy with how you are using your voice, and how much stress you are putting on your vocal cords. Notice where your larynx is when you are not speaking. It should be close to the same position as when you are speaking in a normal voice without much effort.

3. As you raise your pitch, touching your larynx, learn to keep your larynx from moving upward. That is, your larynx stays in position even though your voice is going up. The more you practice, the better you'll get. A trainer can help you do this in the most effective way. But, to be honest, I started practicing before I consulted a trainer. I can't resist experimenting with something that can improve my presentations.

4. Take your voice up to a high pitch (not too high, don't break into a falsetto, and don't cause distortion). As you touch your larynx, modify your voice, noticing what modifications cause it to drop back into it's normal speaking voice position.

5. Do the same thing with your voice down in your low (bass) range.

6. As you get to know this technique, begin applying it as you sing and speak. Over time, practice increasing your range while keeping your larynx fairly relaxed. Especially when you feel like you are forcing your voice, or when you hear distortion, practice getting that effect or pitch from your relaxed larynx position as much as possible.

Soon enough people won't be able to keep up with you, unless they know and use your new "secret" energy sources. If you practice regularly you'll get an obscene amount of energy and balance from this, and I say obscene, because it is like obscene profits, you can get way more than anyone could deserve for how little effort goes into the chi kung and postural work that you do.

ADVANCED GROUP SALES PSYCHOLOGY

Modeling Charisma

Did you know that many charismatic speakers share a common pattern? You can learn it! Try it right now. Do you have a recorder or video camera handy? No? Well try it anyway. Impress and surprise yourself.

Remember learning about using senses in public speaking? Especially sight, sound, and feeling?

Feelings: Start your presentation by including references to feelings. If you know about using your body in producing your voice, originate your voice from your lower torso. Emphasize the lower part of your pitch range, but without straining or sounding artificial.

Sound: Then move to sound. Include sound words. Come from a more middling part of your torso with the mid range of your voice. Step up your temp a little.

Sight: Then sight. Using sight words, speak more from your upper chest and higher pitch. Talk a little faster.

This way, you engage people who favor any one of these senses. You'll make sense to everyone. Also, you will be getting the feeling people first, and pulling them up into the other senses.

You can do this subtly and gently, or in an extreme way. There was a congressperson who did this. But he would start high to begin with, and would not change his tempo. This caused people to joke about him being a robot.

A great time to do this pattern is:

- When you first begin your talk.
- When you are building to a climactic point. Then is when a more pronounced pattern is good for a crescendo.

- When you are making a point that doesn't stand out for a climax, you would do the subtler version of this method.

Ways to Do It

You can do this as a wave, moving up and down, or for a more dramatic style, jumping down and working your way back up. Each new point can be the beginning of a new wave.

When telling a story, I prefer to mix the senses, to carry everyone along in a sensory-rich way. As you use this charisma pattern, you find how, when, and how much to use it in your presentations.

It seems that the feeling-oriented folks are especially sensitive to hearing things in their feeling terms. This is why we start with them. Coming back to them at the end of the cycle is good for everyone. It drops them down from the peak, makes the feeling folks more comfortable, and creates more interest and variety.

Drop into the feelings at the end and an interesting thing happens - the visuals and listeners will follow you into their feelings, and their feelings will have been prepped, so that it is a positive feeling that gives more power to your presentation. It also reaffirms the feelers as you are relating to them in their comfort zone again, sealing the deal for everyone.

HELP FOR THE CHARISMATIC

In the controlled environment of a presentation, you can muster a lot of charisma, make more sales, and as long as you have already handled any public-speaking anxiety, you'll most likely be just fine. But as you build this charisma, and it starts affecting your personal life, people will have different expectations of you and reactions to you.

Here are the guidelines. The full treatment of this topic goes beyond the scope of this book but I'd be doing you a real disservice if I didn't get you sensitized to this issue. If it doesn't apply to you, remember that sooner or later (probably sooner) it will apply to one of your trainees.

1. Know your weaknesses, especially invisible disabilities such as attention deficit disorder (very common among salespeople) or emotional trigger issues (very common among all human beings).

2. Manage others' expectations. If they have high expectations of you, guide them to expect what you can do, and not expect what you can't. But that means you really have to understand yourself, or you will gleefully dive off the high dive into the shallow end of the pool.

3. Manage your own self concept. Evolution has shaped us to create a more perfect impression to the world. This is a survival mechanism. It has helped to keep us alive. Predators are less likely to go after the stronger members of a tribe or herd. But don't be fooled by your own façade and others' reactions to it. And don't be let down by seeing through it to your imperfections, either. Make it a top priority to become comfortable with your strengths *and* challenges, so that you can smoothly manage others' expectations of you, and set yourself up for success. Self knowledge is a great power, so long as you prime your self esteem to handle it.

How to Survive Your Own Charisma

This book will increase your charisma, but will you know what to do with charisma when you increase it? There's one thing I don't want to do, but it is something that some motivational speakers accidentally do. That is the high dive effect.

If you psych someone enough, you can get them to dive off of the high dive. But there is a problem. Did you make sure that the high dive was over the deep end of the pool? You have to do that before they dive! You can see the same thing with getting people psyched up to start a business or develop charisma. Will they know how to handle it once they get it?

If you have lived into your adult life without feeling like you have ever handled charisma, you want to know how to handle it before you get it. At least, you want to have some basics so you don't unconsciously sabotage yourself. You know how subconscious minds are. They are always busy figuring out how to take care of your needs. The problem is, unless you manage them and provide good instructions, they can act like they are mismanaged and need better instructions.

ANCHOR SPOTS

If you misspeak in some way, don't be psyched out. Move away from that spot. If you need to comment, gesture to that spot as you correct yourself or apologize.

Choose spots on stage to represent states you want in the audience. Consistently stand on the spot that matches the mood and material you are covering. Your "good" spot is where you will stand when you talk about your product.

This will tend to foster additional positive feelings about your product. You can guess where to stand when you mention the competition or not buying. Yes. The BAD spot. For an instructive controversy about this, learn about the Willie Horton ad.

If the previous presenter was not good, don't stand where (or how) they stood.

The left side of the stage or area seems to be more dominant for most people. Try to be here when you should have primary attention or leadership. A moderator may put the panel more on that side because the moderator is taking a secondary position to the luminaries on the panel.

People tend to experience the right side as being the less dominant side.

Try to have information up and to the left. Experience suggests that this is helpful. As of this writing, there is not enough research on the subject of positioning.

Keep only a very limited amount of information on a display at one time. You want a very specific point brought out at one time. You do not want people to be absorbed in your display, and getting out-of-synch with you. You usually will want to emphasize feelings a lot. If people are getting pulled into an analytical frame of mind, you may lose your momentum and rapport.

Recovering from Significant Mistakes

A significant mistake is the kind in which you have really misspoken in a meaningful way, like by accidentally insulting your audience.

If you make a mistake like this, immediately step into a different position and face the prior position. Do and say something indicating that you have a reaction to it that many other people would have. If you can add in a little wit, or say something that shows you are beyond thinking like that, all the better.

For example, let's say you inadvertently blurted out a political opinion that turned out to be unpopular with the audience. You could step aside, gesture to the previous spot, and say, *"Well, thank you for blurting that out, and now, for equal time, we present (name of a famous person with an opposing view)."*

Then step to your opposite side, and state, in a compelling way, something critical of the prior opinion.

Saying something critical is better than actually conveying the opposing opinion because it shows that you really understand the weakness of the opinion and are open-minded. Every opinion has its weaknesses, even if it is right. You don't have to believe that your critical comment is the best opinion, just that you can use it to express your understanding. After all, if you do not understand the opposing viewpoint, what good is your opinion, anyway?

Prepare yourself in advance not to be so intimidated by a mistake that you simply gloss over it or are so mortified that you are thrown off altogether.

BE READY FOR PROBLEM QUESTIONS

Be sure to think of the questions and concerns that your presentation will create in a reasonably intelligent person. I once innocently asked a presenter how his product was different from a competing product.

He had implied strongly that his was special, but he became embarrassed, and never recovered his confidence during the presentation. I felt bad that I had made him feel so bad, and I had no idea my question would have this effect.

Take this a step farther, and be prepared for tricky questions and comments from people who want to appear smart or who are shills for the competition. It is amazing what silly questions the occasional wise guy will come up with.

And I say "wise" loosely, because these people really aren't bright enough to realize that they are not asking a sensible question. They are just harming their own credibility.

Enhance your credibility by responding without getting flustered, angry, or sarcastic. In fact, put on a little extra kindness, and briefly, but methodically, respond so that there is no question in anyone's mind that you can answer this as you fully erase any doubts that it raises.

If a question raises an issue that you can't respond to, it's best to say so rather than to fake it. Maintain your credibility, it's priceless. "Oh, I don't have that information yet.

I can get that to you if you'll leave your contact information with us. Thanks for bringing that up." The thank you at the end provides some reverse masking and ends on an upbeat, open tone.

Lecterns

Just in case you've heard of people, *"speaking at the podium,"* the podium not what you speak at, but what you speak on. You stand on the podium. T

he lectern is what some presenters stand behind while they speak.

The lectern may have a light that helps the professor read notes as the students sleep through the Power Point presentation. It's also convenient to clutch and hide behind for those who have anxiety about public speaking.

For a skilled, confident presenter, focused on achieving the right effects for their presentation, the lectern is either a prop, or it is not used at all, unless it is for traditional purposes required by the presenter's role.

Think for a moment of all the things you could do with a lectern. You could get behind it while acting scholarly or like a politician; step out suddenly as a dramatic move; lean on it with limbs akimbo to punctuate an awkward fact or set the mood for a relaxed telling of a story; get right in front of it and move toward the audience to modify your size for various effects.

You could move it out of the way before your presentation.

Your lectern offers a convenient reference point for you to do anchoring using space. It makes it more obvious where you are on stage in relation to it.

A mic stand can fulfill a similar role, and I'm sure you can use your imagination (or watch some comics who use it as a prop). But unless you are very well-practiced, don't try anything that might cause an incident. A corporate presenter, imitating a famous rock star, pitched the stand upside-down, lost control of it, and was knocked unconscious by its base. That is not how you want to be remembered.

NEGOTIATE LIKE A PRO. WAIT, YOU ARE A PRO!

START THE NEGOTIATIONS: DEMANDS AND FIRST MOVES

POWER NEGOTIATORS UNDERSTAND THE IMPORTANCE OF GATHERING INFORMATION

Before the face-to-face negotiations begin, you must learn all you can about the other side. Fortunately, there are many kinds of information that can help you. This business intelligence comes from librarians, the government, portals, and many other outlets. Learn all you can about how to expediently gather information related to the industries and companies that you sell to.

Try to develop a good sense of what these companies are likely to offer, and how they are likely to respond to your potential gambits. You must also know the market, and that includes your competition. If you know what the competition is doing, you'll have a much better idea how to position yourself. In sales, the most aggressive information gatherer is often the one who wins. Don't be that guy that stays lost because he doesn't like asking for directions. Develop an insatiable hunger for business intelligence.

Most of us find that the more we dive into the information pool, the less we realize that we know. This can be intimidating or overwhelming at first, but it gets better. The more skills and sources you acquire, the more powerful and efficient you become; the better your judgment gets as to where to put your time in preparing for a negotiation; the more your knowledge will turn out to be recyclable into new applications, giving you an even more streamlined experience. It's a great feeling to pick up speed that way. It's worth the early investment of time and effort. Learning will become more and more fun as you have more knowledge to put it into perspective with.

GET THE INFORMATION AND THE SOURCES

Definitely get into the habit of asking questions. That means that you have to get into the habit of discovering questions. You'll be surprised at just how much you've been taking for granted as you develop the gift of curiosity. You know those people who always seem to know something you don't? They get that by thinking of questions. Of course, it helps to know people with answers, but I'm getting there.

Remember I mentioned librarians? You'll be surprised how helpful they can be. These people are pretty bored with lame questions, so tossing them something really interesting that they don't already know will get many of them pretty excited. They'll throw out various sources of information that you've never heard of, and maybe even find the answer for you on a slow day. And, of course, the online sources continue to expand and improve. It's important to stay on top of those. Despite the proliferation of professional sources, I still get a lot out of scanning through discussion forums. It's amazing how much information gets bandied about because the people have an illusion of privacy that comes from the feeling that they are having a personal conversation.

LEARN THE ART

Remember to loosen people up with open-ended questions. Those are the ones that are not easily answered with a simple yes or no, for a single fact. Here's a nice open-ended question, *"What is the business climate like now for sensor equipment? I heard that the imports are becoming a problem in some areas."*

You can get all kinds of information without seeming too obtrusive. And this is helpful, because some of your best information will come from personal contacts; sometimes fleeting encounters with people that you don't even know that well. Consider the income taboo. You wouldn't ask someone out of the blue how much money the make. And you wouldn't expect people to freely answer proprietary questions about deals they have made or what they paid a specific vendor. But some people will, sometimes! You want to be there when that happens and you have to ask somehow.

I suggest taking the well-mannered, but taboo-breaking approach of making the question less direct or less personal, by making it a bit more general. Phrase an income question like this, *"Tell me if this is too personal, but what would I expect to make in the purchasing field in a major industry like yours, once I got some good experience?"* The response is much more likely to be forthcoming than if you ask them how much they make at Acme Industries these days.

Of all the question frames, the why question is the most likely to sound invasive or accusatory. If you have a why question, you can soften it, or rephrase it. Instead of, "Why did you quit Acme Industries?" you might try, "Can I ask what people found dissatisfying about working at Acme?" Notice I asked about people, this makes the question even softer than "you." Here are some nice phrases. "Can you tell me about..." "I'd really like to know more about..." "I never really understood..." "My wife and I were just talking about that the other day. I read that..." "My boss thinks... I'm not so sure because... What do you think?" "You're smart about these things, would you consider a move like that in this industry? Something tells me you'd take a different tack."

THE PEOPLE FACTOR

Keep in mind the importance of environment and the power of reciprocity. You are most likely to get people to open up in an informal environment like a shindig at a conference. You are even more likely to lubricate the conversation if you are taking them to lunch, thereby invoking the reciprocity principle. Take them snow boarding at your lodge and you'll do even better. There, you'll have time to develop a more cozy connection.

You'll have to be careful who you trust. Anyone with a vested interest in what you do with the answer may be influenced. Most obviously, anyone that you will be negotiating with. This is another incentive to be well-armed with objective information and good sources. By providing information to your colleagues, you will gain more openness from them. It becomes a mutual relationship. Cultivate relationships with the people who sell to the people you sell to.

Another good source is employees of the kinds of companies you do business with. They will have inside information that is perfectly legal for you to use. Just hold their confidences in trust. The last thing you'd want to do is compromise someone who, perhaps thoughtlessly, told you something their employer would just as soon not have revealed to someone they will be negotiating with. But in this case, take care with reciprocity. You don't want to say anything that you wouldn't want getting back to your opponents.

You can also orchestrate contacts that would work better between other people. This will work for you because people are more open with people who have similar roles in their industry. Get people in or connected with your company to converse with people in the companies you want to negotiate with. Get them to probe in a non-obvious way for the information that you need. Train them on how to do this if they aren't sophisticated at this sort of thing.

If you're selling janitorial supplies and your company has a buyer, then your buyer should be rubbing elbows with other buyers at conferences and the like. It may look like learning, fun, and games, but the networking is the real business of conferences. Take advantage of it. Just train your buyer not to get carried away with your own company's proprietary information. Your objective here is to have the collegial bond soften up the bond that employees have with their employees-- at least enough to gather some helpful information.

Ask for the Moon

This is rule #1 in negotiating. In fact, it is expected. Always ask for more than you intend to get out of a negotiation. If you don't, you will almost always get less then you could have, and you will probably even get less than you want.

Here are the top reasons for asking for the moon:

Better deal: This will get you a better deal in the end. Who knows? They might even give you the deal you ask for. But if they do, you'd better ask for more from your next customer. Otherwise, you'll never know how high the moon really is. If they give you what you ask for the first go round, you didn't ask for enough.

Wiggle room: This practice gives you room to come down. This is essential to your negotiating strategy, because the art of coming down is essential negotiating strategy. You have to have wiggle room in order to do that.

Perception of you: Your high starting point modifies the perception that the other side has about you. If they have much negotiating experience, they understand that you are carrying out the ancient tradition in fine form. If not, then they may thing you are going too far. But you will learn to state your demand in a way that keeps your opponent engaged.

Perceived value: Your high starting demand increases the perceived value of your product. Unless it lacks credibility, it will do the job mostly unconsciously. If your customer is new to this product, it may also affect them very consciously.

Anchor points: In psychological research, they have found that people set anchor points based on the initial numbers they hear. They may be influenced by that anchor point, even when they know they shouldn't be. Your high demand is places the anchor point. You will learn a number of ways to make that anchor point more powerful in influencing your opponent.

Customer needs: Another justification for asking for the moon has to do with the emotional needs of your customer. People need to feel that they are savvy, thrifty, or good negotiators. The higher your starting point, the larger the gap between the starting point and where you settle. The larger the gap, the more your customer accomplished. Aren't they something, getting so many concessions from you? What a deal! If you start too low, they may not be able to satisfy those needs. This can force you into a deadlock. They may have to go away empty-handed. This can lose future referrals as well as today's sale.

Tradition: Most people with some negotiating experience have expectations for how a negotiation will go. If you start too low, they will expect you to go lower than you want, based on their traditional understanding of negotiation. Once again, you risk deadlock if you defy tradition and start too low.

TIPS FOR MAKING YOUR DEMAND

When you make your demand, make it with some attitudes and practices in place. The ones below are the most important. Make sure they are habits. The rest of the pieces on negotiating depend on them.

Highest credible demand: Just be sure you know what your highest credible demand can be. As long as you have credibility, you will have a negotiation.

Validate the demand: When you make your demand, have compelling reasons. This helps validate it in the customer's mind. The reason does not have to be verbal. The way the store is furnished and the attitude with which you display the merchandise and state the price are all non-word ways to convey reasons. Reasons do not have to be logical words, they can be impressions as well.

In the dark? Shoot high: When you have not been able to learn enough about your customer, you need to make a guesstimate of your highest credible demand. Always go higher than your assumptions tell you to go. Do this because your assumptions may be wrong.

Maybe they are willing to pay more than your existing intelligence suggests. If you have not dealt with this person before, you can make larger concessions and make a cooperative impression if you decide you need to. Besides, you are on a teeter totter. If the other side is not familiar with you, they may be playing the same game.

Highlight the value: Create more validity and support for your demand by highlighting the various additional value that is part of the purchase. This can be anything from fantastic customer service to the superior materials used. Depending on your customer, it might even be an altruistic thing such as a low carbon footprint or that it was made by local people and supports employment here.

Be ready for the customer's reaction: Here is a custom you may not quite be emotionally ready for. It is standard negotiating practice for the other side to have an unpleasant reaction to your initial demand. This can include shock, guffaws, pain, or anger, and even walking way in a huff (and later, coming back for more negotiating). Do not allow this reaction to throw you, and do not allow fear of this reaction to prevent you from asking for the moon. It's just part of the work-a-day world.

THE MOON IS NOT JUST ABOUT PRICE

Don't limit yourself to price negotiations. You can ask for the moon in more ways than price. Same thing for those counter-concessions you make along the way to the final deal. Think deeply about all the possible ways you could extract value from a deal. How could the deal be more advantageous. Don't just think about the big, obvious things. There are countless little details that benefit your company.

Does your buyer want to spread their business around among vendors? **Ask for all the business.** Have compelling reasons to help set that anchor point. Is your customer stressing that they are very budget conscious? Start with the very best model and explain why they should stretch their budget in compelling terms. Maybe when they go for a lower model, they won't go as low as they would have without your help. Isn't your customer the type to get the extended service warranty? I'll bet you can think of some very good reasons why they must correct this oversight. If there is more than one version, start at the top and let them consider something less.

What is smaller than these values? How about payment terms? Delivery terms? Volume? Duration of the contract? Conditions for release from the contract? You could go for miles.

YOUR FLEXIBLE ATTITUDE

Here is another one of those customary rules. Just as you start high, you must not imply or state that this is as low as you'll go. A "take-it-or-leave-it" attitude is likely to get at "leave-it" response. By conveying that you have some flexibility on your demands, you can make your outrageous initial demand have a soft enough impact to keep them at the bargaining table.

The yacht you're selling is a real beauty. You are asking quite a bit over the private sale price. You justify this by talking about the guarantees and support, your company's reputation, and the extraordinary condition of the vessel. Then you say, "I would be very surprised to see anything as superb as this selling for much less today." You just gave your customer two signs of flexibility. You would be surprised, but it could happen that there is a competitive deal out there. The customer might go to the effort to give you that surprise. You also used the phrase, "much less." Now just what does that mean, exactly. Apparently you are open to the idea that there is some softness in the price, based on the market.

Another good way to show some price softness is to tie it to a concession from the buyer. *"We do make some very attractive offers when we receive your business with our in-house financing and premium service contract, and both of those are very beneficial to you, for a number of reasons we have on this poster."*

With a move like this, the customer will stay in the negotiation, seeing that there may be a way to get a better deal. So long as the customer is engaged in the process, you are moving toward the sale.

DEFINE THE DEBATE ON YOUR TERMS

In the negotiation for the yacht, you'll recall that you focused your price softness on competitive offers. You know that this is not the only way the customer can talk you down. But it is to your advantage to direct your prospect's attention to the arena of your choice. This may take their mind off of other avenues of negotiation, and it will help you create an anchor point.

The anchor point is set more firmly, because you picked an arena where you are strong. You happened to know that the market is rather competitive at the moment, and there aren't good deals for what your customer wants. And your customer has been pretty specific about his needs. Were the conditions different, you might have chosen a different arena.

You have also firmed up your anchor point by creating another arena for your prospects attention. It was that business about your price flexibility being tied to your customer using your financing and premium service contract. You can now move on price, financing, and a lower or no service contract. And the customer's mind is occupied with the poor market conditions and the ties you are creating for negotiating. This is good negotiating strategy.

Your customer still has his free will, and may already be thinking out of the box, but at least you have helped firm up your anchor point; the point from which your customer gains perspective on the final price; the point that causes customers to settle higher than they otherwise would have.

BRACKET

Bracketing is a negotiating technique that helps you choose a highest credible demand point. The best way to explain bracketing is to start with an example.

Imagine that you have a ruler, and you have one inch. Of what? It doesn't matter. You have an inch. You want two inches. Now make a point that is on the other side of two inches, and puts the two inch point in the middle. That would be three inches, in case you lost track.

To recap: Two inches is in the middle between one and three. You have one inch. You're trying to get them to agree to two inches.

What you want is in the middle of what you have and what you ask for at first.

That's pretty straightforward. But it's also kind of arbitrary, don't you think. I mean, why would you do this? If you don't have good criteria upon which to base your initial demand, bracketing provides a general rule that is usually pretty safe. It is most likely to work when it doesn't cause you to produce an astronomical initial demand. It is best for simple negotiations, but you can use it to help you think about more complicated ones.

It has a psychological advantage that I call a secondary anchor point. When you set your initial demand, the other side tends to guess where you might be willing to land as your final offer.

Let's try this with a real situation, where the buyer is trying bracketing on you. You want to sell a small yacht for $500,000.00, and the buyer offers $400,000.00. You are willing to go as low as 450,000.00, and you assume that the buyer is hoping for this. But you don't tell them that, because you'd end up at a lower price. You make concessions in steps so that they buyer has worked to get you down close to $450,000.00. Then you say you've gone about as low as you can go, and that you aren't sure you can really do any better. Are they sure they have really given the best offer they are capable of? If they come up with $450,00.00, they have a deal. You conceded to their offer, and they had to work for it, so they feel good about the deal. You knew in advance what to aim for.

When you set the $500,000.00 price, you were bracketing. You knew that a customer would probably give a lowest credible offer, and that it would probably be around $100,000.00 lower than anything in the price range of the yacht. Since you were hoping for $450,000.00, you added half of the $100,000.00 to that price and ended up with a $500,000.00 starting price.

There's some kind of psychological fairness principle at work that gives this little gimmick some extra intuitive authority. If you look at a lot of negotiations, you'll see this dynamic in play pretty often. Needless to say, the middle goal outcome is not guaranteed.

You can also keep bracketing in mind when you are in the negotiation. If you make concessions that are similar to those of your opponent, you will probably end up in the middle.

It's easiest, and perhaps best, to get the other side to take the first position. This enables you to define the middle. This acts as that secondary set point in your opponent's mind. Their mind may or may not be conscious of it, but it's in there somewhere. This way, if a customer asks how much leeway there is on the price, you can tell them that, since they approached you, you are willing to consider a sincere offer. That "sincere" word places some onus on them not to attempt a lowest credible offer, and makes you just a little unenthusiastic about reducing your price. Unenthusiastic, yes, but rigid, no.

NEXT MOVES: BUILD MOMENTUM

Put the Law of Diminishing Returns on Your Side

With the law of diminishing returns, you can guide your opponent toward the deal that you want. Much like with that secondary set point caused by bracketing, every concession you make creates an echo point in the opposition's mind. Each step of the way, your opponent is thinking about what they should offer, and where you might be willing to end up. Those are the echo points.

Your first concession needs to be large enough to be credible. This is a little like your maximum credible demand, or their minimum credible offer. Let's call this your minimum credible concession. Your second concession should be smaller than the first. This should produce a sort of curve of diminishing returns in your opponent's mind. Their mind will plot out where these diminishing concessions going. They will have a rough idea of the point at which your concessions will be too small to bother with. That point should be where you are hoping to land the deal.

For an oversimplified example, imagine yourself taking a big step down the sidewalk. Then you take one that is just half as long. Then another, half as long. Your mind will automatically know roughly at what point those steps will seem too tiny to bother with, and that is where you will want to stop.

Like many of the points raised in this section, this is a fairly traditional modus operandi, so if you failed to use it, the other side would get a bigger bite than necessary.

Speed Reciprocating

The time to get a concession is as quickly as possible after you make a concession. This is because the value of the concession will fade over time. You want reciprocation as soon as possible. Be prepared to ask. At that time, highlight the value of your concession, and any other motivational points that you can drop in without arousing resistance.

And don't limit your thinking to money. Anything of value is a kind of concession. Put differently, some concessions are more like a debt that the recipient feels they should repay as an act of reciprocation.

Your company prides itself on customer service for it's large corporate clients. If you work a miracle of some kind for a client, you want to make sure they value it, so you find a way to make sure they understand the effort and ingenuity involved. When they thank you, what concession will you request? Perhaps they should give you a leg up in contacting a company that they have an in with? Maybe a glowing letter of reference for your marketing materials with an impressive signatory or two from their company. Perhaps they should make you their sole provider of miracle widgets. They will be most receptive when your request is not out of proportion to what you have provided.

In the event that you absolutely can't get that concession conversation going right away, be sure to get it as soon as you can. And when you do, remind them of your miracle in a way that makes it as fresh and alive in their minds as possible without wearing out your welcome. If the person wants to talk about it later, create an anchor point in their mind by mentioning briefly the kind of thing you're hoping for and ask if this is the kind of thing they might look at doing for you. Notice the soft language. It's more likely to get that initial commitment. This increases the odds that they will take this seriously when you do talk later, because commitments tend to stick in people's minds and motivate them to be consistent with what they have said.

OBJECTIONS ARE BUYING SIGNALS

Have you learned to love objections yet? If you haven't, then you still need to capture the joy of the game. When you receive an objection, you are still in the game. More importantly, so is your customer.

Think of a spat with a loved one. The discussion is animated and emotions crest. But this is part of love. It is not hate. And it certainly is not apathy. Apathy is the most extreme dilution of love. It is also the most toxic to the sale. Objections, however, are not apathy. They are involvement, caring, and action. They are possibility. They are the challenge that you accepted when you chose your career in sales. They are your mission.

Say the same for reluctance. Certainly say it when reluctance is feigned by an experienced negotiator. Again, it's part of the game. Learn to love the game, whether it's for the money, the glory, or expanding your talent, and you will learn to love objections and reluctance, and all the other charming little gambits that your buyers will trot out for you.

THE FREAK OUT

When your customer makes an offer, they are watching for your reaction. Odds are, the sense that most fills up their brain is what comes in through their eyes. At the moment, that's you and your reaction to their offer. They want to know if they're going to get a good deal. The deal will come from you. How you react will give them a clue what's next. Of course they are paying careful attention to how you react. What should you do?

Freak out. Maybe a little, maybe a lot. It depends on the situation, and we'll get into that. In some way, you should always show some form of negative reaction to their proposal. You want them to feel that they are getting the best possible deal. They won't feel that way if you jump for joy. They certainly won't feel like making any more concessions if you do.

CREATE VALUE WITH YOUR FREAK OUT

Don't just save your little freak outs for cash concessions. Any concession, any value, is something to freak out about. If your customer asks you to throw in a better sound system, you had better start, gasp, flinch, or otherwise display your shock or dismay. When your customer tells you they want high Blue Book for their trade-in, you had better display your surprise or disappointment in their unfortunate belief that their trade-in could be worth anything near Blue Book.

People believe what they see, and if they see you flinch, they are moved by it. Even if they are experience, and know what you are doing, they are still affected. They may take psychological measures to keep their objectivity and play the game as effectively as they can, but at the very least, they know that you are not surrendering easily; they know that the negotiation will require some more work and some more concessions.

If you have the slightest doubt, I implore you, don't misjudge it until you've tried it a few times. Soon, you won't be without it. It will be as necessary and comfortable as a good pair of shoes. Every flinch is worth money to you. Sometimes that will be in the thousands. In a slightly soft rental market, I brought the rental price of my office down five hundred dollars with only two flinches. In eight years, those flinches were $24,000.00 *each*.

WHEN TO FREAK OUT

Freak outs range from a mild gasp or sharp inhalation to jumping up, yelling, and storming out of the negotiation. I have seen the full range used effectively, and ineffectively many times. I use the full range myself, but only very rarely stomp away.

When I was travelling in the Middle East, I had the thrill of watching camel traders negotiate with herders. They negotiated with passion that would make most of the negotiation I've seen appear comatose by comparison. They were so close to each other and so loud, it looked like violence would break out. Contrary to appearances, this was a well-orchestrated and ancient ritual.

More than once, I saw a herder storm away, only to return under some pretext. Once, the trader reached over the herder's head with his whip and actually pulled him back in by the neck. Did the herder get angry? No! He got right back in the trader's face with more intense negotiation as if someone had put two magnets so close that they spontaneously snapped together. His stomping away was merely an attempt to set some kind of anchor point. Next time, I'll bring a recorder and have it translated and transcribed.

Here are the times to use a small, or not-so-small freak out:

1. When your opponent makes an initial offer.

2. When they make a final offer.

3. When you feel they need to make more generous concessions in order for you to have a satisfactory outcome.

4. When they try to play up the value of their offer too much.

5. Any other opportunity that you feel is worth a freak out.

The Small Freak Out

Here are some guidelines that will help you freak out effectively.

You should practice various freak outs, to make sure that they are smooth and convincing. That's what mirrors, recorders, and video cameras are for!

Use small freak outs for conservative or smaller situations. A good-faith offer to a car dealer should not get the salesperson doubled over with guffaws. It would be clear that there was no point in negotiating, unless the customer was pretty thick-skinned or experienced.

A smaller freak out might be of the gasp variety. I almost always provide some commentary as well. For example, "I'm sure you came by that estimate honestly, and I'd like to know more about how you computed it, but really, we couldn't justify coming in at that price." This rebuke was fairly accommodating, because it was not outrageous, and I want the other side to reveal information that will help me respond and maybe even provide me with some market intelligence. I do get valuable information that way! And this favor that they provide is not viewed as a concession, but work on their part to negotiate. When they work at negotiating with me, it hardens their resolve to make their investment in time pay off by getting to a deal, and it helps me set more favorable anchor points.

You can also have a more subtle freak out when offers are made in the thick of negotiation. This can range from being apathetic about the offer, to having an overall uncomfortable, mildly disgusted, or slightly irritated quality. This has to be strategic so as not to break the rapport and motivation to negotiate. It is such an intuitive aspect, that you will get the most improvement from experience. I can tell you though, that these reactions can be very subtle. I believe that the power of these subtle moves comes from their effect on the subconscious mind. It lies in the value of behavior modification. The more intimate you get with this use of body language, the more you will feel like you are a potter working with repeating cycles of behavior to shape the dialogue.

THE LARGER FREAK OUT

You can be more creative with your responses to the more outrageous offers. I know that my opponents certainly have done so with me. When it happens, I don't take it personally. I know it's part of negotiating. Be careful with outright anger. Save it for situations where you have reason to feel frustrated or that you have been abused in some way.

Save hurt for when you have a sufficiently sympathetic connection that you can spell out why you feel hurt about the situation and what would make you feel better about what it going on.

When you are angry, you are not likely to be very rational, but you should drop some kind of a hint that you are still in the negotiation so they won't think it's all over.

"If I hear about this concession another time before I die, it will be too soon! I've made such big concessions on price and service they should have my hide at headquarters. You aren't going to be getting much more from me on this."

Hmmm, what exactly does "much more" mean? It must mean there is some kind of concession possible, but that the other side should think more carefully about what to expect.

And be sure that your body language appears to be taking you away from the negotiation when you do anger or hurt especially. The angle of your body, direction of your glances, and the tilt of your shoulders, all serve to signal that you are on the verge of giving up.

And if you don't start practicing these fantastic techniques in your very next human interaction, I'm going to take this book and give it to someone who's taking their sales career seriously! Don't make me do that!

GOOD COP BAD COP

Good Cop Bad Cop

Everybody knows the good cop bad cop routine from watching cop shows, or maybe being suspected of something and having a little interview at the station. But did you know it is a common negotiating gambit, especially in corporate encounters? You must be ready do protect yourself.

The basic dynamic works like this: You start negotiating with someone who appears to have the authority to at least hammer out a proposal that will go up to a final decision maker. Maybe it will be a competitive process and several proposals will be considered. Maybe that will be followed by another round of negotiation when one company is preferred, but they want to improve the deal. However, you begin to realize that they are starting to play good cop bad cop with you when the negotiator starts consulting with their boss or some other authority figure who is not there. I call this the authority in absentia.

The gambit may start with the authority in the room. That person may pretend to get fed up with your offers and give up. Then the good cop negotiator sticks around and tries to "help" you produce a better proposal. To help rattle you, the big cheese may dramatically react and storm out of the room. That person is now the authority in absentia.

Any time you are negotiating with more than one person, or one person and an authority figure in absentia, you can be pretty sure that you will soon be on the receiving end of the good cop bad cop approach. A funny thing about this is that people can know you're doing it, but it will still usually work so long as you know how to respond to the various tactics used to subvert it. These pieces will go into all that in detail. You will be able to use all of these tactics immediately.

BEWARE THE GOOD COP BAD COP DYNAMICS

This gambit can wear you down, because you have to work harder to get concessions from the good cop bad cop team. Since the negotiator from the other side can say his hands are tied at various points, you have to get him to go explain the benefits of the deal to the authority in absentia. This can throw you off by getting you to make a key psychological blunder, that of thinking that your opponent is on your team, trying to help you get the deal through. It can also make you more squeamish, and make a desperate move or two that can add up to a lot of money down the road. Somehow, the authority of the invisible power person can undermine your confidence.

They may work the dynamic to try to get multiple concessions from you before they make a counter offer. This happens by trying to get you to shape the deal more favorably in the hopes that it will get approval by the big cheese. By activating your automatic desire to get approval from an authority figure, they are undermining your negotiating common sense.

Anyone who has ever purchased a car from a dealer has seen the salesperson go to the boss to see if they can get a concession for you. This also has the effect of getting you to become more invested because of the additional time you are putting in by waiting around. By acting like they are on your side, they are trying to create a bond with you that makes you more willing to give them concessions. If that happens, you have allowed a Trojan horse into your city.

SET UP THE GOOD COP BAD COP DYNAMIC

When salespeople come to my office with IT equipment, advertising, or other things I'm in the market for, I follow a simple process. It's the core of the good cop bad cop dynamic, and I do it out of hand, even in simple negotiations. So I'll share with you the most simple approach to get us started. You can make a habit of this immediately, in your business and personal life.

1. If you are motivated to get the product or service, carry out the negotiation process pretty much as you normally would, getting them to their rock-bottom price.

2. Tell them that you think it looks fine, but, of course, you'll have to run it by (fill in the blank). This can be the budget director, the board of directors, your spouse (who you have to admit really runs everything around here), or any other authority in absentia of your choice.

3. When you reconnect with the salesperson, tell them that the authority in absentia has been pretty tough to get things past lately, and that they just aren't going along with our best-laid plans. They just aren't going to approve the sale unless you can shave four hundred dollars off.

That simple three-step approach works very consistently. Do that a few dozen times, and you're making some real money. In fact, if this ads five minutes to each deal, and you make an average of two hundred dollars per deal, that means that you are making $2,400.00 per hour. Not bad!

Prevent the Good Cop Bad Cop Dynamic

The prevention approach works best with customers who are not very sophisticated, but you should do it with everyone to test the water. Your objective is to prevent them from even brining up a higher authority for the buying decision. You want that decision right in their lap. To accomplish this, before they have a chance to resort to the higher authority, try to get them to deny that there is one. This way, they will make a commitment that they will feel obliged to stick to.

They will, as a result, be more likely to make a buying decision. As you know, the tension that can build before a buying decision causes the customer to seek a way out; a way to postpone the decision. But if they don't buy, at least you will be in a position to find out what the objection is, since it won't be disguised as an appeal to a higher authority. And you know how important it is to unearth those objections so you can work your magic.

So, as the discussion begins, ask this simple question: *"If I can provide the ideal widget for you at a fair price, is there any reason why you wouldn't go for it today?"* or, *"Let me make sure I'm on the same page with you, if you like this widget, and I know you will, will anything keep you from taking it away today?"*

If they say no, there is no reason, they are telling you that they are the decision maker. If they get cold feet you want to respond with language that maintains this reality that there is no higher authority. You might make this query, *"Ah, well, since you mentioned that you were in a good position to make your purchase decision today, I suppose I didn't explain something. After all this is a remarkable deal today. Let me go over this again."* You might want to focus on getting to the objection by asking, *"Oh, well, there are always some concerns that people have about buying something this special, since you mentioned that you are able to make your decision to buy today, what would have to happen for you to love this offer?"*

Let's say they just slip right by their earlier implication that they can decide today. Let's say that they bring up the dreaded higher authority escape clause. If they do, for starters, you can still remind them of what they said earlier. You'll want to do this with some style, and keep their personality in mind. This is no one-size-fits-all intervention.

Eliminate the Good Cop Bad Cop Dynamic: The Direct Approach

If you couldn't prevent the good cop bad cop approach, your next priority is to try to eliminate it. Here are some good ways to do that:

1. Identify it: You can simply point it out, preferably in a way that makes them appear a little silly or amateurish for doing it, unless you feel that a classier approach is best for the corporate culture you are dealing with or want to reflect. Here is an example: "Oh, you folks are still using the old good cop bad cop approach. It's a little old school, but I guess it still works with inexperienced people." Here you are implying that you are not inexperienced, and it's a waste of time to be using it on you.

2. Tell them, convincingly, to stop: If they persist, go ahead and request that they give it up. Say something like, "How about if we pick up the tempo here and dispense with the good cop bad cop routine." You can ask them to stop by indicating that both sides are really above such a transparent and off-putting maneuver. "Josh, I know you want to get the best possible deal, I do too. But this good cop bad cop thing is just wasting our time. Let's give each other a little more credit for being experienced professionals. I don't think it's too much to expect the minimum courtesy of negotiating with the person who is truly authorized to negotiate." There is a lot of classy language. Don't you think? Like, "credit for being experienced, and "minimum courtesy," nice. And there's the compelling rationale of, "wasting our time," and "person who is truly authorized to negotiate." Keep it powerful.

3. Maybe even go over their heads: If you really feel that their good cop bad cop approach is mucking up the negotiations, and you think it's worth it to risk making them mad, consider going over their heads. This is most likely to pay off if someone in your company has a connection with a higher up. The call to the higher up would ask if they really approved of their people using this technique, and to ask them to get them to negotiate more sincerely, because it is taking up the reps' valuable time. You wouldn't have called, but they are stonewalling you and you're running out of patience, options, time, or whatever.

THE APPEAL TO PRIDE

You want as many tools in your toolbox as possible. These less direct approaches to eliminating the good cop bad cop approach will appeal to you more than the direct approach in some situations. They will especially appeal to you where you feel your customer has a big ego or need for control, as so many business people do.

Here are my favorite gambits. I'll start with The Appeal to Pride.

The Appeal to Pride: Some people can resist asserting that they are influential and have approval and good relationships. You can use this to your advantage in preventing the appeal to higher authority by asking about their supervisor early in the process, with, *"So, if you run our final plan by your supervisor, do you think she'd give it her approval?"* A yes to that creates additional commitment to the deal. She may ask for less when she gets back to you, or advocate with more umph with her supervisor.

Put some extra polish on this approach by asking directly for their support. *"So it looks like your really on board with this. Can I count on you to really pitch this to your supervisor?"* You know what I have to say about remembering to ask for what you want. And, at this point, I don't think you'll be hearing any request for a counter concession. Not for confirming that she likes the deal. Not unless she's taking bribes.

THE APPEAL TO EGO

The Appeal to Ego I: But if you have a sufficiently ego-driven opponent, she just might blurt out a different answer, completely upending her resort to a higher authority. *"I don't need approval for these decisions. I have the decision-making authority on this. I'm the one you're dealing with."* How convenient! You are not in a much better position to get this deal wrapped up.

The Appeal to Ego II: In a very constructive, upbeat tone, ask, "But you can count on them going along with your decision, can't you?" If they are really playing it to the hilt, they'll say, *"Heck no, I have been having an awful time because they've gone budget-crazy on me. But at least they're keeping me realistic."* Oooff! Your opponent not only held the higher authority in place, but he also showed deference and appreciation for it. Smooth move. You should try that, yourself, next time somebody tries to dislodge your imaginary bad cop. But there will be plenty of folks who couldn't stomach saying that, or didn't happen to think of it soon enough. Instead, you'll hear something different from them. Perhaps, *"Well, yes, if I say it goes, it goes. But I have to run it by them, that's how things are set up."* At the least, you are now in a position to get a stronger commitment, at best, they'll give up the higher authority and assert their own, with, *"Well, yes, I really am the boss. What the heck. I like the deal well enough. Let's sign and get this over with."*

Right to Reject

You can make the buying decision less intense and take away the price objection from the higher authority at the same time with this. I use this in life insurance pretty regularly. In this approach, you get them to agree to the deal in principle, but subject to approval on both sides. The trick here is to specify whose approval it is subject to, and what the check off is to be about. That is, you are tying the approval to a specific issue, and that issue is NOT price.

You have probably seen this language somewhere, like in qualifying for your life insurance policy. The agent says, "We can just do the paperwork subject to your passing the health exam." In this case, it makes the buying decision seem a little more distant, and pulls on your desire to pass the test. But when we use this to really take price gouging power away from the higher authority, we need something like this, "...subject to the right of your legal department to reject the proposal within 48 hours for a legal reason." Note that the higher authority is specified, and the possible reason in the contract is not price.

IF YOU GET STUCK WITH A GOOD COP BAD COP SITUATION

If you can't eliminate the good cop bad cop dynamic, here's how to play along without getting psyched out. Sometimes, it's just as well to play along with good cop bad cop by responding to the bad cop in a favorable way. Here are the key pieces:

1. Confirm the authority of the bad cop: Tell the negotiator that you appreciate that he is keeping the negotiation open with their superior, and for letting you know who the real decision maker is.

2. Shift the dynamic by negotiating with the bad cop: This one is tricky. The next section lays this out in detailed steps.

3. Be very procedural: From there, know that it may take a bit longer, but that you will be running through your negotiation in the same way as they are there.

4. Use psychological countermeasures: Since you know how the gambit works, you can take psychological countermeasures. You will not be thrown off by the feigned attitude of the authority figure. You will even bring some work along or use your online connection to keep busy if there is a time delay.

5. Don't let the Trojan horse through the gate: Do not allow the underling to weasel their way too far into the role of good cop. You must not let them get the impression that you think they are doing you any kind of a favor.

6. Take the wind out of their sails: By taking a formal, procedural approach to the bad cops moves, you are taking the wind out of their sails. You need to treat their moves as you would a direct negotiation situation, and do the things you are learning in this book to telegraph that.

7. Do not make multiple concessions: A key goal of good cop bad cop is to get you to make multiple concessions, with out the customary tit for tat of traditional negotiation. That means that you have to be ready draw the line; to tell them that you have already made reasonable concessions, and that the bad cop needs to make a complete counter offer. Tell them that if they fail to show good faith, there's nothing you can do. Besides, your boss would kill you.

8. Be ready to walk: If they don't play ball, they need to really get that you'll have to let them sleep on it and see what they are willing to discuss tomorrow. Moves like these make the other side aware of their own time being taken up with this gambit, and they make the bad cop's tempest sound rather hollow.

POWERFULLY SHIFT THE GOOD COP BAD COP DYNAMIC

If you are stuck with a good cop bad cop situation for some reason, you can make some powerful moves to reduce or eliminate its impact. You can attack both the psychological and the practical aspects at the same time. Here's how.

Read this carefully, though. If you don't address each of the dynamics discussed here, you'll be allowing their routine to work its magic on you. You don't want that!

1. Negotiate with the bad cop: One way or another, you need to get as direct a line to the bad cop as possible. Make the bad cop the one you are really negotiating with. Get this idea firmly implanted in your own mind as well as theirs. Treat the underling as no more than a courier. Show that you now know that hammering things out with the negotiator will be a waste of time.

2. Get a favorable rejection from the bad cop: What? What is favorable about a rejection? What's favorable about it is that you get them to reject a very high demand; one that you would not expect them to accept. In other words, you have not allowed them to cow you into making too many concessions before you run the offer up the flag pole. They want you to make multiple concessions so they can reject those and get more, all without making a sincere counter offer. Once they have taken your demands down a few notches, they begin bargaining without having made the reciprocal concessions that you would normally have expected. You must prevent them from manipulating you like that.

3. Get a high demand to the bad cop: There are two basic ways to do this. One is to prevent your negotiator from running to the bad cop piece meal with parts of your proposal. Insist that you two hammer out a complete proposal. But, in reality, keep the hammering to the minimum. What you really want to do is to make sure that the proposal is the same kind of high demand proposal that you would have presented during the first go round of any other negotiation.

You must absolutely make sure that the negotiator is really cringing and insisting that the boss will reject it. Then, when the boss does reject it, and you know that will happen, you do not make more concessions. You demand nothing less than a complete counter proposal.

If the negotiator says he can't present it to the boss, tell him that he is not the person you are really negotiating with, and you want to hear the rejection from the real decision maker. Point out some features to the deal, such as the sterling reputation of the company, that mean the boss should seriously consider the deal as is, and respond with a counter proposal if she doesn't like it. After all, she knows what she wants and should have no trouble spelling it out. I mean, she *is* the boss, isn't she?

Wait! Get that Counter Proposal!

One of their key objectives is to get you to make multiple concessions. They have a few ways to do that, as you have seen. For example, they might get you to make your first proposal, and *then* swap out to the good cop bad cop dynamic. In the confusion, you might actually forget that you have done this, and make an early, unnecessary concession ahead of their offer.

You can make your demand for a counter proposal sound pretty credible and convincing. Insist that you need a counter proposal so you can better understand their needs better. You can even apologize for not understanding their needs well enough and tell them that this will really be good for both of you. It's a little odd to make such an apology and this will tip them off that you are on to them, and that you will need to be treated on a more professional level. They may not admit it, and they may stonewall you at first, but you are going to get through to them, and this is a step in that direction.

You could add that, besides, you don't negotiate blindly, because you don't want a reputation for putting out bogus proposals. Insist that it wouldn't serve either of you if you simply threw out pieces willy-nilly. Including a *"because"* in your rationale improves it's credibility.

Here, you are making it sound like a very bad idea for both sides and something that you would *never* do. In fact, your company would never allow *anyone* there to do it. See how serious I sound? You should sound like that. Besides, if you have something that is complete enough to respond to, you are more likely to come up with something that will fly with your boss. Good! Now YOU have an authority in absentia. Turn about's fair play.

Part of the good cop bad cop routine is to test your patience and wear you out. Don't let them engage you like that. If the underling tries to work with you on the proposal, say you have already worked it out, and these are the concession factors. Insist that you will have no more to say about it until the big cheese comes back with a counter proposal. Not a rejection--counter proposal. Ask, how long they think it will be for them to get that back to you. If they aren't sure, ask them to have the big cheese contact you on your cell phone and leave. There are good odds that they will shape up before they let you out the door.

THE CONTRACT: MORE THAN MEETS THE EYE

When the Talking Stops and the Writing Starts

You have worked it out, sweated it out, acted it out, and feel played out. Maybe you should take a breather, because you are not done. Your verbal agreements need to be confirmed in the form of a contract. The contract is not just a way to bind people to their agreements. It is a way to prevent bad feelings over misunderstandings. It is a way to refer to the document that both sides agreed to when there is a concern. It is also a way to sleep better at night. That's because you have negotiated so well, and created a contract so clear, and are selling to companies of such integrity, that you will never have to go through the misery of suing any of them. Okay, that was a little optimistic. I mean, never say never. But at least you now have better odds of smooth sailing.

The pieces about contracts will help you avoid some common pitfalls, and make some good strategic moves that can save, or make, you some serious money.

We'll talk about how contracting is a process, and how care must be taken at each step. I'll tell you how to avoid misunderstandings, and to make sure that your interests are fully represented in the contract's final form.

I'll show you how the contract process may be part of the negotiation process, and how to be prepared for that.

Audit Your Contract Process Here

Think of this piece as an audit. Like the checklist a pilot goes through to make sure their flight will be safe, go through this little list and see if you have a solid habit of following each one consistently.

Version Control

Be prepared to detect and change any misunderstandings that show up in the contract.

Realize that if the other side wrote the contract, they might have slipped in some things or omitted some details that you will need to negotiate over.

Read or do an automated version check on every version of the contract to make sure there are no mistakes or surprises, no matter which side produced it.

Take Charge

Make every effort to have your side produce the contract, and to make it favorable to you.

If the situation warrants it, have them accept in writing a memorandum of understanding (MOU) that outlines the key features of the agreement, including elements that may appear small, but that are important to you.

Be ready with good reasons for being the side that writes the contract.

In producing the contract, do not overreach or take advantage in a way that will produce animosity. Be attentive to little details that the other side will recognize. Don't take advantage of ignorance or lack of experience of the other side when preparing the contract.

Have all team members review the contract before it goes to the other side, or when it comes from the other side.

Be prepared for the possibility that the contract process my be part of the negotiation process.

Never relax about an issue because you think you can recover the resulting damage with a lawsuit.

If the other side writes up the contract or any portion or change, get a verbal commitment from the other side to not add anything that was not discussed.

CONTROL THE CONTRACT PROCESS ON YOUR END

Manage Your Information, Team, and Advisement

Write up the ideal contract prior to the negotiation just for you as a guide for your own negotiation process.

Take careful notes of all details and mark items for inclusion in the contract.

Stage your note taking and verbal interaction so as to help the other side comply. Clarify and confirm each key point, and visibly write it down.

Make sure the people doing the negotiation on your side have good negotiation personalities for the situation at hand, and considering the personalities, motives, and corporate culture on the other side. They must be able to detect and manage subtleties, gain trust, have judgement about when to quibble, and be experienced and successful in negotiating.

Get appropriate legal advice and review of the contract.

Manage and Enhance Your Relationship, Credibility, and Trust

Prepare good, verifiable explanations for any changes you want in the contract..

Consider using a memorandum of understanding as a non-binding agreement that serves as the basis for the actual contract.

Consider negotiating up front the important details of how the negotiation process will work. Factor in things like whether there will be a memorandum of agreement, timelines, etc.

Have good written and graphic materials to support your points in negotiation, because the written word and pictures are very convincing. When negotiating by phone, use written and graphic support materials sent electronically or as hard copy.

VERSION CONTROL

Translating words and ideas into legalese is fraught with risks to both sides. When you prepare or review your contract, you'll want to watch for errors, omissions, and outright manipulation, especially if the other side is writing the contract. I'm sure you've seen plenty of misunderstandings emerge over the course of negotiations, whether it's between family members or nations. Often, these misunderstandings to not become apparent until the agreements are well under way. The result can be endless and fiery arguments and legal combat; even actual combat.

If misunderstandings can't be discovered during the negotiation, then they should become apparent in the contracting process. It is for this reason that you must not only go over the first draft of the contract with great care, but also review every change that occurs from the other side, especially if they have directly produced the text. Since some contracts can be quite long, loaded with boilerplate text and interminable clauses, you should review the text with an automated version checker. Even Microsoft Word allows you to compare documents for any changes that occur, even so much as a single letter. Human review is imperfect, but a single word may make a tremendous difference in a contract. You'll have enough to go over just reviewing edits to the contract without having to look for differences that may have cropped up in areas that were supposed to be left unchanged.

TAKE CHARGE

Do whatever you can to have your side write the contract and any amendments or changes to it. This way, the resulting contract with be fully sensitive to your interests, including the more nuanced ones that the other side might not represent as effectively, even if they intended to.

You should be prepared with a logical, persuasive, and verifiable set of reasons for being the ones who prepare the contract. You can show how it will save money, because you have access to an experienced attorney, or because your organization does these all the time and has boilerplate that you already know will pass legal muster and take care of both sides. Your satisfied customers and your history of staying out of legal controversy are evidence that they can entrust the contract writing to you.

While you want to turn the contract writing process to your advantage, you must not be swept up in the temptation to try to get away with something. If the other side misses it, they'll be a bear to deal with when the problem emerges. If they catch it, your trustworthiness will be impugned, and they will have more leverage while the final contract is negotiated. When the other side doesn't understand an issue, someone on your team may get the bright idea to take advantage of this. But if you create obligations that they do not adequately understand, you may stir up a hornet's nest of ill will when they come face to face with unexpected demands or losses. They will feel taken advantage of, and they'll be right. The will talk about your company, and that will cost you community good will, which will cost you customers. Sometimes it can be proven in court that there was trickery, and this can be costly as well. If they feel that their relationship with you is disposable, they will not feel obligated to fully support the relationship. There are many ways that an unhappy customer can make your life difficult. And the more complicated the arrangement is, the more ways there are.

And why not take that fairness philosophy a step further, by being attentive to the little details that the other side will recognize as representing their interests? This will show that you deserve their trust, and make the shadings to the contract that are in your interest be more palatable to the other side at the same time.

IF THE OTHER SIDE WRITES THE CONTRACT

If the other side writes the contract, it will be from their perspective. They may even sneak in some things that you didn't exactly agree to. When you raise an objection, they will most likely explain that it's policy, everyone does it that way, it's inherent to doing what was agreed to, or some other officious-sounding non-response. If that happens, now the contract process is definitely part of the negotiation process. Unfortunately, this places you in the position of feeling like you are asking for concessions. But it's quite they contrary; they are. The truth is that they have asked for concessions and disguised them as some kind of tradition or inconsequential legalese. Take care not to fall into that trap.

Put it that way to them, and make it very clear that these were not points raised during the negotiation. Embarrass and shame them for this egregious behavior, in whatever terms fit the situation. Use each and every point as an opportunity to demand a counter-concession, or demand that it be eliminated without any expectation of a concession on your part.

Be sure to forewarn the other side that any mischief will be met with stiff resistance. Get a verbal commitment to not adding anything that was not discussed.

If the situation warrants it, you may want to be more formal about your contracting process, and have them accept in writing a memorandum of understanding (MOU) that lays out the terms of the contract in a rough, plain English format. An MOU outlines the key features of the agreement. Such an agreement is non-binding, but helps make sure that the contract fully reflects what was negotiated. The other side should be familiar with this process. If not, you can reassure them about its non-binding nature. It is "subject to the approval of their attorney," of course.

Get Out of the Lawsuit Frame

While we're on the subject of contracts, never get into the mindset that you should let down your guard because you could make things right with a law suit. It's nice to know that the prospect of a law suit can help keep people honest, but lawsuits are very costly. They aren't just expensive, but the risk of losing or not winning enough takes an emotional toll. And who wants to add risk to their business affairs when it is could be avoided? Sometimes litigants win large, disproportionate amounts of money. In these unusual circumstances, the winnings can actually be worth more than what you could have made by doing what you would rather have been doing with your time and resources. But normally, lawsuits just aren't worth even the personal costs of the insecurity and aggravation. Even when you are on rock-solid legal ground, the process is very distracting and costs you by taking your mental focus away from your business. This alone is a tremendous hidden cost. How do you place a value on lost opportunities, known and unknown, over a prolonged period of time?

Keep it Real

For the sake of time, accuracy, and for making sure you get what you worked so hard to win, take careful notes. When there is a disagreement between your understanding and the contract, you will be able to say exactly what happened. When you review a point, and they acknowledge it, note that that happened so you will be able to point that out with certainty. The mere fact that they see you jotting down these details helps ensure their compliance. You can draw their attention to this. Do it right after you verbally confirm that your understanding is correct. This helps strengthen the agreement in their mind. It makes it more legitimate. Mark each point in your notes that will be in the contract. This will save you some time and frustration.

When you get agreement on a key point, briefly summarize it verbally. Then ask if this is a correct representation of what happened.

You can introduce comments like this with a snappy phrase like, *"Just to make sure we're on the same page, we're offering..."* Then get their confirmation that you are correct. This will do more than just produce an accurate contract, it will help to secure it in their memory. You'll have less trouble down the road. You can get confirmation with a simple phrase like, *"Now tell me if I'm on target, you're saying that you will..."*

TEAM RIGHT

When you are on a negotiating team, be sure to have everyone review the contract before you send it over the transom or sign it. You would be surprised at how often someone realizes that some point was omitted; sometimes a really important one. Hey, we're all only human. Also, in their enthusiasm, your team lead may have put something in that actually exists only in their imagination. If you are intentionally adding some favorable conditions that you have a good strategic reason for, then let your conscience and business sense be your guides. If it doesn't pass those sniff tests, then take care not to alienate the other side or impair your own credibility by letting something like that slip by.

Be sure the right people are doing the negotiation. Consider their personalities.

Be sure that you have at least one person there who intimately understands the business. They will help ensure that the contract is fully supportive of the aims and needs of the business. Never underestimate the importance of this point.

ATTORNEYS ON THE TEAM

You usually want to avoid using lawyers for business negotiations. Lawyers are trained to break contracts, enforce contracts, and be confrontational. Getting to an agreement requires much more than this. Attorneys can miss the point by being too conservative. This actually goes well beyond the topic of negotiation.

At the risk of ruffling some legal features, a person who is good at being an attorney, may not have the personality for sensitive negotiations. I don't want to get carried away by the stereotype, but it's there for a reason. I wish I had a nickel for every attorney who has complained to me about not liking what the field is doing to their personality, or saying that they left the field because they just couldn't go there. But I'm sure that if you are an attorney, dear reader, that you are one of the many exceptions to this unfortunate overgeneralization. I'm sure you have a delightful and profound ability to discuss sensitive issues and win friends.

Business people need to remember that most attorneys are not business people. The attorney cannot always predict the future, and is not taking into account everything that goes into business decision making. Attorneys are trained to be very protective, and this means they may interpret laws and regulations in such a way as to give advice that is too conservative.

Ultimately, the decision maker must decide how much risk to take on, and not simply fall in line with every concern that the attorneys raise. At the same time, the business person must be alert for signs that ignoring legal counsel would be at their peril.

While you consider the conservative nature of legal advice, also remember what they're trying to prove. They want to foster a reputation as an attorney who never looses, and who gets the biggest winnings. This can lead them, from a business perspective, to inadvertently throw the baby out with the bath water. This happens when legal maneuvers create too much damage to a businesses reputation, or cost the deal that is under construction.

Of course, there are attorneys that have extensive experience in negotiation. If you use one, be very sure that you have a solid understanding with them as to their role in the negotiation process.

Perfecting and Changing the Contract

Should your people discover a problem with the contract, you'll want to preserve your credibility and trust by having a very clear, legally-grounded explanation for the change. Point out any ways that it would have been to their disadvantage if you had not caught the problem. Since it is a legal matter, your reasons will be verifiable, and that will preserve your precious reputation for fair dealing.

Having counsel involved in reviewing the contract can be profoundly important. An experienced attorney may find a clause that is unenforceable, a requirement that can turn into a lawsuit, or language that a legal mind could subvert to your disadvantage.

There are three times that an attorney can be helpful for contract review: before, during and after. That is, before you begin, see if they can alert you to some legal issues that you need to bear in mind. During the process, run the emerging contract language with the attorney for a reality check. This can save you a lot of time, because you don't want to have to retreat and renegotiate, or create concerns about whether you know what you're doing. After the final draft is complete, the attorney can do a final check for legal issues.

When you are doing a more complicated negotiation that may involve a step such as a memorandum of agreement, you should have a little negotiation up front as to how the negotiating process will work. At that time, you can talk about timelines, memoranda of understanding. If you include in that preemptive negotiation the matter of any costs that will come from third parties such as a broker or other professional, this may eliminate such costs from the actual negotiation, reducing the number of concessions that they other side feels that they are making. This will, then, reduce the number of counter-concessions that you will feel obliged to make.

Preparation for Power

You can help yourself stay on track and meet your objectives by writing up the ideal contract in advance. At least write up all the elements of a good agreement, including price. This help you get reality checks on how well you are doing during the process, and how well you have done at the end. This can be very motivational, too. It helps you stay clear and strategic during the negotiation.

Keep in mind how important and powerful written and graphic materials can be. They have a special power to persuade. Often, people simply will not question things they see in writing. We are so used to following the commands on signs and the rule of law that, somehow, the written word has some extra authority in our minds. Take advantage of this power. Have good written and graphic materials ready. Use them to support your points in negotiation. When you are negotiating by phone, don't let that stop you. Provide written and graphic support materials that will give your position more meaning and authority. You can send them electronically or by courier or mail. Use professional layouts and impressive materials, because the package lends even more power to the contents. Get used to using things like presentation binders. Don't worry about their cost when the stakes are high. Keep your perspective.

MONEY AND VALUE MATTERS

Don't Get Money-Psyched

As a salesperson, you are probably money-psyched. You are very sensitive to squeezing every dollar you can out of the deal. As an employee, a salesperson knows that their performance turns up in their paycheck. Even a business owner who does a lot of his own negotiating feels the pinch. And then there is the constant drumbeat from customers, saying it's price, price, price.

They dig in their heels and postpone the buying decision, probably to go look for a better price. They look at your showroom, and then go online to find a better price, despite the risks of dealing with someone from out of town.

They tell you it's about price all the time. Well, I'm here to un-psych you, to de-hypnotize you, to take the zombification out of the price equation.

Hear this. More often than you realize, money is several gods lower on the totem pole. Stack up the other side's priorities, and you'll find there are many ways that you can add value and make concessions that matter more to them than money.

Of course there are competitive environments where money reins, but even in those, you offer more than price. Your reputation is a good example of a value that lies outside of the price domain.

Let's get into this subject, and transform your consciousness and your sales practices beyond the money dimension. We'll even cover techniques that will help you figure out where money does fit into their world, and even how much they'll pay. Psychic powers are not needed.

PEOPLE LOVE SPENDING MONEY

Let me guess what you're thinking. Customers love to spend money when it's other people's money, when they have money to burn, when the economy is hot, and when they want to ruin their soon-to-be-ex-spouse. Well, you're right, but don't stop there.

People love to spend money when they have a good reason. But where do good reasons come from? I think they come from some tiny vault in the brain that trots them out in order help them act on their feelings. **Feelings first. Reasons second.** Even when you have a highly analytical, rational, scientific-sounding discourse from a customer or friend as to why they bought *that* car, if you listen carefully, you'll hear another sound underneath all those rationalizations; it's the sound of their heartbeat quickening.

Actually, you might need a stethoscope for that.

This brings me to the Big Price Problem. Anything that makes someone fall out of love with spending money, even for a few moments, will kill the spending fever. And here is the rub. Salespeople are unconsciously sullying that love all the time. They do it by acting on the belief that they can't sell the person a higher priced item or get them to spring for the value add. They do it by acting on the belief that they can't create community good without helping their customers make a frugal purchase.

They do it by acting on the belief that they can't sell as much at the higher price, and can't cross the break point for better profit. But they don't really have to *act* on that belief. All they have to do is unconsciously, accidentally, passively put out a *vibe* that they can't. If the salesperson is at a point in their life when they must be very frugal, there is some internal set point that sets off an alarm when certain conditions occur, like getting the fully-featured item, or the luxury item, or the convenience package. Hence, the *vibe.*

EXORCISE THAT FRUGAL-NOMIC POSSESSION

Purge yourself of this accursed possession. No, not the luxury item, the fact of being possessed by the demon of frugality, the frugal-nomic possession. Expunge preconceptions about the customer from your mind. You must liberate your customer's potential to spend. You really don't know their values and needs like they do.

Nearly every customer will haggle over price or act squeamish regardless of how moneyed they are. How did the moneyed class come by their wealth? By giving it away? Even people with old money have usually learned to negotiate by the time they were, oh, about three. And here lies that powerful source of price-hypnosis, that that drum that pounds out price, price, price. Haggling.

No wonder salespeople are psyched about price.

From this moment forward, stand in awe of the luxury item, the quantity purchase, the value add, the maintenance contract, the features, the label. No glitz, no glory! And in that cherished mindset, you will radiate a new vibe spectrum; the vibe of permission, of excitement, of satisfaction. Your customers will absorb from merely basking in your presence a contact high. They will inhale. They will buy. And not just with the frugal self-deprivation of the humble peasant. They will buy with the mighty thunder of the empowered consumer.

Okay, I'm sure that's quite enough. I've made my point. The take away message is to rid yourself of any glitches that can hold your customers back from buying, or hold you back from selling. Are we inspired yet? No? Well, consider one more thing. Why is it that salespeople can sell more bigger ticket items when they are earning more money? Because they have a more personal connection with financial well being. Because they know what it feels like not to tense up around buying decisions. Because their body language, their vibe, creates no barriers between the customers and their dreams.

I discovered a problem like this with my own sales reps. Left to their own devices, customers would select substantially more life insurance than they did when my reps were helping them. As I helped my reps become more successful in terms of volume, they also began to sell bigger policies and higher end packages. And I'm not just talking about reps that were under my tutelage. It always seems that their comfort around money is a key factor in their ability to sell higher-priced items. And this is independent of their volume. Those are telling factors. Now I always work on their comfort with money, and the results are very gratifying.

What Matters More than Price?

From now on, think of your customers as wanting to spend more money. They only need two things. The certainty that they are getting the best deal, and a reason to close the deal.

Fortunately, many of the things you are learning in this book will help you convince the customer that they are getting the best deal. While the customer needs to know that they will not turn around and find the same product for a much lower price somewhere else, they also need to know that they bought from a reputable company. This, too, is a value, and it helps to mollify price concerns and buyer's remorse.

But this piece is about reasons that people buy that are not price. Let's just give you a list of examples. Here goes:

- *The company's experience*
- *The workers experience*
- *The management team on the product*
- *The team's capacity to complete the job by the deadline*
- *The company's ability to adhere to the specifications*
- *The certainty that the company is getting the best deal you're prepared to offer*
- *The quality of the product or service.*

- *Your terms*

- *Your delivery schedule*

- *Your experience in providing the product or service*

- *Your guarantees and ability to stand behind your promises*

- *Your return policies*

- *Your capacity to inventory stock*

- *Your capacity to automate your processes and make data available in harmony with their systems*

- *Your willingness and track record in building a working relationship with them*

- *Your capacity to offer credit, especially to start ups and companies in cyclical markets*

- *Your staff's competence and attitude*

THIS IS TRUE FOR GOVERNMENT AND BUYERS, TOO

Consider these factors that come into play when you are being considered to manufacture directly for a company:

- *The skill and quality of your workers, low turnover*

- *The management FTE's and level assigned to their projects*

- *Your capacity to package and ship product according to their needs*

- *How much you will make them a priority. You might have an advantage as a smaller company because that will make them a bigger part of your workload and, thus, value them more*

- *Reliability and consistency of quality*

- *Your capacity to ramp up to a high level of production in a timely fashion when needed*

- *Your ability to coordinate outsourcing for more complex projects*

- *Your ability to provide competent, honest, objective expert consultation as needed*

- *Your ability to deliver on a tight schedule, as with the just-in-time delivery business model*

- *Your experience and comfort in conforming to the demands of that company's type of business*

And consider the frame of mind of government agencies. There is a widely held belief that they MUST go with the lowest bidder. This is a myth. They must buy from the lowest bidder who can meet their specifications. If they really like a particular supplier, they'll make sure the specifications match that supplier. Government agencies are not operated by robots, despite the stereotypes. They develop an intimate understanding of the vendors, and they want to work with the most knowledgeable ones. You develop a relationship with them and stay on the cutting edge, and you have the advantage. And yes, I know there are notable exceptions where cronyism, nepotism, and outright bribes can trump the public interest. But these situations change when they come to light.

DEATH BY PRICE

Consider also the idea that products that have become commodities hinge entirely on price. Even Wal-Mart, a chain that achieved a reputation for taking over markets on price alone, did not actually always have the best prices. They did succeed in creating that reputation, but they also succeeded by having a very broad selection of merchandise that made it possible to do all your shopping in one place, so long as you fit a certain broad range of demographics. If commoditization made price the only factor, the shakeouts in the industries offering those products would be much more serious than they have normally historically been.

To be fair, there are market conditions that occur in which price makes or breaks deals and even companies. But the situation must be severe. The intrusion of Chinese into the American market, notably through deals with Wal-Mart, occurred because of Chinese government subsidies that broke treaties (as documented in a successful lawsuit), and because there was a profound difference in labor costs between the two countries. This difference was not a matter of who was a better haggler, this was an overwhelming difference in base costs that no negotiation could overcome. The result was not some lost deals, but many lost companies and American factories and other sources of employment.

WE'RE TALKING REAL MONEY

Have you ever found yourself thinking in percentages to decide whether to pursue more money. It could be in deciding whether to file a small court claim, how much time to spend negotiating, how hard to work in developing a proposal, any number of things like that.

It might go like this. We're $500.00 apart, I need to send back my response. If I rework these clauses in the memorandum of understanding like so, and talk them into it, there will be some back and forth, but maybe I can get them down another $200.00. Well, that must be a good idea, after all, it's a $2,000.00 deal, and you don't want to get screwed out of a whole 10%, do you? You might! You're talking about something that will add up to maybe four hours of work, and maybe even lose the deal. That's risking the deal and hoping to make $50.00 per hour.

I get very excited about some of the great returns I get from these negotiating tactics. But, as you've noticed, those returns are far greater than $50.00 per hour. So will you please stop thinking in percentages and think in real dollars? And, when appropriate, dollars per hour. When you get down to $50.00 per hour, you need to start thinking about other profitable ways that you might be using your time. Especially when there is risk to a deal.

This is a good reason to watch over any attorneys that you end up working with. Like a dog chasing a squirrel into the street, they can really lose perspective, chasing after some cash at a net loss (or a lousy profit-to-risk ratio) after their time is paid for.

Always ask yourself what your time is worth as you chase after a sum of cash. How long will it take to get that money? How much is your time worth? Does this really compute?

STRATEGY GRAB BAG

PROTECT YOURSELF FROM TRICKY BUYERS WITH SYMMETRY

I suppose there are countless ways that a buyer can be tricky. I'll cover some common tricks that you may not be prepared for, and what to do about them. The buyer's goal here is to see how low you will go.

First, we must look through the sophisticate buyer's eyes. Of course, they're trying to look through your eyes. What do they see as they try to get into your head. They start with the basic premise that the you, the seller, have a range from the high of your highest credible demand to your walk-away price; the price below which you cannot or will not sell. That can be a fuzzy line, of course, because there are all those other factors besides price, such as volume. And they are aware that you know they have a range themselves.

Let's get the painfully obvious tactic out of the way first. They'll simply ask. Yes, I had to say it. It's there, hiding in plain sight, and I hope you're prepared for them to ask what your lowest price is, as in, *"What's the best deal you can offer."* Your response will be to propose something that will keep them interested and make comments that keep negotiations going, depending on their sophistication, body language, and so forth.

SYMMETRY WORKOUT

Now let's assume that you are dealing with a good negotiator, and they ask in a sophisticated way. They might use any of the opening gambits that I have shared with you. For example, they might do a variation of the reluctant buyer, as in, "I've been half thinking of going in with my uncle on a yacht. We were thinking of a model around this big, like this here. We've been thinking of a used one, but I thought I'd sneak a peek at your boats, I mean, um, yachts here just out of curiosity. What kind of a deal can I guy get on a yacht around this size?"

Oh boy, this good ole' boy even knows to play dumb. He knows Yankees will fall for the dumb southerner routine because they love feeling superior. But you know better than that.

You take a symmetrical approach, and decide to risk losing him. But you doubt you will. You say, "We are getting quite an influx of demand for our yachts, because the big thing now is resort properties with waterfronts, and people doing business while traveling on their yachts to places like Dubai. It's amazing. Oh, anyway, you were interested in one of our most in-demand models. If you move quickly, I can secure this for you without the long wait. It's our last one."

You are using a variation on the reluctant seller. This isn't really so much a reluctant seller as one who really doesn't care who buys it as long as they don't want to haggle much.

BE READY FOR REAL TRICKERY

Your sophisticated buyer might absorb a lot of your time to get you invested, and then tell you that it isn't really quite what he's looking for and wish you luck in selling it. As if you needed luck. But you don't bristle, because you are enjoying the game as much as he is. When his is one foot out the door, he appear to have a spontaneous idea, and tells you he'd really like to be fair, since you gave him so much time, and asks you what the very lowest price is that you would let it go for. Now that's asking, but with quite a torturous twist.

The buyer might even use a surrogate, as a variation of good cop bad cop. He says he might have a friend who might want to look into it. But he doesn't really have a lot of dough. Again, the question will be what the lowest price you'll take.

They might even try the finder's fee angle, asking you if their friend bought, if you'd offer a $300.00 finder's fee. They might have this set up with their co-buyer or something to really double team you.

They may juggle some angles to see how soft your price is, like talking about getting the yacht without various add-ons that this fully-featured one has, or offering to pay cash up front, and so forth. Then, after they have a feel for the parameters, bargain more directly for what they want.

If they are really ready to con you, they may even have a couple people come by and make super low offers. Once your confidence is dashed, they come in for the kill.

And don't forget all that good cop bad cop info we covered. That's the most common of all.

TURN ABOUT'S FAIR PLAY: GET TACTICAL

Add these tactics to your arsenal. Their purpose is to test factors such as their price softness and unspoken interests.

Raise and test their top offer by getting tentative agreements about what your authority in absentia might do. For example, if the buyer is paying $1.00 for widgets, and you know that he wants a company with your consistency and experience, you need get a feel for just how eager he is. You might say, "Since you see how superior our product and service are, if I could get my boss down from $2.00 to $1.50, would that work for you?" In this case, you're looking at high volume sales and can come down to $1.50, but you expect to do better. You're using your authority in absentia to test their responsiveness and raise their anchor point to a higher level. You don't have to sell it for that amount, but you have gotten them to a higher place to negotiate from.

Find out what their quality standards really are. If you offer a more basic model for a lower price, you are associating that lower price with lower quality or features, and seeing if they actually want to discuss this option. Their response might plainly tell you that quality is a big deal, and their real walk away price is higher than it first appeared.

Do the same tactic with higher quality as you did with lower quality. You'll get a sense of their walk away price this way. If they turn their noses up at a higher-quality version they may even let slip a higher price that they would settle for.

Anytime that you can't provide the item a corporate buyer wants is an opportunity to gather some intelligence. It's worth a try, anyway. You could say, "We really appreciate every opportunity to do business with you, but this isn't really something we can offer right now. Please keep us in mind though." Before too long, you'll want to ask what they might expect to get the item for. If you get an unguarded answer, you can factor that into your thinking about the industry, and whether you want to go after the market for that product.

You know that price is not the only consideration, but you certainly want to play the game so that you understand the price dynamics of your potential customer as much as you can.

THE ULTIMATE WAY TO NOT SPLIT THE DIFFERENCE

Refrain from splitting the difference by getting the other side to split the difference at least twice. Here's how. And, by the way, after this bare-bones explanation, I'll provide a complete example in a real-world situation.

1. Once the negotiation has come down to a more-or-less small gap, you will both feel tempted to split the difference.

2. Talk to them. Emphasize how close you both are, but how you just aren't in a position to go any lower. You're really sorry, especially after all the time you've both invested, but you're just going to have to pass.

3. Talk like that, and before long they offer to split the difference.

4. Get them to confirm this new amount. This helps them feel a little more like it's their commitment than just splitting the difference.

5. Tell them you will do your best to get your authority in absentia (partners, board, spouse, whatever) to approve it, and you get back to them with the result.

6. When you get back to them, explain how tough they were, and how hard you worked trying to justify it, and that it just didn't fly.

7. Tell them that you really hope you, together, can find a way not to let the deal fall through, since you're so close. Remind them of the legitimate reasons why you are unable to flex much more and how far you have already come down.

8. I'll give good odds that they will, again, offer to split the difference.

9. Now you can accept the deal. Or you can go through these steps again (or some variation) to get them to split the difference yet again. Or you can accept the deal on a condition that some other concession by the customer is in place.

Thus, you have *quartered* the difference by getting them to split it *twice*. Or *eighted* it. And look how little time it took. Well, in actual practice, it takes very little time, especially compared to what led up to it.

Keep this key point in mind the entire time: You are framing this so that they feel that they have won. Right up to the very end, reinforce this perspective. Make sure they feel good about what savvy, hard-working negotiators they are.

A WARM, ENTERTAINING EXAMPLE

Here's that example of NOT splitting the difference. Or should I say, how to eighth the difference.

Let's say a nice, wealthy couple bought a cottage in the Santa Cruz mountains and they want you to rehabilitate a small bridge from their home to a convenient road so they can get into town faster. You've been negotiating. Here's where the fun starts.

1. The negotiation has come down to a much smaller gap than you started with. In fact, it's small enough to tempt most people to split the difference between your $65,000.00 and their $61,000.00. Especially since, if you offered to do it, they'd probably say yes! Do you feel that tension building? It's the call to split the difference. Quick. Before you answer the call, go to step two.

2. Get your opponent into a position where it makes sense to them to split the difference. To achieve this, you might say something like, *"Well, if it weren't for our tight margins, I'd like to be more accommodating, but I think I'm going to have to pass. It's a shame though after we put so much time into this. I mean, we're only $4,000.00 apart."*

3. Stay on those talking points, and it's likely that they will offer to split the difference.

4. Respond to the offer by getting them to confirm the amount. *"Well, so that would mean $65,000.00 minus half the difference, that's $2,000.00 off my discounted price, to take me down to $63,000.00. Is that what you're offering?"*

5. When they confirm (and it is helpful that they confirm that as an offer, since you are taking some of the emphasis off of the idea of splitting), you say, *"I might be able to get this to fly. Let me talk to my partners and see if I can go with this. I'll let you know first thing tomorrow."*

6. When you contact your customer, you tell them how difficult your partners are on this because of tight margins or whatever you'd care to say. Emphasize that you spend a good deal of time going over the figures. Tell them that they are insisting that you'll lose money if you fall under your original $65,000 stopping point from yesterday. Emphasize the fact that you are now only $2,000.00 apart, now. Look what you've done, you have redefined their offer as being $63,000.00 as if it was their new position, thereby establishing an *anchor point* in your favor. You are trying to turn their split-the-difference offer into a *concession* of $2,000.00.

7. But you aren't going to drop out of the bidding just yet. You put them, again, into a difference-splitting attitude, by saying, *"Can we find a way not to let this fall apart now that we're so close? We're only $2,000.00 apart."* As you talk, stick with those talking points, including your tight margins or whatever.

8. They will probably surrender to the temptation to split the difference again. This puts them at $64,000.00, which is another $1,000.00 higher. Now, they have come up a total of $3,000.00. If you had split the difference, you would have struck the deal at only $62,000.00.

9. You might accept the deal at this point, making $1,000.00 more than if you had split the difference. This means you have *quartered* the difference by getting them to split it *twice*. This took you maybe ten minutes. Right now, I'm thinking you're a genius, because you made the equivalent of $6,000.00 an hour. Since I like to negotiate, I can't even spend that fast.

Be sure to emphasize that you are coming down $1,000.00 and that you're going to take heat for it, but they are a nice couple and you've all worked hard to hammer out the deal, and you are really motivated to rehab that bridge, it's going to be so beautiful; a point of pride.

You have worked this all along so that the couple can take pride in having won, while your pride is in the opportunity to do something beautiful.

But you missed something! When you said you were willing to come down so far (I mean $1,000.00 isn't chicken feed), did you ask for a concession? No? What? Did you think that they made two concessions and you were only making one? Banish the thought. Next time you quarter the difference, work in some kind of nibble, even if it's just some additional time to complete the project, or them doing the clean up that you might normally do in preparation for the project.

They might feel obliged, and be so excited about the project that they want things to be all ready for you when you arrive. It could save your crew a couple hours.

One more thing. Sometimes you can play out this pattern three or more times. Instead of quartering, you could eighth or sixteenth the difference!

Deep Breath, Let's Summarize This

Here are the key points for this maneuver:

1. You don't get into thinking that splitting the difference is fair. You don't use it as a way to escape the tension of negotiating over the remaining gap between you and the other side.

2. You're version of this is to end up quartering or eighthing the difference. You can do it multiple times.

3. They offer to split the difference, not you. You work them into the position of wanting to offer the split.

4. You make sure they feel they've won because you emphasize how far you're coming down, and you're reluctant but give in, etc.

5. You get them to confirm what the split amount is, so that it is more like they are making a commitment. It's a subtle, psychological bit of leverage that helps you out.

6. The good cop bad cop is a required part of this example. But there are other variations you can come up with, depending on the situation.

7. You can plug in any of your other negotiating techniques into this framework. For example, when you emphasize the reasons why you can't come down, you are playing a version of the reluctant seller.

8. This doesn't take a lot of time in practice, and the gains make for a real return on your investment!

BETTER THAN THAT

Hardly a negotiation should go by without at least one use of this venerable technique. This one technique, which is so brief and so simple, has made me such an obscene amount of money, that should be X-rated, and for so little effort!

The key words are, **"better than that."** Here are some phrasings. I'll bet you'll see right away how handy they are.

That's promising, but the deal has to be better than that.

I'll be able to take a deal before the board if it's better than that.

I'm sorry, you'll have to do better than that.

You gotta do better than that.

Look at what we're offering here. C'mon, you can do better than that.

I'm taking enough heat already, throw me a bone, fer crissake.

I got nothin'. You wanna deal, get serious or I'm walkin'.

Ah, I admit, the phrases got more Godfather as I went along. But I'm making the point that you can say it a lot of different ways, and to any kind of person. Whatever your choice of words, the Better Than That is a very effective tactic, so long as you use it's key ingredient, *silence.*

You say the phrase, and wait. Silently. Feel the tension build. Gaze into their eyes, softly, with a very slight and gentle, almost invisible smile, and count in your head or chant your mantra or something to keep yourself occupied. Once, when I did this, I was so relaxed about it, that when the person blurted out their response I almost jumped. They were releasing tension, and I was just floating on a cloud. And I think I only got up to six. That silence can really get people talking!

By the way, this is a nice one to use when you think you've already done it all. Just when you are on the verge of accepting a bid, try the magic words, wait, and see what happens. You might take a written bid, write those words with a medium point red marker, and send it back. It might stir the ghost of a perfectionistic teacher in the recipient's mind, and he'd just *have* to do better than that.

SILENCE WORKOUT

There is a problem with this, though, when two people are using silence, waiting for the other to speak. And this happens. It's because there are points in a negotiation where you know that the first person to speak loses. Neither one wants to lose, so neither one speaks.

I found myself in this position once. I had made an offer, and the other party told me I'd have to do better than that. I did a slight shrug, and tilted my head to the side with a smile, as if to say, *"Well, really, I don't think I can."* After I grew tired of looking beatific and counting to myself, I said, *"Knock knock... Man... Man oh man, we're both good negotiators, using that silent close. They say the first one to speak loses. I lost. So what is your counter-offer?"*

He chuckled, and said, *"Okay, you're offering this amount and we need to have these items in place to even come close. If we move on price, can you flex on these?"* To which I said, *"I think we can, but what kind of offer are you willing to make for that?"* and we were back into negotiating full speed ahead.

Oh! I almost forgot. What about if this technique is used on you and you don't want to do a knock-knock joke? Try saying, "Well, gee, just how much better are we talking here? What did you have in mind?" Then, silence.

IS THAT A PROFIT, I MEAN PURE PROFIT?

Did you know that a negotiated dollar is worth way more than a gross-income dollar? If you work your buns off for a $100,000.00 contract, sweating out many an hour, and involving many staff people, your boss will be thrilled that it came through. You're a hero. But if your in an industry that has a margin of, say 2%, the profit is going to be $2,000.00. Yes, I know it isn't quite that simple because of fixed costs, community good will, and the like. But, still. Compare that to making some moves that bring that contract in at $101,000.00. Let's say you spent an extra two hours and got that concession. Doesn't look like much, really. But it was $500.00 per hour, bottom-line profit. Compare that to many staff hours for the bottom-line equivalent of about $2,000.00, and the art of negotiation takes on quite a sheen, doesn't it?

Don't be so dazzled by bringing in a big contract that you feel too grateful to negotiate. This is akin to that basic rule I brought up about not needing the sale so much that it throws you off. Remember how much you are contributing to your company's financial well being by carrying out this essential part of your job, as a negotiator. Don't let your job description, job title, or other preconceptions distract you from your power to product profit; bottom-line profit; really fast per-minute profit.

Win in Second Place

Don't go first! It's not that it isn't polite to go first, and you wouldn't say to the other side, "Age before beauty!" It's just a matter of good negotiating sense. In negotiation, you always want the other side to make the first commitment. I'm not even talking about concessions yet. You may well make the first concession. That's better than making the first commitment. Consider the reasons:

1. Whatever their first offer is, it's business intelligence for you. What have you learned? This is especially true when you are talking about multifaceted deals.

2. Getting that initial offer is what you need in order to do your very best at bracketing, where you create a price point that places your goal price exactly in the middle between the two. Conditions may allow you to do something a little different, but at least you can take the lead in bracketing. You are much more likely to end up where you want to be. And maybe better if you work in some tactics such as eighthing the difference, as I describe in this book.

3. If you don't show your hand first, you could get an offer that is better than you expected. Why ruin that by risking them finding out that you would have settled for less?

4. Let's say they refuse. I suppose that tells you a little something right there. Both sides know that the other knows something about negotiation. But you can't sit there all day in silence, waiting for the other to do something. That would be too much like my starter marriage.

But what if you are in a setting where there is a price right there on the product, like a car showroom, for example? Same difference, really. The customer tells you that they want to know what you can do for them. You might ask, *"Well, really, what price range can you afford right now?"* That should loosen them up. If they say they don't know, then you really have to wonder if they aren't just window shopping. Not that this would put any damper on your creativity. *"But you can afford to buy a new car today?"* and so forth.

Light the Way with Your Dim Bulb

The streets are paved with gold if you travel them on the short bus. Good negotiators know to keep their gleaming sword of brain power snug in it's scabbard, so as not to lose the sale. In most sales situations, you really do need to act dumber than you are. Or at least dumber than your customer. Since you can be dumb and do a perfectly serviceable job of applying most techniques in this book, I don't have to act at all. At least that's how I feel some days.

There are some really serious advantages to putting some dumbness in your day. If you talk a bit more slowly, and take a little time to chew things over, thinking out loud, this is very helpful. It allows you to take time to think strategically, while keeping your customer preoccupied with what you're saying. It allows you to frame things to your advantage. But, since you're do dumb to do that, the customer may not think anything of it. They don't feel threatened, and the don't feel competitive.

For your own psychology, it actually helps keep your own ego in check, as well. We salespeople can get a little ego heavy. Well, some of us do, anyway. So try this on and see what it does for you. You can probably find a television character who is smart, but in a dumb way. You can use them to hammer out the personality you present to your customers. See what happens.

There's also a psychological advantage in how you influence your customers. They not only feel less competitive, but many of them will actually feel a need to help you a bit. They might help you understand how to sell them, or just not bring out their harshest negotiation techniques so that you at least have a chance. But if they are opportunists, you can reel them in like a strong fish, and reshape their expectations. By the time that happens, they'll be very invested in the sale, and still have the comfort of knowing they're superior.

THE GUIDELINES OF DUMB

Follow these guidelines, and you will be dumb rich:

- *Don't act so dumb that it ruins whatever credibility and trust you need.*

- *Don't act so smart that it ruins whatever trust you need.*

- *Don't act so dumb that it looks like you're acting.*

- *Don't act so smart that it's obvious you're acting.*

- *Don't act so dumb that you have to fumble things that matter.*

- *Don't act so smart that you bring out the competitiveness in the other party.*

- *Don't act so dumb that they can't help you.*

- *Don't act so smart that they don't want to help you.*

- *Don't act so dumb that you take too long to think.*

- *Don't act so smart that you think you don't have to think.*

- *Don't act so dumb that you can't keep things straight.*

- *Don't act so smart that you think you don't need to take complete notes.*

- *Don't act so dumb that you can't do a thing without checking with your boss.*

- *Don't act so smart that you just don't need any approval for anything.*

High-Concept Value: Break it Down

You're doing so much to make sure the customer feels that they are getting a good deal, winning at negotiation, staying invested, and really desiring the product or service. You are also doing your attitude wizardry to make sure the customer does not dig in their heels as you prepare to close. Let's apply some psychological elbow grease to the cost and sacrifice fear factor. How can you make the cost of an item less intimidating? I told you that, deep down inside, customers really want to spend money. But you also know that they need a reason. Let me add excuse, rationalization, outlet, permission, or approval.

If you can break the cost down into smaller units, you can really take away some of the sacrifice or intimidation in the price. You also get their mental gears turning, and this absorbs them more in the negotiation and anticipation of having the product. One reason for this is that the broken-down cost is more animated and more connected to the actual use of the product. This is a key to the psychology of sales, recruiting the mental resources of the customer into the dream and into the buying process. That last sentence spoke volumes. Seriously. You might want to read it again just to commit the principle to memory.

You'll recognize a broken down price immediately. But are you taking advantage of all of your own opportunities to mount this classic gem?

You can present the price in broken-down terms at the outset, to help establish a frame of reference. Sometimes this makes practical sense, as in a per mile charge for a rental car.

You can also break it out as a reframe, as when you say, "Well, you know, that is just a quarter a day, and for such entertainment value!" Well, since you put it that way, it's no sacrifice. I'd have to be a real Scrooge to deprive my family of all that entertainment value for just a quarter.

Look for opportunities to break down your price into units of time, item, use, kilobyte, or whatever else you can think of. The more relevant you can make this to your customer's life and frame of reference the better. Look at cell phone service. They would never talk in annual costs. That would be suicide.

HIGH-CONCEPT ATTENTION FOCUS

You've admired the prestidigitation of magicians as they make objects disappear. They have their ways of directing, or misdirecting, your attention in order to preserve the illusion. Salespeople work attention magic as well, all to make it easier for the customer to make their buying decision, and to get better products and services.

I mentioned cellular providers. They will certainly keep your attention away from the costs of going over your minutes unless you want to bring up the subject yourself. And look at loan providers, even mortgages. They keep the customer's attention away from the total cost, and focus it on the monthly cost. This keeps the discussion firmly rooted in the customer's tendency to think in terms of their monthly budget. That monthly paycheck tells them what they can afford. Most consumers don't think much beyond that convenient reference point. Remember what I said about the importance of keeping things connected to the customer's frame of reference. And when does any company tell you what the interest will cost over the life of a loan? Most people have no idea what that total will be, even if it is for a house. And that's usually the largest purchase they will make in their lives.

The customer's attention is also directed away from customer borne costs, such as the cost of gasoline for a rental car. I'll bet you think it sounds petty even bringing that up. That's exactly how I'd want it to sound if I were renting you a car. But why don't I also charge you for tire wear? How about oil changes and depreciation? Well, that's factored into the overall cost. Then why not gasoline. Because people are so used to putting gas in a car, and it is such a familiar tradition in the industry, that no one would ever expect to have their gasoline for free. Customer borne costs were borne to be invisible.

CUT THE C.R.A.P. - CUSTOMER REPEAT-ACTION PILFERING

I'd like to share with you exactly what I do when the negotiation gets past the point of good-faith moves, and turns into a time-wasting grind for small amounts of money. I call this Customer Repeat-Action Pilfering, other wise known as C.R.A.P.

The technique I'm about to share can stop this cold. Or, perhaps I should say, cut the C.R.A.P. Sometimes you will have a customer who is thinking about how much they can make per hour by shaving a little more. However, they don't make a lot per hour, so they don't mind taking up your time with what feels to you like petty concerns. Don't get mad, just create a little change in perspective, a change in accountability, a change in motivation.

Here's how I put an end to negotiations and seal the deal. I discover that I have made a small error, or maybe a big one. Either way, the price is actually somewhat higher, I'm sorry to say. Or the feature actually doesn't come for free. Or buying just one includes a handling fee.

This really shifts the power dynamic. The person feels remorse for digging themselves into this hole. They could just blame you, because you either made a mistake, or returned from the powers that be with bad news. But deep inside, they feel at fault for not grabbing a good deal, or being too greedy to see that it was a good deal. You just made a good deal out of what was not feeling so good to them a moment ago. That's a kind of inflation I can live with.

Well, they may say something about it, like, *"Aw, c'mon, you told me..."* bla bla. And you can say, *"I'm really sorry, but we had a special on this extra feature and normally it costs."*

But you don't leave them feeling bad. They could still get the good deal that they missed out on when they were busy trying to get the better deal. And you give them that opportunity, appearing to offer a concession when all you are really doing is coming back to your earlier price. You raised the anchor point to a higher price, and coming down provides some relief for the customer from the artificial pain you inflicted with your bad news.

"Look, I feel really bad about this. Let me go back to them and admit what I did, and maybe I can get it for what I promised. Would that do it for you?"

There you go!

MORE ABOUT CUTTING THE C.R.A.P.

So far you've learned that this gambit involves a take away. The price was not so low after all, or the feature was not free, after all. This redefines the game right on the spot. You do this when the customer is grinding you for too much time and too little money to negotiate over. You think this gambit will put a stop to it, based on what you know about the customer. You have used an external bad guy so that you can blame them, even though you made the mistake. And since it is your mistake, you will try to help them out by restoring the take away. Now they accept the original price and stop the grinding. It's a done deal.

You know that there is some risk involved, so you only use this when you really feel that it will work. You normally would not try this with bigger gaps in the negotiation. You would do the NOT splitting the difference technique before you would do a take away.

We have talked about money so far. But you can also do this with product features, or features of the deal. For example, you can't wave the maintenance fee, after all. Or you can't include the installation cost, after all. Or you can't wave the training charge.

But remember, the more you value the customer, the bigger the gap, and the higher the stakes, the more you should look at other approaches.

How to NOT Argue Your Way to Sales Success

If a customer says something bad about your company or product, don't you feel an urge to jump to the defense? Of course you do. But don't. Sure, they're wrong, but don't argue. I have an even better idea. Show understanding and support for their position, without giving your position away. To do this, you go into stealth mode for a moment, as in, *"Yes, that's something that has a lot of people worried. I've been hearing about that from new customers all too often."*

This works because their concerns are there for a reason. Why would you want to destroy their trust in you and your own credibility by denying what is real for them? You wouldn't! And there is another great reason for this, it gives you some time to frame things.

Did you catch the framing in my response? When I said that it has a lot of people worried, I was gaining trust and credibility, but when I said I was hearing about it from new customers, that is the set

up for telling her that is a problem with other companies. I'm prepared
to show verifiable information to prove that we are different, because
it's true. Also, I said the magic words, *"all too often,"* showing that I,
too, have feelings about this, and have ethics that are against it, and
have concern for how it affects people. I can even add that it affects my
profession, because it hurts reputable companies like mine.

I have, in effect, moved her concern onto other companies
instead of arguing about the nature of my own company, profession,
product, or service, any of which might receive a tongue lashing from
a customer at any time. It just depends on what they've experienced.
And this is a key point. You can't deny what people have experienced,
even if it is just a thing they picked up from the news that biased them.
It was still a commanding voice, and a powerful image. It's as good as
reality once it becomes a memory. Maybe even stronger.

YOUR PRICE IS TOO HIGH

Can you avoid direct argument on something as specific as
price? What do you do with someone telling you that your price is
too high? "Well, I hear this quite a bit, and that's because people have
not had a first-hand experience of the kind of quality that we offer. We
have created an actual kitchen right here in our showroom, and you
will not believe how a floor this beautiful can be this resistant to wear!"

And what if they have heard some bad things directly about
your company. You can't push that off onto another company. But
you can credibly push it to another time and circumstance, as in, "Yes,
that is a rumor that's been going around since before our company
purchased this business and got rid of the customer service people
they were using overseas. Now, any time you call, 24/7, the person
who picks up the phone will treat you right, and understand every
word you say. And you can try that any time, by calling our customer
service number, you can use my phone or yours right now if you want

to see how they sound." How's that? Note that the sales person is prepared to verify their claim.

PULL THE IRON OUT OF THE FIRE: SALVATION THROUGH SMALL CONCESSIONS

Don't you just hate it when negotiations stall. It's the doldrums. You are going nowhere. Worse, you fear you'll lose the sale because you are running out of wiggle room, and they are digging in their heals. What's a poor salesperson to do?

And have you noticed that this tends to happen with really experienced negotiators? Maybe there's some ego in the works, or maybe they are trying a silent close, or maybe they are running out of wiggle room themselves and are beginning to lose hope.

Come to the rescue with a small concession. Especially when it is one of those stalls that happens when you're so close to a deal that you can just taste it. This helps the other side feel more enthusiastic, because it creates more hope. It also positions them as winning another concession, even though it's a small one. Ah, but why would a small concession work any magic with these big time, experienced negotiators? Because you're close to an agreement and they want things to pick up just like you do. They have invested a lot in the deal and they want to come back to their HQ as the victors, reveling in glory, the stuff of legends, or at least worthy of a round of drinks.

Think of small concessions that you can make for customers that you negotiate with. But don't just think dollars. Small dollar concessions seem small, and when they are unit prices, they seem smaller than they are, so your doubly damned. Think about meaningful gestures. And when you do, start with things that you would have done anyway. How about telling them that you just don't have any ability to budge on the price at this point, but you promise to devote your best manager to oversee the project? And be sure to rave about her extraordinary success and experience. That might be all the excuse they need to say, "Can you guarantee that? Because if so, then we can go along with this price." See how they helped you make it into a concession? They wanted to get this put to bed just like you did.

There are all sorts of things you can offer. Training, additional customer relationship management features online for their convenience, locking in the price for future orders for a period of time (that's a popular one!), promising a renegotiation of the price because market conditions are changing (you worked in a because, good, that was from another lesson), offer longer payment terms, extend the warranty period. Now we're brainstorming. What else can you think of?

The other side is going to feel good about winning that last concession. They won!

How 'Bout a Little Nibble?

Employ the nibble principle at the end of your negotiation. At the last moments of a negotiation, you will usually have an opportunity to squeeze in one more concession of some kind. In fact, so that you are asking for less concessions during the main body of the negotiation process, you might want to strategically hold back an item that you think may make a good nibble concession until the right moment at the end of your negotiations.

Here's why this works so well.

At the end of the negotiation, people have the highest level of commitment that they could have during the negotiation. People automatically tend to justify their commitments when they make them. People's sense of the odds of a gamble even increase once they have placed their bets. This makes a small concession seem even smaller when the timing coincides with that peak of commitment and justification.

People tend to let their guard down at the end of a negotiation. They are more fatigued, and less inclined to expect any demands to be place on them. Their minds are already leaping ahead to getting away and relaxing, or maybe rolling up their sleeves and putting things in writing, or getting back to the office and basking in the glory of victory. In any case, that last-minute nibble slips right past their defenses and gets a yes response far more often than it would if it came much sooner.

People are more generous and undefended when they are feeling good. Of course, you helped them feel good by making sure that they feel that they have won, too. So, of course they can be magnanimous and entertain one more small concession, maybe it will make you feel better about them, since you gave up so much.

The other side feels the way you do. The last thing they want after all this work is to hunker down for more negotiation. Their nerves are flayed enough. The effort-to-gain ratio is tilted toward the, "aw, just give it to them and let's get out of here," side at this point.

But remember, just a nibble. You don't want to get into an uproar, either, do you? That means going for something like this, "Oh, and just so there are no surprises, you'll be coordinating the training with the vendors, won't you? That's how everyone normally does it." It's a nibble for some hours of staff time, nothing terribly big. I'm sure you can think of things in your industry that would be to your advantage, but wouldn't cause a big to-do at the end of the negotiation.

You may be wondering about the technique of providing a small concession at the end. Remember that that technique is mainly to save a stalled negotiation. But if you can come up with one that you're okay with, to help them feel better about giving you your nibble, then you will have better odds of getting it.

NIBBLE-PROOF

After all that talk about the irresistible nature of the nibble principle, you'd think no one was immune. But you are, because you have this book full of inoculations. Here, I offer the prevention and the cure for the nibble principle.

Expect the nibble and be psychologically prepared. Have your response style ready to go. There's an example in the next paragraph.

Make the other person feel cheap. No need to get carried away here, I mean you don't want cause any kind of problem at the end of the negotiation. But then, neither do they. Just give them a kind smile, and say, *"We all know you have negotiated a great deal, and we're all ready to pack it up. Don't make us start doing the work that is expected of you, too. Fair enough?"* Honestly, I'd say, *"Well, it doesn't hurt to ask, but if you feel that way about it, we'll take care of it, then."* That's because the nibble is just a nibble. If you get it, that's nice. You might get it because it isn't a big deal. But, then again, if you don't get it, it still isn't a big deal. Let it go. Neither side needs to take this too seriously.

Try the symmetric approach. It's hard enough to deny a nibble. Try denying one when you have just asked for one and the other side says, *"We'd be happy to do that. And, I'm sure you won't mind your graphics people handling the announcements and press releases."* Oh boy. *"Oh, why, how can I say no?"* How, indeed?

Prevent nibbling by being very careful with your language at the end, getting very clear commitments that this is it. That will make it easier to use your friendly nibble rejection response should a nibble occur. This includes making it very clear that there are things you are not entirely satisfied with, but that you are letting go to show your good faith commitment to making the relationship work. Not only do they feel victorious, but it's hard to say, and let's add something to your dissatisfaction, then, shall we?

As you think about what to turn into a nibble, consider the following:

Anything that you didn't quite get satisfaction on in the main negotiation, but is small enough to fly under the radar.

Something that might just be better kept to the end so as not to use up your concessions in the body of the negotiation.

WIN OR LOSE, CONGRATULATE

Why gloat? You don't punish a dog when it comes to you, you reward it so it will come when you call. You don't gloat in front of a customer or any negotiation opponent. You want them to come back again. And you want them to have a good relationship with you during any follow up, such as when repairs are needed. And you certainly want goodwill in the community.

Refraining from gloating is like dieting by not bingeing on sundaes. Go the extra mile. Well up your best social skills and deliver a hearty congratulations. If a victorious general can congratulate the defeated one, who is responsible for thousands of his soldiers deaths, you can congratulate a negotiation opponent, whether you feel like you won or lost. If you lost, you congratulate them for winning. If they win, you congratulate them for winning. Yes, that's what I said. It's a timeless principle of negotiation. It's the cherry on top of your strategy to make them feel good about their deal. And that is at the core of negotiation philosophy. Sorry for the mixed metaphors. I think the comment about the sundae distracted me.

THE FIRST OFFER IS NEVER ENOUGH

Never go for the first offer in a negotiation. There are so many reasons. **Where do I start?**

You want to practice negotiation because it will earn you so much bottom-line money. Don't pass up this opportunity to practice.

You can't make the person feel like they've one if there was no fight. If anything, they'll be certain that they could have done much better. They will be convinced that they offered too much. You are living proof of that, because no one in their right mind says yes on the first go round unless it's a screaming deal.

If they don't think they offered too much for what they thought they were buying, they will think they didn't get what they paid for. They'll think the car was a lemon, or the clothes must be going out of style, or the computer system must have a chronic problem of some kind. Now they will lose sleep, or try to back out, or overreact to any small problem.

Even if you get a person who doesn't know how to negotiate, and they put something up for sale at their rock bottom price so they can move it quickly, at least get them to work a little, resolving your concerns about it. If it's a screaming deal, and you're sure, then take it before someone else races up the driveway.

But as a salesperson, you won't be making offers like that, or you would just be a cash register clerk. Expect the person to be offering their lowest credible offer, and use an assortment of methods from this book to perfect your art as a negotiator and master of influence.

NEGOTIATION POWER

Part of your power as a negotiator lies in your knowledge that people tend to feel that they have the lower hand in negotiation.

They feel that time pressure is against them.

They feel that the other side knows things that they don't know.

They believe, maybe subconsciously, that this is the last, best deal of its kind. And the advertisements may have reinforced that feeling with great skill.

They want the item, and don't want to experience the loss of letting it go.

They have invested time in the negotiation, and don't want to feel that it was wasted.

They think the other side is greedy, and they feel powerless to anything but get some meager concessions and swallow their pride.

They over-value the item (or the deal) by bathing it in an aura of anticipation, as if it were some kind of capital A Answer.

The under-value the negative side of the item (or the deal): the follow up, customer service, depreciation, maintenance, loss of luster, going out of style, and evaporation of that new car smell, or whatever it is that makes it seem extra special before they own it. Call it covetousness.

I want you to ponder each one of those items a little bit and think about how your approach to sales is relevant to that human tendency. How do you use it when it occurs in your prospect, and how to you mitigate for it in yourself. Think over a variety of customers and negotiations that you have had. How does each of these human foibles play out, and what might you do to take your approach and your own psyche to a new level in light of these insights? Isn't that something that both you and the person you're negotiating with may feel that they have the lower hand at the same time?

SUPER-SYMMETRY

This boils down to a simple rule. Ask for something in return every time. Every time the other side asks for a concession, show your interest in providing that concession, show your interest in keeping the negotiation alive, and show your interest in your own welfare. Do it by asking this magic question, "If I do that for you, what can you do for me?" Or, if you are very clear about what you want at that point, don't be coy. Say, "Well, we can look at that. If we do that for you, can you give us right of first refusal on renewal for five years?" or whatever tosses your confetti.

This is a good idea because the other side expects this kind of sea-saw symmetry. It's good because you don't want to miss a single opportunity for a concession. You know how those add up! And it's good because you wouldn't want your opponent to get out of the habit of feeling very accountable for a square deal. Besides, you don't want them feeling like maybe they could have gotten more. They would fear that they'd lost their edge, or that you were keeping something form them, or that they started too high in the first place. They'd remember that the next time they did business with you, and that would make for some difficult negotiating.

You can add a little umph to your something-in-return principle by buying a little time. "Well, I can talk to shipping about that. But if I do, will you be willing to use our online management system for the drop shipping?" You get the concession, and then give the concession, after you talk to shipping, of course.

And always make sure that your concession is valued. Make a bit of a process out of giving a concession. Never give the impression that it comes out of you like some kind of a reflex. You aren't *easy*. Your mother taught you better! By punching up the value of the concession, you create more obligation for counter-concessions. Invoke the value of your concession when you ask for a concession back. It's the stuff of business.

With this persistent response, you will be relieved of any tendency that the other side might have to become a repeat offender, asking for unrequited concessions or grinding away for all sorts of little nuisance items. It's behavior modification. Work and sacrifice are the mild punishments for seeking a concession. **They ask, they have to work and cough up a sacrifice.**

BEWARE THESE MANIPULATIONS

Time Pressure

Consider the effects of time pressure in negotiation.

People become more desperate, or should I say more flexible, as time pressure increases.

If both sides are not experiencing the same time pressure, the most pressured side is at a disadvantage, *if* the other side knows.

If one side thinks it has more time pressure than the other side, it is at a *real* disadvantage for imaginary reasons.

The guidelines that flow from these insights:

Never allow the opposition to be aware of your time situation unless it is advantageous, even if it is imaginary.

If the other side might buckle to time pressure, find ways to increase the pressure, such as stretching out the negotiations or keeping key aspects for the end, as if they were hostages. For those are the ones for which you most want the advantage. Work on others first as the other side builds both its investment in the process, and it's sense of urgency.

If you have any time urgency, make sure that the most important aspects are resolved early in the negotiation, so that you will feel pressured to cave on the less important items.

If you can create the impression that some less important items are more important than they really are, the other side may force you to postpone dealing with those unimportant items until you feel pressured to buckle. The other side will feel very cunning.

DECOY DUCK

Sometimes the other side tries to get a concession from you by pretending something is important to them when it really isn't. They will try to pick something that you can't do for them, so that it can't be negotiated. Or they will try to pick something that is really unimportant to them, so that their sacrifice isn't really a sacrifice. They just act like it is.

This only works in situations where you will not be getting to know each other all that well, where a complex, nuanced relationship is not in the works, and where you're pretty sure it won't backfire. But I've seen it backfire, and it's a real embarrassment.

I once saw a girl at a campground put all the good stuff in her bowl of soup. She offered the other two campers somewhat fuller bowls to show how nice she was to the big, strong men. One of the campers thought it would be funny to swap bowls, because he saw what she had done. He graciously insisted that she take the larger soup, and whisked away the one she had intended for herself. She was very disappointed with her bowl of soup that day. But what could she say? "No, I really want that one, I took most of your vegetables and meat for myself." Charming.

As you can see, it isn't really an ethical tactic, but you will want to be on the alert for it. Someone will use it sooner or later. But if you do have the opportunity to use it appropriately, it's a great time to ask, "Well, if I do this for you, what will you do for me?"

DEFEAT THE DUCK

You can act against the decoy duck if you think it's happening. You'll want to prevent them from switching to another decoy if they are wrong the first time. Isolate the demand. First, ask if it is the only thing bothering them. Then get the agreement written up.

Let's say, for example, that they were upset that you did not have leather seats and they got a promise of a concession from you if you could not get a model in leather within two weeks. You make sure that this is the only thing bothering them. They insist that it is.

Then, you get it written up and take it to the higher authority. Then you get back with them, tell them that the leather is available, tell them what it will cost, and see how important it is to them then.

If they pass on the leather after all, you have already gotten their agreement, so you won't have any more decoys or other surprises. You thought you sniffed a decoy in the leather seat issue, so you isolated it by using it as your own decoy. In effect, you out-decoyed them.

A counselor friend of mine had a client who wanted to break her 24 hour cancellation notice requirement. She asked if he would mind, because work was really a zoo that day. He said no, because he didn't mind being flexible, but he said she'd have to be responsible for a 14.00 office rent charge that he'd be stuck with. Suddenly, she decided that she could get away from work after all. For a couple of lattes, work wasn't really such a zoo. In this case, it wasn't all that important to her. She was asking for a convenient concession, but it wasn't as important as it appeared after all.

TASTES LIKE DUCK

This little trick is a cousin of the Decoy Duck. In this, the customer has a decoy that they intend to sacrifice, but it is not important to them. They expect to get a concession for that "sacrifice," though. They act like this issue is a big deal, but it isn't. You might detect this by sniff test. Somehow, you just don't think the issue is really that important to them.

Your counter to the Tastes Like Duck, is to try to tie it to a reciprocal concession at the time that it is under discussion. Otherwise, the person will time shift the sacrifice and use it to trade for something they really do want. It's a bit of a shell game. If you catch it at the time it comes up, you say that you'll concede to the demand, but you extract a price for it by playing up the effect on you, and refusing to table it for later. These decoys have a funny way of evaporating when handled that way. "Well, that's quite a demand. We'll think about it and get back to you." Like maybe never.

However, if the decoy is something that you won't concede because it is very onerous or outright unacceptable, they can gum up the works with it until things come to a head and you are manipulated into offering up more than it's really worth to them. In effect, they have increased their concessions artificially, and made it into a major one at that. This can be done with urgency and deadlines, packaging, what vendors will be brought in and coordinated, and countless other things.

Do your best to prevent them from extracting too much for their demand. Try to call attention to how unimportant it really is. Point out how over-dramatic they are being. Point to information that shows that they are making too much out of it. Tell it like it is. If you can get away with it, call into question the relationship, and talk about the kind of people you normally have lasting business relationships with.

And since you want to be convincing, you do have to be above this sort of thing yourself.

Unfair Comparison

This is a tactic that some buyers will use against sellers. In Unfair Comparison, buyers will compare the features of one seller with another, but without considering the entire deal. This gives them a case of buyer's remorse in advance. They feel that way because no single seller has all the advantages of each other seller's biggest advantage. No surprise there, if you live in the real world.

But the buyer tries to cure their advance buyer's remorse by driving a seller crazy with demands that are based on unfavorable comparisons to other providers.

The cure for you as a seller is to know your competition so well, that you will know exactly what is going on. By being very courteous and educational, you can help them see the advantages of working with you. You will have an easier time getting them to see the big picture by being very reassuring, understanding, and courteous, because people can see the big picture more easily when they are not so anxious and defensive.

If your prospect is doing this on purpose, then you can still use pretty much the same approach, except that you will need to get a feel for whether they are wasting your time. If they are intent on finding someone they can manipulate that badly, then the sooner they figure out that you can't be manipulated like that, the sooner they'll get out of your hair.

ERROR TERROR

This one is done by unscrupulous sellers. It's more of an outright con, rather than a negotiation tactic. Like many con jobs, it relies on the greed of the mark in order to work. (The "mark" is con artist slang for the targeted victim.) If you, as a seller, are the mark for error terror, it could cost you. You have to keep your eyes out for this one.

This is done more by sellers then buyers. But the more complicated the deal, the easier it is for one side or the other to come up with a variation of this ploy.

The basic idea is that one side pretends to make an error in the favor of the other side. If the other side is greedy enough, they will become eager to complete the deal before the error is discovered. If it's a seller, they might fail to charge for a feature or service. When the deal is closing, they pretend to discover the error, and shame the buyer into paying the correct price. All would be even except for one thing.

By getting the victim to hurry, the seller short circuited the negotiation process. The buyer did not try to negotiate. They thought they were getting away with something.

Come to think of it, if your buyer ever seems to be in a hurry, you might want to double check to make sure a charge was not left off!

It's conceivable that a buyer could come up with a variation of this, but it will be rare. Have you ever had a buyer shame you for trying to get away with a mistake that they made, and then realize that in your hurry to take advantage of it, you failed to negotiate and ended up with a poorer deal that you would have otherwise negotiated. And all because they buyer held you accountable for covering the mistake? I suppose they could leave something out of a contract, and notice just before signing. But the reason buyers are not likely to try to get away with this is that most sellers are too perfectionistic to try to get away with this, it would cause buyer upset and be bad for their reputation, and because buyers would not expect it to work.

CONCLUSION INTRUSION

This isn't exactly a con job, but it's more on the manipulative side. It is performed mostly by sellers. In this tactic, the seller gets the buyer to reveal important information that puts them at a disadvantage, sometimes to the point of committing themselves to the deal. The seller "accidentally" makes an inaccurate assumption, like, "You won't be needing us to include the radar on the yacht, will you?" The technique is more like a con job when the seller gives the buyer the impression that they will get something for nothing. They don't, but they made a commitment that is hard to wiggle out of for all but the more assertive and astute buyers. To avoid embarrassment and disappointment, the buyer might just end up buying the radar they thought they were getting for free.

The seller might get the buyer to reveal urgency by asking a question that assumes they won't need delivery today. Their response might give it away. Now the seller knows they have urgency on their side. As a seller, you'll want to watch for manipulative questions. Of course, playing things a little dumb gives you a chance to feel your way into these things, and asking a question or two before you actually answer one.

Sellers don't generally do this because they want to have a good reputation and just prefer not to cultivate that kind of sleaze factor in their personality.

Presumption Gumption

Sellers may have to watch out for this from vendors and other providers, even in their own private lives. Credit card companies have been notorious for this. The provider makes a unilateral presumption that works to their advantage, and sneaks in the condition, hoping it will get through the buyer's defenses. Anyone who has been amazed at all the miscellaneous charges in a hospital bill or mortgage broker's contract knows how it feels. It feels like some piranhas got into the pool

This can take the form of unwanted charges or conditions. These can be handling feels, unilaterally imposed deadlines for acceptance of conditions, changes in due dates or late charges, changes in fees or interest, or even nonexistent steps that a nonexistent provider is getting paid for. It might even take the form of additional services or materials that weren't really agreed to. And if they, too, are imaginary, you really have a con artist on your hands.

This nasty tactic works best on people who are distracted and busy, or cognitively impaired, such as many elderly or disabled people. It's a sad fact of life that con artists have their own personal radar that detects vulnerable people. In fact, they have a con for every human weakness, whether it is a character flaw or disability.

You can protect yourself by having quality time set aside for going through your bills and contracts with a clear head, and making it a habit of aggressively following up. Getting used to using small claims court can be helpful. Trying to do business mostly with outfits that are in your region helps too, because you don't really want to travel to a small claims court out of state.

UNFAIR LEVERAGE

Unfair Leverage befalls a seller or buyer when the other party makes a demand after everyone thinks things are settled, but the party with the new demand has seen an opportunity to take advantage. This might happen when there is so much in place, that the other party really can't afford to cope with the disruption it would cause. The vulnerability might be the commitments made, family illness, a natural disaster, and major supplier problem, or any manner of things.

Obviously this is not someone who has much to lose. So your best protection, as with the other more manipulative tactics is to work with people who work to cultivate a good reputation, and who are committed to it. They are known quantities. They may charge more for their services, but the additional cost functions a lot like insurance.

This tactic is a kissing cousin to extortion, except you are not threatening to break their kneecaps or post their sister's nude pictures online.

If you truly are over a barrel, you might have to give in. But you should do what you can to circumvent. It depends on the person's motivations and personality. If they are a died in the wool con artist, an appeal to their conscience won't work, because they don't have one. You can try to get a counter concession, but why would they entertain the idea. Only if you can settle them down and get an honest discussion of their motives. Sometimes, it will turn out that they are just to clueless to realize the full implications of what they are doing, and you can exercise some courteous, skillful leadership in the relationship to reshape their expectations and understandings. They may have some kind of beef, and are paranoid and reactive enough to think that they can't work it out with you. Again, your diplomatic skills will be needed to settle them down and get things right.

By getting legally-binding agreements, you have better odds of getting justice. This means not leaving too many things on a handshake basis with people, especially those unknown quantities. The larger the deposit you get, the less likely they will be to back out. The more up front exposure and commitment you have, the larger your deposit should be.

Planted Information

The other side may try to throw you off with fake information. A favorite way to provide it is surreptitiously. If you think you are overhearing something through sheer luck, it might be there to trick you. This is a common practice, so keep your guard up. Even information that is provided to you is suspect if you can't verify it.

Misleading Behavior

Poker is a microcosm for negotiating. Everyone is trying to disguise the effect that their hand is having on them. But you have to do more than act the opposite. People expect you to do that. So you size up the situation in broader terms. If you have a hand that is unexpectedly good, you might think you have it in the bag, but if you raise your bet too much, you could lose more than you gain as players fold.

In negotiation, you need to keep your eye on the real issues and the numbers. If you're up against even marginally seasoned negotiators, they probably have some ways to give the wrong impression. Sometimes this involves dramatic displays. Whether it is shock and dismay at your counter offer, or yelling and stomping out of the room because you will not budge on an issue, look for more than there reaction in order to size up the situation.

THIS IS THE END OF OUR JOURNEY
TOGETHER.

NOW GO OUT THERE AND MAKE US PROUD!

CONTENTS

Keys To
Motivation And Sales

Core Ideas

Motivation & Income Through Advanced Self Management

Sheer Persuasion

Hidden Influence Factors

People Reading
for Fun and Profit

Becoming Trustworthy

Influence Power Tools: Word Magic

Decisions on Fire

Persuasion Without Products

Activating Core Needs and Values

Memory Magic and Belief

Momentum Magic

Stephen's Sales Process: From Contact to Close

Contact Phase

Momentum Phase

Agreement Phase

Nailing Down Phase

Closing Phase

Working the Sales Process

Zen Archery: Acting in the Optimal Moment

Deep into Objections

Objections, Mind Massage Style

The Psychology of Money and Budgets

Advanced Skills and Knowledge

Automatic Behavior

More Ideas for Absolute Fanatics

Also by the author:

Get Anyone to Quit
SMOKING

ISBN: 978-965-7489-00-0

Can you believe some of the things that smokers say?

They say they LOVE to smoke. They'll quit SOME DAY. They usually make sense. But not when it comes to smoking. If it's about smoking, it just has to FEEL right, and it's "TRUE."

The manufacturers could put hundreds of chemicals into cigarettes to make them more deadly and addictive. They could even add pesticides. They could even freebase the nicotine the way cocaine is processed for crack-heads. Smokers would STILL smoke! **Oh, wait, that IS what they do to cigarettes... and people still smoke!**

If you want someone to stop smoking, you need to come in through the back door. Instead of logic, you have to sneak up on the source of the crazy ideas: the subconscious.

Stephan will show you exactly how in this book.

NO fancy hypnosis or subliminal messages. Stephan, a master of persuasion and the author of **"Persuasion Mastery"**, gives you easy ways to tip the scales of their motivations. Once that happens, your "client" will quit without knowing why...

Get Anyone To Quit Smoking, by Stephan Thieme - available on Amazon and selected book stores.

Visit **InnerPatch.com**